Catholicism in South Florida
1868–1968

Catholicism
in
South
Florida

1868 – 1968

Michael J. McNally

University Presses of Florida
University of Florida Press
Gainesville

Library of Congress Cataloging in Publication Data

McNally, Michael J.
    Catholicism in south Florida, 1868–1968.

    "A University of Florida Book."
    Bibliography, p.
    Includes index.
    1. Catholic Church—Florida—History.   2. Cuban
Americans—Florida—Religion.   3. Florida—Church
history.   I. Title.
BX1415.F55M33   1984   282'.759   84–7389
ISBN 0–8130–0788–7 (alk. paper)

    University Presses of Florida is the central agency for scholarly publishing of the State of Florida's university system, producing books selected for publication by the faculty editorial committees of Florida's nine public universities: Florida A&M University (Tallahassee), Florida Atlantic University (Boca Raton), Florida International University (Miami), Florida State University (Tallahassee), University of Central Florida (Orlando), University of Florida (Gainesville), University of North Florida (Jacksonville), University of South Florida (Tampa), University of West Florida (Pensacola).

    Orders for books published by all member presses of University Presses of Florida should be addressed to University Presses of Florida, 15 NW 15th Street, Gainesville, FL 32603.

    The author acknowledges the following archives and publishers for permission to use material: Adrian Dominican Sisters, Adrian, Michigan, for archival material; the Archdiocese of Baltimore for archival material; the Costello Publishing Company, Inc., for a quotation from the translation by Austin Flannery, O.P., of the Vatican Council II Conciliar and past conciliar documents; the Diocese of St. Augustine for archival material; Harcourt Brace Jovanovich, Inc., for lines from "Little Gidding" in *Four Quartets* by T. S. Eliot; the U.S. Catholic Conference for excerpts from Cecilio J. Morales, Jr., *Hispanic Portrait of Evangelization—The Shrine of Our Lady of Charity*.

Printed in the U.S.A. on acid-free paper

Contents

Maps

Foreword

History tells us of the past. Good history brings some portion of the past to life and enriches our understanding of the human condition by showing us what the world was like for those who came before us. But a certain kind of good history does even more—it adds a new dimension to our understanding of the here and now by showing us how the present was shaped and conditioned by the past. *Catholicism in South Florida, 1868–1968* is that kind of good history. It brings the past to life, to be sure; but its special merit is that it succeeds so well in linking past to present and in identifying elements of continuity and change in the story of Catholicism in South Florida over the past century.

In view of Father McNally's extraordinary success in demonstrating the relevance of past to present, it is interesting to note that he did not start this project with the foreknowledge that he would be able to do such a thing. Of course, all historians are persuaded in a general way that studying the past equips us better to deal with the problems of our own time. But that is a different matter from knowing that one can show precisely how specific developments in the past actually influenced the way things are in the present. In other words, Father McNally did not know in advance that the past was relevant to the present in this concrete sense; rather, he *discovered* that such was the case in the course of his research. The circumstances of that discovery merit a word of elaboration. They are, of course, better known to the author than to me. But it is a prerogative of foreword writers to talk about matters that modesty and the conventions of the craft inhibit an author from enlarging upon.

When Father McNally first discussed his project with me, he had in mind a history of the Roman Catholic diocese of Miami from its establishment in 1958 to the present. But as he began the actual research, he found it necessary to push further and further into the "background" of the founding of Miami as an autonomous ecclesiastical unit. Eventually he concluded that the story he wanted to tell began properly over a hundred years ago and reached a decisive turning point in the late 1960s. As I understand what happened, a specific historical discovery, as well as more general considerations, persuaded him to enlarge the chronological scope of his study.

Generally speaking, he came to the conclusion that one simply could not understand the situation that existed in 1958 without taking a long look at how it had developed historically. This was something of a surprise to Father McNally because, like other Catholics in South Florida, he had assumed that 1958 was, more or less, when significant ecclesiastical activities began. Then he discovered that this very assumption was to a considerable extent the product of a specific historical episode connected with the establishment of the diocese of Miami itself. That episode was the jurisdictional quarrel between Coleman F. Carroll, the first bishop of Miami, and Joseph P. Hurley, the incumbent bishop of St. Augustine, whose see had hitherto encompassed the entire state of Florida.

The Carroll-Hurley dispute, which Father McNally treats with exemplary fairness and candor, is a fascinating chapter in his story. But what matters most for our purposes is that, in researching and reflecting upon it, he became convinced that it affected attitudes toward the past in an unfortunate way. Indeed, he speaks of it as having created a "historical caesura," a kind of psychological chasm separating the diocesan era from the earlier history of Catholicism in South Florida. This separation came about because the tension and ill feeling that grew out of the controversy did not dispose Bishop Carroll to link his own efforts with those of his predecessors. The same thing was true of the priests and religious of the diocese, many of whom underwent considerable stress as a result of the financial and jurisdictional uncertainties arising from the dispute. Lay people were unaware of what was going on, but their historical sense too was affected in a negative way because they heard little or nothing about the past from their pastors or their bishop. This unplanned and largely unconscious neglect of history contributed to what Father McNally calls the "moment-to-moment mentality" that has characterized the Catholic Church in Miami over the past quarter of a century. Other factors—the fact that most Catholics are relative newcomers to the area, the vast influx of Cuban refugees after 1959, and the dramatic religious and cultural shifts of the 1960s—reinforced this ahistorical mentality, but the Carroll-Hurley controversy illustrates vividly how an incident in the present can affect the way the past is understood—or in this case not understood, or even adverted to.

After having attained this insight about the historical effects of the controversy, and considering also what he had learned of the formative influence of earlier developments, Father McNally concluded that a larger scale history of Catholicism in South Florida was needed than he had at first been aware. Catholics of the region will be grateful that he did, for this book makes possible a far deeper and richer appreciation of their past development and present situation than could have been attained without it or that can be matched in very many other places in the Catholic world. Scholars interested in American social history will also be grateful, for his findings illuminate the larger story of American Catholicism and religious history in general. I cannot review all of the book's virtues here, but let me call attention to a few points that struck me most forcibly.

In the first place, Father McNally strengthens the work by dealing with a sufficient span of time to bring out long-range developments. Moreover, by going back to the 1860s, he has linked his account to the excellent treatment of early Florida Catholicism provided in Michael Gannon's *Cross in the Sand*, which brings the story from Spanish times up to 1870. In dealing with a long time span, however, it is essential to devise a convincing periodization. Here the author has succeeded admirably: the division of the pre-diocesan story into three distinct epochs—the pioneering era from 1868 to 1914, the period between the two world wars marked by growing pains and economic distress, and the years of booming expansion from 1940 to 1958—assists the reader immensely in grasping the main lines of development and keeping them in mind as the account proceeds. The same organizing power is evident in the chapters dealing with the establishment of the diocese and the multifarious developments of the 1960s.

The periodization highlights change, the succession of developmental stages that have marked the history of Catholicism in South Florida. But Father McNally is equally sensitive to elements of continuity, to persistent themes that recur in different epochs or that run through the whole century. One of the most interesting of these themes is what he calls the "missionary" character of Catholicism in the region. This quality—which refers to the fact that the Church is not self-sustaining but dependent on support from outside the area—affected virtually every aspect of Catholic life. It was, of course, most notable in the pioneering stage, but it persisted into the post–World War II years and, in respect to ministering to the Cuban refugees, continued into the contemporary era.

The relatively unformed "missionary" conditions that characterized the Church for such a long time meant that leadership was especially important. Here we can be grateful that Father McNally has analyzed so carefully the role of the seven bishops who guided Catholic developments in the area. In doing so, he has by implication defied the recent tendency to deprecate the traditional emphasis on the role of bishops in Catholic historiography. Impatience with what is sometimes called "the episcopal synthesis" is certainly understandable, and other aspects of Catholic life, neglected in the past, need more attention. But Father McNally's treatment demonstrates that, as leaders of the institutional church, bishops do indeed play a crucial role which must be inquired into and understood if we are to make sense at all of the history of Catholics as an organized group. It is an added bonus that the ensemble of bishops he portrays for us includes some colorful personalities and that we get to see two of them engaged in a hard-fought contest over conflicting interpretations of their respective rights.

Finally, Father McNally handles with great skill the two closely related, and very persistent, themes of diversity and complexity in the fabric of Catholic life in South Florida. We often think of diversity in ethnic terms and of complexity in organizational terms. There is nothing wrong with that, but the long-continued dominance of foreign-born Irish priests among the Florida clergy indicates how ethnic and organizational factors often interact. The same is true in the case of Spanish-speaking Catholics. They have been a significant presence in South Florida Catholicism since the 1860s; their presence has added to the ethnic diversity of the Church and to the organizational challenges confronting it. The account presented here of the coming of the Cuban refugees and the Catholic reaction, both in providing material assistance to the new arrivals and in trying to assimilate them into the religious life of the diocese, would alone justify publication of the book.

But that is far from being its only merit. There is much more than I can touch on here, as the reader will soon discover. This is a genuinely informative book written by a man who is not only a conscientious scholar but also a humane and compassionate interpreter of the struggles of his fellow men. It is a pleasure to commend the book to the public and to congratulate the author on its appearance.

Philip Gleason
University of Notre Dame

Preface

Religion is often an overlooked factor when historians write about America. They discuss politics, economics, military affairs, and social groups but rarely mention religion as a force that shapes and is shaped by history. This study is about American religious history, specifically Roman Catholicism in Florida. Michael V. Gannon's *Cross in the Sand: The Early Catholic Church in Florida, 1513–1870* (1965) covers Catholicism in Florida until 1870. Since no work has yet gone beyond 1870, this book fills a lacuna by taking up where Gannon left off, at least for South Florida. The lower sixteen counties of Florida, which became the Diocese of Miami in 1958, provide a geographical area and unit of population for investigation of the growth and development of Catholicism.

A century (1868–1968) provides a chronological and thematic unity for the study. Arising from the life of the local Church, the narrative begins with Key West in 1868 when parochial life was stabilized and Cuban immigrants arrived in significant numbers and ends with the creation of the Archdiocese of Miami in 1968, a watershed year for South Florida Catholicism because of the upheavals in American culture, the "spiritual earthquake" created by Vatican Council II, and shifts germane to the Diocese of Miami.

Growth means a quantitative increase in people and institutions to serve them; development suggests how people organize and structure growth; both concepts imply change, the very stuff of history. Growth and development are investigated in this work from many perspectives: social groupings, such as priests, religious, and laity; organizational patterns, such as personnel, parish building, social services, education, and ministries to blacks and Hispanics; individual leaders, such as bishops, pastors, women religious, and benefactors; structural development, such as financing, recruitment, planning, and policy.

The historical method used arises more from the nature of Catholicism in South Florida than from any preconceived theoretical system. It might be called a synthetic approach in that it looks at the totality of Catholicism by investigating a specific place during a specific time, drawing together constituent elements to grasp the organic whole. For example, since Catholicism embraces many different cultures and ethnic groups, the impact of culture and ethnic groups on the Church in South Florida is surveyed. The local Church or the particular expression of Catholicism in South Florida is an organic unit composed of bishop, priests, religious, and laity. (The words *Catholicism* and *Church* will, incidentally, be used interchangeably in this study, even though a distinction between them might be argued.)

This book falls into the diocesan category of Catholic religious history, although it does not follow the methodology of older "episcopal" or "institutional" histories such as Joseph L. J. Kirlin's *Catholicity in Philadelphia* (1909) or *History of the Archdiocese of Boston* (1944) by Robert Lord, John Sexton, and Edward Harrington. Nor, on the other hand, does it follow the methodology of recent French diocesan history such as Louis Gerard and Yves Marie Hilaire's *Une Chrétienté aux XIXe Siècle? Le Vie Religieuse des Populations de Diocèse D'Arras, 1840–1914* (1977) or Claude Langlois's *Le Diocèse de Vannes au XIXe Siècle, 1800–1830* (1974). Rather, this study's methodology resembles more recent American diocesan histories such as Alice O'Rourke's *The Good Work Begun* (1977). Although this work attempts to go beyond traditional institutional diocesan history, it remains more institutional history than social history, as those two terms are used in contemporary historiography. This designation reflects both the nature of the sources used and the dominant role played by the juridical institutional elements of Catholicism during the period under study.

Although scholarly work is the product of solitude, it cannot be produced in isolation. It is the result of and contributes to scholarly dialogue. In addition, it is the flower of the benefaction of many people. I would be remiss indeed if I did not pay tribute to those whose generosity assisted me in bringing this work to completion.

I owe a debt of gratitude to my Ordinary, Edward A. McCarthy, Archbishop of Miami, who released me from my archdiocesan assignment in order to pursue graduate studies, supported me financially and spiritually during my absence, and contributed to the publication of this book by means of a generous grant. The two Auxiliary Bishops of Miami, John Nevins and Agustín Román, showed a lively interest in my work, as did the Poor Clare Nuns of Christ the King Monastery, Delray Beach, who donated the art work for the maps contained in this book. While I traveled the east coast of the United States in the summer and fall of 1981 to conduct my research, several people were particularly helpful, either by providing hospitality or by going beyond their required duties to furnish archival material, and I should like to pay special tribute to them: Sr. Joyce LaVoy, OP; Sr. Mary Philip Ryan, OP; Rev. Edward F. McSweeney; Rev. John Maloney; Rev. Omer Kline, OSB; Sr. Veronica Rodrigues, OSF; Msgr. Vincent L. Burns; Rev. Frederick J. Easterly, CM; Rev. John B. DeMayo; Sr. Rose Bernard, IHM; Sr. Martha Marie Kelly, OP; Sr. Kathleen Reilly, SSND; Br. Thomas Spalding, CSFX; Rev. Peter Hogan, SSJ; Rev. Michael Scanlan, OSA; Sr. Mary Albert Lussier, SSJ; Bp. John Snyder of St. Augustine; Rev. Philip Gagan; Msgr. John McNulty; Rev. Robert Lynch, Rev. Gerald LaCerra; Sr. Lorean Whiteman, SNJM; and Mrs. Martha Chisholm. Also I am especially grateful to all those who granted me interviews; meeting these living resources of history was one of the most pleasurable aspects of my research.

Finally, the University of Notre Dame has been crucial in the production of this work. Through its generous tuition scholarships during the three years of my graduate work, through discussions with fellow graduate students and gifted professors, my thoughts about the science and art of history germinated and bore fruit. To the Cushwa Center for the Study of American Catholicism at the University of Notre Dame I am grateful for a fellowship awarded during my last semester. To two people at Notre

Dame I owe a very special debt of thanks. Mrs. Thomas Box, secretary of the History Department, typed the final manuscript. Last, and most especially, I have been enriched through association with Notre Dame Professor Philip Gleason, whose respectful patience, keen intellect, professional excellence, gentle wit, and rich humanity have been a profound inspiration to me.

[T]he Church on earth is endowed already with a sanctity that is real though imperfect. However, until there be realized new heavens and a new earth in which justice dwells (cf. 2 Pet. 3:13) the pilgrim Church, in its sacraments and institutions, which belong to this present age, carries the mark of this world which will pass, and she herself takes her place among the creatures which groan and travail yet and await the revelations of the sons of God (cf. Rom. 8:19–22).

Austin Flannery, ed., *Vatican Council II*,
"Dogmatic Constitution on the Church,"
par. 48, p. 408

What we call the beginning is often the end
And to make an end is to make a beginning.
The end is where we start from. . . .
A people without a history
Is not redeemed from time, for history is a pattern
Of timeless moments. . . .
We shall not cease from exploration
And the end of all our exploring
Will be to arrive where we started
And know the place for the first time.

T. S. Eliot, *Four Quartets*
lines 214–16, 233–35, 239–42

Yet time will prove where wisdom lies.

Matthew 11:19b

To my mother, Francesca Ilacqua McNally,
who taught me to love and seek the Truth.

1

Prologue:
Frontier Catholicism
in Florida, 1565–1876

Established on the "Rim of Christendom" as a missionary en-
terprise, frontier Catholicism in North America began in St.
Augustine, Florida, in 1565 and ended in 1876 with the death of
Florida's first ordinary in residence, Augustin Verot.

Colony, Territory, and State, 1565–1857

St. Augustine was founded by Pedro Menéndez de Avilés, captain-
general of the Indies Fleet, in order to establish an advantageous
place for Spanish colonization, to search for traces of unauthorized
intruders and expel them, and to claim Florida for Philip II of
Spain. Menéndez's royal *asiento* also charged him with the missionary responsibility of seeing that the Indians under his jurisdiction were converted to "our Holy Catholic Faith." After sighting
land on August 28, 1565 (the Feast of St. Augustine), Menéndez
and his party of about four hundred men and four diocesan priests
landed on September 8, 1565 (the Feast of the Nativity of the

Blessed Virgin Mary) at a site named Nombre de Dios that would be called St. Augustine. Mass was said at Nombre de Dios, thereby establishing Catholicism and the first permanent European settlement in what would become the United States of America. Soon afterward, an Indian mission was built at Nombre de Dios and Father Francisco López de Mendoza Grajales was named pastor by Menéndez with the concurrence of the Bishop of Santiago de Cuba, within whose jurisdiction the parish lay.[1]

In October 1565, Menéndez petitioned the Compañía de Jesús (the Jesuits) to supplement the diocesan priests as missionaries to the Indians.[2] Early in 1567, two Jesuits left the Spanish Caribbean headquarters in Havana for South Florida. Father Juan Rogel went to a military outpost near present-day Charlotte Harbor to minister to the Calusa Indians; Brother Francisco Villareal went to Biscayne Bay to work with the Tequesta, establishing a mission outpost of strategic importance since it was the closest in Florida to the military and mission headquarters of Havana. Following the custom in the establishment of such mission garrisons, Menéndez himself officially inaugurated the Biscayne Bay (Miami) outpost by staying there for four days in 1567 and erecting a cross, venerated by Indians and Spaniards alike, to signify the initiation of Catholicism in the area.[3] This first attempt at establishing Catholicism in South Florida was short lived, however. The mission garrison there was abandoned in 1569 due to the severity of the climate, the incompatibility of the Spanish soldiers with the Indians, the difficulty of supplying the outpost, the problems of ministering among migratory Indians, and the tensions between the soldiers and the Jesuits.[4]

The Jesuits did not return to South Florida for nearly two hundred years. In 1743, two Italian priests from Havana opened a mission chapel for the Indians in the Florida Keys and, later, at Biscayne Bay. However, since they had no garrison of soldiers to protect them, the governor of Cuba forced the priests to return to Havana.[5] Although an extensive system of Indian missions was constructed in northern Florida by Franciscans in the seventeenth century, no recorded attempts to establish Catholicism in South Florida exist beyond the Jesuit efforts of 1567 and 1743.[6]

The political and military changes that caused the destruction of the Franciscan Apalachee missions by Col. James Moore of South Carolina in 1702–7 also transformed the status of Florida. In 1763, by the terms of the First Treaty of Paris ending the Seven Years' War (the French and Indian War), Spain ceded Florida to Britain. Most Spanish colonists left Florida by mid-1764, and the number of Catholics remaining was negligible.[7] At the conclusion of the American Revolution, Florida was ceded to Spain by the United States as a reward for Spanish aid during the conflict. After a second Spanish colonial period from 1783 to 1821, Florida became a territory of the United States.[8] Although the Second Seminole War (1835–42) had damaging effects on the state as a whole, it benefited South Florida. Unmapped territory was explored; forts such as Ft. Lauderdale, Ft. Dallas (Miami), Ft. Jupiter, and Ft. Harvie (Ft. Myers) were established; and the Armed Occupation Act of 1842 provided homesteads to settlers who might not have otherwise come. At the same time, Florida's open-range cattle business began in earnest, with huge tracts of prairie land opened up north and west of Lake Okeechobee. On March 3, 1845, Florida entered the Union as its twenty-seventh state.[9]

American Catholic Juridical Structures, 1857–70

Catholicism in Florida was transformed. In January 1857, Pope Pius IX created the Vicariate Apostolic of Florida, which included all lands east of the Apalachichola River. Augustin Verot, a French-born Sulpician who had worked for twenty-seven years in Maryland, was appointed head of the Vicariate in December 1857. At fifty-three, he became the first prelate from the American Church in residence in Florida, arriving on June 1, 1858, at his Vicariate headquartered at the former Spanish colonial city of St. Augustine. Before Verot's arrival, Catholicism in Florida had been under the ecclesiastical jurisdiction of the ordinaries of the dioceses of Santiago de Cuba, Havana, Louisiana and the Floridas (East and West), Louisiana, Mobile, and Savannah (1850–57).[10]

In spite of the difficulties, limitations, and poverty of his situation, Bishop Verot was a churchman who could see beyond the immediate present. He was an active participant in Vatican Council I. In 1866, he suggested as a topic for the Second Plenary Council of Baltimore the creation of the Diocese of St. Augustine for the whole state of Florida, including the territory west of the Apalachichola River which belonged to the Diocese of Mobile. With foresight and hope he wrote in 1866, "Florida is exceedingly poor, if it is not assisted by the French Propagation of Faith, it could scarcely support one priest: things however may improve."[11]

Following the suggestion of Verot, the Holy See erected the Diocese of St. Augustine on March 11, 1870, with the French bishop as its first ordinary (an ecclesial term used here to mean a local residential bishop who has canonical jurisdiction over persons and things of a specific administrative unit called a diocese). Florida Catholics were no longer on someone else's frontier but a juridical entity with a corporate identity of their own. However, the new diocese did not comprise the whole state, as Verot had suggested, but territory east of the Apalachichola River, comprising 46,959 square miles of the state's total 58,560 square miles.

The state in which the new Diocese of St. Augustine was inscribed included 1,350 miles of coastline (today second only to Alaska among the states), a top elevation of 345 feet, a subtropical climate with wet, humid summers (in Miami an average annual temperature of 75.1° F. and an average annual 66 percent of sunshine).[12] In a state population of 187,748 in 1870, the number of Catholics was quite small; a generous estimate made in 1876 reckoned it at "around 10,000."[13]

The creation of the Diocese of St. Augustine had little practical, immediate impact upon Florida Catholicism and the leadership style of the ordinary. Yet the disposition of property and personnel did create difficulties for Verot and had implications for another new Florida diocese to be created almost one hundred years later.

While in Rome attending Vatican Council I, Bishop Verot became ensnarled in the difficulties surrounding the division of properties between the Diocese of Savannah and the new Diocese of St. Augustine. Since he had resigned as ordinary of Savannah in order to become the ordinary of St. Augustine and since he was also head of the Vicariate of Florida, an understandable mixture of finances, property titles, and personnel existed. At first, Verot made little of the actual division of the properties since he and the new Bishop of Savannah, Ignatius Persico, had signed a document of settlement. But soon after the actual division of the diocese and for the next several years, Verot faced controversy with Persico and his successor in Savannah, William Gross, over properties, railroad certificates, back pay for several priests, and some other financial matters. Also at dispute was the jurisdiction over the diocesan religious community, the Sisters of St. Joseph, claimed by both bishops. These matters seem to have been settled by the time Verot died in 1876.[14]

Characteristics of the Period

With the creation of the Diocese of St. Augustine in 1870 and the death of Verot in 1876, the era of frontier Catholicism in Florida ended. From 1565 to 1876, both continuity and discontinuity were in evidence. During the first Spanish period, Florida was considered a political and ecclesial backwater with both a military and an ecclesial frontier. The Spanish military frontier ended with Spanish withdrawal in 1763; the Spanish Catholic evangelical frontier ended with the destruction of the Apalachee Missions in 1702–7 and the British occupation of 1763. The second Spanish period (1783–1821) was ineffectual both politically and ecclesially. By the time Bishop Verot arrived in St. Augustine in 1858, what remained of Florida Catholicism was concentrated at St. Augustine and Jacksonville. He found a Church that was barely surviving, with a scattered, small, untutored flock mostly southern in culture and poor in material resources, ecclesial personnel, and social or educational institutions of a religious nature.

As old as Catholicism was in Florida—311 years from 1565 to 1876—it did not have much to show for itself; yet Florida Catholicism survived with a resiliency, an adaptability, a mysterious dynamic of its own which transcended economic dislocations, social upheaval, political discontinuity, and cultural differences. The Church had a life of its own.

2

Pioneer Catholicism in South Florida, 1868–1914

No longer at the "Rim of Christendom," no longer in confrontation with Indians or colonial officials, Florida Catholicism in 1870, at the creation of the Diocese of St. Augustine, was developing an identity and character of its own. The challenge for pioneer Catholicism in South Florida reflected that of the entire diocese at the time: how to cope with the poverty of finances and ecclesial personnel while at the same time providing basic Catholic structure such as churches and schools to ensure the survival of a small and scattered flock. This challenge was met by the three pioneer bishops of the period—Verot, Moore, and Kenny—whose task it was to guide the development of Florida Catholicism under pioneer missionary conditions.

Three Episcopal Leadership Styles and Solutions

Augustin Verot (1805–76) was born in Le Puy, France. Having joined the Society of St. Sulpice, he came to this country in 1830 to teach at St. Mary's College in Baltimore, Maryland. Later he served as part-time pastor of St. Paul's Church, Ellicott's Mills, Maryland, while teaching at St. Charles College. In 1857, he was appointed vicar-apostolic of Florida, arriving in St. Augustine in

1858. Three years later he was given added responsibility as bishop of Savannah, while remaining vicar-apostolic of Florida. In 1870, at his own request, he was transferred from Savannah to St. Augustine as the first bishop of the new diocese, a post which he retained until his death on June 10, 1876.[1]

Bishop Verot was a man of extraordinary energy, insight, and character. When named to the Vicariate of Florida, he tried to decline the appointment and the episcopacy concomitant with it by citing poor health, age, discomfort in heat, and the fact that he "always wanted to live and die a Sulpician." However, both his Sulpician superior in France and Archbishop Francis P. Kenrick of Baltimore persuaded him to accept the new responsibility out of obedience.[2] As bishop of the Vicariate of Florida for twelve years (1858–70) and ordinary of the Diocese of St. Augustine for a little more than five years (1870–76), he visited yearly the outposts of his scattered jurisdiction. With the vigor necessary for a missionary frontier bishop, he endured "sleepless nights, protracted fasts, exposure and long and interminable rides through roads often impassible. . . . Not one day, not one hour was not full, and which did not see him at work."[3] A man of deep faith, Verot loved to pray the Mass and to live a simple life of poverty, his wardrobe having "the mark of destitution." Disregarding "even the ordinary comforts of life," Verot's apostolic life was compared to other missionary French-born bishops—Flaget, Maréchal, Bruté, Cheverus, Odin, Portier.[4]

Verot was the last of the frontier French bishops in America and the first pioneer bishop of Florida. Through his leadership and his tireless creativity, he formed something out of practically nothing. He set the style for a renewed tradition of Catholicism in Florida by meeting the challenge of the poverty of material resources and personnel and planning for a time when things might improve. Throughout his episcopacy, he was a man to whom truth mattered much, for whom personal comfort counted little, and to whom concern for those in need meant everything. A man for his time, Verot's vision and leadership style extended beyond his time.

Verot's episcopacy in Florida from 1858 to 1876 represents a continous creative leadership despite the changes of his title and jurisdiction. When Verot arrived in Florida in 1858, he found three parishes, seven mission chapels (only one of which was in South Florida—Key West's St. Mary, Star of the Sea Chapel), no schools, no convents, and no ecclesial social service institutions. He had three priests, two Frenchmen of the Society of Mercy and an Irish diocesan priest. The number of Catholics in the Vicariate was unrecorded, but they were literally few and far between. The largest and most significant concentration of Catholics was in St. Augustine, where an estimated 952 white and 376 black Catholics lived.[5]

One of the most pervasive and manifest characteristics of Catholicism during the seventeen-year episcopacy of Bishop Verot in Florida was the poverty of the Church in real estate, buildings, finances, personnel, and Catholic population. What few Catholics there were had slight inclination to give of the little they had to the Church; Verot wrote in 1858, "The people are not like the Irish, fond of giving to the Church, even out of their poverty." He expressed similar feelings in an 1860 letter to his metropolitan, Archbishop Kenrick, as he apologized for the size of a collection taken up for the Holy Father: "I am ashamed at the small amount of our offering, but the country is very poor and the number of Catholics is small."[6]

Bishop Verot, like most of his people, supported the southern cause before and during the War between the States and defended it afterward. At the beginning of the conflict, he was made ordinary of the Diocese of Savannah (July 22, 1861) while remaining the head of the Vicariate of Florida.[7] The war did not enhance the material well-being of either the church or the state. The Union effectively blockaded the South, Florida in particular. Jacksonville suffered more than any place in Florida during the war, invaded and abandoned four times by the Union forces. In March 1863, during the third occupation, one-third of the city was burned, including Immaculate Conception Church and rectory. In South Florida, Key West (mostly southern in sympathy) was in northern hands for the duration of the conflict.[8] During the war about 14,000 Floridians (one-tenth of the total 1860 population) entered Confederate service, most seeing action outside the state. At least one-third lost their lives either in battle or from disease. Some 1,200 white Floridians and a like number of black Floridians served with the Union forces.[9]

The war and Reconstruction produced economic, social, and political dislocation in the state. The decline of property values in

Florida was exceeded only by that in Arkansas in all of the former Confederate states. Over 198,000 government rations were distributed to white and black Floridians from late 1865 through 1868. Martial law went into effect in May 1865 and was reinstated in 1867 with the rise of the radical Republicans. Soon thereafter, moderates took over the Florida Constitutional Convention, drew up the Constitution of 1868, and returned the state to civilian government and to the Union in July 1868. Yet considerable societal dislocation and turmoil still existed. Prewar Democrats wanted to oust the Republicans and moderates and used terrorism, violence, and murder to achieve this end. Between 1870 and 1876, contested elections and unseating of those elected were commonplace.[10]

Social instability was not widespread enough, however, to discourage new settlers or tourists. Whites as well as blacks continued to move into the state, whose population increased by 33.7 percent from 1860 to 1870. Visiting Florida, William Cullen Bryant reported that Jacksonville and St. Augustine were thriving with two new hotels apiece, all of them full. Another northern visitor in 1875 quoted a Floridian's answer to how one makes a living in Florida: "We live on sweet potatoes and consumptive Yankees . . . we sell atmosphere." By 1876, land development and planned real estate sales took hold, beginning with Henry De-Land, a New York manufacturer who founded a Florida community named after him.[11]

Reconstruction was not simply a political slogan or a social experiment but a literal fact faced by Bishop Verot and his fellow Florida Catholics. They were confronted with rebuilding the Church both materially and spiritually in the midst of economic, social, and political dislocation. Besides the burning of Immaculate Conception Church and rectory in Jacksonville, the chapels at Mayport and Fernandina had been ransacked and wrecked during the war. Since no money could be gotten from Florida Catholics, Bishop Verot begged for financial assistance from Archbishop Martin J. Spalding of Baltimore and other northern bishops, as well as the Society for the Propagation of the Faith in Lyons, France.[12] Yet beyond the material rebuilding and financial destitution, the spiritual impoverishment of war, defeat, and occupation required a moral regeneration. Although Reconstruction in Florida was somewhat chaotic, Bishop Verot's zealous pastoral solicitude led him to initiate a spiritual Reconstruction by two means: the establishment of private Catholic schools for blacks and the introduction of parish missions.

The plight of the black Floridian was the predominant concern of Verot's spiritual Reconstruction. Even before he had come to Florida, he cared for plantation slaves around Ellicott's Mills, Maryland.[13] As a bishop of the antebellum South, he had explained the rights and duties of both slave and master in his *Tract for the Times* (1861).[14] Concerned as he was with missionary activity among the Negroes in the South, Verot influenced the composition of the section of the bishops' 1866 pastoral that dealt with the American black.[15] He also established schools for black children throughout Florida in spite of postwar impoverishment, an expression of concern for the American black unequaled in success and scope by any Catholic ecclesial jurisdiction in the South.[16]

Before 1869, all education in Florida was through private schools. In 1866, Florida law allowed for the education of Negroes, although military occupational forces refused to enforce it.[17] After negotiating with the Sisters of St. Joseph of Le Puy, France, Verot welcomed them to Savannah in 1866 "in order that they consecrate themselves to the service of the poor Negroes."[18] Amid local opposition, the sisters opened their first school for blacks in St. Augustine in January 1867. By 1876, the Sisters of St. Joseph were staffing five black schools in Florida, serving 248 pupils.[19]

The second component of Verot's spiritual Reconstruction was the introduction of parish missions (a popular revival of Catholicism done at the local parish by a priest from outside the parish and usually lasting a week). After the war, he often commented to other bishops on his desperate need for priests and asked them for "infirm or disabled priests" who might be able to winter in St. Augustine.[20] Having little success, Verot changed course by inviting the Redemptorists to St. Augustine to conduct a parish mission in 1868. Redemptorist Father Joseph Wissell preached the mission before "large crowds," as a contemporary non-Catholic newspaper reported, stating that "there seems to be something magic about the Mission" and that it was sure to improve the moral tone of the city. In a less complimentary tone, the article said the "spectacle alone would well repay the curiosity of the visitor." Verot had the Redemptorists conduct parish missions at other places as well in order to bring about a spiritual Reconstruction.[21]

Verot's successor, Bishop John Moore (1834–1901), struggled similarly to develop the material and spiritual life of Florida Catholicism, in spite of the poverty of the missionary diocese. Moore was born at Rossmead, Ireland, and studied in Rome, where he was ordained in 1860 for the diocese of Charleston. In 1877, he was named the second ordinary of St. Augustine, a position which he held until his death in 1901. Because Moore never forgot his Roman training or his Roman friends, he had a keen and steadfast interest in Church politics during such Catholic ethnic controversies as the Abbelen Memorial, the "German Question," and the McGlynn case.[22]

Following the informality of his predecessor, Moore had no elaborate chancery structure, though he did introduce the practice of requiring every parish and school to submit an annual report, a *notitiae*. He handled other administrative matters in ad hoc fashion. Often, when a priest was sick or away, Moore took over the pastoral duties of the parish. His personal preoccupation as bishop was the restoration of the cathedral which had been destroyed by fire in 1887 and which he struggled for his remaining fourteen years to rebuild.[23] But his most significant contribution to the Church in Florida was not the erection of buildings but the building up of ecclesial personnel so essential to Catholicism. Besides installing the Benedictines in what is today Pasco County, north of Tampa, Moore introduced the Jesuits into South Florida and initiated the recruitment of priests and sisters from Ireland, all groups that would play crucial roles in South Florida.

Within Catholicism, spiritual and intangible elements of religion are made present and tangible through a hierarchy of persons who have complementary roles—bishops, priests, religious, and laity. American Catholicism could and did exist in the nineteenth century with scant material resources or organizational structure, but it could not exist long without priests, whose presence makes possible the very core of Catholicism—the Eucharist. Without sufficient priests, Catholicism becomes insipid and lacks vigor, orthopraxy, and, in time, orthodoxy. As Bishop Moore lamented to his metropolitan, Archbishop James Gibbons of Baltimore, about the situation in Florida in 1883: "I could not express to your Grace the anxiety I feel on account of the want of priests in this diocese. Catholics are coming to all the little towns that are now springing up so rapidly all over the Southern part of the state, and

I find everywhere I go the very bad distortions of our religion on the part of non-Catholics. Oh, if I only had priests to minister to them all."[24]

Native vocations for the priesthood were extremely rare in Florida. Of a handful of young men from the state Moore sent to northern seminaries, the only one ordained was Edward Aloysius Pace, born July 3, 1861, in Starke. After Pace went to St. Charles College from 1876 to 1880, Bishop Moore sent him to North American College in Rome for six years. Having been ordained in Rome in 1885, Pace received his S.T.D. (Doctorate in Sacred Theology) in 1886. In October of that year, Pace was back in his home diocese as rector of the cathedral and chancellor. During his extended absences from the diocese in 1887, Bishop Moore delegated to the young priest all episcopal faculties. Unfortunately, Pace had no opportunities in his missionary diocese to exercise his academic inclinations and intellectual gifts. Moore denied a request that Pace be released from the diocese to teach at North American College, but in 1888, when Bishop John J. Keane requested to have Pace assigned to the faculty of the projected Catholic University of America, Moore reluctantly acquiesced.[25] He wrote Keane, "I have reason to believe that he will do better work in teaching than he is likely to do on the missions."[26] Pace's gifts would have been welcomed and utilized in a more advanced diocese than St. Augustine, but a pioneer church has little need for an academician.

Upon his return to the United States in 1891, after getting his Ph.D. from Leipzig in psychology, Pace began a long and fruitful career at the Catholic University.[27] One of the original thirty-one members of The American Psychological Association founded in 1892, he became the most influential figure of his time in gaining acceptance of psychology as a science in American Catholic colleges and universities.[28] In addition, he was the cofounder of the Sisters College at the Catholic University, in the summer of 1914; he encouraged the foundation of the National Catholic Welfare Conference and was instrumental in the drafting of the Bishops' Pastoral of 1919.[29] In recognition of his service to the Church, Pace was made a protonotary apostolic in August 1920. By 1934, his health had begun to decline, and he died at seventy-seven on April 26, 1938. Ironically, the Diocese of St. Augustine's first native vocation served his own Floridian Catholics for only two years of his fifty-three-year priesthood.[30]

Meanwhile, Bishop Moore had to look outside his diocese for

priests. He needed a more reliable source than the other American dioceses which occasionally sent a few priests who asked to stay on, several for health reasons.[31] His solution was to recruit Irish seminarians and bring in New Orleans Jesuits.

By far the most important source of priests for Florida from Moore's time on was Ireland, although recruiting priests from Europe was not new for the diocese. Bishop Verot had recruited seven from France in 1859 and at least four from the Missionary Seminary of Genoa, Italy.[32] However, Moore, himself Irish-born, was the first to bring priests from Ireland to Florida. Mungret College, Limerick, was his primary place for recruitment; by the 1890s a half dozen Irishmen were studying for the Diocese of St. Augustine. During Moore's episcopacy, at least ten Irish priests came to Florida.[33]

Moore's Irish recruitment during this period included women. Under less than ideal conditions, he separated the Sisters of St. Joseph from Le Puy in 1899, thus making them a diocesan community under the direct authority of the ordinary. At this point, leadership moved from French to Irish control. As early as 1900, under Moore's direction, two sisters of St. Joseph were in Ireland looking for recruits.[34]

The Benedictines from St. Vincent Archabbey in Latrobe, Pennsylvania, came to establish in 1886 St. Leo's Abbey, 30 miles north of Tampa, but their pastoral ministrations only occasionally took them into South Florida.[35] For South Florida, Bishop Moore's most significant move was the reintroduction, after an absence of 146 years, of the Society of Jesus. Bishop Moore invited the Jesuits of the New Orleans Province in April 1889 to take over the missions of South Florida, which, according to the Bishop, had "greatly increased in population and commercial importance" and had excellent promise for future growth. The bishop defined "South Florida" as the lower one-third of the state (map 1). The only place not offered to the Jesuits was Key West, where the Italian diocesan pastor, Felix Ghione, was canonically irremovable until he wished to leave. Moore expected the Jesuits' takeover to be gradual and gave them full liberty to establish any institutions that they desired to conduct. The Jesuit authorities accepted this arrangement, and on the feast of St. Ignatius, July 31, 1889, Moore and James O'Shanahan, SJ, provincial, signed an agreement giving the New Orleans Province of Jesuits the care of souls in South Florida's eight counties.[36]

Map 1. Southern Florida mission territory given to the Jesuits, 1889. Source: Edward C. Williamson, *Florida Politics in the Gilded Age, 1877–93*, p. 164.

What was extraordinary about this document was that it gave to the Jesuits "exclusive and perpetual right" to the missionary territory—only Jesuits were to staff the parishes and missions for the care of souls in southern Florida in perpetuity! Since the agreement was so unusual, Roman authorities refused to approve it without some clarification. Moore explained that O'Shanahan had inserted the exclusivity clause in the agreement because the Jesuits felt strongly on several points: they feared that diocesan priests and Jesuits would not be able to live in harmony in the territory; they thought that the Jesuits needed full liberty of action without interference, that religious were better suited for many reasons to missionary work than diocesan priests, and that diocesan priests were unable or unwilling to serve the 10,000 Cubans in Key West and Tampa. A second contract, signed in 1891 by Moore and O'Shanahan, mentioned the Jesuit takeover of Key West "in perpetuum."[37]

A bishop does not easily hand over one-third of his diocese, an area which he himself thought had a bright future, to a religious community as its exclusive preserve. Only the most extraordinary circumstances would have driven Moore to seek help from the Jesuits and to sign an agreement so unfavorable to the interests of the ordinary and his successors. Such circumstances existed, caused by disease and death among a clergy already in short supply and by the pastoral needs of Cuban Catholics in southern Florida.

Between 1873 and 1879, the whole South had been hit by epidemics of cholera and yellow fever. In Jacksonville in 1877, yellow fever erupted and panic seized the population. Another and more devastating yellow fever epidemic broke out in Florida in August 1888, striking the Bishop himself and killing four of the fourteen diocesan priests, three in Tampa. It was in the midst of this situation that Moore called upon the Jesuits, who sent Philip de Carriere to Tampa on October 17, 1888.[38]

A second important factor in Moore's decision to invite the Jesuits was the pastoral problem of trying to serve the Cubans in Key West and Tampa. Moore told Edward Pace in May 1889 that he was unable to care for the 10,000 or so Spanish and Cuban Catholics in any other way than through the assistance of a religious order. He could not get Spanish secular priests to come. Moore was negotiating quietly with the Jesuits of Spain, Mexico, and South America to establish on the Florida West Coast a house of study "as big as Woodstock."[39] The Bishop wrote the Jesuits of Castille, Spain, as late as March 1891 to put into effect his plan for a house of study and for the pastoral service of the Hispanic community.[40] But this plan did not become a reality, and Moore signed his second agreement with the New Orleans Jesuits in September 1891 to assure adequate care of souls in southern Florida.

The arrangement with the New Orleans Jesuits was unworkable from the beginning. As Father de Carriere, SJ, who had five years' experience on the missions, wrote in 1893: "The intentions of both sides are perfect and do much honor to your Lordship and Father J. O'Shanahan, S.J. . . . However, the intended agreement could not be accepted and has been refused de facto. Because it included too much and asked too much. . . . Let both parties agree that the Society will be allowed to have, belonging to her, some lands and Churches in the said counties without limiting the Ordinary in establishing other Parishes, and that Agreement will surely be accepted also by the Propaganda."[41] Apparently, we can conclude that the agreement (both the 1889 and 1891 pacts) was not seen as final and was deemed unworkable in regard to exclusivity and the expanse of the missionary expectations and that Rome had not ever officially approved of any agreement between the Diocese of St. Augustine and the New Orleans Jesuits. The ambiguity of the arrangement would be clarified thirty years later by the fourth bishop of St. Augustine, Michael J. Curley.

The last bishop of this pioneer period 1868–1914, was Florida's first American-born ordinary, William J. Kenny (1853–1913), who was born in Delhi, New York, and grew up in Scranton, Pennsylvania. Ordained at the Cathedral of St. Augustine in 1879 (the first ordination in the history of the diocese), pastor in Jacksonville in 1885, vicar general (1889–1901) and administrator of the Diocese (1901–2), Kenny was Bishop of St. Augustine from 1902 until his death on October 24, 1913.[42] He continued Moore's policy of Irish recruitment of ecclesial personnel, as well as the yearly notitiae required from parishes and schools of the diocese, but he initiated some policies of his own during his episcopacy—more efficient administrative organization, intensified recruitment, and missionary evangelization efforts.

More than any of his predecessors, Bishop Kenny expressed an interest in more efficient administration of the diocese. He took steps to see that his priests did not disregard diocesan statutes. He organized more efficiently some of the internal affairs of the diocesan chancery operation.[43] He responded to the perennial problem of a pioneer church, the lack of finances, by taking a corporate rather than a personal approach to seeking financial assistance. Unlike Verot and Moore, who both sought funds on begging tours to northern bishops and dioceses, Kenny sought monetary aid from such corporate organizations as Mother Drexel's fund, the Commission for Catholic Missions among Colored and Indians, the Catholic Church Extension Society, and, through a series of lawsuits, the United States government.[44] Kenny also inaugurated more intensive and creative recruitment techniques. He sought unattached seminarians from the North, in particular from St. Bonaventure's College, Allegheny, New York, from 1903 to 1907; unfortunately, this attempt produced few practical results. He was, however, able to get a scholarship for one of his seminarians for the 1902–3 school year at St. Mary's, Baltimore.[45]

Although Kenny was not an Irishman, he intensified the practice of Irish recruitment, especially from Mungret, and made at least one trip to Ireland between 1905 and 1913. The Irish seminary system allowed a young man to enter certain "missionary" seminaries for diocesan service outside of Ireland without being attached to any bishop. The seminarian's parents were expected to pay for room, board, and tuition until the young man was attached to a diocese, after which arrangements varied from one diocese to another. The Irish seminarian found a bishop (a necessary requisite for ordination) through his own contacts or those of his seminary rector, who might act as an intermediary between a bishop and the young man, or through a personal visit to the seminary by a bishop or his delegate.[46]

Relying on the special connections that Moore had established with Mungret College, Kenny arranged for a burse for St. Augustine seminarians at Mungret and All Hallows. However, he did not allow all of his Irish seminarians to be trained solely in Ireland: he sent Michael Curley to the North American College in Rome, and Patrick J. Bresnahan, William Barry, and Francis Conoley to St. Mary's, Baltimore. Not only did these Irishmen replace the French priests brought over in Verot's time but they formed a natural fraternity within the diocesan priesthood, since a native clergy trained at a local seminary did not exist. Most of these Irishmen made a fine showing in the Florida missions; they became the backbone of the diocesan clergy; three became bishops, two serving in Florida.[47] Furthermore, with Bishop Kenny's full support, seventeen Irish female candidates for the Sisters of St. Joseph were recruited in 1904.[48]

William Kenny also encouraged evangelical missionary efforts among black and white non-Catholic Floridians. As was Bishop Verot, Kenny was particularly sensitive to the plight of blacks, expanding the diocese's commitment to Negroes, Catholic or not. To open a new school in Jacksonville, he carried on negotiations with Mother Katherine Drexel, founder in 1891 of the Sisters of the Blessed Sacrament for Indians and Colored People. With Drexel money, Kenny built the first black parish in Florida, St. Benedict the Moor (St. Augustine), dedicated in 1911. After visiting Turpentine Camp (a farm labor camp one mile from the Benedictine Abbey) in 1907, he encouraged the Benedictines to establish a black Catholic congregation there. The diocese under Kenny staffed seven black schools, continuing the tradition established by Verot. Although black conversions were few, those who were converts came from the Catholic schools.[49]

Undoubtedly influenced by the growing national interest among non-Catholics in Catholic preaching missions, especially in the South, Kenny organized evangelical efforts among non-Catholic Floridians. After finishing his studies at St. Mary's Seminary, Baltimore, an Irish-born Mungret College alumnus, P. J. Bresnahan, was assigned in 1904 by Kenny to the Apostolic Mission House, run by the Paulists at the Catholic University of America.[50] Besides training Bresnahan, Kenny convinced the abbot of St. Leo's Abbey near Tampa to relinquish one of his priests for non-Catholic missionary work. After training at the Apostolic Mission House, Fathers Aloysius Delebar, OSB, and Bresnahan began their missionary work, the latter taking the northern part of Florida, the former covering the area around St. Leo's Abbey. In general, South Florida was not touched by their efforts because of the exclusivity of the Jesuit presence there. Apparently, Delebar did not get the kind of cooperation from some of the local clergy that had been expected. Although he had promised to work for five years on these home missions, he was pulled out by his abbot after only one year.[51]

Bresnahan's first mission was to Lake City. From November 1904 to June 1910, Bresnahan conducted missions in forty-five locations.[52] Most were held for non-Catholic Caucasians, though

Catholics were often also reached, and there was at least one mission to the Negroes at Madison (1908). Lynchings were by no means infrequent in Madison County, and Bresnahan, having received a personal threat, mentioned the next time he preached that he was prepared to defend himself: "I kept on with my services, with a newly secured revolver, ever ready, but screened from view of the hearers." An armed layman guarded the front door and another stayed in the sacristy with a shotgun, but nothing happened.[53] Bresnahan's only recorded mission to South Florida was to Ft. Pierce in January 1906; there he had two missions which resulted in the Catholic laity purchasing a site for a future church.[54] In 1908, Bresnahan was one of five priests who constituted the Catholic Missionary Union in the South and West. The figures show that Florida's missionary measures up well during the first six months of 1908:[55]

	Number of Missions	Days	Aggregate attendance	Converts
P. O'Reilly, Natchez	6	60	1,940	—
O. Weisneth, OSB, Mobile	12	131	4,325	24
P. J. Bresnahan	15	106	5,059	11
J. F. Mahoney, Charleston	10	61	5,570	25
W. Huffer, Oklahoma	16	120	6,730	6

The end of full-time evangelization of non-Catholics in Florida came in 1910 with Bresnahan's appointment as pastor of All Soul's Church, Sanford. His missionary endeavors had been important for pioneer Catholicism because through "drumming for the Church," as he called it, he was able to contact Catholics who had been isolated and separated from more established parish life due to distances and location.[56] He gathered together Catholics, some for the first time, and organized them to raise money to buy property or build a church, while at the same time he restored and renewed the faith of lax or fallen-away Catholics. Moreover, he reached non-Catholics, most of whom had never seen a Catholic priest before. Although conversions were not numerous, it was remarkable that there were any at all, given the brevity of their contact with the priest, the general lack of ecclesial support within pioneer Catholicism for a convert, and the ostracism that probably resulted from such a decision.

Centers of Parochial Development

The parish is a primal unit in Catholicism. In South Florida, the beginnings of parish life were nurtured at Key West, an island 161 miles from Miami and 90 miles from Cuba. Incorporated in 1828, the island was described in 1831 as "settled by persons of almost every country and speaking almost every variety of language." The population grew from 582 persons in 1835 to 5,016 in 1870, which made it one of the largest and most important settlements in South Florida and in the state. The majority of the 5,319 foreign-born Cubans in the United States in 1870 lived in Key West.[57]

In 1846, the first recorded Mass was celebrated by a Havana priest in the city hall at Key West. A year earlier, the Catholic population of the island had been estimated at perhaps 15 families numbering not more than 100 persons. Between 1850 and 1852 the Catholics erected a small wood-frame chapel on Duval Street near Eaton, and on February 26, 1852, Bishop Francis X. Gartland of Savannah personally dedicated the chapel as St. Mary, Star of the Sea. From 1852 to 1857, pastors were appointed to Key West by the bishop of Savannah, though their tenures were brief.

When Verot became the vicar of Florida he asked the Havana Jesuits to attend Key West. In February 1860, Verot assigned as pastor Sylvanus Hunineq, who died of yellow fever in August 1862. During his episcopacy, Verot did his best to supply Key West with priests.[58]

The landmark year for Key West and South Florida Catholicism was 1868, when three important events occurred: the first group of religious women came to the region and established the first Catholic school in South Florida, Cuban exiles began immigrating in significant numbers, and parish life became more stabilized.

The Sisters of the Holy Names of Canada arrived in Key West on October 24, 1868, through the instrumentality of John B. Allard, OMI, who had been associated with their founding and early years. Bishop Verot sought the sisters because he was concerned

with education in a broad sense or, as he put it, with the "regeneration of the moral and religious life of the Island." The Holy Names'
original purpose had been the education of poor youth, which was
financed by the operation of private girls' academies. Upon leaving Montreal, one of the sisters wrote, "Voluntary exiles, we go
into a distant isle to make God known, to extend His kingdom and
do His Will." [59] One of the sisters described her shock at her first
impression of Key West: "The town, built in the northwest section, is noteworthy more for the number of its inhabitants than for
the progressive development that charcterizes the other growing
cities of the Union. One can see no important public buildings,
and the private residences, rarely more than one story in height, are
all built of wood. The channel encircles the island in such a fashion
that one gets a pastoral view of the whole, even before landing." [60]
With the sisters' arrival in 1868, a women's religious community
and Catholic education were under way in South Florida. The sisters began their ministry in Key West with an academy in an abandoned Union barracks, on a site owned by Stephen R. Mallory,
former secretary to the Confederate Navy and a Key West Catholic. Mallory let the sisters use the barracks and land free of charge
and soon deeded them the property outright. [61]

Beginning in 1868, Cubans in more significant numbers than
ever before were emigrating ninety miles by sea and settling in
Key West. The Ten Years' War (1868–78) forced some Cubans, especially from the western provinces, to emigrate for both political
and economic reasons. Thus Catholicism in Key West came to be
influenced by the cultures of both Cuba and the southern United
States. [62]

Finally, in 1868, for the first time in its history, the Key West
Catholic community had two priests who remained in residence
for longer than two years. The South Florida Catholic community
had not yet experienced such a stabilization and continuity of
priestly service. [63]

The next important events for Catholicism in Key West took
place thirty years later. In April 1898, the Sisters of the Holy Names
offered the U.S. Navy the use of the Convent of Mary Immaculate
(built in 1875) in the event of hostilities between Spain and the
United States, an offer the Navy gladly accepted. The convent/
academy was remodeled as a general hospital, staffed by nine doctors, four trained nurses from Washington in charge of the four

TABLE 2.1. St. Mary, Star of the Sea, Notitiae, 1878–1910

Year	# of Catholics	Easter duty	Children's catechism	Children in school	Baptisms	Marriages	Mixed and disparity of cult	Year's receipts
1878								
Cubans	4,000				97	8		
American whites	560	230	120	116	126	12	0	$2,638.36
1880								
American whites	564	–	140	103	130	12	1	1,829.69
1885								
Americans	718	225	100	180	130	14	4	4,824.46
White	648							
Black	70							
Cubans	7,000				127			
1890								
Americans	619	328	100	483	147	15	3	2,190.53
White	465							
Black	154							
1895								
Americans	514[a]	202	–	400[b]	56	8	5	1,323.88
White	375							
Black	139							
1898[d]	463	115	110	–	114	12	0	2,897.50
1900[d]	475	200	150	505[c]	119	17	5	2,536.75
1905[d]	–	–	–	–	131	14	7	1,501.72
1910[d]	653	280	175	215	139	8	6	4,166.67

SOURCE: ADSA, St. Mary, Star of the Sea, Key West, notitiae, 1878–1910.
a. Two-thirds were practicing.
b. Three-quarters were Protestants.
c. Half were Catholic if the Cubans are counted.
d. Total black and white Americans.

wards, and twenty sisters who assisted the nurses. The Spanish-American War became a reality, and the first wounded sailors arrived on May 12. During the week of July 5, the hospital cared for 200 patients. Thus the Sisters at Key West expressed a Catholic patriotism at a time when many Americans of the 1890s looked down on Catholics, many of whom were recent immigrants, as intruders who threatened the American way of life.[64]

Another significant event of 1898 was the transfer of St. Mary, Star of the Sea parish to the Jesuits. After Pastor Ghione's retirement in July 1897, the Jesuits of the New Orleans Province took charge of the parish according to the terms of the agreement with Bishop Moore.[65]

Later, in September 1901, St. Mary, Star of the Sea Church burned down, the work suspected to be arson. The whole parish, including some Protestants, supported a drive for a new church. From October 1901 to July 1905, priests, sisters, and lay people banded together to raise money. Black and white parishioners gave separate suppers and held raffles. The new church cost $24,444 to furnish and construct. Over more than four years, monthly collections and pew rents totaled $6,411.69; fairs, raffles, suppers, and donations of $5 or more raised $2,646.41, for a total of $9,058.10. The property on Duval Street on which the former church was located, owned by the Church since 1850–52, was sold.[66] The uniquely constructed new church was the first nonwooden place of Catholic worship in South Florida.

Catholicism in Key West was pioneer Catholicism, reflecting a characteristic lack of practice of the faith and lack of orthodoxy, especially as evidenced by the sacrament of matrimony. In 1906, a Jesuit priest there lamented that he had many marriage problems to contend with: "Key West is an exceptional place for contempt of church laws and everything holy. It is not want of knowledge, for I have explained this matter . . . repeatedly in public and in particular cases."[67] Another characteristic was poverty. From 1868 to 1914, the parish in Key West struggled continually to raise enough money to support its services (table 2.1).[68]

Parish records reflect the growth and development of Catholicism in Key West parochially and educationally. Statistics indicate (tables 2.1 and 2.2) three quite distinct cultural groups and religious expressions: American southern whites, Cubans, and blacks. Generally, the white Americans formed the core of the practicing (churched) community. Parish baptisms and marriages remained fairly constant throughout the period, with a higher proportion of intermarriage with non-Catholics beginning around 1900. By 1910 all areas show a general increase. With the coming of the Jesuits in 1898, parochial lay organizations decreased in number. The Apostleship of Prayer and the League of the Sacred Heart involved more people, but less was expected of them in terms of personal, corporate involvement. Since private prayer fulfilled the "dues and duties" of membership, more people were attracted to join.[69] What was consistent throughout the period was the unbroken existence of a white American women's group, the absence of any parish organization for Cubans, the rather consistent presence of a children's organization that bonded school to parish, and only two instances of a men's organization.

Schools were also an important part of Catholic communal life in Key West, and from 1868 to 1914 several Catholic schools operated on the island (table 2.3). Both Cuban and black schools were free. A high percentage of students of the Catholic-run schools were non-Catholics; thus the schools were simultaneously Catholic and private. Protestants sought out Catholic schools for their discipline and rigor and because few other private schools existed. The schools were happy to have the Protestants since they provided needed income and since the Catholic community alone could support the institutions neither numerically nor financially. For example, in 1912, the percentages of non-Catholics in the parish school, the Convent of Mary Immaculate (the academy), and the black school were 63, 74, and 67, respectively.

The period from 1868 to 1914 marked further growth and development in West Palm Beach–Miami, as South Florida Catholicism shifted its geographical focus northward. Catholic ministry had begun on the South Florida mainland in 1872, when Bishop Verot sent one of his French recruits, Father Peter Dufau, to deliver a letter not to the Catholics of the region but to the Seminole Indians. Verot offered in the letter to send priests as well as sisters to teach the Indian children how to read, write, and "please the great Spirit." While in Miami, Dufau stayed with the only Catholic family in the area, the Wagners. At that time the Miami area was inhabited by about fourteen families and a few single men, most of whom lived on Biscayne Bay. Scattered from Cutler, eighteen miles south of the Miami River, to ten miles north of it, their live-

TABLE 2.2. Number of Members, Parish Organizations, St. Mary, Star of the
Sea, 1878–1910

Year	Organization	Members
1878	St. Mary's Temperance Society	–
	Ladies Benevolent Society	40
	Young Ladies Society of IHM	15
	St. Monica Society of Colored Women	14
1880	Ladies Benevolent Society	30
	Young Ladies Society of IHM	15
	St. Monica Society for Colored Women	12
1885	Ladies Benevolent Society	25
	Young Ladies Society of IHM	12
	St. Monica Society for Colored Women	20
1890	Ladies of the Sacred Heart of Jesus	31
	Young Ladies of the Sacred Heart of Mary	16
	St. Mary's Gentlemen's Organization	24
	Children of Mary	12
	Holy Angels	20
1895	Ladies Society of the Sacred Heart	38
	Young Ladies of the Sacred Heart of Mary	18
	Men's Society of St. Mary	35
	Children of Mary	40
	Holy Angels	35
	Infants of Jesus	50
1898	Apostleship of Prayer	260
	Ladies Benevolent Association	25
1900	Apostleship of Prayer	370
	Children of Mary	28
	Ladies Benevolent Association	22
1910	League of the Sacred Heart	415
	Children of Mary	56
	Daughters of St. Ann	52

SOURCE: ADSA, St. Mary, Star of the Sea, Key West, notitiae, 1878–1910.

lihood was based on starch-making, sponging, or wrecking. Only
a few traded with the Seminoles. Dufau's mission to the Indians
was unsuccessful because he could find no one who would or
could take him into the Everglades to meet the Seminole chief and
deliver the letter.

In 1875 Bishop Verot celebrated Mass and confirmed the entire
Wagner family in a wooden chapel built on the Wagner property in
honor of his visit. Over the next two decades, diocesan priests visiting Miami from time to time celebrated Mass there.[70]

TABLE 2.3. Key West School Enrollments, 1868–1912

| Year | St. Joseph's Parish School | Convent of Mary Immac. (academy) | | St. Francis Xavier (black) |
		Boarders	Day students	
1868–69	–	7	7	–
1873–74	–	15[a]	0	–
1875–76	–	4	382	–
1887–88	40	8	245	125
1890–91	120	16	260	67
1895–96	100	6	295	69
Total Catholics, 252				
Total non-Catholics, 218				
1904–5	166	Total convent enrollment 472		33 Cath. 50 non- Catholic
1906–7				
Catholics	59	5	132	69
Non-Catholics	115	3	361	87
1911–12				
Catholics	64	Total convent enrollment 120		41
Non-Catholics	110	Total convent enrollment 340		83

Sources: ASHN, School Reports; ADSA, St. Mary, Star of the Sea, Key West, notitiae, 1888–1912.

a. There were 250 part-time boarders.

This leisurely pace changed dramatically with the coming of the railroads to South Florida, easily the most important development during this period of pioneer Catholicism. When the War between the States ended, Florida's four hundred miles of railroad were in shambles and they remained so throughout Reconstruction. The return of native white Democratic leadership after the 1876 elections marked the beginning of Florida's Bourbon era, a time when the South's political leadership returned to many of those Democrats who were in power before the war. The railroads were the principal beneficiaries of state assistance during Bourbon rule. Ninety-two legislative acts between 1879 and 1899 dealt with railroad land; by 1900, 2.2 million acres had been given to the Florida railroads by the U.S. government.[71]

It was Henry Morrison Flagler's railroad that opened up southeast Florida. Flagler, originally from Connecticut, had amassed a fortune as a collaborator with John D. Rockefeller in Standard Oil. After visiting St. Augustine in 1883, he began the second major business venture of his life. In 1888, he opened in St. Augustine the Ponce de Leon Hotel, the first of a series of hotels which were tied intimately to his railroad construction. By November 1894, Flagler's railroad reached West Palm Beach, which at that time had about 1,000 residents. In Palm Beach, Flagler built the Royal Poinciana Hotel to accommodate 1,200 guests; a dining room that seated 1,600 made it one of the largest wooden structures of its kind in the country. In 1896, he built The Breakers in Palm Beach, then Whitehall, his private residence, in 1901. A railroad bridge across Lake Worth connected his hotels to the mainland.[72]

Fearful that the southern terminus of the railroad might be located in the Palm Beaches, two principal landowners in Miami, Mrs. Julia Tuttle and William Brickell, offered Flagler one-half of their considerable landholdings to induce him to continue rail construction to the Miami area. When a severe freeze during the winter of 1894–95 killed most of the state's citrus, except in Dade County, Mrs. Tuttle sent Flagler orange blossoms to convince him of the desirability of extending his line farther south. Flagler did so, and in April 1896 the first train reached Miami. Early the next year, Flagler opened Miami's first large hotel—the Royal Palm on the north bank of the Miami River. By 1912, after both labor and engineering problems were overcome, the railroad extended to Key West. One year later, Flagler died at the age of eighty-three.[73] For the first time all of South Florida's east coast was connected with northern Florida and the northern United States.

Encouraged by railroad interests, the U.S. Army stationed soldiers in several Florida locations during the Spanish-American War. Although Tampa was the principal port of embarkation for the U.S. Expeditionary Forces to Cuba, Miami had an encampment of 7,500 soldiers for a month. Although Florida's military camps' records were no better or worse than other states' during the war, sanitation problems that led to breakouts of typhoid fever in Miami and other Florida cities damaged the state's reputation as a health resort. Yet, despite the unfavorable publicity, Florida became better known as a result of the attention focused on it during the war.

TABLE 2.4. St. Ann and Holy Name Parishes, Notitiae, 1899–1910

Year	No. Catholics	Easter duty	Children's catechism	Baptisms	Marriages	Mixed and disparity of cult	Year's receipts
1899[a]	245	96	45	7	4	1	$ 369.85
1900							
St. Ann	–	–	–	–	–	–	–[b]
Holy Name	70	35	15	7	4	2	–[b]
1901							
St. Ann	70	67	–	10	3	2	–[c]
Holy Name	150	50	15	9	1	0	339.90
1904							
St. Ann	100	74	18	4	3	2	649.21
Holy Name	135	85	20	14	2	0	1,054.41
1905							
Holy Name	170	110	30	15	2	1	886.16
1906							
St. Ann	60	57	3	3	1	1	843.65
1910							
St. Ann	60	28	16	4	0	0	–[c]
Holy Name	–	–	–	–	–	–	–

SOURCE: ADSA, St. Ann's and Holy Name, notitiae, 1899–1910.
a. Data from St. Ann's and Holy Name were combined.
b. Financial statements of both parishes were sent from St. Louis, Tampa.
c. Included with the Miami accounts.

Catholic institutional growth was naturally affected by the new developments in the region. The first parish on the southeast coast was not in Miami but in West Palm Beach. In the early 1890s, Jesuits from Tampa visited Catholics in the Palm Beaches, and in 1896 St. Ann Church was dedicated in West Palm Beach. Catholics and non-Catholics alike contributed to the construction of the church west of town, property for which had been donated by Henry Flagler. Later the building was moved to its present location closer to the lake (Lake Worth), more convenient to the winter visitors across the lake in Palm Beach. The expenses for moving the church and building a rectory were met by Flagler.[74]

In Miami, Flagler once again displayed his favorable disposition toward the Church by donating property in 1896 for a church and school. Through the benefaction and encouragement of two Catholics—Joseph McDonald, an architect for the Flagler hotels, and John B. Reilly, the first mayor of Miami—Holy Name Church was completed in January 1898, at a cost of $3,534. A Jesuit attended both St. Ann's and Holy Name from the Jesuit headquarters for southern Florida at Tampa. By 1901, a Jesuit resided in each parish, though finances were figured as one unit. Also in Miami, St. Catherine's Academy, named for a recently deceased child of Joseph McDonald, opened September 1905 under the direction of the Sisters of St. Joseph. Ninety children enrolled, non-Catholics comprising 58 percent of the student body. Since the sisters were unable to pay the school debt, a school collection averaging $12 was taken up every third Sunday at the parish Mass. The parish was also having money problems. In February 1907, the church mortgage-holder warned that unless the past-due interest was paid immediately, "we shall be obliged to call the mortgage." Despite the poor economic situation and lack of funds, both parish and academy survived their fiscal problems.[75]

A statistical comparison of Miami's Holy Name and West Palm Beach's St. Ann's (tables 2.4 and 2.5) shows that both parishes were small (about 100 Catholics) but that Holy Name had a more stable population. Ethnic diversity did not seem to be as prevalent in Miami and West Palm Beach as in Key West. After 1902, St. Ann's congregation was diminishing because of a layoff of railroad workers, while Holy Name's numbers were increasing. The number of mixed marriages (those between a Protestant and a Catholic) was notable in both places. The existence of only two parish

TABLE 2.5. Parish Organizations, St. Ann's and Holy Name, 1899–1910

Year	Name	Members
1900		
St. Ann's	Apostleship of Prayer	25–30
Holy Name	–	–
1901		
St. Ann's	Apostleship of Prayer	30
Holy Name	–	–
1904		
St. Ann's	Apostleship of Prayer	Almost all parish
Holy Name	Apostleship of Prayer	Almost all parish
	Benevolent and Altar Society	40
1905		
Holy Name	Apostleship of Prayer	Almost all parish
	Benevolent and Altar Society	35
1906		
St. Ann's	Apostleship of Prayer	Almost all parish
1910		
St. Ann's	Apostleship of Prayer	35
	Altar Society	10

SOURCE: ADSA, St. Ann's and Holy Name, notitiae, 1899–1910.

societies reflected the Jesuit influence. (When the Jesuits had taken over in Key West, six parish societies were reduced to two.) Only the women had a real parish society which met and set up activities. Not until 1914 was the pastoral care of St. Ann's and Holy Name split into separate and autonomous administrative units by the Jesuits.[76]

Ministry to Ethnic Groups

Within the Catholic community of South Florida from 1868 to 1914 were two significant ethnic groups, the Cubans and the American blacks.

Of the Cuban refugees who fled to Key West during the Ten Years' War, virtually all were Catholic; but the weakness of Cuban Catholicism in the nineteenth century meant that most were not practicing the faith (attending Mass and receiving the Sacraments regularly). Bishop Moore, who journeyed to Havana in 1886, commented that only about 2.5 percent of the Catholics of the city were practicing. The Diocese of Havana had 120 parishes served by 400 priests, practically all of whom were Spanish. Moore found the clergy in a poor state of moral decay and the Spanish bishop of Havana frustrated in trying to discipline his priests canonically. "There is a scarcity of native priests," Moore wrote, and the faith of Cubans "degenerates into superstition . . . the state of religion here is practically sickening."[77] A more sympathetic view of Cuban Catholicism is presented in an 1875 newspaper article that begins by observing the presence of 2,000 Cubans in Key West. Although they were exiles from their native land, said the writer, they still had patriotic sympathies with Cuba. They were Catholics, though without understanding their faith "from want of early instruction." Their laxity of practice could be "traced to the influence of secret associations among them. . . . Yet to accuse them of infidelity—of straying from the Catholic faith—they deem a gross insult." They were proud of being Catholic yet were neither active contributors nor practitioners.[78]

The Catholic Cubans of Key West found employment in the 91 cigar factories that had sprung up on the island. In 1892 about 18,000 people inhabited the city, but inflation and strikes among cigar makers in that same year forced over 2,000 Cubans to move to Tampa (Ybor City). Key West's population in 1898 was 44 percent Cuban, 22 percent black and 34 percent American Caucasian, the last representing every state in the Union.[79] A Jesuit at St. Mary, Star of the Sea Parish wrote in 1898, "The practice of Religion among the Cuban population, at least of the men, is not encouraging, but the women as a rule are better disposed." It should be noted that the same commentator was equally unimpressed by the fervor of the American Catholic population in Key West: "Even the American portion of the parish is largely made up of lukewarm Catholics. A great deal of work lies before us."[80]

The state of Cuban Catholicism in Key West presented challenges that demanded a pastoral response: the need to kindle faith, to educate youth in Catholicism, and to respond to Hispanic Protestant ministers.

At the instigation of Bishop Verot, two missions were given by the Redemptorists at St. Mary, Star of the Sea Church in 1869 and 1870 for the purpose of rekindling the faith of both American and

Cuban Catholics of the island. A particular concern was that some of the non-practicing Cubans were being wooed by a Methodist minister.[81] In 1876, another mission was conducted in the parish, for both English-speaking and Spanish-speaking Catholics. Although the Anglo mission was successful, the Hispanic attempt bore less fruit.[82]

As an educational response to the influx of 4,000 Cubans, the Sisters of the Holy Names opened a school for Cuban girls in 1873. One of the sisters gave her impression of Cuban Catholicism and the school's purpose: "The ever increasing immigration of Cubans brings to Key West only the lowest classes of the population— classes shrouded in deepest religious ignorance. 'Faith' is an idle word for them. To receive Baptism and Extreme Unction is the extent of their religion. The other practices of Holy Church, according to them, are of use only to amuse children or to satisfy woman's sensitiveness and sentiment. Strange illusion! To preserve children and youth from such harmful principles is our purpose in opening a school for the Cuban children."[83] Great expectations were held for the effects of the school upon the Cuban population. One parish priest said a year after it opened, "The present generation is irrevocably lost to the faith and all our efforts towards saving the rising generation should receive a stronger impulse than ever—free schools for Cuban boys and girls should no doubt go far to achieve this end."[84]

Enrollments in the school were cut in half after 1875. In addition, the sisters had a $7,794.54 debt outstanding from their new $24,678.11 convent built in 1875.[85] The economic, practical, immediate institutional decision was to cut back someplace, and the Cuban school was deemed most expendable. So the sisters closed down Our Lady of Mercy School on August 1, 1878, five years after its founding: "We have had to discontinue Our Lady of Mercy School for the Cuban children in view of the small number who enrolled. Nevertheless, in order not to abandon the Cubans who would wish to profit from our instruction, we still receive them at the Convent with the American girls, and give both groups the same care and solicitude."[86] However, good short-term administrative and economic decisions do not always make good long-term decisions for the nourishment and growth of the faith. The need for the Cuban school was repeatedly noted by those in pastoral care, but the choice to close it and take in those who could afford the academy served the sisters' economic needs more than the pastoral needs of Key West's Cuban children.

A challenge on another front were the Protestant preachers, some of them Cubans themselves, who evangelized among the exiles. As one Jesuit bemoaned, "These preachers call themselves Catholics, in fact 'the Catholics' and thus deceive the Cubans, who by the way do not mind much to what denomination they belong."[87] However, this criticism indicates a misperception. The Cubans did care what denomination they belonged to. They thought of themselves as Catholic, and that is exactly why the Protestant preachers identified themselves with Catholicism.

One pastoral accommodation initiated in response to the Protestant challenge came in 1876, when Bishop Verot gave permission for the priests of Key West to conduct marriages and Nuptial Mass in Cubans' homes. The priests had been having difficulty getting Cubans to the church, and the Protestant minister had been most accommodating, since he did both baptisms and marriages in their homes. In addition, a special service each Sunday and holy day was offered for the Cubans at the parish church—a sermon was preached in Spanish and a Cuban choir sang. In 1879, a separate Cuban chapel (Our Lady of Charity del Cobre) was established for the immigrants. The pastor at the time, Father Ghione, mentioned that when no priest was at the chapel, the people went to the Protestant church; when there was a priest, they would not go to the Protestants. The chapel was still in use in 1895 but was apparently not used after the Jesuits came in 1898.[88]

In spite of attempts to meet the pastoral challenge of Cuban Catholicism between 1868 and 1914, priests at Key West continued to express consternation over working with the exiles. Their perspective might best be summed up by this statement in 1904 by a Jesuit stationed there: "I never once asked for money, on the contrary I always explicitly said to them that I would baptize, marry, and bury them *gratis*. . . . We cannot visit them socially; if we try, as I have tried it hundreds of times, we are misjudged, sinister intentions are attributed to us. We should not dare go when the husbands are not at home and when these are home, the women are relegated to the back rooms of the house. It is a God-forsaken race, at least those we have in Key West. Nothing but a miracle of grace will save them."[89]

The basic source of the pastoral frustration of many of these

priests was that they and the Cuban people had different perceptions of the meaning of *Church* and *Catholicism*. The American
Jesuit quoted above defined Catholicism from his experience of
American Catholicism and his knowledge of official Church teaching; the Cubans defined it from their experience of nineteenthcentury Catholicism in Cuba, which was lacking in knowledge of
official Church teaching and which expressed itself in popular religiosity nourished within the family rather than at the parish church
or school.

For the second major ethnic group in South Florida's Catholic
community, American blacks, ecclesial records between 1868 and
1914 are slim. Bishop Verot, who had a special concern for black
Floridians, had brought the Sisters of St. Joseph from France to
teach black children. It was he who persuaded the Sisters of the
Holy Names to open the first school for blacks in South Florida.
After false starts in 1870 and 1875, St. Francis Xavier School opened
in 1876 with fifty black students of both sexes, as many non-
Catholics as Catholics; it would serve Key West for eighty-six
years.[90]

Keeping a black Catholic school open in Key West for that length
of time was no easy task, given the unfriendly milieu of the small
southern town, the school's financial difficulties, the pedagogical challenges and cultural misapprehensions, and the constant
problem of getting black Catholics to send their children to a
black Catholic school. As one Jesuit who taught in the school remarked in 1904: "If we had the means to furnish books and in
some cases shoes, we would have more Catholic children in our
colored school. . . . There are also some parents too proud to send
their children *gratis*."[91] For these and other reasons, Catholic black
children were often sent by their parents to public schools.

Key West had the only significant black Catholic population in
South Florida, about 125 by 1900 (see tables 2.1–2.3). As was true
among Cubans and white Americans, women seem to have been
the most influential in the black family in religious matters. St.
Mary, Star of the Sea Parish had a black women's organization until 1890; its demise perhaps reflected the growing sense of segregation and alienation of blacks from whites that accompanied the rise
of Jim Crowism in the South.[92]

Characteristics of the Period

A precise determination is difficult, but data from tables 2.6 and 2.7 seem to indicate that there was considerable growth in the South Florida area from 1868 to 1914 but that the growth of the Catholic population was not proportional. In 1914, the 15,600 Cubans outnumbered the 10,000 native-born American Catholics in the Diocese of St. Augustine, although by then the Cuban presence was concentrated in Tampa.

What characterized pioneer Catholicism of the period was the importance of episcopal leadership and poverty. It was because of the poverty that episcopal leadership was so crucial.

All the bishops of pioneer Catholicism faced a common problem: lack of resources. Begging trips and letters to northern bishops and benefactors were frequent, along with supplications to the French Society for the Propagation of the Faith. Another aspect of this poverty was the shortage of ecclesial personnel. Bishop Moore summarized the feelings of all the bishops of the period when he wrote to Archbishop Gibbons: "I am struggling down here with poverty, fewness of laborers for the vineyard and the wants of the missions growing yearly beyond what anybody expected in [sic] a short time ago, and trying to do my best. I dislike the idea of going out to beg in some of the rich diocese of the country, but I have a Father White down here and I may be compelled to undertake the labor myself sometime or another."[93]

Pioneer Catholicism was distinguished by its lack of centralized diocesan structure: most diocesan business was handled on an ad hoc basis by the ordinary, a modus operandi that resulted in a personalized leadership. No central diocesan planning existed for the formation of parishes; rather a local Catholic community would ask for a priest after demonstrating its ability to support itself as a parochial entity. Parishes thus developed mostly from the bottom up, rather than from the top down. Catholic laity, both men and women, were essential for raising money for property purchases and church building. Benefactors were an essential source of funding, at least initially. Money-raising and church building united parish subgroups in a common cause, as well as bringing together Catholics and Protestants. Catholic schools, both parochial and private academies, were another unifying source, especially for Prot-

TABLE 2.6. Diocese of St. Augustine, 1870–1914

Year	Diocesan priests	Religious priests	Religious women	Parish schools	Academies	Churches	Catholic population
1870	8	2	–	–	–	–	–
1877	8	2	–	–	7	20[a]	
						70[b]	c. 10,000
1902	14	17	121[c]	11	9	15[d]	
						25[e]	
						83[f]	c. 7,000
1914	18	28	170[c]	18	12	23[d]	
						20[e]	
						60[f]	40,600[g]

SOURCE: *Sadlier's Catholic Directory* 1871, pp. 281–82, 1878, pp. 376–79; OCD–1903, p. 512; OCD–1915, p. 680.

a. Churches and chapels.
b. Stations.
c. With novices and postulants.
d. With resident priest.
e. Missions, no resident priest, but chapel.
f. Stations, no resident priest or chapel.
g. This figure broke down as 15,600 Cubans, 4,000 Spaniards, 8,000 Italians, 13,000 other aliens, 10,000 native Americans.

TABLE 2.7. General Population of South Florida Cities, 1870–1910

City	Year	Population	Increase	
			Number	Percent
Ft. Myers	1890	575	–	–
	1900	943	368	64.0
	1910	2,463	1,520	161.2
Key West	1870	5,016	2,184	77.1
	1880	9,890	4,874	97.2
	1890	18,080	8,190	82.8
	1900	17,114	−966	−5.3
	1910	19,945	2,831	16.5
Ft. Pierce	1910	1,333	–	–
Miami	1900	1,681	–	–
	1910	5,471	3,790	225.5
West Palm Beach	1900	564	–	–
	1910	1,743	1,179	209.0

SOURCE: U.S. Bureau of the Census, *Population*, 1950, 1: 10–8.

estants and Catholics, and were recipients of benefaction. Women were a particularly important segment of the Catholic population. The sisters were educators and occasionally nurses. They communicated the Faith to their students, many of whom had little catechisis at home. Women's parish organizations were active and pervasive. The religiosity of Cuban women noted by several Key West pastors significantly influenced both husbands and children in the home.

The events of 1868 in Key West mark the beginnings of Catholicism in South Florida. The pioneer Key West community, the most developed South Florida Church, with all its diversity and difficulties, represented an archetype of the Catholicism that would later develop in South Florida. Diocesan and pastoral concern for ethnic groups characterized both pioneer Catholicism and South Florida Catholicism after 1868.

Beginning around 1914, a series of changes indicated a shift. With the completion of the railroad to Key West in 1912 and the initial stages of the Dixie Highway to Miami in 1911, areas previously inaccessible became available to Floridians and other Americans. South Florida was on the threshold of a new era of growth and development.

Two events of 1914 affected women religious of South Florida.

That summer, the Sisters of St. Joseph and the Sisters of the Holy Names sent some of their numbers to the newly opened Sisters' College at the Catholic University of America to upgrade their professional preparation as teachers. And the Holy Names Sisters of Key West ceased to keep their convent chronicles in French after 1913, a shift which signified their acculturation.[94]

The year 1914 also signified a change in pastoral administration in South Florida. Parishes were beginning to abolish the pew-rent custom of social segregation and money raising in favor of the envelope system, which emphasized a certain democratization, since everybody (as long as they were white) could sit any place in church. Also in 1914, the Jesuits finally split the pastoral care of St. Ann and Holy Name into two separate and distinct spiritual, financial, and jurisdictional units, signifying that both had come of age.[95]

Bishop Kenny died on October 24, 1913. A new episcopal administration began in 1914, bringing its own administrative style to South Florida.

3

Riding Out the Storm,
1914–40

The population of Florida doubled between 1920 and 1940, rising to almost two million. Population growth in the 1920s reflected the economic boom, while more modest growth in the 1930s showed the effects of the "tropical depression." With the exception of Key West, South Florida's cities grew at astronomical rates in the 1920s; Miami increased by 247.1 percent, West Palm Beach by 207.3 percent, and Miami Beach by 908.4 percent (table 3.1). Miami became the most important city in South Florida and the second largest in the state, although still small compared to other American cities.[1]

The common characteristic uniting frontier and pioneer Catholicism in South Florida with the Catholicism of 1914–40 would be its missionary character. The Church would remain poor in material and personnel resources, necessitating outside assistance; Catholics would continue to be a small proportion of the general population; and the faithful, still scattered over an expansive territory, would need mobile priests and bishops. Formal ecclesial structures and institutions would remain less established than in older northern dioceses—the parish church and modest school, if they existed at all, were the basic ecclesiastical institutions. During the period 1914–40, the South Florida Catholic community, with its missionary character, was to face a series of tempests which simultaneously challenged and strengthened the developing Church.

TABLE 3.1. General Population of South Florida Cities, 1920–1940

City	Year	Population	Increase Number	Increase Percent
Ft. Myers	1920	3,678	1,215	49.3
	1930	9,082	5,404	146.9
	1940	10,604	1,522	16.8
Key West	1920	18,749	−1,196	−6.0
	1930	12,831	−5,918	−31.6
	1940	12,927	96	0.7
Ft. Pierce	1920	2,115	782	58.7
	1930	4,803	2,688	127.1
	1940	8,040	3,237	67.4
Miami	1920	29,571	24,100	440.5
	1930	110,637	81,066	274.1
	1940	172,172	61,535	55.6
West Palm	1920	8,659	6,916	369.8
	1930	26,610	17,951	207.3
	1940	33,693	7,083	26.6
Miami Beach	1920	644	–	–
	1930	6,494	5,850	908.4
	1940	28,012	21,518	331.4

SOURCE: U.S. Bureau of the Census, *Population, 1950,* 1: 10–8.

Bishop Curley: Clearing the Deck, 1914–22

The two bishops of Florida between 1914 and 1940 provided indispensable leadership during difficult times. The first, Michael J. Curley (1879–1947), born in Athlone, Ireland, attended Mungret College, then Propaganda College, Rome. Ordained in 1904, Curley eventually became pastor of St. Peter's in DeLand, Florida. On April 3, 1914, he was appointed Bishop of St. Augustine at the age of thirty-four, making him the youngest bishop in the United States.[2] He was a missionary bishop in a missionary diocese: "From December to June, I am 'on the road' traveling through the diocese."[3] As a defender and promoter of the faith, Curley provided strong, energetic, confident leadership at a time when Catholicism was numerically weak and under ideological attack. He spoke and wrote with wit, intelligence, and refreshing directness. His cogent argumentation and confrontational style ended the thirty-year Jesuit monopoly in South Florida and reopened the region to diocesan priests. During World War I, he displayed a patriotism that verified the Americanness of Florida Catholicism. Throughout his episcopacy, he continued the work of the Church among Florida's blacks, for whom he had a special concern. In writing of his episcopal qualities, a committee of Florida priests described Curley as "very zealous . . . had good judgment . . . had a mind of his own and is not afraid to act."[4] Like Verot, Curley was a man who loved poverty and embraced it. He never drove or owned a car. Living simply, he gave away most of what he had. An example of his sense of poverty and integrity can be found in a letter he wrote after a ceremony in Baltimore:

> Thanks for yours of January fourth. I appreciate, of course, your generous offering, but I am scandalized beyond telling when a Jesuit Superior with Vows of Poverty and Obedience wants me to violate my holy "vow" made on June 30, 1914. Since that day, I have never accepted one single, solitary penny from any man, woman or child, clerical or lay, on the occasion of any pontifical work. That means refusing tens of thousands of dollars during the past twenty-eight and a half years. I am richer because I am poorer than I might be if I had any taste whatsoever of money. So I am sending you back the check reminding you of my holy "vow" never to accept any money on such occasions. Thanks just the same. It is too late for an old man to change his ways now.[5]

Not ambitious for his own ecclesial career, Curley was as surprised as everyone else when he was chosen to succeed Cardinal Gibbons as archbishop of Baltimore in 1922. Perhaps he was even a little disappointed, since he loved the Church of Florida; he retained an active supportive interest in Florida Catholicism throughout his Baltimore episcopacy.

> I have never gotten the sand of Florida out of my shoes or should I say, out of my hair. It takes seven years, according to our old tradition way back in the nineteen hundreds, to make a "Florida Cracker." Well, seventeen and a half years must have done a fairly good job on this writer. I am free to admit that whilst I have been living up here the better part of twenty-three years, still south of the Mason-Dixon Line, my heart is in Florida where I spent ten of the happiest years of

my life as a Priest. My years as a Bishop down there were happy years too. Somehow, however, I still look back with sincere pleasure on the years in the tall timbers from DeLand to Smyrna and from Smyrna to Fort Pierce.[6]

During his Florida episcopacy, Bishop Curley responded to the external challenges of anti-Catholicism and the patriotism of World War I as well as initiating action affecting matters internal to Catholicism. Edward Cuddy wrote of the period, "The religious life of the United States turned sour during the years following World War I. . . . The Ku Klux Klan, fueled by the resurgent anti-Catholicism, spread like wildfire across the nation in the early 1920's. In a decade marred by many hatreds—against immigrants, Jews, Negroes, radicals—anti-Catholicism was probably the strongest."[7] Militant anti-Catholicism did not exist in the South prior to 1910 because few Catholics lived there. In fact, during the Tom Watson–Progressive Era, the American Protective Association (a national secret anti-Catholic group founded in 1887 in Iowa) was disdained in 1893–94 as a tool of the Republicans. But from 1910 to 1917, bellicose anti-Catholicism erupted in the South, especially in Florida, a product of expectations that Progressivism failed to fulfill. Tom Watson, the Populist leader of the 1890s, led off the August 1910 issue of *Watson's Jeffersonian Magazine* with an article called "The Roman Catholic Hierarchy: Deadliest Menace to Our Liberties and Our Civilization." By 1914, Florida's rural population was sensitized to the issue by the broad circulation of both *The Menace* (begun in 1911) and Watson's magazine.[8]

The April 1915 meeting of the American archbishops expressed apprehension over the national trend toward anti-Catholicism. In Florida, Bishop Michael Curley wrote his priests in 1915: "We Catholics of the United States are victims of organized vilification and the government itself through the mails takes a hand by the distribution of lewd and lascivious anti-Catholic filth."[9] He asked all pastors to conduct a special meeting with their people in order that each parish might send a formal protest to its senators.[10] Against this background three events occurred—one in South Florida, one in North Florida, and one throughout the state—that would test the mettle of Catholicism.

In Ft. Lauderdale, Julia Murphy, a graduate of normal school with teaching experience, was given a teaching appointment in the

Dade County public school system. Later the principal discovered that Miss Murphy was a Catholic. In mid-July 1915, the school trustees signed a note of protest to the superintendent of schools, Robert E. Hall: "Our attention was called to this by local tax-payers and patrons of our school and while we do not in anyway desire to interfere with your arrangements, we are opposed to hir-ing and placing in charge of any of our school work any but Prot-estants."[11] By August 10, Father James McLaughlin, SJ, pastor of Holy Name Church, Miami, referred the whole matter to the *Miami Herald*, whose editor called Hall and asked him to explain the situation. Meanwhile, the *Miami Daily Metropolis*, a *Herald* rival, reported that a citizens' gathering in Miami backed the ac-tion of the trustees in the ousting of the Catholic teacher: "When 181 out of 188 citizens express their wishes not to have a teacher of the Roman Catholic faith in their school, it may be assured that neither the teacher herself—or none of her fellow churchmen— would desire to have the situation."[12] Meanwhile, the *Herald* edi-tor arranged a meeting with the superintendent and trustees, in-forming them that the whole matter would not go unnoticed in print. The *Herald* entered the fray in order to undermine their competitor while upholding principle.[13]

Kept posted of developments by McLaughlin, Bishop Curley entered the fray. On August 28, 1915, he sent a telegram to Mc-Laughlin to buy up all the issues he could of the three issues of the *Herald* that exposed the bigotry against Catholicism in the Mur-phy episode and to send one of each issue to Catholic and secular newspapers inside and outside the state. Twenty-six newspapers were contacted, including the *Boston Pilot*, the *Philadelphia Stan-dard and Times*, and the *Sunday Visitor*. That next Monday, Curley sent the *Herald* a letter which was published in the paper. Ten days later the public debate was still being fueled by the *Herald* and the *Metropolis*.[14]

The upshot was that, although Miss Murphy did not get her job back,[15] the incident and the issues became known throughout the state and, in Catholic circles, throughout the nation. But more than this, the episode showed Curley to be a bishop who acted de-cisively in the public defense of the Church. Not since Verot's talk on slavery in 1861 had Florida seen a bishop speak out in the public civic forum.

A second event damaging to Catholicism had statewide repercussions. By the winter of 1914–15, Sidney J. Catts made it known that he was running for the office of governor of Florida. The other four Democratic candidates' platforms differed little, so it was Catts, an outsider in Florida politics, who injected controversy into the campaign. Three issues set him apart from the other candidates: Prohibition, anti-Catholicism, and anticonservation laws. Catts campaigned for the 1916 election in a Model-T, taking his message to the back roads where people had never heard a railroad whistle or seen a Catholic. Ignored by newspapers and other candidates, Catts was listened to by less sophisticated audiences.

Catts did not originate anti-Catholicism, but he exploited it by increasing its intensity through inflammatory campaign rhetoric. Since Catholics made up less than 3 percent of Florida's total 1916 population, Catts had nothing to lose politically by alienating them.[16] In Miami, he promised to open convents for inspection, force religious to pay taxes, and make priests "turn their collars right." The *Herald* commented that only ignorant people would believe Catts could actually do such things,[17] but Father P. J. Bresnahan maintained that Catts himself was anything but ignorant. He felt that Catts had the ability to size up an audience better than anyone he had ever seen. The Irish priest also revealed that Catts had once told him in Tallahassee that his campaign tirades against Catholics were "all politics."[18]

Having lost the primary, Catts surprised many by running as an independent and winning the governorship. Although the anti-Catholic promises of the campaign were not matched by executive action or significant legislation,[19] Catts's gubernatorial campaign and administration created a rhetorical milieu which made Florida Catholics defensive about themselves and uncomfortable with their non-Catholic neighbors.

The third anti-Catholic event during the Curley episcopacy was occasioned by a 1913 act of the Florida legislature titled "An Act Prohibiting White Persons from Teaching Negroes in Negro Schools."[20] In fact, the only persons affected by the law were the Catholic sisters teaching in black schools throughout the state. So that they would not be forced to make arrests, officers of the law appealed to Bishop Curley to have the sisters stop teaching blacks. Curley forced the issue by refusing to pull either the Holy Name Sisters or the Sisters of St. Joseph out of their black apostolate and by telling the officers to do their duty.

In early April 1916, three Sisters of St. Joseph who taught at St. Benedict the Moor School in St. Augustine were charged with "unlawfully teaching Negroes." The sheriff had been ordered to arrest the women religious by the lame duck governor, Park Trammell, who said that he had been petitioned by six Negroes to enforce the law against the sisters. The arrests staggered Catholics in St. Augustine. Two sisters were released on their own recognizance; a third, Sister Mary Thomasine, SSJ, refused to accept liberty and was placed in the custody of the cathedral rector.

The trial of Sister Thomasine began on May 16, 1916. On May 20, Judge George Cooper Gibbs, in an eighteen-page opinion, ordered her release, stating that Chapter 6490 of the Laws of Florida (1913) did not apply to private school teachers or schools. In addition, Judge Gibbs stated, the law was constructed improperly. More to the point, however, he concluded, "To say that such teaching would have a tendency to promote social equality among the races . . . is to insult the superior race." Even more than the Murphy episode in Dade County, Bishop Curley used Sister Thomasine's publicity as a national platform to defend the Catholic school system, to draw attention to anti-Catholicism, and to protect black Catholic education in Florida. Curley paid the legal fees of the trial and financed subsequent litigation to have the law declared unconstitutional.[21]

These outbreaks of prewar anti-Catholicism neither diminished Florida Catholicism nor discouraged its bishop. Early in 1916, Bishop Curley wrote to Cardinal Gibbons, "In spite of bitter bigotry, the Church in this poor diocese is making progress, thanks be to God." Curley mentioned having ten new churches to dedicate, a new parochial school, and twenty-three young men preparing for the diocesan priesthood, assuring Gibbons that "there is a splendid spirit of co-operation everywhere in the diocese."[22]

With the wave of patriotic and Wilsonian rhetoric surrounding World War I, Catholics in Florida were anxious to show themselves as true Americans, especially after the attacks of southern anti-Catholicism. During World War I, five of the thirty-five military flying schools in the United States were in Florida: Dinner Key Aviation Camp (Navy), Curtis Field (Marines), and Chapman Field (Army) were in the Miami area, and, in Key West, a naval training station and Ft. Jefferson, a seaplane base and wireless station.[23] Father McLaughlin of Holy Name said Mass at the Miami area camps. The Miami Knights of Columbus offered their recreation rooms to servicemen free of charge and pledged their support of the president. The Knights assisted their pastor in ministering to the camps and aided the Red Cross in raising $5,300 in less than a year. The Daughters of Isabella, the women's auxiliary of the Knights, had a hospital visitation committee, made surgical dressings for the Red Cross, and raised money for the fourth Liberty Loan. In West Palm Beach, St. Ann's War Council reported that the women's Altar Society helped the Red Cross and put on a luncheon for "L" Company. Although Catholics in Palm Beach County made up only 1 percent of the total residents, they purchased 20 percent of the third Liberty Loan and 14 percent of the fourth.[24]

Bishop Curley was as vocal a defender of his adopted country as he was of his Church. As early as 1915, at a public reception in Jacksonville, the Bishop stated, "patriotism of the highest order flows from the very essence of Catholicism."[25] In April 1918, when Gibbons wrote Curley that the U.S. bishops had recently formed the National Catholic War Council, Curley immediately informed all pastors that a Diocesan War Council was to be established and mandated that chapters be set up in each parish with detailed reports to be sent to him monthly. Moreover, Curley, who was well known for his eloquence, was asked to give a series of talks in Florida cities for the United War Work Campaign and in Miami for the Liberty Loan Committee. He even went so far as to grant permission for the War Department to install an anti-aircraft battery on unused Church property in Jacksonville and for one of his priests, John F. Conoley, to remain an Army chaplain an extra six months.[26]

Although Bishop Curley laid the groundwork for a stronger Catholicism in Florida through his battle with the bigots and his patriotism during the war, his most significant contribution to the future of South Florida Catholicism was opening up the territory once again to diocesan priests.

In 1919, Curley wrote to the apostolic delegate, John V. Bonzano, explaining the history of the agreement between Bishop John Moore and the Jesuits, the resultant tenure of diocesan property, and the difficulties of diocesan administration that arose from the implementation of the agreement, not the least of which was the lack of progress in the development of Catholicism in southern

Florida. The crux of the problem, reasoned Curley, was the Jesuits' exclusive and perpetual right to exercise the care of souls in the region. Curley indicated that no evidence of Rome's approval of this agreement was extant up to 1893, and no approval was ever given by Rome after that time. Curley further stated that, although the second agreement between Moore and O'Shanahan in September 1891 omitted the word "exclusive," the Jesuits had taken de facto exclusive charge of southern Florida for twenty-six years. Curley went on to comment: "I do not believe that said contract gives any such right, and yet, 'mirabile auditu,' this is just the defacto status today. 'Only Jesuits can enter here' is written over the gateway into South Florida, and the Bishop's hands are tied and he is powerless to grasp the splendid opportunities for the multiplication of labourers in the Vineyard and the upbuilding of God's Church in that particular part of the Diocese."

Curley granted that no mention had been made in contract or correspondence in regard to the title of diocesan property, but he emphasized that Moore had in fact deeded to the Jesuits all land— every piece of diocesan property which had been purchased from money collected from the faithful. This fact, commented Curley, "has made this diocese a 'joke' in the eyes of many Bishops and priests in the United States." Curley was particularly concerned with the erosion of episcopal authority since the jurisdiction of the ordinary was, he felt, reduced to nominal supervision. In addition, Curley said that many places in the area needed resident pastors, which the Jesuits could not supply. "The whole situation amounts to this: I am the Bishop of this Diocese and I am not. . . . Secular priests . . . have been discontented with the present status and plead for unity and uniformity in the administration of the diocese." He concluded by stating that Moore's agreements "stand in the way of the Church's progress and are detrimental to the interests of religion and souls." Curley sent to Bonzano what amounted to a legal brief of supporting documents and asked for adjudication regarding the validity of the contract, the binding force of the exclusivity clause, and the tenure of diocesan property in southern Florida.[27]

Thus began a series of negotiations between the ordinary and the New Orleans Jesuits that was to last through the remainder of Curley's episcopacy. The Jesuits made their first move by suggesting the negotiation of a new contract in June 1919. Curley responded with a list of items which for his part were nonnegotiable in any contract; the list dealt with the bishop's right of jurisdiction in his own diocese, especially in regard to diocesan property. Maintaining that the matter of the contract should deal with canonical questions, Curley asserted the real contractual matter was which parishes of the diocese would be entrusted to the care of the Jesuits "in full canonical form." He concluded by hastening to assure the Society that they were "dealing not with an enemy but with a friend." In the course of the negotiations, Curley wished the Jesuits to retain Key West but neither Holy Name (Miami) nor St. Ann's (West Palm Beach). However, an agreement drawn up in August 1920 gave the Society permanent charge of Holy Name, continuation at Key West (though "not with the idea of permanency"), and certain properties.[28] Curley objected to the terms of the agreement on two grounds: Holy Name in Miami, which the Jesuits retained, was one of the "finest parishes in the whole Diocese," and the deeding of property to the Jesuits might enable them to create on it a commercial building for profit in Miami. "But I cannot see the justice of turning the property over to the Jesuits in such a manner that they can . . . without any consideration whatever for the needs or good of this diocese . . . pack it up and carry it off to New Orleans if they so wish. There ought to be some limitation."[29]

Under the direction of the apostolic delegate, a second agreement was drawn up between the Society of Jesus and the Diocese of St. Augustine in June 1921. The Jesuits were given permanent charge of St. Louis Church (Tampa) and Holy Name (Miami). All other parishes and missions administered by them would be handed over to the ordinary at his convenience, including St. Mary, Star of the Sea and St. Ann's; the vacant lot in Miami was deeded to the Jesuits, but it was to be used for educational or ecclesial purposes only within the limits of the diocese. On October 7, 1921, this second agreement was approved by Rome.[30]

Curley's confrontation with the Jesuits involved both his personality, which was direct and forceful, and his principles, which governed his actions more than did pragmatic necessities. His basic concern in this classic confrontation between the episcopacy and religious was the rights and responsibilities of his episcopal jurisdiction. His specific pastoral concern was for both the unity of his diocese (a third of which was virtually beyond his control) and the growth of a rapidly developing part of his diocese. Moreover, he was getting pressure and support from his priest consultors and clarification from the new code of canon law (1918), which helped him sort out the rather dubious legality of the 1889 and 1891 agreements. From the beginning of the negotiations, Curley had been interested in delineating the canonical dimensions of the dispute.[31] Although the Jesuits actually gave up no South Florida parishes until 1941, since no Florida ordinary demanded it of them, Curley's settlement with them opened up South Florida once again to diocesan administration at a crucial time and prepared the way for the development of the Church on the southeast coast.

Bishop Barry: The Storm Breaks, 1922–40

Curley's successor, the fifth bishop of St. Augustine, was Patrick Barry (1863–1940). Born in County Clare, Ireland, he attended Mungret College and St. Patrick Seminary, Carlow. Ordained in 1895, he was chaplain to U.S. troops in Jacksonville in 1898. He subsequently served as cathedral rector, vicar general, and diocese administrator, and on February 22, 1922, he was named bishop of St. Augustine. Like his predecessors, Bishop Barry was constantly on the road, residing in St. Augustine for only brief periods of time; unlike his predecessors, he drove a car. Beginning in 1925, he faced the dual problem of a demand for new parishes and a monetary crunch, so that much of his eighteen-year episcopacy was loaded with financial headaches. His papers are full of account books and innumerable pencil jottings on scraps of paper. Remarkably, Barry steered the Church away from financial ruin; indeed, he did more than simply ride out the storm: significant growth and development of Catholicism took place during his episcopacy.[32]

While remarkably competent financially, Barry's leadership style was pastoral rather than bureaucratic, although he organized the first diocesan clergy conference in November 1923, as well as several lay conventions in the 1930s.[33] Dropping the practice of yearly notitiae begun by Bishop Moore, Barry preferred to run the diocese informally and personally. He had a warm, easygoing relationship with his priests, often taking charge of a parish himself when a pastor needed some time off. Barry modeled himself after the simple, humble parish priest of rural Ireland; he was what the Irish call "fair and easy." As his brother William wrote, "He ran the Diocese with the fountain pen . . . he was careful to hide his achievements."[34]

Any discussion of Patrick Barry and his episcopacy, especially in South Florida, cannot omit the mention of his brother William and his sister Catherine. Twenty-three years younger than Patrick, William was born in County Clare, Ireland, in 1886, decided to join the same diocese as his brother, and was ordained June 1910, at St. Mary's Seminary, Baltimore. He became assistant pastor at the Cathedral parish, St. Augustine, in 1910, and, after several other assignments, was founding pastor of St. Paul's, Jacksonville, where he spearheaded the erection of a combination church–school building, one of the first of its kind in the state. Although the people of St. Paul's petitioned to have their pastor remain with them, the bishop transferred him to Miami Beach, where he remained as pastor of St. Patrick's for forty years, building an outstanding parish plant and wielding influence with South Florida Catholics and non-Catholics alike.[35]

The Barry brothers' sister Catherine (1881–1961) joined the Dominican Sisters of Adrian, Michigan, in 1913 and took the name Sister Gerald. Both she and the superior of the Adrian Dominicans attended the consecration of Bishop Barry in 1922, at which time the congregation was invited into the Diocese of St. Augustine. Sister Gerald encouraged the foundation and expansion of the Adrian Dominicans in Florida, especially South Florida. In 1933, she became Mother Gerald when she was elected superior of the Adrian Dominicans, a position which she held for more than twenty-five years.[36] In that time, she did much to increase the professionalization, prestige, pride, and expansion of her congregation. She was a woman of vision, ambition, and energy, whose personality resembled William's more than it did Patrick's. Both individually and corporately, the impact of these three Irish persons upon South Florida Catholicism cannot be overestimated.

Unlike Bishop Curley in 1914, Bishop Barry did not have to confront virulent anti-Catholicism when he took over in 1922, although the Ku Klux Klan and anti-Catholicism grew strong in the 1920s in other parts of the United States. Perhaps the rapidly souring post–World War I economic boom riveted South Florida's attention on financial rather than ethnic, religious, or cultural concerns.[37]

With both Dixie Highway and the Florida East Coast Railroad in place, South Florida had been prepared to capitalize on the boom. In addition, the Everglades Drainage District, comprising 4.3 million acres, had been created in 1906, and the prospect of draining South Florida lands had triggered a land sales boom beginning in late 1911, although drainage projects lost steam with the outbreak of war.[38] But with the creation of the Miami Chamber of Commerce in 1913, and its 1915 advertising campaign in nineteen northern newspapers, Miami had become more widely known as a winter resort and consequently frequented by more tourists than ever before.

From 1915 to 1925, Miami's population grew from 7,000 to 130,000, that is, by 1,857 percent.[39] Anxious investors fed South Florida real estate development, which was raging out of control by 1921. Land prices soared and speculators realized quick, substantial profits. National magazines flaunted the possibilities of fast fortunes that could be made in South Florida real estate, even by "little people," attracting even more investors to the Gold Coast. By 1925, $7 billion worth of Florida real estate had changed hands.[40] This frenzied buying and selling inflated real estate prices and caused organizational difficulties for the Church as it attempted to meet the demands generated by the influx of people. Barry ended up buying two strips of property in the Miami area for future church sites in November 1925, a purchase which he claimed cost $550,000 and one which later proved to have been a very bad price at a very bad time.[41]

Much of the profit from the land speculation in Miami was a "paper castle," due to the method of buying and selling, and it began to be blown away by the fall of 1925. Florida received bad press in stories of land fraud, overspeculation, and failures of the newer and smaller banks.[42]

Although the boom was over by the fall of 1926, its finale was the hurricane of September 17–18, 1926, stilling once and for all any hope of economic revival. Miami, which had not experienced a major storm since 1910, was hit with winds exceeding 125 miles per hour. When it was over, 392 people were dead, 6,281 were injured, and 17,784 families were directly affected by property damage. Structural losses resulted from flimsy construction and the lack of building codes. Immediately after the hurricane, Bishop Barry instructed his pastors to take up a special collection throughout the diocese for storm relief, netting $4,502.30. Donations totaling $8,126.75 came from outside the diocese. The physical losses to Church buildings were relatively small.[43]

The Great Depression thus began in South Florida in late 1925 and did not abate until about 1940; this "tropical depression" had its effects on Catholicism. By December 1926, properties the diocese had bought in Miami for $550,000 in 1925, plus another $100,000 parcel of South Florida real estate, were threatened with foreclosure.[44] Barry described the situation to his sister in late 1927: "Florida is fine but suffering a severe purgatory now. It may be all for the best, but everyone seems bankrupt. Fr. William [Barry] is getting plans for his church in shape on a modest scale. His congregation is reduced on account of the general exodus and lack of employment. . . . In spite of financial collapse we are still building and planning and hoping."[45]

To make matters worse, South Florida was battered with another hurricane on September 20–21, 1928. This time most of the damage was in Palm Beach County. It was estimated that 2,381 homes were past repair; some 8,220 whites and 4,000 Negroes were homeless. Three Palm Beach County churches and a Dominican Sisters' academy suffered uninsured damages of over $40,000.[46] William Barry, pastor of St. Patrick's, Miami Beach, wrote of a personal car tour he took the day after the hurricane:

> Up to the last these poor people had been led to believe that the hurricane would miss them. . . . The property damage is exceedingly great. I do not think that in the area referred to [Delray to Palm Beach] there is a single house or building which is not seriously damaged. A great percentage of structures are a total loss. . . . No more tall churches or schools for me in this territory. We must build carefully. We must likewise refuse to get ourselves in large financial obligations for costly churches.
>
> The unfortunate people in all this territory have been hard pressed by losses and debts; they can hardly meet this terrible visitation with any hope. In 1926 we had some money left,

but now after two years of poverty the poor unfortunates are in the saddest plight.[47]

Catholicism in South Florida was able to survive the tropical depression and to avoid financial ruin by three means: the generosity of wealthy benefactors, the bishop's begging letters to northern dioceses, and the bishop's own financial skill, along with his association with William C. Bitting, a non-Catholic financier from St. Louis.

Benefactors had always been key in the development of Catholicism in South Florida and were particularly important between 1925 and 1940. Mr. George E. Merrick, the developer of Coral Gables, donated the grounds for a church, school, and support facilities opposite the St. Joseph's Academy plot. Liguori H. Matheson donated some lots for a church in the center of Coconut Grove in 1925. Mrs. Mary Kerr of New Jersey donated land for a church in Hialeah. Mr. George Beck of Brooklyn, who admitted losing a lot of money in the South Florida land boom, wanted to build a church before he lost everything and donated the construction of a wood-frame church called St. Mary's in Little River in 1930.[48] By far the most generous and important benefactor of the period was Edward Riley Bradley of the Idle Hour Stock Farm, Lexington, Kentucky, a winter visitor to Palm Beach since 1898. Bradley was that rare benefactor whose generosity came with no strings attached and no fanfare, whose concern was for the best interests of the Church, whose generosity was always covered by anonymity. Two examples of his style of giving are his substantial contribution to the construction of the Catholic Center at the University of Florida (he expressly refused to have his name placed on any plaque or tablet there)[49] and his quiet deeding to Archbishop John McNicholas of Cincinnati of a building in Palm Beach for a Catholic institute for scientific research.[50]

Bishop Barry further supplemented diocesan income by continuing the Florida episcopal tradition of begging for money. During the crucial period of ecclesial financial crisis, Barry wrote to Archbishop Curley in Baltimore in December 1926, mentioning the $650,000 Miami real estate debt and the threat of foreclosure. Barry thought that the diocese was on the brink of financial ruin and begged Curley for help. He wrote a similar desperate letter to George Cardinal Mundelein of Chicago. Curley sent checks; Mundelein sent pastoral and brotherly advice. In the 1930s, Barry gave speeches not only in Chicago and Baltimore but in other dioceses as well, appealing for funds for his "poor and missionary" diocese.[51]

By far the most crucial factor in keeping the diocese solvent during the years 1925–40 was Bishop Barry's association with W. C. Bitting, Jr., a St. Louis broker and financial advisor. Bitting's business relationship with the diocese and Bishop Barry began in 1927, at which time he was instrumental in arranging for the diocese two loans of $190,000 and $100,000 from the American Trust Company of St. Louis. These loans were decisive in getting the diocese through the worst of its financial crisis.[52] At the time, Bitting assured Barry that the bishop could borrow from the Bitting Company solely on his signature: "We would not make a single loan in Orlando today, although we are willing to loan the Bishop of St. Augustine as much money as he wants to borrow, realizing that he will not borrow more than he ought to borrow . . . we know that the Episcopal Signature is all of the security we need."[53] Bitting was a businessman and charity was not his line. He loaned the diocese money because he felt it was a good risk, and, through his business association with Barry, he was introduced to other ecclesiastical clients. He asked Barry's help in making loans to the Church in Argentina, Chile, Peru, Brazil, and Cuba. Also, through Barry, he made a loan of $800,000 to the Archdiocese of Baltimore in May 1928. Bitting continued to expand his dealings with Bishop Barry and the diocese. In March 1928, Bitting reminded the bishop again that the credit of the Church of Florida was good. The bishop could borrow at rates "tremendously lower than those others can obtain, if indeed, the others can obtain loans at all." Bitting reiterated that his company was prepared to loan the bishop any amount.[54]

Yet the relationship between Bitting and Barry was not simply financial. As early as 1928, Bitting was expressing his personal admiration for Barry. In 1930, he took the Bishop to a private club in New Hampshire for two weeks. As Barry later wrote, Bitting "derives so much pleasure in parading his dearest friend the Bishop whom he loves to entertain in his home." Patrick Barry, however, was not the kind of man who sought or enjoyed the company of the rich. He told his sister that the New Hampshire stay involved the discussion of financial matters: "My visits to Bitting have been principally on financial affairs . . . otherwise I would not have gone." The bishop had a great influence on Bitting,[55] who grew more appreciative of the manner in which Barry handled his financial responsibilities: "The performance of the Diocese of St. Augustine, has far and away exceeded in spirit, as well as in literal performance, that of any other one with whom we have ever come in contact, in your Divine Church. . . . I do not believe that there is a single Diocese in the United States that has done that which Bishop Barry did in sending the cheque, receipt of which is acknowledged in the enclosure."[56] Bitting had less than amicable monetary dealings with other American Catholic dioceses.[57]

Bishop Barry's financial problems did not end with the settlement of the Miami property debt but continued throughout the 1930s. In fact, most of his episcopal preoccupations involved obtaining or refinancing loans for parishes and schools to keep them from going under.[58] Barry commented on the financial situation of 1930: "Continued financial troubles here have chained me to a post. . . . It has been one crash after another until our people are helpless, their distress is reflected in bankruptcy of parish finances. . . . I have met the obligations so far by my own resources and my borrowing power. The people can do but very little."[59] Pastors scrimped to meet parish loans, some of which were refinanced several times. But since most Catholic Floridians were either broke or poor, pastors simply could not keep up with their outstanding loans and had to rely on the resources of the ordinary, a most abnormal situation because parishes were expected to be self-supporting.

Barry, being the corporation sole,[60] was responsible for both the spiritual and temporal well-being of his flock. In 1931, the bishop had $1,028,500 in loans outstanding for the diocese.[61] Although Bitting supplied most of the money and financial acumen for refinancing schemes, even his firm was on the ropes by 1933; he could lend no more. Ultimately, it was Barry who paid the loans and kept the diocese solvent, although precisely how he did this needs more investigation. He did use some of his own financial patrimony to aid the diocese, with the result that his personal accounts became entwined with those of the diocese, creating problems for his heirs. It was not until 1940 that Florida parishes returned to financial independence so that Barry could write, "Our individual units in par-

TABLE 3.2. Diocese of St. Augustine, 1914–40

Year	Dio. priests	Rel. priests	Rel. women[a]	Parish schools	Acad-emies	Churches[b]	Missions	Stations	Semi-narians	Cath. pop.
1914	18	28	170	18	12	23	20	66	12	40,600
1922	29	28	189	20	5	32	45	150	13	51,014
1933	71	44	255	30	5	61	41	150	15	67,802
1940	75	62	373	–	–	62	41	150	21	65,767

SOURCES: OCD-1915, pp. 678–80; OCD-1923, pp. 589–92; OCD-1934, pp. 644–47; OCD-1941, pp. 563–66.

a. Includes postulants and novices.

b. With resident pastors.

ishes seem to be able to take care of themselves now. I do not have to bolster them up by my personal finances."[62]

Bow to the Wind, 1914–40

Even the critical cultural and monetary issues of the Curley and Barry years could not altogether sway pastoral attention from concerns about personnel, the erection of parishes, and ministry to black Americans.

Like his predecessors, Bishop Curley was interested in the development of ecclesial personnel, especially priests. Curley sought burses (endowments) for his seminarians in the United States and Ireland.[63] Native Floridian vocations during the Curley years (1914–22) were virtually nonexistent. A few northern seminarians studied for St. Augustine and a few northern priests expressed interest in working in the diocese,[64] but the most important source of seminarians and priests continued to be Ireland. Curley had Irish seminarians in four seminaries in Ireland, at St. Mary Seminary, Baltimore, Mt. St. Mary Seminary, Emmitsburg, and in Europe at Fribourg and Rome.[65]

During the Barry years (1922–40), the number of diocesan priests increased from 29 to 75—by 158 percent—and the total number of priests serving the diocese increased from 57 to 137—by 140 percent (table 3.2). A 1928 report from the apostolic delegate encouraged Barry to increase his efforts, so far unproductive, to supply native priests—"a most important point which can scarcely be overemphasized."[66]

Barry did pick up a number of northern seminarians (especially from the Josephinum), some of whom would later become well known in South Florida. Northern priests continued to petition for temporary or permanent positions, and Archbishop Curley often referred surplus or problem priests to Barry. In the 1920s and early 1930s, both Baltimore and New York, for example, had surplus vocations and priests.[67] Barry was not always happy with the quality of extern priests who applied to St. Augustine, observing in 1925 that "all the cripples and undesirables in the American continent want to help us out in Florida" and repeating much the same sentiments the following year.[68] He was not willing to sacrifice quality for quantity. Ireland continued to be an important source

of priests, and Barry visited there at least twice to recruit seminarians and priests. From 1922 to 1940, Barry had Irish seminarians in four Irish and three continental seminaries, as well as in St.
Mary's, Baltimore. American-born seminarians for Florida studied in the Pontifical Roman Seminary, Rome, and various American seminaries.[69]

Although Barry had inherited $76,000 in burse money from his
predecessor, in 1924 he instituted an annual collection for seminarians—the first diocesewide collection in Florida and the only
such annual collection at the time. The South Florida parishes of
St. Patrick's (Miami Beach), St. Ann's (West Palm Beach), Gesu
(the name since 1922 of Holy Name, Miami), and St. Edward's
(Palm Beach) were consistently the highest donors to this annual
collection, which in 1940 amounted to over $8,000.[70]

Bishop Barry introduced two communities of religious women
who were to have tremendous influence in South Florida during
his episcopacy and in the years to come: the Adrian Dominicans
and the Allegheny Franciscans. The former were the third group
of religious women to be introduced into South Florida (the Holy
Names and the Sisters of St. Joseph of St. Augustine preceded
them), but they became the most powerful and influential in the
area.[71] As early as 1915, Father Patrick Barry, then pastor of Assumption Church, South Jacksonville, intended to ask the Adrian
Dominicans to help in his parish. However, it was not until his
consecration as bishop that the congregation was invited into the
diocese. South Florida was undergoing its boom years, and the
Adrian Dominicans were expanding their apostolic commitments.
The Adrian Dominicans' first Florida foundation was at St. Ann's
School in September 1923.[72]

Having been given a seven-acre tract on the shore of Lake Worth
by benefactor E. R. Bradley, the Dominican Sisters went about
building a convent and private academy of their own, at a cost of
$106,126. It was opened in October 1925 and called St. Ann on-
the-Lake Academy until 1939, when the name was changed to
Rosarian Academy. Begun with about twenty boarders in 1925,
the academy had seventy-three by 1938. Boarders and students of
the parochial school shared the same facilities until 1934, when
they were separated.

Rosarian became a social as well as educational center in the latter half of the 1930s when the apostolic delegate, Ameleto Cico-

gnani, stayed there for six weeks each winter. The delegate's presence brought many members of the hierarchy to South Florida, including Cardinals Dennis Dougherty of Philadelphia, Edward Mooney of Detroit, and Samuel Stritch of Chicago and Archbishop John McNicholas of Cincinnati. In addition, as other Adrian Dominicans were assigned throughout South Florida, Rosarian became the gathering-place for parties and fellowship. When the Allegheny Franciscans arrived in West Palm, the two communities came together at the academy almost weekly for a social event.[73]

By the early 1930s the Adrian Dominicans staffed not only Rosarian but also four parochial schools in South Florida. They were the most influential and most favored women religious in South Florida by reason of the Barry family ties (the bishop, the pastor at Miami Beach, and the superior of the congregation), as well as by educational reputation. By 1931, the Adrian Dominican Sisters were seeking to have their members receive recognized bachelor's and graduate degrees, beginning with the novices. The educational upgrading led the energetic Mother Gerald to approach her brother William Barry in 1937 about founding a Catholic women's college in Miami, and in March 1939, he located a suitable piece of property in Miami Shores. His knowledge of the area, his innumerable contacts, his financial and real estate acumen, and his common sense, sound advice, and wealth of experience made him an invaluable ally in the monumental task of establishing a Catholic college in Miami. He steered benefactors toward Mother Gerald's project; Bishop Barry contributed funds.[74] The school was named "Barry College," ostensibly in honor of the bishop, who died the summer of 1940 just before it officially opened. However, the name "Barry College" was not preceded by the word "Bishop." Perhaps the chosen title was more appropriate, since it was through the cooperation and vision of the Barry triumvirate that the first Catholic college in South Florida was founded.

Unlike the Adrian Dominicans who were educators, the principal contribution of the Allegheny Franciscans was health care; they began with the first Catholic hospital in South Florida, established in Miami Beach. (As early as 1915, a proposal had been made to have the Sisters of the Holy Names take over the operation of the Mercedes Hospital in Key West, but nothing came of the idea.)[75]

James A. Allison, a long-time partner of Miami Beach developer

Carl Graham Fisher, built a three-story, forty-room, $3,652,000 hospital on a Miami Beach island donated by Fisher for the purpose. It opened January 1, 1926, with the finest, most modern equipment, complete with exquisite china and a chef from the Waldorf-Astoria in New York. Not surprisingly, costs soon exceeded budget, and, burdened also by the failure of Allison's health and the poor economic conditions, the hospital was forced to close. It was suggested to Allison that a group of sisters be asked to take over the management of the hospital. Father Barry of St. Patrick's was consulted, and in October 1927, Mother Alice, former administrator of a New York City hospital and now administrator/superior of the Miami Beach foundation, and five other Allegheny Franciscans came to staff the Allison Hospital. They set about at once to pare operating expenses. Allison disapproved of the sisters' economies and informed them that he would not renew their contract; when he died in August 1928, his heirs sought to turn the building into a casino. Fisher intervened, saying that the property was donated with only one purpose: having a hospital erected on the spot. With help from Bishop Barry and a benefactor, Robert Graham of Detroit, the sisters bought Allison Hospital for $250,000 in 1928 and renamed it "St. Francis Hospital," the first Catholic hospital in South Florida.[76]

In November 1938, Mother Alice and a few Allegheny Franciscans opened a nursing home for the poor in West Palm Beach, having received encouragement, land, and money from a group of Catholic women in Palm Beach and from E. R. Bradley. From the beginning, Mother Alice had in mind establishing a hospital to serve the needs of the poor and middle classes, who were not being well served by another private hospital in the area, Good Samaritan. The Board of Governors of Good Samaritan voiced strong public opposition to a Catholic hospital on the grounds that the community did not need, and was unable to support, another hospital. Nevertheless, St. Mary's Hospital was established in 1939 and had prospered into a 110-bed facility by 1942. Although their contribution to South Florida was primarily in medical care, in 1938 the Allegheny Franciscans also opened a parochial school in Ft. Myers.[77]

In addition to the growth in personnel between 1914 and 1940, the number of parishes in the diocese tripled and stations, missions, and parish schools doubled. The estimated Catholic population in the diocese increased by 62 percent to approximately 65,000, indicating that South Florida Catholics did not grow proportionally as fast as did the general population. This growth and the development of ecclesial personnel meant larger parishes and missions in South Florida. During the Curley period, St. Theresa of the Little Flower Parish, Coral Gables, was established in 1919. Holy Name Parish, Miami, replaced its wooden church with a more permanent structure and changed its name to Gesu in 1922. Bishop Barry, during his first visit to South Florida in December 1922, placed the cornerstone of Gesu, with a public parade of the Catholic population and lay societies. The previous Sunday, St. Anthony's in Ft. Lauderdale had been dedicated. Both events signified to the rest of the populace, and to Catholics themselves, that Catholicism was firmly established in South Florida.[78]

Several former stations and missions became parishes during the Barry period.[79] Many parishes still had missions and stations attached to them; for example, Father Gabriel Ruppert, OSB, and later Father Michael Beerhalter at St. Anastasia's traveled all week on the missions, returning to Ft. Pierce on the weekend. Parishes founded during this period started from scratch with a small group of people, usually drawn from different places of origin. In many instances, missions and parishes grew new-born in places where no people or no community had existed before.[80] But the key parish of the period was St. Patrick's, Miami Beach, and the key pastor of the period was Monsignor William Barry.

Although William Barry was the first pastor of St. Patrick's, he was not the first priest in Miami Beach's Catholic community. A winter visitor, John J. O'Leary of the Diocese of Scranton, said a regularly scheduled Sunday Mass at Miami Beach Gardens Theater from February 21 to May 17, 1926. In conjunction with Father James McLaughlin, SJ, pastor of Gesu, O'Leary organized a lay financial committee and selected a site for the church. O'Leary asked Bishop Barry if he might stay on to build the church and went so far as to make arrangements for twelve sisters from the North to come to Miami Beach. Bishop Barry was not very excited about O'Leary's suggestions and sent his brother, William, to take over the parish. William arrived May 12, 1926; O'Leary left for his home diocese on May 18.[81] Thus began Bill Barry's forty-year pastorate on Miami Beach at St. Patrick's.

Like his sister Catherine, William Barry was a person of vision, ambition, and energy, who wasted no time in getting things done. The parish school was opened by six Adrian Sisters in 1926 in five polo stables donated by Carl Fisher. Though battered about by the 1926 hurricane, the pastor, parish, and school forged ahead. Barry was instrumental in getting the Allegheny Sisters to take over Allison Hospital. He got the lay financial committee to work. Financed by Bitting, the new Romanesque-style church was dedicated and the Spanish-style school opened, both in 1929. Father Barry was working at such an intense pace that the bishop expressed concern to Sister Gerald about his physical and mental health. In 1931, St. Patrick's Patrician Club was organized, affiliated with the national Council of Catholic Women, and divided into two departments, the Altar Guild and the Study Club. The parish debt had to be refinanced in 1932 and Barry was slowed somewhat by the depression. However, in 1936 he built an auditorium, clubrooms, and cafeteria and in 1937 the first Catholic gymnasium in the area.

Bishop Barry made his brother a domestic prelate in 1937 and vicar general in 1939. In 1939, Monsignor Barry founded the *Florida Catholic*, the first Catholic diocesan newspaper in Florida, and built the Campanile, a tower which housed a set of bells donated by Carl Fisher in 1929. As mentioned, Monsignor Barry was a key figure in the establishment of Barry College in 1940. His ambitious building program was fueled by a yearly fund drive during the winter tourist season for some specific parish project.[82]

Although unequaled by any of his priest contemporaries as a financier and builder of an enviable parish plant, Monsignor Barry's interests extended beyond bricks and mortar. He took an active interest in community affairs and was well known as a friend of Miami Beach's Jewish population, who often sought him out for advice. He had an Irishman's interest in local and national politics. One of his guests for his Silver Jubilee in June 1935 was Father Charles Coughlin,[83] about whom he wrote to Mother Gerald in 1938, "I am glad Father Coughlin came to St. Joseph's. He is still a power in the land and is working for the interest of the Church and the glory of God."[84] Monsignor Barry initiated a social service program in the parish in September 1936 with an Adrian Dominican in charge. The development of St. Patrick Parish and the involvements of its pastor continued long after 1940.[85] While not the biggest or busiest parish in South Florida, St. Patrick's from 1926 to 1940 outdistanced others in reputation and organization.[86]

Parish expansion in South Florida from 1914 to 1940 owed much to lay energy and interest. Parishioners in South Florida were extremely active on a local level during this period. Letters of complaint about priests were common.[87] Father William Mullaly, for example, seemed to give grounds for complaint wherever he went. His parishioners in Seabreeze would not pledge money for a church. His pastoral style so disturbed his parishioners at St. Anthony's, Ft. Lauderdale, that they wrote individually and collectively to both Archbishop Curley and Bishop Barry. Lay pressure and financial chaos caused Mullaly's transfer to St. Helen's, Vero Beach, though he wanted to go to Miami. Complaints continued from Vero, and parishioners refused to make further payments on a debt.[88]

Members of the laity also petitioned for schools and parishes. They organized into committees, raised money, and signed petitions to muster the 150 members that Bishop Barry's policy required for creating a mission or parish. Building committees proliferated, with women and men equally involved in founding and supporting parishes and institutions.[89] As in earlier periods, lay benefactors, as exemplified by E. R. Bradley, were important in institutional building. Catholic communities too poor to support themselves were often funded by outside agencies such as the Catholic Extension Society. Giving the faithful a sense of pride in ownership and identity, church and school building was a great unifying element for a parish.

But the laity did more than complain, petition, and raise money. They also volunteered to provide services not otherwise available. The Catholic Instruction League, begun in September 1921, was made up of women who taught public school children after school in Catholic homes. The Miami Knights of Columbus, Father Brown Assembly #1726, was established March 29, 1914, with the help of David J. Heffernan of Miami, a judge of the Dade County Civil Court for thirty years, who came to Miami in 1911. He was also instrumental in organizing the Miami Saint Vincent de Paul Society and the Catholic Daughters of America. Mrs. Agnes F. Dillon and Miss Edna Kyle worked with blacks in West Palm from 1927 to 1938. In December 1930, Michael McNally, SJ, pastor of

Gesu, called a meeting of Miami laity to organize an agency to act as a liaison between the Community Chest and the St. Vincent de Paul Society. The result was Associated Catholic Charities, formed in March 1931 with lay officers. The newly formed Community Chest allocated $7,460 to the new Catholic agency with the stipulation that a trained social worker be employed. In 1939, the agency changed its name to the Catholic Welfare Bureau.[90] Each of these lay movements was either approved, encouraged, or guided by local clergy. Some diocese-wide-sponsored lay groups were the Holy Name Society (first annual convention in 1928), the Diocesan Council of Catholic Women (first annual DCCW Convention in 1931), and the Knights of St. Gregory (1937).[91]

Besides personnel and parochial expansion, a third area of the growth and development of South Florida Catholicism was ministry to ethnic groups, especially black Americans. Pastoral problems with the Cubans of Key West seem less acute from 1914 to 1940 than in the pioneer period, perhaps because the Cubans were no longer mostly immigrants or unfamiliar with American culture. From 1914 to 1940, the ministry to black Floridians continued and even increased as a result of the heightened social consciousness brought about by the depression, as well as the impact of the social teachings of popes and bishops.[92] Black apostolates of the period emphasized the establishment of black missions or parishes, encouraged by black Catholics themselves.

Bishop Curley showed an ongoing interest in blacks during his episcopacy, in one of his first acts asking for a census of black Catholics in his diocese. Miami reported 30 black Catholics, Key West 150. In mid-1914, Curley invited the Josephites to take over St. Benedict the Moor Church in St. Augustine, thus making it the first independent black parish in the diocese, not simply a mission of the Cathedral. Following the example of his predecessor, Curley sought and received money from national organizations for the black apostolate.[93] When Curley asked for another black Catholic census in 1915, Father McLaughlin of Holy Name, Miami, added to his report, "No lasting results can be made unless a priest lives and works in their midst."[94]

During the Barry years, activity in the black apostolate increased. In Miami, black Catholics attended Gesu but had separate seats and received communion last. In June 1927, a committee of six black Catholic men asked the pastor of Gesu to establish a sep-

arate black Catholic mission. In July 1928, a Mass for black parishioners in the basement of Gesu drew 150; in November, Mass was
celebrated in a vacant store on Northwest 11th Street. A wood-
frame church, built and dedicated "St. Mary of the Missions" in
April 1932, subsequently became a school; a Spanish-style stucco
church, built entirely by parishioners, was completed in October
1937 and dedicated "St. Francis Xavier Church" in February 1938.[95]
In Key West, where St. Francis Xavier School for blacks was still
operating, seventy adults attended Mass for black Catholics in a
large classroom in 1934. This chapel for blacks was closed in 1941.
In West Palm Beach, two white women, Mrs. Agnes F. Dillon and
Miss Edna Kyle, and Mrs. Victoria Huyler, a black Bahamian,
conducted a catechism class and the Sacred Heart Club for Adults
for Negroes of the area from 1927 to 1938, when the Adrian Dominicans took over the work.[96]

The Adrian Dominicans, under the dynamic aegis of Mother
Gerald, were interested in work among black Floridians as early
as 1936:

> What I would like to do is to establish a school for the colored
> children. . . . Right here in West Palm Beach. There is a flock
> of them and I wonder how many of them are Catholics. . . .
>
> Perhaps you are frowning on this and that you think I am a
> little crazy but I have been besieged by Sisters for Porta Rico
> [*sic*] and for China. . . . Since I am here I realize that we could
> do some missionary work right at home and now that Blessed
> Martin de Porres is being presented for canonization, the col-
> ored question is rather in the limelight. . . .[97]

In West Palm Beach, Blessed Martin Mission, attended by a Jesuit
and with classes conducted by two Adrian sisters, opened in December 1937; the sisters soon had thirty-one children and sixteen
adults in classes. Much energy was expended by the two sisters to
make the mission a success, as illustrated by the Christmas cards
and pageant invitations sent throughout the North and Midwest to
friends of the Adrian Sisters, generating local and national publicity
and contributions. Mother Gerald also spearheaded the founding of
St. Martin de Porres Mission in Ft. Pierce in conjunction with St.
Anastasia's Parish. Two Adrian Dominicans began work there in
1940, with forty-eight children as their charges. Since there was

only one black Catholic family in Ft. Pierce (the Browns), most of the students were non-Catholics.[98]

Catholic ministry among the blacks during the years 1914–40 was conducted for Catholics and non-Catholics. Although the ecclesial personnel were white religious men and women, black Catholics were organizers, teachers of religion and, in some cases, of grade school, as well as supportive coworkers. Although these black Catholic institutions never reached large numbers, they were highly visible in both the black and the white communities.

Characteristics of the Period

The general population in the State of Florida increased by 92 percent from 1920 to 1940, while the Catholic population increased by approximately 62 percent and the number of parishes tripled. The most dramatic diocesewide growth and development took place between 1922 and 1933. During the Barry years, eleven South Florida parishes had built new parochial structures by 1932.[99] Laity petitioned for parishes and supported their construction. Women were particularly involved with religious education, altar societies, and charitable-social parochial clubs.

During the period, the number of diocesan priests tripled, the number of religious priests and sisters doubled, and the number of diocesan seminarians changed little. Seminarians were recruited vigorously in Ireland, which continued to be the chief source of priests for Florida. In 1914, none of the four South Florida pastors had been Irish-born; in 1922, one out of six was, and in 1940 nine out of seventeen (with a concentration in Miami).[100] The Irish clergy predominated, especially in Palm Beach, Broward, and Dade counties, led by their two Irish bishops, yet both bishops needed native vocations.[101] Both were concerned about this matter, but neither had much success with recruitment, an indication of the missionary character of the diocese. Priests of the period became somewhat more stationary than their frontier or pioneer predecessors, though most parishes still had missions and stations. Through the foresight of Curley, South Florida Catholic communities by 1940 were primarily ministered by diocesan clergy. Due to the depression, pastors and parishes were unable to remain financially self-sufficient. In spite of Patrick Barry's personal inclinations, the bishop and diocese administered the financial burdens of the individual parishes, though it was the bishop himself, and not a bureaucratic structure, who performed this task.

Between 1914 and 1940, three male and five female religious communities came to work in the diocese. The Adrian Dominicans and the Allegheny Franciscans added to their respective fields of education and hospital care a professionalism hitherto lacking in Catholic South Florida. Pastors with a parish of any size were expected by their parishioners to provide a school and sisters to teach in it. After World War I, the popularity and necessity of academies declined. More and more, sisters taught and administered parish schools, with the parish paying operating expenses and sisters' expenses. The crowning achievement for Catholic education in the period was the opening of Barry College for Women. In the late 1930s both Adrian Dominicans and Allegheny Franciscans became active in the black apostolate, joining the Sisters of St. Joseph and Holy Name Sisters. Religious priests, especially the Jesuits, played an important role in the ministry to Cubans, blacks, and other ethnic groups during the period.

What ties the period 1914–40 to previous eras is its missionary character. New parishes and schools were being opened. Many parishes still had missions and stations attached to them. The bishop, the key to growth and development, was constantly on the move both within the diocese and on begging trips to the North, always emphasizing the missionary character of the diocese.[102] As Bishop Barry commented: "I have been making headquarters here [St. Patrick's] for the past three weeks during visits to West Palm Beach, Lake Worth, Lauderdale, Hollywood, Miami, and Coral Gables. In this way I get a chance to rest up between Sundays. Wherever confirmation is administered they expect me to speak at all the Masses, visit missions, boost their appeals for finances, etc., and when Sunday is over, I'm about finished too. I've been on the road continuously since New Year's Day. Every Sunday a heavy programme . . . almost half my time I'm on wheels going over the entire territory."[103] Missionary Florida always had problems with finances, but the strains of the depression almost capsized Florida Catholicism. Through benefactors, Bitting, the Extension Society, the Catholic Board of Missions, the Propagation of the Faith, and Bishop Barry's own financial skills, the Church not only rode out the storm but made headway. The personnel situation improved, though the missionary diocese still lacked native vocations and relied heavily on Irish missioners.

The year 1940 marked another shift in the growth and development of South Florida Catholicism. The depression was over, and America was being pulled into World War II. The death of Patrick Barry on August 13, 1940, brought a new ordinary (appointed only three days later) to the See of St. Augustine. South Florida entered an era of prosperity and boom which called forth from the Church a fresh response.

4

Prophetic Vision and Pragmatic Implementation, 1940–58

The informal, unstructured leadership style of Patrick Barry gave way in 1940 to the vigorous prophetic vision and pragmatic organization of his successor, Joseph P. Hurley. The seeds of more centralized organization had been sown during the depression with Barry's personal financing of diocesan parishes. But it was the force of Hurley's personality more than anything else that created an "organizational revolution" within the diocese, especially in South Florida, enabling the missionary Church to respond to the unprecedented demands of the post–World War II period and to prepare for the future.

The Episcopacy of Joseph P. Hurley

Archbishop Hurley had more influence upon the course of Catholicism in South Florida than had any of his predecessors during their terms of office. A native of Cleveland, Joseph P. Hurley (1894–1967) studied philosophy at St. Bernard Seminary, Rochester, and theology at St. Mary's Seminary, Cleveland. Ordained in 1919, he was six years an assistant at Youngstown and Cleveland

and secretary to the ordinary. When Edward Mooney was named the apostolic delegate to India (1928–31), he asked Hurley to be his secretary. After three years in India, Hurley went with Mooney to Japan in the same capacity, and in the winter of 1933, Hurley was the chargé d'affaires of the apostolic delegation in Japan in Mooney's absence. From 1934 to 1940 he was attaché to the Secretariate of State, Vatican City State, succeeding Francis Spellman. Consecrated bishop of St. Augustine in Rome on October 6, 1940, and installed on November 26, Hurley sought advice from his mentor, Mooney, now the archbishop of Detroit. Hurley also numbered among his friends some of the ecclesiastics in Rome: Giovanni Montini, Alfredo Ottaviani, and Walter Carroll, a priest from Pittsburgh who succeeded Hurley at the Vatican.[1]

For part of his episcopacy Hurley had problems with arthritis, although he remained outwardly vigorous and energetic; an indefatigable worker, he expected the same performance from his subordinates. He often said that there were two kinds of bishops: one sits behind a desk; the other rides the fences. Hurley was the latter. In his efforts to learn everything he could about the diocese, he set up bases or "co-chanceries" at St. Edward's in Palm Beach, Holy Family in North Miami, in St. Petersburg, and in Orlando, besides his St. Augustine chancery. Often he worked in the back seat of the car which a priest drove for him. Although he kept in touch with St. Augustine by mail or messages delivered by train or bus, much diocesan business was conducted over the telephone. Hurley was a well-read man of European tastes who considered himself an intellectual. In the mid-1950s he commissioned Yugoslavian sculptor Ivan Mestrovic to create several works for the diocese; he had an interest in history and sought to make the Shrine of Our Lady of Leche a pilgrimage site for the diocese as early as 1941.[2]

More important, Hurley had a vision of the future of a larger, more developed, more influential Catholicism, a vision which was beyond the grasp of most of his contemporaries. His organizational mind and indomitable will enabled him to take practical steps to make that vision a reality. He worked for the development of parochial and diocesan institutions that would serve white, black, and brown Catholics, as well as the larger Florida community. Although a difficult and demanding taskmaster, Hurley knew his priests personally and was generally respected by them. When a priest was sick in the hospital he was there to visit him; when a priest was in trouble he was there to help him. He was not, however, close to the laity; even children made him nervous. Priests were instructed to keep the laity away from him after confirmations.

Archbishop Hurley was a churchman. He had the best interests of Catholicism in mind and at heart in whatever he did, but he was insular and insulated in his view of the Church and the episcopacy. He responded as a creative innovator under extremely difficult circumstances where demands for the services of religion far exceeded available resources of material and personnel. Setting a style of leadership, he also established policies, procedures, and structures that the Church in South Florida would follow for years. Beyond his physical and organizational testament, Hurley gave to South Florida Catholicism a confidence, a sense of destiny and of vibrancy.[3]

The most pervasive concern of Hurley's episcopacy was to organize and structure the diocese so that his vision of the Church might be implemented. The first organizational problem he had to deal with was $2 million left from the Barry episcopacy. The Barry family, headed by William Barry, demanded from the diocese a personal settlement from the deceased bishop's estate. This settlement was drawn out over several years because Bishop Barry did not keep his personal accounts separate from the diocesan accounts: in fact, he often did not keep accounts at all. In addition to this financial confusion, marriage forms and dispensations from the Barry years were found stacked in a chancery closet. It took two years for them to be registered by the assistant chancellor.[4]

After traveling extensively around the diocese visiting far-flung parishes and confirming, Hurley began his organizational efforts in earnest in June 1941. At that time he wrote to the Catholic University of America School of Social Work to arrange a sociological survey of the diocese; it was completed in 1944. Also that June, he instituted at St. Leo's Abbey an annual priests' retreat. So he might know his priests better, he compiled an alphabetical list of them— ninety-nine in all, twenty-six of whom were stationed in South Florida. Meanwhile, he applied for money from the Extension Society.[5] By the end of his first year, Hurley had asserted his position with even the powerful Adrian Dominicans and Monsignor Barry over the issue of a controversial conference to be held at Barry College. After working out a compromise with the sisters, he added to a letter to Monsignor Barry a paragraph that reveals his personality and position: "May I add a word of more general advice? You will always find me most anxious to promote the various good works in which you are interested and to enhance them, as best I may, by my approval and assistance. . . . But you will have to understand, once and for all, that I am running this Diocese, and that in matters of grave moment I shall set the policy. The present difficulty could have been entirely avoided if you had used frankness and courtesy in your dealings with the head of the Diocese. Believe me when I say that I am not in the habit of accepting the fait accompli."[6] By the end of 1941, it was clear to all but the most obtuse that Hurley was a different sort of bishop than Barry, that he was in charge of the diocese, and that he would confront all those who might think otherwise.

In subsequent years, Hurley continued to centralize the diocese around the office of bishop. In 1942, he reinstituted his predecessor's practice of having clergy conferences. From the results of a 1943 survey he had conducted, Hurley drew up a map of the diocese showing the boundaries of all seventy-three parishes, twenty-one of which were in South Florida, including one in Monroe, eight in Dade, two in Broward, and four in Palm Beach counties. The bishop also centrally organized the popular parish Eucharistic devotion of Forty Hours, giving out a yearly schedule for each parish in the diocese.[7]

In the midst of this organization of the diocese, much of Florida was co-opted to meet the military aviation needs of World War II. In 1941, Florida had six air training schools; by 1945, forty military airfields had been constructed. Unique to Florida, a number of tourist facilities were converted into military housing, and by April 1942, the Army Air Force was using 70,000 hotel rooms on Miami Beach. One-fourth of the Army Air Force officer candidates and one-fifth of the enlisted men trained at Miami Beach.[8]

The effects of the war added to Hurley's organizational problems, the most serious difficulty to provide enough priests for the ever-increasing number of servicemen in the state. In December 1942, Hurley sent a begging letter to eleven northern bishops asking them to lend him priests to augment his personnel for the upcoming Christmas holidays. Fifty priests were sent as temporary help, which pleased Hurley and got his priests through the Christmas pressures.[9]

By March 1943, Bishop Hurley was feeling the pinch and pressure of the military invasion of his diocese even more. The diocese had 300,000 servicemen but only 35 chaplains—9,000 men for each chaplain. Because several northern ordinaries were under quota in sending military chaplains from their dioceses, and these same ordinaries had ignored his attempts to solicit priestly assistance, Hurley was indignant over what he called the "callous indifference to our plight by our brother Bishops of the North."[10]

Besides serving the American military during the war, Florida priests also ministered to non-American servicemen. Clewiston had a military training base for English soldiers, some of whom were Catholic. Also located near Clewiston toward the end of the war was a German prisoner-of-war camp housing soldiers from Rommel's North Africa Corps, a high percentage of whom were Catholic. They built their own chapel from discarded lumber. Peter Reilly, who said Mass for them, was struck with their singing the *Gloria* and *Credo* in their native tongue, a liturgical practice unheard of in the United States. Two German-speaking priests, Michael Beerhalter from St. Anastasia's and Abbot Francis from St. Leo's Abbey, came to the camp every month to hear confessions.[11]

In spite of wartime pressures, during these years Joseph Hurley set out to build a financial base for ecclesial growth. Toward the end of his episcopacy, Patrick Barry had instituted an "Orphan Collection" in all the parishes. Hurley expanded this annual collection into the Catholic Charities Drive, with the first collection taken up in February 1944. Priests and lay volunteers went from door to door for the collection, which turned out to be successful. The beneficiaries were the nursing homes and the homes for the aged in the diocese, such as Villa Maria in North Miami.[12]

Later that year, Hurley launched not only the 1944 census but also the Second Annual Catholic Charities Drive, for which Miami was the headquarters. It was during this drive (February 1945) that Hurley introduced his most famous and infamous fundraising technique, the parish quota. Other methods included designating certain affluent individuals as "special givers," publicly advertising in the *Florida Catholic* and seventy-five secular newspapers, hiring the John Price Jones Corporation to coordinate the campaign, soliciting corporate gifts (which included luncheons for corporate representatives), and using pledge cards, radio spots, and volunteer lay workers. Laymen chaired various committees. The drive netted $765,548.78, and from its proceeds, in an act which many local pastors felt was foolish, Hurley purchased forty acres of property from the Deering Estate (Vizcaya) in June 1945 for the site of a proposed Catholic hospital.[13]

For the Third Annual Catholic Charities Drive, Hurley again focused his attention on Miami, with the object of the drive a new Catholic hospital to serve Miami as the "Mayo Clinic of the South." To realize his goal, he introduced another new technique in Catholic fundraising in Florida, the fundraising dinner. At the first such occasion, Hurley addressed his affluent audience of prominent Catholics and non-Catholics: "Money, like nobility, has responsibilities . . . if Miami is to become great, let it not become a community where wealth accumulates and men decay." At this time, he appointed Sister Theresa Joseph, SSJ, administrator of the new institution, to be named Mercy Hospital. The $2 million hospital drive, with the slogan "Mercy for all," would occupy the energies of Bishop Hurley and his associates for the next five years.[14]

The second phase of the growth and development of South Florida Catholicism during Hurley's episcopacy, 1945–50, was characterized by the absence of the ordinary from the diocese. In November 1945, Hurley, a former Vatican diplomat, was appointed regent of the apostolic nunciature in Belgrade, Yugoslavia, and in early December 1945 he left the diocese for his papal appointment.[15]

As planned by the bishop, the Mercy Hospital Fund Drive continued in his absence. The former chancellor, Auxiliary Bishop Thomas J. McDonough, newly consecrated on April 30, 1947, was delegated to run the day-to-day operations of the diocese as well as to oversee the hospital drive's new phase with its $1.5 million goal. Besides the yearly Mercy Hospital dinner, priests and laymen knocked on doors canvassing funds to meet parish quotas. Miami businessmen were invited to luncheons to muster a broad base of community support. Father Lamar Genovar, a native St. Augustinian, was in charge of the details of the Mercy fundraising. An office was set up in downtown Miami, for the twelve fund drive committees, all of which had Protestant and Jewish members in addition to prominent Catholics.[16]

In spite of all the effort, energy, and planning, the drive brought in only 10 percent of its projected goal, and considerable opposition to Mercy Hospital was expressed both within and without Catholic circles. The sisters and doctors of St. Francis Hospital

were against the idea. Pastors were unhappy because of the parochial assessments that had to be met. Many Miamians could not
see the point in giving to such a venture since hospitals already existed in the community. At the same time, Miami-area Jews were
ready to start building Mt. Sinai Hospital, a project which shrank
the donor pool. To add to these problems, freshwater springs
were encountered in excavating the construction site, pushing expenses $250,000 over budget. Related expenses included training
twelve sisters of St. Joseph as nurses for the new hospital. When
the campaign began to bog down, Hurley appointed Monsignor
James E. Enright as its new executive director in November 1949
and Sister Mary Edith, SSJ, as new hospital administrator.[17] As
McDonough reported to his absent superior: "The situation here,
as you know, is quite serious in view of Mercy Hospital. I certainly
am at my wit's end trying to figure out how we are going to finance this project without jeopardizing our complete diocesan
financial structure. It is so easy to make a mistake, but so terribly
difficult to extricate oneself from it, particularly where money is
involved. Even when Mercy Hospital is opened, we shall still be
faced with a deficit each year."[18] The one man who unswervingly
believed in the Mercy Hospital project, and who pushed it through
to completion from thousands of miles away, returned to Florida
in 1950. He dedicated Mercy Hospital in February 1951, after it had
opened in December 1950.[19]

Although Mercy Hospital took a great deal of time and energy,
the establishment of new parishes was a continuing preoccupation
in the years 1945–50. Many servicemen who had trained in South
Florida during World War II returned after their military service to
settle down with their families. The addition of over 1,560 miles of
highway in Florida during the war and the growth of commercial
airlines and airports made South Florida easier to reach. Electrical
refrigeration, the use of pesticides (DDT), air conditioning, Vet-
erans' Administration financing for new homes, a rising standard
of living, and literature extolling the advantages of life in tropical
Florida all attracted residents to South Florida. The postwar building boom was hampered only by a lack of building materials.[20]

The center for major growth and development of the Diocese of
St. Augustine was South Florida from 1945 on. Miami grew to the
north and west, including the parishes of St. Michael's (1946), St.
Rose of Lima (1948), and Holy Family (1950). By February 1949,

nine diocesan parish projects were under way. By June of that year, ten of the eighteen parish projects of the diocese were in South Florida. Most of the construction was not of churches but of a "chapel/auditorium" or "school/auditorium/chapel/cafeteria," indicating rapid growth and scarce capital, as well as a pragmatic approach to parish building. The Diocesan Development Fund was the "instrument in helping our parishes financially."[21]

When Hurley returned in 1950 from Yugoslavia, he was a different man. He carried the personal title of archbishop in recognition of his service to the Church in Yugoslavia, but, more important, he had acquired a broader vision of the world and the Church, and he set about transforming this vision into reality.[22] At the same time, South Florida continued its postwar boom from 1950 to 1958, the third segment of ecclesial growth and development under Hurley.

Hurley added a new dimension to the diocesewide collection instituted by Bishop Barry in 1924 for educating seminarians and establishing seminary burses. On December 3, 1952, at a clergy conference at St. Anthony's, in Ft. Lauderdale—a meeting which pastors of the diocese would long remember—Hurley's announcement that he was initiating a new "Missionary Burse Appeal" in all parishes was met with complete silence. Although not sure of the details, the priests knew their bishop well enough to understand that this project was going to mean more assessments. In a follow-up letter, Hurley informed the pastors of the purpose of the appeal, which was a special one not related to the yearly Diocesan Development Fund: "The Burse Appeal is designed to give us an endowment fund for a part of the heavy expenses we shall incur in the education of these future priests." Quotas were established for each parish in the diocese, and the assessment was an incredible 160 percent of the income of each parish for the year 1953, payable over the span of two years. The dismay of the pastors was understandable, but most met their obligation by 1957, although some pastors had to take out loans to do it.[23]

What the archbishop did not tell his priests either at that memorable conference or in the letter was that he wanted to collect the staggering sum of $5 million to invest in Florida real estate. The money (of which about $4 million was collected) was to finance his plans internally, to provide for the future growth and development of parishes and institutions, and to finance clerical education.[24] It was a creative, ambitious, bold, and, as it turned out, farsighted scheme.

Hurley went about converting the money from the Missionary Burse Appeal into real estate. He already had a reputation throughout the state as a shrewd purchaser of land, but it was only after he had the financial base from the new assessments that he was able to buy property methodically and in quantity. The properties purchased were speculative only in the sense that the archbishop was making an educated guess as to where future growth of Catholicism might take place. His intention, which he carried out successfully, was to purchase the land as sites for future parish or institutional development. With the rapid growth of South Florida real estate values in subsequent years, Hurley's foresight in the early and mid-1950s was accurate and immensely valuable for the development of Catholicism for decades to come.

Hurley's method of land purchase in South Florida was based on cooperation from local pastors and eventually on the work of four priests: Monsignors John O'Dowd, John McNulty, John O'Looney, and James Nelan. These men were instructed by Hurley to visit the county school board property office, officers in Florida Power and Light, the district manager of the phone company, and several real estate developers, to inform themselves about future plans and probable growth trends in South Florida. Based upon knowledge thus acquired, they were to buy property suitable for future parishes or institutions: parish property was to be ten acres, institutional property twenty-five acres. Larger tracts were purchased for special purposes, such as the Camp Matecumbe property (150 acres) and Biscayne College Property (130 acres). Generally, parish property was to be located on two main roads and approximately three miles north or south of the nearest existing or prospective parish property. In time, a chain of present and prospective parish sites extended along the southeast coast, with a second chain three miles west and even a third chain in formation (map 2). Hurley himself normally inspected all property before it was purchased and, in most cases, had the land rezoned when he bought it. This land would provide an important legacy for Hurley's successor in South Florida.[25]

Throughout the 1950s, South Florida and its Catholic popula-

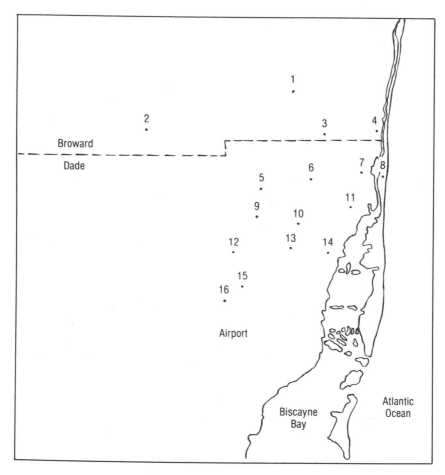

Map 2. Pattern of Archbishop Hurley's land purchases in the 1950s, North Dade and South Broward counties.

1. St. Stephen's
2. St. Bartholomew's
3. Annunciation
4. St. Matthew's
5. St. Monica's
6. Visitation

7. St. Lawrence's
8. St. Mary Magdalen
9. St. Mel's (OLPH)
10. St. James's
11. Holy Family
12. Immaculate Conception

13. St. Vincent de Paul
14. St. Rose of Lima
15. St. John the
    Apostle
16. Blessed Trinity

TABLE 4.1. General Population of South Florida Cities, 1940–60

City	Year	Population	Percentage increase
Ft. Lauderdale	1940	17,996	107.7
	1950	36,328	101.9
	1960	83,648	130.3
Ft. Myers	1940	10,604	16.8
	1950	13,195	24.4
	1960	22,523	70.7
Ft. Pierce	1940	8,040	67.4
	1950	13,502	67.9
	1960	25,256	87.1
Hialeah	1940	3,958	52.2
	1950	19,676	397.1
	1960	66,972	240.4
Key West	1940	12,972	0.7
	1950	26,433	104.5
	1960	33,956	28.5
Miami	1940	172,172	55.6
	1950	249,276	44.8
	1960	291,688	17.0
Miami Beach	1940	28,012	331.4
	1950	46,282	65.2
	1960	63,145	36.4
North Miami	1940	1,973	–
	1950	10,734	444.0
	1960	28,708	167.4
West Palm Beach	1940	33,393	26.6
	1950	43,162	28.1
	1960	56,208	30.2

SOURCE: U.S. Bureau of the Census, *Census of the Population, 1960, vol. 1, Characteristics of the Population*, pt. A, pp. 11-9–11-10.

tion continued to grow, for the same reasons as it had in the postwar period but even faster. Northern, southern, and western portions of Dade County were all developing; parts of Broward and Palm Beach counties grew at a somewhat slower pace. In North Dade, two parishes were established; in South Dade and the Keys, four; in West Dade, six (map 3 and table 4.1). Development outside of Dade County included Resurrection, Queen of Martyrs (named for the Yugoslavian martyrs under Cardinal Stepinac), and Assumption in Broward County, and St. Mark's, St. Vincent Ferrer, St. Juliana's, and St. Joan of Arc in Palm Beach County.[26]

Parochial and Extraparochial Planning

As the diocese grew and developed under Hurley, systematic planning in parish building, education, and social service helped the Church meet the increasing pastoral demands created by rapid growth. Hurley laid down basic principles of parish building. After property was secured by the diocese, and after consultation with the pastors of the area, the archbishop sent a priest into the locality to "start a parish." At this point, with some seed money to rent a residence, the pastor or administrator was on his own. He was to find a place to say Mass, such as a tent, theater, school auditorium, or hotel lobby; he was to get Catholics of the area to attend; and he was to organize fundraising for the church and school that were to be erected. The church was to be a provisional structure, often a multipurpose hall. Since the laity wanted Catholic schools, and because schools would bring parishioners to church, a school was usually put up before a rectory and often before the provisional church. The pastor then had to find sisters who would teach in the school and in the CCD program (Confraternity of Christian Doctrine, religious education for public school students held after school or on weekends). Teaching faculties almost always included both lay people and religious.

Fund drives for churches were often conducted by professional companies, which Hurley liked but pastors did not because they took a considerable cut of the donations as a professional fee. Construction could not begin until a quarter of the total building cost was at hand; when the temporary church was built, the diocese began billing the pastor for the land at cost plus 6 percent interest. Parishes took out loans from banks with which the diocese did business at 5.5 percent interest. The pastors, most in their thirties and forties, had all they could do just to keep up with the interest.

Parish building created a unique spirit. Parishioners, most of whom were recent arrivals, became caught up in the excitement. The pastor was responsible for getting the parish started, but lay people also felt an obligation and pitched in. Shared efforts by pastor, sisters, and lay people created an exhilarating sense of unity, cooperation, and pride as the church, which symbolized the parish community, took physical form from sacrifice and struggle.[27]

Laity of the period were involved with parish building differently than in previous years. Efforts were more centralized and guided from above than they had been in the past. No longer did people have to raise petitions, money, and even churches in order to create a parish, since parishes were now usually erected according to a central plan based on properties purchased by the archbishop. Occasionally, however, lay people did appeal for parishes, since the central plan had a certain flexibility.[28] One example of the give and take between the laity and ecclesiastical authorities is a 1947 petition by the Polish Roman Catholics of Miami asking for a Polish language church. But even with the formation of a schismatic Polish National Catholic parish in 1950, Hurley steadfastly refused to build a Polish language church in Miami. In 1954, with the arrest of Cardinal Wyszynski in Poland by the Communists, Miami Poles organized a large demonstration at Notre Dame Academy, where they erected a cross to commemorate the event. Soon a Polish Catholic priest was assigned to St. Michael's so that Mass and confession could be administered in Polish.[29]

Catholic lay benefactors continued their important role, although Hurley was not one to curry their favor nor to acquiesce to their demands. Frank J. Lewis of Chicago was an outstanding benefactor of the Church in South Florida. Born in 1867, Lewis sold his coal tar chemical business in the 1930s, moved into the investment business, bought Florida land during the real estate bust (12,000–15,000 acres in Palm Beach County alone), and set up the Frank J. Lewis Foundation to channel his benefactions. As an enthusiastic supporter of the Extension Society, Lewis donated twenty chapels and churches to the Diocese. St. Francis Assisi in Riviera Beach, St. Philip Benizi in Belle Glade, and St. Juliana's in West Palm Beach were all built with Lewis money. He also helped with the establishment of burses.[30]

The Knights of Columbus continued to function in the Miami community, though perhaps not with their former visibility. Because certain firms had an unwritten policy of not hiring Catholics, Catholic professionals in South Florida had difficulty finding acceptance in their given professions, a situation that improved by the early 1950s. The Holy Name Society dwindled in importance, fading by 1958 into virtual extinction on a diocesan level. Since its basic purpose was to get men to Mass, confession, and communion, and since more men were doing so in the 1950s than ever before, the organization became superfluous.[31]

The Diocesan Council of Catholic Women was active in the

period 1940–58. Every parish had a chapter. In the days before women had many other outlets for their time and talents, some 300 to 400 Catholic women of Southeast Florida were actively helping migrant workers, teaching CCD, transporting children to CCD, raising funds for Catholic charities, and carrying on other worthy projects. Women were secretaries, teachers, and nurses in Catholic parishes, schools, and institutions. Several women had important roles in the Catholic Service Bureau, and a Miami woman reporter for the *Florida Catholic* was one of eleven women among the national correspondents for the National Catholic News Service. According to the 1944 census, Catholic women in Florida were more faithful in all religious obligations than were men.[32]

Adding to the retreats held at diocesan institutions beginning in 1943, the Florida West Coast Laymen's Retreat Association was founded under the guidance of Monsignor Charles Elslander in 1945, the only organization of its kind in the state at the time. In 1948, the Knights of Columbus of Tampa organized a motorcade from Miami, with 120 men from South Florida parishes, to the Miami Men's Retreat, which would be held annually at St. Leo's for another ten to fifteen years.[33]

Parish development was closely related to the development of Catholic education, an area in which Hurley was especially interested. In one of his early actions, he appointed Father Romuald Philbin superintendent of schools in 1941, sending him to Catholic University of America for a graduate degree in education which was completed in 1943. In December 1947, Hurley ordered a survey of all diocesan elementary and high schools to determine the status of educational facilities in relation to resources and needs. Beginning in 1949, Hurley established a Newman apostolate for the University of Miami.[34]

Hurley sought excellence in the schools within his jurisdiction. Up to 1950, except for a few academies run by religious, Catholic grade schools and high schools were on the parish grounds, often occupying the same building. The consolidated public high school was developing in Florida in the early 1950s, and small parish high schools could not compete, especially for accreditation purposes. In 1950, Hurley decided to create a central Catholic high school system, the first two schools being Bishop Kenny in Jacksonville (1952) and St. Thomas Aquinas in Ft. Lauderdale (1952). Bishop Curley High School for Boys in Miami was opened in September

1953, along with its sister school, Notre Dame Academy. Hurley wanted his diocesan priests to teach in the central high schools to help instill native vocations, a decision that caused consternation in the minds of many pastors who ended up with part-time assistants as a result. To prepare these diocesan priest-teachers, Hurley sent them to Catholic University or other universities. To help bolster his diocesan high school plans, Hurley initiated a new fund-raising drive in 1957–58.[35]

As part of the reorganization of education in the diocese in the 1950s, Hurley appointed Father William McKeever superintendent of schools (January 1951). McKeever had the difficult tasks of implementing Hurley's education plans and acting as mediator between the diocese and religious educators, as well as begging motherhouses for personnel.[36]

Parochial education in South Florida in the 1950s had a missionary quality about it. McKeever wrote in 1953 that thirteen parishes had to open schools immediately, "even though we do not have religious communities committed to staffing them." In September 1956, three Allegheny Franciscans began Holy Name School in West Palm with 213 students in a converted World War II Air Force warehouse. The parish chapel had used an adjoining warehouse since 1953. The interior of the school-warehouse was partitioned by beaverboard into six classrooms, a small cafeteria, and an office. Across the state in Naples, St. Ann's School was started by the Sisters of St. Joseph with no school building at all. Classes were held in the fall of 1956 under a tree in the churchyard and in the church building.[37]

Besides parish building and Catholic education, the bishop and his people responded to the diocese's tremendous population growth by planning for the development of Catholic social services. Bishop Barry and his predecessors had a nineteenth-century concept of Church charity as a local and individual matter. Hurley had a more modern notion of Catholic charities as centrally organized and professionally staffed. In 1941, he invited Father Thomas Mitchell, dean of the School of Social Work at Catholic University, to survey the diocese with an eye to setting up a diocesewide Catholic charities program. When Mitchell stressed the necessity of having trained social workers for the project, Fathers Paul Leo Manning and Rowan Rastatter were sent to Catholic University for the necessary preparation. In 1942, Hurley sent four young women to Catholic University's School of Social Work on diocesan scholarships to prepare them to staff diocesan Catholic charities. In June 1943, Father Manning was appointed diocesan director of Catholic charities. Hurley commissioned a second study, which suggested that Manning organize agencies in Tampa and Jacksonville to complement the one operating in Miami. All three then joined to form a diocesan unit. In February 1947, the Miami charter of the Catholic Welfare Bureau, Inc., was surrendered to the diocese, and the Miami agency became a regional office of the diocesewide organization, the Catholic Charities Bureau.[38]

The bureau was supported by proceeds of the annual Catholic Charities Drive (by 1950 called the Diocesan Development Fund). From the abundance of the 1945 drive, St. Joseph's Villa for dependent children, staffed by the Sisters of St. Joseph, opened in Miami; it operated until 1961. Other social service projects sponsored by the diocese from this period included the first Catholic Home for the Aged, Villa Maria, staffed by the Carmelite Sisters, and, in West Palm Beach and Miami, Morning Star Schools for mentally retarded children, staffed by the Sisters of St. Joseph of St. Augustine. A regional office of the bureau was opened in Ft. Lauderdale in 1957. Also in that year a small group of Hungarian refugees was processed by the Miami regional office; the experience from this resettlement procedure would prove invaluable to the agency in a few years. The directors of Catholic Charities during the Hurley period were Paul Manning (1943–54), Rowan Rastatter (1954–58), and Bryan O. Walsh (from February 1958).[39]

Personnel

Besides parish building, education, and social service concerns, Catholicism in South Florida had the ever-present missionary problem of too few ecclesial personnel. Ireland continued to supply most of the seminarians for the Diocese of St. Augustine in this period. In Bishop Barry's time, Irish seminarians were usually from County Clare, men the bishop knew. Under Hurley, the system of Irish recruitment broadened. Of the twelve major seminaries in Ireland in the early 1940s, only two were for those studying for Irish dioceses; those two accepted only students who were at the top of their class intellectually. The other ten, called "missionary seminaries," were filled with young men who had to seek out a non-Irish bishop. One seminarian who became a priest in South Florida had written one hundred letters to bishops in the United States, Canada, Australia, New Zealand, Scotland, and England. One of Florida's selling points for the Irish seminarians and rectors was the missionary character of the diocese. For most of Hurley's episcopacy, Father Thomas O'Donovan was in charge of Irish recruitment, managing to find more than eighty seminarians for Florida. In 1949, the diocese had college and theology seminarians in six Irish seminaries and in Rome.[40]

In 1948, the diocese had American college seminarians (mostly nonnatives) in seven U.S. seminaries. Hurley preferred those who were intellectually able to have a European education in Rome or Louvain. In the summers of 1949 and 1950 when Hurley was in Yugoslavia, a villa was rented in northern Italy for the bishop and his European seminarians. Life at the villa was an extension of the controlled atmosphere of seminaries of the period.[41]

Ordained priests with intellectual and administrative promise were sent away for graduate study, a policy that complemented Hurley's plan to have diocesan priests, rather than male religious, teach in the central Catholic high schools. But parochial coverage was often stretched thin by this policy, especially in conjunction with the scarcity of native vocations and the missionary demands of a rapidly expanding Catholic community. As a result, Hurley often had to rely on extern priests: in 1957, the diocese had twenty-three priests who were there on loan, six Spaniards, nine Americans, and eight Europeans.[42]

Like his predecessors, Hurley was concerned with native vocations. To encourage them he tried a variety of techniques, such as giving awards to outstanding altar-boys throughout the state, ordering the *Florida Catholic* to give good coverage to ordinations, and organizing a vocation campaign in Catholic high schools by having priest-students at Catholic University of America come to Florida to give high school retreats. (Coleman F. Carroll of Pittsburgh, who was to become Miami's first bishop, was one of those priests in 1944.) Hurley also ordered pastors, principals, and chaplains in the armed forces to emphasize Vocation Sunday.[43]

The number of native diocesan priests increased slightly during the Hurley years, though not in proportion to the effort expended in trying to attract them. On November 24, 1945, the first native vocation from South Florida, Father David Heffernan, son of Judge Heffernan, was ordained at St. Theresa of the Little Flower Parish, Coral Gables. Lamar Genovar (1943), Harold Jordan (1949), and Louis Roberts (1953) were other Florida-born priests of the period.[44]

The work of a diocesan priest was demanding, especially during the work of parish building; some priests burned themselves out under the pressures. Although priests attended meetings relatively infrequently during the period either on a diocesan or parish level, a call to St. Augustine meant a twelve-hour car trip up U.S. Route 1. In Barry's time, priest transfers came once a year, in October; few were affected. Under Hurley, priests were more frequently transferred as burgeoning needs dictated. Thomas O'Donovan was pastor of six parishes between 1943 and 1958, Rowan Rastatter was in thirteen in the years 1941 to 1964, and William McKeever was in seven from 1945 to 1958. Their parish duties were augmented with extraparochial assignments. To illustrate what this explosive growth meant for some priests, Monsignor James Nelan held the following positions between 1952 and 1954: administrator of St. John the Apostle, pastor of Blessed Trinity, president of Notre Dame Academy, administrator of Immaculate Conception, administrator of St. Mel's, administrator of Blessed Trinity, and pastor of Immaculate Conception.[45]

The diocesan priesthood in South Florida was still predominantly Irish, and these missioners had to adjust to a new land and a new expression of Catholicism, usually with little preparation. One young Irish priest formed his first impression of American Catholicism from attending Easter Sunday Mass at St. Patrick's Cathedral, New York, and listening to Fulton J. Sheen preach. All eyes and ears were riveted on the preacher; in his innocence this young Irishman thought that all American Catholic congregations were amazingly attentive and accustomed to Sheen's kind of eloquence. After a long train ride, the same young Irish priest was almost bowled over by the heat in St. Petersburg, where he was assigned. He received a further shock when he tried to hail a taxi and the black driver, under a segregated cab system, would not pick him up. Older Irish priests often took these young Irishmen under their wings. In Miami, for instance, Monsignor Barry was known as a patriarch of the Irish brigade, hosting a card game for Irish priests every Sunday night for thirty years. Barry was strict with his assistants (in by eleven and no free days) but was well respected among the clergy of the area, among whom he had considerable influence. In many ways, Barry represented the model of pastoral success—an enviable parish plant, a financially secure parish, and recognized community influence.

American-born diocesan priests in South Florida were a minority. Native and near-native vocations had increased but were not numerous enough to develop a base of native clergy in the presbyterate. Some felt at home among the Irish. Others felt that some pastors ostracized the Americans, disrupting the bonds of priestly fraternity.[46]

Confirmations and Forty Hours Devotions (solemn exposition of the Blessed Sacrament during forty hours) provided opportunities for socialization among the priests in the times before days off and when many priests were in single-man parishes. Retreats and clergy conferences also filled this need for priestly fraternity. Hurley rewarded his outstanding clergy with the title "monsignor" to a degree unequaled by his predecessors; from 1940 to 1958, at least twenty-three were named as a reward for work faithfully accomplished.[47]

During the entire Hurley period, only two institutions received new male religious: Barry College (1940), a Dominican campus minister, and Our Lady of Angels Parish, Jacksonville (1952), Augustinian priests. The paucity of religious priests stemmed from Hurley's basic distrust of religious due to his experience of them in Yugoslavia, where he felt that they had turned on Cardinal Stepinac. Also, with native vocations in mind, he wanted his diocesan priests to be involved with youth work, so as to foster diocesan vocations. Some Florida men entered religious life, among them Curtis Washington, SVD, a native of Coconut Grove, the first black from South Florida ordained to the priesthood (1949), and Raymond Brown, SS, ordained at St. Rose of Lima Parish (1953) for the Society of St. Sulpice.[48] Charles Mallen, CSSR, conducted parish missions during the 1950s throughout South Florida. The model used for these missions was the same as in the nineteenth century, that is, the method advocated by Joseph Wissel, CSSR.[49]

In decided contrast to the way he froze religious order priests out of the diocese, Hurley brought in no fewer than sixteen communities of sisters between 1940 and 1958. He took a more benign attitude toward the sisters' communities because of the demand for parochial schools and sisters to teach in them.

The superintendent of schools and the vicar of religious were searching constantly for religious women's communities. Diocesan officials and pastors who went North on begging tours found that getting sisters to come to Florida was not easy in the 1950s, one of the biggest obstacles being Florida's distance from northern and midwestern motherhouses. Another problem was that in the post–World War II period the demand for sisters in the schools exceeded the supply. Pastors sometimes opened parish schools even if they had no sisters. Five parochial schools opened in the diocese by 1956 were staffed exclusively by lay teachers.[50]

Among the teaching communities new to South Florida in the Hurley years were Sisters, Servants of the Immaculate Heart of Mary (Monroe, Michigan), 1951; Sisters of the Holy Family of Nazareth (Chicago), 1955; Sisters, Servants of the Immaculate Heart of Mary (Philadelphia), 1953; Irish Sisters of Mercy of Clogher and Kinsale, 1955; School Sisters of Notre Dame (Baltimore), 1957.[51]

Not all of the newly introduced communities taught in parochial schools. Carmelite Sisters of the Aged and Infirm came to Florida first at St. Leo's Abbey north of Tampa in 1941. From 1951 until 1958, they staffed Villa Maria Nursing Home in North Miami. The Religious of the Assumption established Assumption Academy in Miami for affluent young American and Latin American women.[52]

Women's communities that had been in South Florida before 1940 expanded their work. The oldest, the Sisters of the Holy Names, carried on their educational efforts, in 1957 teaching more students in their three schools in Key West—997 pupils—than at any time before or since. In 1879, the first vocation from Key West came to the Sisters. From 1879 to 1959, the Holy Names accepted eighteen young women into the community from South Florida, six during the period 1940–58. In 1958, of the 234 sisters of the province, 36 were stationed in South Florida.[53]

The Allegheny Franciscans continued their hospital ministry at St. Francis and St. Mary's, with Pine Ridge Hospital for blacks moved to a forty-bed wing of St. Mary's in 1956. In 1950, the sisters opened a school of nursing at St. Mary's, later expanding their work into four South Florida parochial schools. In 1958, of the 847 professed sisters in the community, 55 were stationed in South Florida.[54]

The Adrian Dominicans continued to staff four parochial schools, a black mission, Rosarian, and Barry College. From 1940 to 1958 their added commitments included five parochial schools, a black mission, and a diocesan high school. Although they were no longer the most favored religious community in the diocese, the Adrian Dominicans had the most prestige, the best reputation as educators, and the largest number of sisters of any community in South Florida—127 assigned to South Florida in 1958, out of 1,934 in the congregation. Through Barry College, where from the beginning sisters from various communities in South Florida attended summer courses, they exerted a professional educational influence upon other South Florida religious. Because of their repute and the constant demand for teaching sisters, they could choose their assignments. The Adrian Dominicans did well in getting vocations from South Florida, with 10 percent of their postulants from that region in 1953.[55] In spite of occasional "family spats" between the Adrian Dominicans and Hurley, correspondence was always cordial between them, and South Florida benefited from the Dominican sisters' service and stature during the period.[56]

The Sisters of St. Joseph of St. Augustine, Florida's oldest religious community, went through a period of rapid expansion of services, stretching resources to the breaking point as they responded to the needs of the diocese as indicated by the ordinary. Hurley called on the Sisters of St. Joseph time and time again to render help that was needed and which no one else would provide, his intention being to give them the opportunity to serve in key apostolates, an opportunity they did not have in the Barry years.[57]

In the 1950s the small community of Sisters of St. Joseph was becoming too diversified and dispersed. In South Florida they were staffing four high schools, three migrant ministry teams, a home for dependent children, homes for the retarded, two hospitals, several elementary schools, and a school for blacks. Worse, they were constantly being shifted from one place to another to fill in gaps until other help came or needs changed.

In 1956 they began a mission in Corazal, Puerto Rico, and at the same time were asked by the archbishop to withdraw from their diverse existing commitments in order to open more elementary schools. The next year they dedicated a new novitiate in Jensen Beach, while they reduced their novitiate training to eighteen months, a change pushed by Hurley.[58] More than any other religious community, the Sisters of St. Joseph reflected the missionary character of the diocese.

Although many of their members were native Floridians, the Sisters of St. Joseph also recruited young women from Ireland. A number of Irish women had joined the community in the Barry years (1937–39); efforts at Irish recruitment were renewed between 1947 and 1956. By the mid-1950s native vocations, mostly from North Florida, were sufficient without further Irish recruitment, but by then the Irish sisters were an important leadership core of the Sisters of St. Joseph. However, whether native or Irish, vocations were never sufficient to match the missionary needs of the diocese. By the end of 1957, the diocesan community had a total of forty-one commitments statewide, eighteen of them in South Florida. Ninety-one sisters were in ministry in South Florida out of about two hundred professed sisters.[59]

Although life for religious women in South Florida was basically the same as in other places in the country in the forties and fifties, there were some differences. Virtually all the sisters who came saw South Florida as a missionary land, as they would China or Brazil. Religious from the North saw the South in general, and South Florida in particular, as populated by lukewarm Catholics untutored in their faith.[60]

The sisters who came had considerable adjustments to make. Educational institutions and facilities were often disappointing compared to their northern counterparts. Although priests and laity often were more friendly and worked more closely with the sisters than in the North, sisters involved in nonparochial institutions such as high schools and hospitals were more isolated and got less of a sense of the diocese, priests, or people than did those teaching in parochial schools. The sisters had to work with lay faculties and not just with their fellow sisters as in many northern schools. In Florida, the sisters taught not only in the parochial school but also CCD on the weekends. The greatest initial adjustment they faced was the heat: "That first day in Miami we took five years off our lives—the heat and humidity were intense. And, as we learned later, the worst was yet to come."[61] Some northern sisters loved South Florida Catholicism and did not want to return to the North. Others, far away from their culture, their mother-house, and their family and friends, could not make the adjust-ment. "We are anxious to be back once again among many more IHM's. So we bring to a close another year of toil in God's Vine-yard in our Southern Mission of Florida."[62]

Another unique feature about religious life for women in South Florida was the comradeship among the different communities serving in the area. The sisters gathered with other religious not only for meetings but also for social events. The Irish Mercy Sis-ters of Immaculate Conception visited the Holy Family Sisters at St. Brendan's; such a social gathering of Irish-born and Polish-American sisters would have been a rarity in northern dioceses with their rigid national parishes and neighborhoods. Rosarian was the social hub of the Palm Beaches; Barry College was an edu-cational center as well as a social gathering place.[63]

Ministry to Ethnic Groups

As in the past, the Church continued to allocate resources and per-sonnel for ministry among Florida's blacks and Hispanics. Among the new developments under Joseph P. Hurley were black conven-tions, black missions, a black hospital, Latin American education programs, parochial Hispanic ministry, and migrant ministry.

Organized by the Josephite priests and supported by Hurley, a Convention of Colored Catholics was held at St. Benedict the Moor Parish, St. Augustine, in May 1941. Black Catholics from Ft. Pierce, Miami, and around the state attended, along with the bishop himself and the women religious who taught in the dio-cese's black schools. In preparation for a second convention of Florida's black Catholics in May 1942, Hurley organized a Com-mission on Negro Work in the Diocese, to propose a definite plan "for the advancement of the Church among Colored." Meeting in January 1942, members presented a report suggesting that prop-erty be purchased at favorable sites in Florida's Negro commu-nities, social centers be established in black communities, better black hospital facilities be secured, black vocations be fostered, and Negroes be delegates to all religious and business sessions of every other diocesan convention.[64] This last suggestion from the all-white commission was the most controversial in segregated southern Florida.

Only the first of the commission's suggestions—purchasing property in black communities—was ever implemented. Because of the legal and social segregation of blacks in Florida, the Church's position with Negroes was difficult. For example, a Miami Beach city ordinance forbade "colored people" from residing in Miami Beach. As late as the 1950s, Gov. LeRoy Collins (1955–61) accepted segregation as part of Florida custom and law, in March 1956 appointing a committee of jurists and lawyers to study legal means to retain segregation in defiance of the Supreme Court's ruling in the famous *Brown v. Topeka Board of Education* case (1954).[65]

Segregation had created suspicion between blacks and whites, and Florida Negroes seemed less than enthusiastic about the Catholic missionary approach, as evidenced by the paucity of black converts. Part of the difficulty, too, rested in the mentality of Florida's white Catholics. For example, in the fall of 1945, Hurley sent a letter to all pastors asking what they were doing for blacks. The response to the survey was uninspiring in quality and quantity; only twenty-three of the seventy-three parishes answered. No followup ensued from the chancery.[66] Such lackadaisical response and follow-up were not allowed in other matters, such as the Catholic Charities Drive, even with the ordinary's absence in Yugoslavia.

Of the difficulties of ministry to blacks in Florida and his own approach to the task, Bishop Hurley wrote in 1944:

> Perhaps it is just as well that you [Fr. M. J. Ahern, SJ] declined this invitation as it is extremely difficult to touch at this time the question of race relations in the South without arousing emotions which would becloud the real issues of justice and charity, and which would prejudice our practical missionary approaches to this problem. The difficulty is not concerned with the statement of principle; it is rather with applications here and now when feeling runs high and tension mounting [*sic*].
>
> I myself have preferred to go ahead with a program of missionary and scholastic expansion in colored areas, in the hope that the preaching of Christian charity by example will be

more potent in the long-run than academic discussion of rights and wrongs of prevailing attitudes.[67]

With only a few exceptions, the specialized work done among blacks in Miami, Coconut Grove, Key West, West Palm Beach, Clewiston, and Ft. Pierce was done by religious men and women. The Adrian Dominicans continued to work at Blessed Martin Mission, Ft. Pierce, under the energetic leadership of Sisters Mary and Marie. In 1944, they rented a storefront as a recreation center. Attendance was small, but regular baptisms, first communions, and confirmations continued year after year, though the numbers decreased by 1948 and the Dominican Annals for the mission stop in 1952. However, the work of the sisters did not go on without qualitative effect. When the energetic Sister Mary was transferred in 1943, Ruth Bullard, a young black woman who attended the mission, wrote: "Now for Sister Mary. We enjoyed her very much. . . . We could always depend on a Sister that was very kind to us. I mean the children of my race. The Black Race, if you don't know. She was white, the color of her skin meant nothing. It was her pure soul that was so sweet. We love you, Sister Mary. Not as a Sister of the Nuns, but as a Sister of our own. We feel that you will come back, and be with us again. We were a little confused at you going away, but now we understand. We asked among ourselves why you went away. But then another nice sister took your place."[68] Although only one black family in Ft. Pierce was Catholic, the Adrian Dominicans began St. Martin Day School there in early 1940 with thirty-three students. In 1962, the school of twenty-four students was closed for financial reasons and in order to integrate St. Anastasia's Parochial School.[69]

The only hospital for blacks in a five-county area, Pine Ridge Hospital, was a segregated thirty-bed facility in West Palm owned and operated by Good Samaritan Hospital. When it was abandoned in 1947, the Allegheny Franciscans at St. Mary's Hospital took over, along with fourteen black nurses.[70]

Two diocesan priests were directly involved in the missionary effort to blacks, Father Michael Beerhalter and Father Joseph DeVaney. Beerhalter supported St. Martin Mission in Ft. Pierce. In 1951, DeVaney founded Holy Redeemer Parish in Miami, and six years later he was named pastor of the newly established St. Augustine Parish for blacks in Coconut Grove, continuing as pastor of Holy Redeemer. In January 1956, the diocese opened two out-patient clinics, one near Holy Redeemer under the supervision of Mercy Hospital and Dr. Franklyn E. Verdon, which served 250–300 patients per month, and the other in Gesu Parish.[71]

One noteworthy product of ministry among South Florida blacks during the period was the 1949 ordination of Curtis Washington of the Society of the Divine Word, the first native black South Floridian ordained to the priesthood.[72]

Blacks were not the only ethnic group ministered to by the Church during the Hurley years. The traditional connection between South Florida and Hispanics continued. Monsignor William Barry organized an exchange program of students and professors between the United States and Latin America with the blessing of the ordinary. Both Rosarian and Assumption academies, as well as Barry College, had students from Cuba and other Hispanic-American countries.[73]

Pastoral concern also touched the more permanent Hispanic community in South Florida. Spanish surnames began to appear in South Florida parishes in the 1940s and 1950s. At a clergy conference in May 1951, Hurley told all priests ordained after 1940 that they were to study Spanish because of the increase in Spanish-speaking people on the west and southeast coasts. Forty-seven follow-up letters were sent to priests to this effect; of that group, about five actually learned Spanish.[74] As in the work with blacks, diocesan performance did not measure up to the archbishop's expressed concern.

The impact of Hispanics was also making itself felt in South Florida's Catholic schools. As one of the sisters at Epiphany Parochial School observed in 1953: "Many of our children are Spanish-speaking, and are just learning English. In this Spanish atmosphere I do not feel that I have left Peru [the sister had previously been stationed there]."[75] Most of the Hispanics were Cubans and Puerto Ricans who had come to Miami for various economic and political reasons. A Nicaraguan had founded the newspaper *Diario de Las Américas* in Miami by 1953, and a Miami radio station had introduced two or three hours of Spanish language programming a week by 1954. In 1955, the Miami Catholic Service Bureau hired its first bilingual social worker.[76]

By far the most ambitious diocesan project for Hispanics was

Hurley's plan for a ministry to migrants. As early as 1944, he had sought priests from Spain but with little success. In 1951, Hurley invited Obra de Cooperación Sacerdotal Hispano Americana (OCSHA), an organization of diocesan priests formed by the Spanish hierarchy in 1949 to aid Latin American missions, to come to Florida to assist in the ministry to the Spanish-speaking. Sent only to regions considered missionary, OCSHA priests were to take up work in dioceses that already had parishes and to live in rectories alongside local diocesan priests. They volunteered for a five-year commitment, at the end of which they could either return to Spain, stay on, or be transferred to another location. Monsignor McNulty and Father McKeever, who had studied for a time in Madrid, were sent to Spain to recruit OCSHA priests.[77] Luis Altonaga, the first OCSHA priest to come to South Florida, went to St. Margaret's in Clewiston in 1953; five others soon followed. In the harvest season all six were to serve the Hispanic migrant workers who lived and worked in camps in the agricultural areas of South Florida.[78]

Having received the Spanish priests, Hurley now implemented the second phase of his plan for ministry to migrants. Sizable numbers of Hispanic migrant workers had moved into the state around 1950; the OCSHA priests had come in 1953 and 1954; now the archbishop asked the Sisters of St. Joseph, the only diocesan community of religious, for nine sisters to work in the migrant ministry. The nine volunteers took a crash course in Spanish at Corpus Christi Parish for six weeks in the summer of 1954. In November, three station wagons were purchased and the sisters were divided into three groups, one for Ft. Myers, one for Palm Beach–Glades, and one for South Dade. On Thanksgiving Day, Hurley had the sisters, the OCSHA priests, and the station wagons come to St. Augustine Cathedral for a special Mass and commissioning, at which he told them, "Hold the line until help will come." At Ft. Myers, Sister Mary Aquinas, SSJ, was one of the three sisters living in a small house in town and traveling each day to one of five different camps, where she met the people, told them about religious instruction for the children, found out their needs, took them food and clothing, transported them to the doctor, and made arrangements either for them to come to church or for the OCSHA priest to say Mass in the camp. This type of dif-

TABLE 4.2. Diocese of St. Augustine, 1940–58

Year	Dio. priests	Rel. priests	Rel. women[a]	Parish schools	Churches[b]	Missions	Stations	Baptisms	Marriages	Cath. pop.
1940	75	62	373	41[c]	62	41	150	1,396	575	65,767
1945	85	67	325	32	68	59	14	4,380	1,752	70,573
1950	109	73	593	44	81	57	4	5,672	1,508	72,636
1958[d]	155	77	775	83	106	47	16	11,285	2,443	192,748

SOURCES: OCD-1941, pp. 565–66; OCD-1946, p. 676; OCD-1951, p. 527; OCD-1958, p. 632.

a. Includes postulants and novices.

b. With resident pastors.

c. No distinction is given between private and parish schools.

d. Actually as of December 31, 1957.

ficult missionary work using an established parish and the station wagons continued for seven years, with the diocese paying all expenses.[79]

Characteristics of the Period

Florida's population grew by 161 percent between 1940 and 1960. In 1940, Florida was the twenty-seventh most populous state; by 1960, it was tenth. Most of that expansion was in South Florida.[80]

Unlike previous periods, in 1940–58 Florida's Catholic population growth kept pace with that of the general population, increasing 193 percent. Statistics point to a considerable growth in personnel and institutional service (table 4.2). Taking into account increases in marriages, baptisms, diocesan priests, parishes, and schools, the Hurley period was the period of most rapid growth in the history of Florida Catholicism.[81]

In the post–World War II years, nonnatives swamped the small native Catholic population. As in the North, Catholicism in South Florida centered in cities. Some new residents remarked upon the number of lapsed Catholics, broken homes, and mixed marriages. (The 1944 census indicated that half of Florida Catholic marriages were mixed; 32 percent of these were invalid.) Parish communities were often unstable in South Florida because of constant migration from the North and the character of South Florida neighborhoods. On the other hand, there were many people who liked South Florida's Catholicism—its newness and lack of entrenched traditions. They felt closer to the priests and sisters than they had before, although the ordinary was an extremely distant figure, and parish building gave them a sense of creating the Church anew. Parish building did have adverse effects: priests were moved more frequently than in northern dioceses, and people were constantly being asked to give money and make sacrifices. Some South Florida Catholics claimed to have been part of thirteen parishes from the 1940s through the 1960s without ever moving from their original domicile![82]

Archbishop Hurley, as well as most priests and sisters, referred to the diocese as "missionary." The Irish priests who served in the diocese came with the thought of serving "the missions." The ordinary lived like an American bishop of the nineteenth century, constantly "riding the fences," except that Hurley worked out of the backseat of an automobile. The priests were building parishes, churches, and schools, living in small houses, and saying Mass in warehouses, theaters, public school auditoriums, all-purpose buildings, and "provisional" churches. The Extension Society still contributed money to the diocese and South Florida; the bishop and his delegates still went on begging trips and sent letters for money and personnel.

The years 1940–58 were a time of progress, rapid growth, and tireless energy for South Florida Catholicism. One unique aspect of the period was its new, more centralized organization, which gave the ordinary more power and control, at the same time allowing resources to be allocated for present and future needs. It was this leadership, this vision, this pragmatic implementation of structure and style which moved South Florida Catholicism toward an independent Church, the Diocese of Miami.

5

A Vision Realized, 1958

The Diocese of Miami was created 391 years after the first cross was planted and the first mission established by the Spanish on Biscayne Bay and 100 years after Bishop Verot came to Florida as the vicar apostolic. Because of postwar Catholic population growth, as well as the development of ecclesial structures under Hurley's leadership, South Florida was ready to become an independent and self-sustaining local Church.

Reactions to the New Diocese

Archbishop Hurley had known for some time that a new diocese was going to be created in Florida, and in 1957 he made several lists of clergy in order to have a proper tabulation of personnel when the expected split took place.[1] In the summer of 1958, Hurley was vacationing in Switzerland when the apostolic delegate, Ameleto G. Cicognani, made an unannounced journey to South Florida. In July, Hurley hurried back from Europe to attend the funeral of his chancellor, Monsignor John Love. Throughout that summer, a substantial reshuffling of diocesan clerical personnel was taking place, involving about forty priests, so that by the end of July priests had already been moved from southern to northern

Florida. About twenty priests had been told by Hurley that in the first part of August they would be transferred from northern to southern Florida.

When word from the apostolic delegation arrived unexpectedly, it upset both the archbishop's plans and the archbishop's person. On Sunday, August 11, Hurley was informed of the division of the diocese. On Monday he stayed at the cathedral rectory in St. Augustine, a departure from his usual practice of going to the chancery. On Tuesday, August 13, 1958, the apostolic delegation in Washington announced the creation of the Diocese of Miami.[2]

Hurley's initial reaction was surprise and agitation. He felt that the timing was inopportune and that the authorities had caught him unprepared. He was in the midst of the high school fund drive which was not yet completed. He had just lost his right-hand man, Monsignor Love. He was halfway through an extensive transfer of priests, the second part of which (the movement of priests from north to south) he now canceled, giving St. Augustine approximately twenty more priests than it would otherwise have had. He was particularly disturbed over what he saw as the ill-conceived manner of the division, a latitudinal split which cut off the lower sixteen counties. He had promoted a longitudinal split, with the whole Florida east coast as one diocese and a new diocese created along the west coast, with Tampa–St. Petersburg the See city. Under his plan, Hurley would still have been the ordinary of both Miami and St. Augustine. The archbishop's proposal had merit, apart from his personal preference. Communication, transportation, and commerce ran along the Florida coasts in longitudinal patterns. Connections between the two coasts were poor. The longitudinal split would have been logical and workable. Not only had Hurley been uninformed of the split until the last minute, but he was not offered the new See when it was formed, although it was well known that he had never been fond of St. Augustine and had spent a good deal of his time at his co-chanceries of Palm Beach (St. Edward's) and North Miami (Holy Family).[3]

Clerics and sisters reacted to the news of the new diocese somewhat differently than had the archbishop. Monsignor William Barry commented to his sister: "The creation of the diocese seems to have been the greatest surprise. I saw Arch. Hurley yesterday. He seems highly pleased and is working for a grand reception for Bishop Carroll. I am his chairman of the reception committee.

I spoke with Bishop Carroll by phone from New York. I think he is a very friendly person. He left for Lourdes today."[4] It seems unlikely that Barry was privy to the inner feelings of Hurley on this matter or any other. The surprise that Barry refers to above was not so much from the creation of a new diocese but rather how and when it was done. In clerical circles, rumors had circulated for some time about the division of the Diocese of St. Augustine into two or three new dioceses with Tampa–St. Petersburg as one of them. Among clerics, the element of surprise was the way the split took place. The clergy of South Florida were also surprised that Coleman Carroll got the new See, since some felt that a local man might be appointed (Monsignor Barry or Auxiliary Bishop Thomas McDonough). But most pastors were happy about being in a new diocese that would not feel the heavy assessments and the heavy hand of Archbishop Hurley.[5]

Religious men and women seemed to welcome the change. Mother Gerald wrote to her brother: "I wonder that the creation of the new diocese was a surprise, but then I suppose everyone thought there would be simply a change in administrators and that the structure would not be touched. From all reports, the new bishop is a very fine person."[6] Religious in Florida too were aware of the rumors of the split and were likewise surprised at the way it happened. Some thought the change overdue, especially because of Hurley's unsympathetic stance toward male religious. Some sisters became apprehensive when they learned who the new ordinary was to be, since he was reputed to have been a strict vicar of religious of Pittsburgh.[7]

The reaction of the laity was milder, since most of them simply did not give the matter much thought. The Diocese of St. Augustine seemed to most a distant reality which never much affected their lives. Of course they had donated money for parish building, Mercy Hospital, and the Diocesan Development Fund, but most effects of such contributions could be seen locally. Meeting assessments and interests on loans were the problems of pastors, not laity. The ordinary himself was a distant figure, seen by the laity only on rare occasions. For most lay people, the diocese meant their own parish and pastor. Many other diocesan structural arrangements, although designed for their benefit, did not involve them directly and did not rouse their concern.[8]

Coleman F. Carroll, Ordinary of Miami

The creation of the new Diocese of Miami was not just a territorial and jurisdictional matter but also one of new leadership in the person of the new ordinary, Coleman Francis Carroll. His father, William J. Carroll, came to the United States from County Offaly, Ireland, with his three brothers and two sisters in the late 1890s, at which time they settled in Rochester, N.Y. The senior Carroll was a brakeman for the Buffalo, Rochester, and Pittsburgh Railroad. He married Irish-born Bridget M. Hogan at Corpus Christi Church in Rochester in September 1901, soon afterward moving to Pittsburgh, where he got a job with Carnegie Steel as a clerk. Coleman, the second of three sons, was born February 9, 1905, and baptized at Holy Rosary, one of the finest parishes in Pittsburgh at the time. Father D. J. Malady, pastor of Holy Rosary, had national and Roman ecclesial connections and became a lifelong advisor and benefactor of the Carroll family. Holy Rosary was considered an upper-middle-class Irish parish, slightly above the Carroll family's social-economic position.[9]

His immediate family strongly influenced Coleman Carroll's loyalties and perspectives. With a forceful Irish mother who had curried clerical support and with two successful churchman brothers with national and international contacts, Carroll had a consciousness about the Church and about himself almost unique among his fellow clergymen. He owed to his mother and brothers an independence of movement, a total self-confidence, and a dimension of insight which drove him to emulate his brothers' ecclesial success.[10]

Coleman Carroll's father died in October 1922, leaving his mother to care for three adolescents. After William's death the Carroll family moved to a less affluent neighborhood in Blessed Sacrament Parish. Mrs. Carroll, who sometimes worked at menial jobs to support her three sons, was a powerful force in their lives. Cordial, diplomatic, strong, intelligent, this Irish mother had high aspirations for her sons in the Church. Until her death in 1952, she took an active interest in their careers. By her encouragement and presence, she partook of their triumphs.[11]

The relationship of the three Carroll brothers was always close, both personally and professionally. Howard Joseph Carroll, born in 1902 and the oldest of the brothers, received his education at

Holy Rosary, and in September 1919 entered Duquesne with the financial help of at least one priest friend of the family, Father Joseph Lonergan. Duquesne was an inner-city Catholic college to which a considerable number of young men went before entering the seminary, since the Diocese of Pittsburgh did not have its own seminary. After two years, Howard, having been accepted as a seminarian for the Diocese of Pittsburgh, entered St. Vincent Seminary, Latrobe, in September 1921. After one year, he dropped out of the seminary, then spent a year at home while still officially a Pittsburgh seminarian. He was next sent to study philosophy and theology at Fribourg, Switzerland. Hugh C. Boyle, ordinary of Pittsburgh, wrote to the rector of the Albertinum in Fribourg to explain that Carroll was being sent there so that his "talent and skill in music" might be developed while he matriculated in philosophy and theology. The tight-fisted Boyle informed Howard of the financial obligations he would have to the diocese after ordination as the result of his studies. In addition, the ordinary stressed the importance of his theological studies—his musical inquiries must come second. Being sent to Europe to study after a year's absence from the seminary was highly unusual, especially since Boyle rarely sent priests anywhere for further studies and never sent seminarians to Europe. One explanation for his exceptional conduct in this case is that Howard Carroll had become interested in a young woman. Both his mother and Father Lonergan urged Boyle to send him to Europe so that his priestly vocation might be preserved.[12]

Ordained in 1927, Howard Carroll remained in Switzerland to defend his doctoral dissertation in January 1928, graduating summa cum laude. Upon his return to Pittsburgh, he was assigned to the affluent parish of Sacred Heart. While remaining as assistant at Sacred Heart, Howard assisted at the diocesan marriage tribunal from 1930 to 1938. The most academically inclined of all the Carroll brothers, he taught Italian at Duquesne from 1932 to 1934 and Italian and philosophy at Mt. Mercy College for Women from 1931 to 1938. He had been offered a teaching position at Seton Hill College, Greensburg, but the bishop would not let him accept it.[13]

After ten years at Sacred Heart, Howard was assigned in May 1938 as assistant to Monsignor Michael J. Ready, the general secretary of the National Catholic Welfare Conference. Archbishop Edward Mooney of Detroit, chairman of the NCWC administrative board, was instrumental in the appointment, which lasted from 1938 to 1957. Howard Carroll was named the bishop of the Altoona-Johnstown diocese on December 5, 1957, a position which he retained until his death in 1960.[14]

Walter Carroll, the youngest, born June 18, 1908, attended elementary and high school at Holy Rosary and received his B.A. degree from Duquesne in 1930. Supported by priest friends of the Carroll family, he spent the next three years studying at Fribourg, where Howard had gone. After earning a doctorate in philosophy from Fribourg in 1933, Walter arranged to transfer to the North American College in Rome for theology. In November 1933, from the North American College in Rome, Walter applied to the Diocese of Pittsburgh as a second year theologian, thereby setting a course for his ecclesial career and short-circuiting Boyle's conservative, provincial treatment of his seminarians and priests. After being ordained in Rome in 1935, receiving his licentiate in sacred theology in 1936 and his doctorate in canon law in 1940, Walter finally returned to Pittsburgh, where he was assigned temporarily to St. Basil's, Carrick. In September he was appointed to the office of the papal secretary of state, replacing Joseph P. Hurley who had been made bishop of St. Augustine in August. Hurley had proposed Walter Carroll for that vacant position, since they had become friends in Rome, a relationship which would extend to the whole Carroll family and grow through the 1950s.[15]

Walter Carroll, as a papal diplomat in Rome, worked very closely with Monsignor Giovanni Montini, the pro-secretary of the secretary of state after 1944. During World War II, Carroll went to North Africa to facilitate communications between the Church and the Allied armies and to work with war prisoners. In June 1944, he acted as a liaison between the Church, the Italian government, and the Allied forces in the liberation of Italy. After the war, he aided refugees and concentration camp victims and represented the Holy See in the International Refugee Organization.[16] His unique position during the war and after allowed him numerous international and American contacts, both secular and ecclesial.

In 1943 and again in 1947, he flew to the United States on home visits. Returning in early 1950, he traveled by plane to Florida to visit St. Edward's in Palm Beach to meet his mother, who made a yearly visit there. Complaining of an attack of gastritis, he quickly flew back to Washington, where he died, after several days, at

Georgetown Hospital of gall bladder or liver malfunction. His sudden death at the age of forty-one brought great grief to the whole Carroll family.[17]

Like his brothers, Coleman Carroll was educated at Holy Rosary elementary and high school. Encouraged by his mother and like all his brothers, he took piano lessons from the Sisters of St. Joseph at Holy Rosary. Neighborhood children called him "Cokey," a nickname for Coleman, but did not pick him for their sandlot baseball or football games because his mother always called him away to practice the piano. Both in high school and college, Carroll was the organist for Holy Rosary Parish. In 1923, he entered the sophomore class at Duquesne, having received credit for special work done under the guidance of his pastor. Never involved with athletics or extracurricular activities, he graduated from Duquesne in June 1926.

Immediately upon graduation, Coleman Carroll applied to become a seminarian for the Diocese of Pittsburgh, entering first-year theology at St. Vincent's in the fall. As a seminarian he did not play team sports and went alone to his room to study during recreation periods. He did, however, organize the Choral Society and Orchestra while at St. Vincent's. At ordination (June 15, 1930),[18] the seminary yearbook described him: "more than average ability in each of the several fields of endeavor . . . his cheery, good natured helpfulness, a developed personality . . . who can forget his polishing of an untrained organization from which resulted the Choral Society. Whatever he did, he did well, from wielding the baton or the tennis racket to achieving a brilliant scholastic record."[19]

From 1930 to 1949, Carroll had four pastoral assignments as assistant pastor. Following Howard Carroll's example, he taught philosophy at Mt. Mercy College from 1938 and at Duquesne during the 1945–46 school year, both positions voluntary and not official diocesan appointments.[20]

Because his interests were not particularly pastoral, Coleman Carroll managed to have the Bishop of Pittsburgh, Hugh C. Boyle, assign him to Catholic University to study canon law. Father Henry A. Carlin, pastor of Holy Rosary and a consultor of Boyle's, was instrumental in the appointment. It was understood that to further one's ecclesial career, a degree in canon law was necessary during the pre-Vatican II era. From 1941 to 1944, he studied at Catholic University of America, where he received his licentiate in canon law in May 1943.[21]

Coleman Carroll was not enamored of parochial life, especially as it existed at the time for Pittsburgh priests. Besides his extra-parochial teaching at Mt. Mercy and Duquesne, he left the parish for trips, especially to visit Howard Carroll in Washington, and to visit clergy and laity in Pittsburgh. These activities resulted in a confrontation with his pastor at St. Basil's late in 1945[22] and led Boyle to make inquiries of Carroll: "I have authentic information that you spend much of your time away from your parish . . . and that other priests are employed by you to look after your work in the parish while you are away. . . . I beg that I may have a word from you in the matter."[23] Carroll defended himself by maintaining that his absences were infrequent and legitimate and expressing his regrets that the bishop had to be bothered with a matter that could have been easily settled within the rectory household.[24] Coleman was a man of energy, and the narrow parochialism of his German-American pastor did not satisfy his restless intellect. He was at St. Basil's only one year.

It was common practice in Pittsburgh for priests to bid for pastorates that would be opening up, the parish going to the priest with the most seniority and best record. Coleman Carroll had been a curate for nineteen years in four different parishes. Both of his brothers, with high national and international positions in the Church, had bright futures, while he seemed to be standing still. In May 1949, he put in his bid for the existing parish of St. Irenaeus, Oakmont. The bishop did not grant his request but did assign him to begin a new parish, St. Maurice in Forest Hills, something of a rarity during Boyle's episcopacy when few new parishes were created. It was a great opportunity for a man with Coleman Carroll's energy.

Carroll began the task of parish building by residing at Holy Rosary (not at nearby St. James) with his friend Monsignor Henry Carlin, and he said St. Maurice's first Mass in July 1949 at Melody Lane Skating Rink. The parish was suburban and solidly middle class. In characteristically swift and aggressive fashion, Carroll called upon his wealthy friends in Aspinwall and Fox Chapel for funds to purchase a Coca-Cola bottling plant, which he converted into a parish complex of church, rectory, and hall. He also bought a fine piece of property for a future church building. With outside help, he was able to set up the physical parish more rapidly than would have been possible if he had depended solely upon contributions from people in the Forest Hills area. However, his ability to get the parish going so quickly also reflected his organizational skills. A man of almost impatient energy, Carroll thought big and painted with broad strokes.[25] His methods and style of parish building at St. Maurice were the prototype for his pastorate at Sacred Heart Parish and his subsequent episcopacy in Miami.

Carroll's performance as pastor of St. Maurice impressed Auxiliary Bishop John Dearden, who had become more powerful in the diocese as Bishop Boyle's health declined steadily. In addition, Dearden became friendly with the Carroll family and friends. He took the initiative of moving Coleman Carroll in April 1951 to Sacred Heart Parish, considered one of the finest in the diocese.[26]

Sacred Heart Parish had developed its reputation under Father Thomas F. Coakley, who had been educated at the North American College in Rome where he acquired European tastes and perspectives. Named pastor of Sacred Heart in 1923, Coakley initiated ambitious plans for a new church. Construction began in 1928. Its interior appointments made by European craftsmen, and in size almost as big as a continental cathedral, the church had an elaborate blessed sacrament chapel and the third largest stained glass window in the world. Coakley also initiated a social service department with a sister in charge and in 1930 opened a girls' high school which became coed in 1946. A new elementary school, with a convent penthouse above the school, was dedicated in 1947. Even before Coakley took over, the parish had its own organist and was acclaimed for its fine liturgical music, a tradition he continued and enlarged. At Coakley's funeral Mass in 1951, the main celebrant and speaker, Francis Cardinal Spellman, said that Coakley called his parish "the finest parish in the world."

It was this tradition that Carroll inherited when he became pastor in April 1951. He was familiar with the parish not only because he knew Coakley but also because his brother Howard had been an assistant there for ten years before going to Washington. At Sacred Heart, Coleman Carroll showed himself to be an organizer and a builder. Coakley had not finished his dream church and parish; Carroll went about completing the work. His masonry orchestrations included yearly improvements to the parish plant from August 1951 until September 1958: five clerestory windows installed; a high school building dedicated; a Lady Chapel built and dedicated; a new rectory and offices opened; bells and a bell tower constructed and blessed; an altar of reposition and tabernacle installed; an activities building begun; a narthex organ installed. Under the pastorate of Coleman Carroll, the Kingdom of God was made triumphantly and splendidly tangible in the various building projects that he initiated. Rather than being original, Carroll's gifts amplified existing structures or patterns at Sacred Heart. Later, in Miami, he would elaborate upon the creative structure already put in place by Archbishop Hurley.

The Sacred Heart building projects initiated by Coakley in 1923 had not been financed only by parishioners. Since it was impossible to sustain a building drive for twenty-five to thirty years, Coakley had developed a network of wealthy friends in Pittsburgh who fueled his building machine. Carroll employed the same technique for raising money by adding to Coakley's benefactors his own personal contacts. Through Carroll's teaching at Mt. Mercy, which was attended by many young ladies from well-to-do families, through his former parishioners at St. Scholastica in Aspinwall and Fox Chapel, through his associations among clerics, through his connections with the friends of his brothers Walter and Howard, Coleman was able to move in social circles of philanthropy and benefaction. His charm and wit encouraged the wealthy to generosity. Carroll tapped Coakley's friends to fund the Lady Chapel erected in his memory and gave them a victory dinner at the exclusive Pittsburgh Athletic Association. When the bell tower was to be erected in the name of Carroll's brother Walter, Walter's friends were the primary source of money. Coleman Carroll also used his contacts in the hierarchy: Fulton J. Sheen preached at the dedication of the Lady Chapel, and Ameleto G. Cicognani, the apostolic delegate, officiated at the dedication of the bell tower.[27]

Although Coakley had operated his parish quasi-independently of the diocese and Carroll brought the two closer, he continued many of the former pastor's traditions, such as fine liturgical music, ceremonious rites, and European artworks. Carroll's liturgical and musical interests were also influenced by his boyhood parish of Holy Rosary, noted for its elegant liturgy. An example of Carroll's liturgical progressivism at Sacred Heart was his institution of the Revised Easter Vigil in 1952; his parish was the only one in the diocese with permission to have such ceremonies. His leadership style instilled confidence: he was sure of himself, sure of his position, sure of his Church's tradition, and all of this gave his mostly Irish-American parishioners self-confidence, dignity, and pride in being Catholic Americans.[28]

Beginning at Sacred Heart and for the rest of his life, Carroll's private dinners with friends were his trademark and his primary form of entertainment and human interaction. He served the best food and drinks and, even as he demanded formal dress, made his guests feel relaxed. He did not invite only the rich and powerful but all classes and ethnic groups to his regular Sunday night dinners, including bishops, priests, lay people, or a mixture. His humanity, hospitality, wit, and inquiring mind came alive on such occasions. When the papal secretary of state, Giovanni Cardinal Montini, came to Pittsburgh to express his sorrow to Mrs. Carroll over the death of her son and his good friend, Walter, Montini and the ordinary, Bishop Dearden, had to come to Sacred Heart for dinner rather than dining at the ordinary's house.[29]

To his assistants at the rectory, Carroll delegated authority freely; in turn, he expected tangible results. Woe to that assistant who did not measure up to expectations.

Carroll's achievements and organizational skills did not go unnoticed or unrewarded under the episcopacy of Bishop Dearden. In 1952, Dearden made Carroll vicar for religious and the same year awarded him the honorific title of domestic prelate. The following year Carroll was named titular bishop of Pitanae and auxiliary bishop of Pittsburgh. Consecrated bishop by the apostolic delegate, Carroll took the motto *Primum Regnum Dei* ("the Kingdom of God first"—Matt. 6:33) as part of his episcopal coat of arms.[30]

Carroll won considerable notoriety in his role as vicar of religious. As a canon lawyer, he took his new job seriously, issuing diocesan policies and visiting convents frequently. These convent visitations, which had not been done in Pittsburgh before, were to determine what the sisters might need materially and spiritually, as well as to provide a forum to deal with certain internal problems. At a typical visitation in 1957, Carroll made a list of recommendations, among them a burglar alarm for the tabernacle, roofing and soundproofing for the confessionals, all entrances to the convent clearly marked with the word "cloister" in English, and discontinuing two practices, that of two sisters from the motherhouse going out twice a month to beg at the mill gates and that of receiving communion by seniority. All appropriate legal citations of the local and universal Church accompanied each recommendation.[31]

Activities and jurisdiction of the office of vicar of religious were greatly expanded under Carroll's tenure. His regime, with its rigid, legalistic tone backed by an equally unbending Bishop Dearden, was interpreted by both women religious and priests as overly strict. For example, following the letter of canon law, no woman religious was permitted out of the convent after 6 P.M. The office of vicar of religious was feared by many sisters and disliked by most. They found the canonical visitations, or rather inspections, offensive. So bad was the feeling that the Sisters of Charity of Seton Hall, who had taught at Sacred Heart Parish, refused to accept a later invitation from Bishop Carroll to come to the Diocese of Miami to work.[32]

Pittsburgh's brand of Catholicism influenced Coleman Carroll from boyhood through twenty-three years as a priest and five years as an auxiliary bishop, shaping his understanding of himself and the Church. Since he brought this understanding with him when he became the first bishop of Miami, Pittsburgh Catholicism in Carroll's time contributed to the shape of the Church in South Florida.

From 1921 to 1950, Hugh Boyle was the ordinary in Pittsburgh. Boyle kept a low profile in the diocese; he was conservative in theology, personality, and action, although he never stood in the way of labor priests like Monsignor Carl P. Hensler (who had taught Coleman at Duquesne) or Father Charles Owen Rice or lay Catholic labor leaders. Boyle preferred the status quo; he refused to change or be disturbed by any new ideas. Boyle was a saver; his habit of spending little on diocesan programs or further education of his seminarians or priests made the Carroll brothers notorious for Boyle's breaking his policy of no higher education for his priests. The bishop ran his chancery by not going there, allowing six to eight priests to operate the simply structured chancery in the small Old Synod Hall next to the cathedral. Boyle was surrounded by priests who kept other people away from him, with resulting isolation. It was common for the Bishop to appoint men as administrators some time before naming them pastors. He never transferred priests unless they asked for it. If an assistant complained about his pastor, he was moved to an undesirable pastor, and then moved again to another undesirable pastor.[33] In this way complaints and transfers were kept to a minimum.

The mostly urban Diocese of Pittsburgh was a cornucopia of many ethnic groups, whose enclaves were rich and diverse. Its mixture led to the creation of national parishes, which preserved the faith of the different immigrant groups and at the same time caused tensions and frictions within the local Church. On the south side of Pittsburgh, for example, in a half-mile square, nine Catholic churches were established: an Irish territorial parish, two Ukrainian Rite churches, two Polish churches, a German church, a Passionist chapel, a Slovak church, and a Byzantine Rite church. These national parishes eroded any sense of unity within the diocese. Laity tended to identify themselves with *their* parish, *their* school, *their* pastor, *their* ethnic expression of Catholicism, rather than with the diocese as a whole or their Catholic neighbor who went to another national parish down the street.

The diocese was a kind of confederation of national and territorial churches. Priests, religious, and laity generally identified with and socialized within their own ethnic enclaves. Although the German-Americans and the Irish-Americans mixed socially, Coleman Carroll generally associated with his fellow Irish-Americans. For Forty Hours Devotions, a big clerical social event in the diocese, Slovaks or Poles never invited Irish or Germans and vice versa. Moreover, ethnic resentments existed among the clergy; the Slovaks and Poles resented the Irish in particular because the latter were in the seats of power. The Irish and Germans resented the Eastern Europeans who, because of shortages, became pastors in single-man parishes after only about five years of assistantship, compared to eighteen years of assistantship for a priest of Irish or German descent.[34]

Boyle did not want an auxiliary, let alone a coadjutor, but both were forced upon him in the person of John Dearden in 1948. From the time Dearden arrived, Coleman Carroll initiated a friendship with him, introducing him to Pittsburgh. It was not by chance, then, that Coleman's star began to rise with the coming of Dearden. When he became the ordinary at Boyle's death in December 1950, Dearden began to structure the diocese along more up-to-date bureaucratic lines. He developed a stronger, more unified administrative structure and replaced national parish schools with

TABLE 5.1. Comparison of Dioceses of Pittsburgh and Miami, 1958

	Pittsburgh	Miami
Active diocesan priests	496	63
Religious priests	203	21
Parishes	298	53
Religious women	4,470	392
Parochial schools	207	44
Total baptisms	27,227	6,084
Total marriages	7,329	1,212
Mixed marriages	1,669	492
Catholic population	826,589	185,000

SOURCES: OCD-1958, p. 573; OCD-1959, p. 529.

parochial elementary schools and regional high schools. He generally discouraged national parishes and ethnic enclaves. Coleman Carroll was part of this organizational revolution in his role as vicar of religious. Dearden also encouraged the practice of the priest-in-residence, whereby a priest with a special administrative or ministerial assignment would be placed in residence at a particular parish but would take on little or no pastoral duties. Carroll received one such priest at Sacred Heart in 1955.[35]

The Diocese of Pittsburgh that Carroll left when he went to Miami had over 825,000 Catholics in 298 parishes, 496 diocesan priests, and 4,470 sisters. The newly created Miami diocese was a missionary situation in comparison (table 5.1). Bishop Carroll had to adjust to more than just the weather.

The Move South

Through his brothers, Coleman Carroll was well known in both national and Roman ecclesial circles. The fact that he was made a bishop and given a see was no surprise to anyone in Pittsburgh who knew anything of his energy, zeal, and organizational skills. He knew personally the apostolic delegate, the powerful Cardinal Mooney, and Bishop Dearden.[36]

But why Miami? That question can be answered only by circumstantial evidence construed from a network of personal associations. First, Cardinal Mooney knew Archbishop Hurley; the apostolic delegate visited Florida every year, along with other American prelates. Second, Hurley knew the Carroll family through Walter, whom he had recommended as his Vatican replacement in 1940. Hurley actually visited Pittsburgh and stayed at Sacred Heart Rectory twice in the 1950s. While he was studying at Catholic University, Coleman Carroll came to Miami in 1944, at Hurley's invitation, to lead a high school retreat at St. Mary's High School. By 1950, both he and his mother visited every year at St. Edward's in Palm Beach when the apostolic delegate and Hurley were there. Walter had journeyed to Palm Beach to visit his mother just before he died. Third, Carroll could have expressed some interest in a new Florida diocese, and Hurley might have expressed some interest in having Carroll in the state. Finally, certain influential residents of Palm Beach may have wanted Coleman Carroll, whom they knew.[37]

Whatever the circumstances of his selection, Coleman F. Carroll was to be the first bishop of Miami. Carroll sent several priest friends to Miami to prepare the way, among them his lifelong friend from Duquesne and seminary days, Father Larry O'Connell, and his assistant at Sacred Heart, Father John Unger. The most helpful cleric in Miami was Monsignor Patrick O'Donoghue, pastor of St. Mary's, and not the Miami Beach patriarch, Monsignor William Barry, who was less than enthusiastic about the new arrangements. With O'Donoghue's help, Unger rented two rooms of an office building at 6301 Biscayne Boulevard in which to begin the Miami chancery; he also rented a house for the new ordinary on Sunset Isle #1. In addition to these preliminary arrangements, Unger was to be in charge of entertaining the Pittsburgh people who came for the installation. O'Connell went to Miami early to oversee preparations. Concern was expressed by some of the priests about Carroll's reputed sternness and the possible creation of new parishes. Even before the installation, Miami priests were aware of Hurley's hurt feelings about the manner in which the new diocese had been thrust upon him. In Pittsburgh, on October 1, a Mass was celebrated at St. Paul's Cathedral for Carroll, followed by a testimonial luncheon at the Pittsburgh Athletic Association, at which time a testimonial fund was established for the new ordinary of Miami.[38]

On October 7, 1958, Coleman F. Carroll was installed as the first bishop of Miami; he took possession of the see which com-

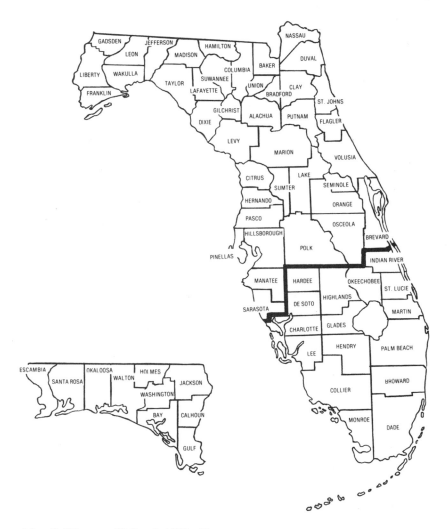

Map 3. Diocese of Miami, 1958–68.

prised the lower sixteen counties of the Florida peninsula (see map 2). Archbishop Hurley attended the installation; Bishop Dearden delivered the sermon; the installing prelate was Francis P. Keough, Archbishop of Baltimore, the Metropolitan See; Monsignor William Barry was the notary. The coat of arms of the new bishop was publicized at the ceremony. The day after the ceremony, Pope Pius XII died, signaling the end of an era for the Church universal and the local Church also.[39]

Carroll invited to Miami people he knew from Pittsburgh to help him establish the new diocese. Agnes Conlin, his secretary from St. Maurice and Sacred Heart, was his secretary in Miami for the first few years. John Ward, the editor of the *Pittsburgh Catholic*, became the editor of the Miami diocesan newspaper, the *Voice*, when it was established in 1959. Victor Lalli, an auditor at Sacred Heart, set up the financial accounts of the Diocese of Miami and initially visited there once a month to care for the books. Clayton Brenneman, organist at Sacred Heart from 1944 to 1959, became organist and choirmaster of St. Mary's Cathedral in Miami in 1959. In the early 1960s, Mrs. Mary Lou Maytag McCahill, a convert of Carroll's, settled in Miami to become an important benefactress of the diocese. In addition, Carroll asked every community of religious women in Pittsburgh to come to Miami. Not surprisingly, few sisters wanted to go, but some did move south, including the Sisters of St. Joseph of Baden, who staffed the school of the first parish Carroll established in the Diocese, Holy Rosary, named after the parish of his youth. For the first few years of his episcopacy in Miami, Carroll continued to travel to Pittsburgh four or five times a year to visit friends.[40]

For the Diocese of Miami, a sixteen-county jurisdiction of 16,457 square miles (see map 3), Carroll replicated the basic administrative structure of Pittsburgh and extended the organizational framework implemented by Hurley. Eight parishes existed in the city of Miami, fifty-three in the whole diocese. There were 63 active diocesan priests, 21 religious priests, no brothers, and 392 sisters. Two men's and fourteen women's religious communities ministered within the confines of the diocese. (For a statistical comparison of the Dioceses of Pittsburgh and Miami, see table 5.1.) By the end of 1958, the Diocese of Miami had eight black churches with eight priests serving them, five black parochial schools serving 624 pupils, and an estimated black Catholic population of 1,000.[41]

Before Carroll could take hold and deal singlemindedly with diocesan needs, he was confronted by a grave problem relating to his succession to full authority over the Church in Miami. It had been thought by some that the splitting off of the Diocese of Miami from that of St. Augustine would go smoothly on account of the friendly relations between Bishop Carroll and Archbishop Hurley.[42] Such was not to be the case.

The Hurley-Carroll Controversy

From the beginning of the new diocese, Hurley felt a deep sense of injustice, perhaps even of betrayal. Not only was he not properly prepared for the split, but he realized that it was a rejection of his wishes. Insult was added to injury by the fact that the man chosen for Miami was someone he knew personally. At Carroll's installation, little reference was made to the work of Archbishop Hurley in building up the Church in South Florida, a historical oversight and a painful personal slight.[43] Hurley's sense of indignation and injustice focused on the issues of seminarians, real estate, and finances.

The resultant disagreement was not caused only by hurt feelings. Creating a new diocese from an older one often introduces tensions concerning temporalities and jurisdiction. When the Diocese of St. Augustine was created in 1870, problems had arisen between Bishops Persico and Gross of Savannah and Bishop Verot over these matters (see chapter 1). The 1918 Code of Canon Law did not clarify matters to any significant degree; Canon 1500 stated:

> When the territory assigned an ecclesiastical moral person has been divided in such a way that either a part of it is given to another moral person or a distinct moral person is created for the separated part of the territory, an equitable and proportionate division shall also be made, by the ecclesial authority authorized to make the division, of the common property (*bona communia*) which was destined for the benefit of the whole territory, as well as of the debts which were contracted for the entire territory, provided, however, that there be respected the intentions of pious founders or donors, legally vested rights, and special laws governing the moral person involved.[44]

The controversy between Hurley and Carroll revolved around application of this canon to the particular conditions of the Church in Florida, especially in regard to the *bona communia.*

The dispute involved money and the fair distribution of seminarians studying for Florida at the time of the split. Archbishop Hurley had shrewdly purchased 328 parcels of real estate totaling over 10,000 acres throughout the state with the proceeds from the $4 million Missionary Burse Appeal of 1953. Pastors, who had been assessed 160 percent of the parish gross income for the year 1953, met the levy in one of three ways: paying the entire sum from parish reserves, taking out a bank loan, or spreading payment to the diocese over up to three but not more than four years. The monetary issues of the dispute centered on the equitable division and reimbursement for the 328 parcels of land, 159 of which were located in the Diocese of Miami, and the resultant financial problems, along with other financial entanglements, including the funds collected for the Catholic High School Building Fund (a collection in progress throughout the state at the time of the split).[45]

Just fifteen days after Carroll was installed, the opening salvo of the dispute was fired at an October 22 meeting chaired by Monsignor McNulty, who represented Hurley. At the outset of the meeting the unfortunate impression was created that the Diocese of Miami was responsible for the delay in the settlement proceedings, setting an adversary tone which continued and worsened in subsequent meetings. Some basic agreements were reached at the first meeting. First, priests were to be incardinated in whatever ecclesial domicile they resided at the time of the division. Second, the curriculum vitae of Miami priests, parish boundary information, and marriage case files were to be handed by St. Augustine to Miami (although St. Augustine expressed a reluctance to hand over to Miami certain other files). Third, seminarians would belong to the diocese of their parents' domicile. Decisions about nonresident seminarians (northerners and Irishmen) and the diocesan religious community of the Sisters of St. Joseph were tabled.[46]

A second and third meeting were held on October 23 and a fourth and fifth on November 4. The November meetings covered questions of real estate, of the Catholic High School Building Fund and parish loans associated with it, and of the fair distribution of other collected monies. Miami proposed a division of nonresident seminarians, since in the next four years St. Augustine would ordain sixty-three men and Miami would ordain only twelve under the present arrangements. Seminarians too represented the *bona communia*. Various proposals were suggested for the distribution of properties and funds.

At the sixth meeting, November 26, Miami requested the complete files of priests and seminarians, parish files, boundary files, and others which had been promised at the first meeting but not delivered. Miami said that non-resident seminarians should be split into two equal groups and promised to appeal to the proper ecclesial authorities unless an equitable division of seminarians took place. Miami also proposed to pay all debts on used property, as well as the cost of unused property parcels, along with a fair percent of interest. However, the new diocese would not pay the increment or appraised value for the properties. If this was unacceptable, proper ecclesial authorities would be called upon. St. Augustine maintained that the cost, charges, and 20 percent should be paid for the property. As the discussions deteriorated and positions hardened, Miami representatives announced that Carroll had a canonical right to all properties held by Hurley in the Diocese of Miami and that he would not consent to arbitration by a board of laymen since these were ecclesial matters. St. Augustine felt the property was not an ecclesial matter and pushed for arbitration by a lay board.[47]

After meetings that took a little more than a month, the chasm between the two negotiating sides was widening. Neither bishop talked with the other directly, only through representatives at the meetings. After the deadlock of the sixth meeting, the dispute was brought to the attention of the apostolic delegate, who in turn referred it to the Holy See. By August 5, 1959, the Sacred Consistorial Congregation set up a three-man commission to study the dispute and make a definitive decision, not subject to appeal until the terms of the adjudication were fulfilled by both parties. The commission was composed of Archbishop Egidio Vagnozzi, apostolic delegate; Archbishop Francis P. Keough of Baltimore; and James H. Griffiths, auxiliary bishop of New York and an expert in canonical matters. They had no easy job. Griffiths commented that the issues over the finances and property were particularly complex, canon law was "regrettably vague," and no precedents of any note existed.[48]

From the beginning, the commission met with many delays.

Carroll wrote to Griffiths in April 1960 to comment that any postponement in the settlement of the dispute might favor St. Augustine on the matter of seminarians, since Hurley had already ordained one class of seminarians who were on the disputed list and the next class was coming up. On May 15, 1960, Pope John XXIII personally entered the dispute: he divided the nonresident seminarians (mostly Irishmen) evenly between the two dioceses by going down the alphabetical list choosing one man for St. Augustine, the next for Miami. The papal order was executed immediately, thus solving the problem of nonresident seminarians relatively early in the controversy.[49]

The financial and property problems remained unsettled. In July 1961, Carroll expressed confidence that a decision would be forthcoming "in the very near future."[50] But the dispute was not even close to settlement and indeed was on the verge of being taken to the civil courts. The immediate object of the possible civil action was the 130-acre property designated for Biscayne College. Even though the legal title was not in its possession, the Diocese of Miami had requested Dade County's Building and Zoning Department to rezone the land. Highland Realty, owner and holder of the option to purchase by the Catholic Burse Endowment Fund, Inc. (the Diocese of St. Augustine), requested that the zoning board hearing be canceled. In spite of these obstructive tactics and threats of civil litigation, the Diocese of Miami went ahead with the rezoning proceedings. To buttress this move, Carroll went to Rome in August 1961 to request that Hurley be made to desist from obstructive action over the Biscayne College property, as well as the Boynton Beach property, the proposed site of a major seminary. As a result, the Sacred Consistorial College in October 1961 authorized the apostolic delegation to persuade Hurley to withdraw his action in both cases.[51] Such persuasion was effective.

About this time, the controversy became a matter of public record and a potential scandal. Hurley's attempt to stop the rezoning of Biscayne College property made public the differences between the two dioceses. The *Miami Herald* in October 1961 reported "a squabble between the two Florida dioceses," adding that the proposed multimillion-dollar education center on the Biscayne–Golden Glades property was in jeopardy. Fortunately for the Church, the newspaper reported only this one aspect of the disagreement and the broader dispute was not revealed.[52]

On November 3, 1961, the investigating commission met with both Hurley and Carroll to collect necessary information about the properties and finances toward drafting a tentative decision. The commission decided that Hurley should make available to Miami immediately the title to both the Biscayne College and the Boynton Beach properties. Before meeting the commission, Hurley had given over the deeds to the Boynton property to Miami authorities. At this meeting, Hurley refused to accept several points which the commission ruled on, demanding instead that the issues be referred to the Holy See. Was the Biscayne College property to be regarded solely as Miami property? Was the Diocese of Miami entitled to receive from the Chancery Building Fund more than $420,000 (of which $229,000 had been contributed by South Florida parishes)? Did the cemetery lands (parcels in Dade and Broward counties designated as Catholic cemeteries) belong to Miami? How were the unused lands to be divided? This last question was the most difficult to settle since it involved an interpretation of the *bona communia* of Canon 1500. At this November meeting, Hurley made it clear that he would recognize no authority in the settlement of these issues other than Rome itself. For him, the controversy was a matter of principle, not simply personal whim or vengeful stubbornness: "I, myself, could not understand why my pastoral foresight in the southern counties of Florida should be used to deal a crippling blow to other and poorer parts of the Church of Florida."[53]

The work of the commission was further delayed by the death of Archbishop Keough on December 8, 1961. Lawrence Shehan, his successor as archbishop of Baltimore, took Keough's place on the commission. Meanwhile, in order to give some answer to the question of lands not yet used for a specific purpose, Griffiths collected documents on all 328 parcels of property, including the location, date of purchase, price paid, and designated purpose of each, as well as the assessed valuation of each parcel for 1958. He wrote, "This subsequently proved to be a task of most formidable proportions and of endless detail."[54]

On September 3 and 5, 1958, after the announcement of the new diocese but before the arrival of Carroll, Hurley, without notifying the pastors, had taken out loans on six Miami parishes. The purpose of the loans was to assure the Diocese of St. Augustine of the assessed money for the Catholic High School Fund Drive from those parishes. In February 1962, the Sacred Consistorial College in Rome ordered Hurley to assume obligation of the loans and promissory notes, totaling $1,070,000. Carroll was understandably pleased with the decision, since it allowed the Diocese of Miami to have a good credit rating among the Miami banks for the first time in its existence. Previously, Miami banks would not extend credit to the new diocese because it lacked title to much Church property, and certain loans, including those on the six parishes, were not being paid off by either diocese during the dispute.[55]

The newly staffed commission met in 1962 to try to hammer out proposals to break the logjam. The new diocese wanted $229,004.52 of the chancery fund of the Diocese of St. Augustine, representing the contributions of Miami parishes. Miami took the position that these funds represented the *bona communia* and that it needed them to construct a chancery for the new diocese. The commission ruled in Miami's favor concerning the chancery fund. In addition, the hotly contested cemetery sites were to be retained, as they were located within each of the respective dioceses with no other recompense to be paid. The commission also ruled that the 151.8-acre site of Camp Matecumbe was to be deeded to the Diocese of Miami. Other funds were discussed and solutions formulated by the commission by September 1963.

The most persistent problem was the equitable distribution of undeveloped lands which had been purchased through the Missionary Burse Fund. Under ordinary circumstances with the division of a diocese, each jurisdictional unit simply kept the land and buildings within its respective territory. It was Hurley's contention that such a solution would be unjust to the Diocese of St. Augustine, since the most valuable land was in South Florida, even though the number of disputed parcels was almost equally divided between the two dioceses: 169 were in the Diocese of St. Augustine, 159 in South Florida. Hurley maintained that the South Florida parcels were valued at 300 percent over the value of those in St. Augustine territory. The Diocese of Miami, on the other hand, pointed out that South Florida parishes contributed 46 percent of the Missionary Burse Fund used to purchase the disputed land; St. Augustine parishes had contributed 54 percent. In September 1963, Griffiths proposed a tentative solution that each diocese simply keep the lands within its own boundaries. This solution, in Hurley's view, did not do justice to the complexities of the situation. Growing impatient over the lack of settlement, Carroll wrote twice to Shehan in early 1964 and asked a conciliation as soon as possible.[56]

Another inadvertent delay was caused when Bishop Griffiths, the key commission member who was on the verge of drafting a final decision, died in February 1964. The material related to the dispute was scattered throughout his room in piles whose classifications were known only to Griffiths. The archbishop of New York gathered the documents from Griffiths's room and sent them to the apostolic delegate, who in turn entrusted the packet of material to Shehan to sort through and use for a final decision. Because the decision had to meet every requirement of canon and civil law, Shehan enlisted the help of the former secretary of Archbishop Keough and the attorney for the archdiocese of Baltimore. Shehan and his assistants met at the apostolic delegation in Washington on July 2, 1964, with the entire commission and signed a twenty-seven-page decision, which was immediately sent to the Consistorial Congregation in Rome. A summary decision was sent to each bishop that put forth the essentials of the case and stated the mandates imposed on each Florida bishop. The summaries were delivered July 10, and both ordinaries promised to carry out the terms of the ruling by August 10, as stipulated by the commission.[57]

The matter finally seemed settled, when suddenly on August 7, 1964, Shehan received a telegram from Hurley: "I am unable to comply with the direction of the Episcopal Commission dated July 2nd. Stop. Legal counsel advises me that the execution of proposed conveyance is in violation of Florida Law. Stop. We have advised the Ordinary of the Diocese of Miami of our position. Stop. I respectfully ask your indulgence in granting at least three months for clarification of decision. Stop. Detailed letter follows."[58] Without waiting for the letter promised by Hurley, Shehan responded that the commission's decision must be put into effect before August 10, 1964, and that no three-month delay could be granted. After consulting legal counsel, Shehan was convinced that Florida law presented no insurmountable obstacle to the pronouncements of the commission. Moreover, the archbishop of Baltimore stated emphatically that Canons 2333 and 2334 stipulated that any Catholic who attempted to impede the actions of the Holy See or its representatives by recourse to lay or civil power incurred excommunication reserved to the Holy See. On September 2, Hurley responded that he had carried out the mandates of July 2, but intended to appeal directly to the Holy See. In October, Carroll traveled to Rome with two South Florida lawyers, Clyde Atkins and Joseph Fitzgerald, to explain Miami's position. The apostolic delegate sent Shehan a copy of Hurley's appeal to the Holy See in January 1965. Shehan and his aides composed a sixty-four-page rebuttal to Hurley's appeal and sent it to the apostolic delegate in May 1965. Finally on November 18, 1965, while Shehan, Hurley, Carroll and most of the bishops of the world were in Rome for the fourth session of the Second Vatican Council, the Sacred Consistorial Congregation ruled that the complaints submitted by Hurley against the commission's decision of July 2 were unfounded. The Sacred Congregation presented its decree to the Holy Father, Pope Paul VI (Giovanni Montini, the old friend of Walter Carroll), who signed it. Beyond the Petrine Office there were no further appeals or delays; Archbishop Hurley submitted at once. The commission's decision of July 2 had been upheld, settling the controversy after almost seven years of disputation. Cardinal Shehan maintained that although neither bishop received all that he had originally claimed, both got more than they expected.[59]

The Hurley-Carroll controversy had baleful effects upon Catholicism in the Diocese of Miami in particular and Florida in general, both during the dispute and after the final settlement.

The ill feeling between the two ordinaries and their representatives affected the Sisters of St. Joseph of St. Augustine more than any other women's religious community in Florida, catching them in the jurisdictional and emotional aspects of the split. Technically a diocesan community for the Diocese of St. Augustine and under the jurisdiction of the ordinary of the Diocese of St. Augustine, the division of the diocese caused the sisters to rethink their mission. A similar trauma had occurred for them when St. Augustine was made a diocese in 1870, since some of their sisters were assigned in Georgia and were cut off from the St. Augustine sisters at the time of that split. At the end of October 1958, in an action that showed an absence of malice or pettiness on his part, Hurley granted permission for the Sisters of St. Joseph to travel freely between the two dioceses, thus permitting them to continue their South Florida foundations and remain united.[60]

The controversy presented massive financial difficulties for the newly established Diocese of Miami, since it did not have legal title to the properties under dispute. The corporation sole of the diocese, the ordinary, was unable to get credit from South Florida banks in order to finance much-needed development. In February 1960, out of desperation, Carroll negotiated a $1 million loan at 6 percent from the pension fund of the Teamsters' Union headed by Jimmy Hoffa. This transaction became public knowledge through local and national newspapers, which quoted Carroll as calling the loan "a simple business deal," the money from which would "be used for homes for the aged." A spokesman for the bishop reportedly said that the loan "could not be construed as an endorsement of Hoffa or the Teamsters Union."[61] As the *New York Times* was at pains to point out, "No previous mortgage loans to any faith have been reported by union pension or welfare funds." The Teamsters already had $13 million invested in Florida at the time.[62]

Carroll received a letter from the apostolic delegate expressing his surprise, and the surprise of the other bishops whom he had seen at a recent meeting, on reading about the diocese's loan from the Teamsters. Archbishop Vagnozzi commented, "Recent investigations would, it seems, make it unwise to deal with the organization involved because of the accompanying unfavorable publicity which is actually taking place."[63] Jimmy Hoffa, other Teamsters' Union officials, and officials of other unions were at the time being investigated for improprieties.[64] As a result of all this unfavorable publicity in the secular press, Carroll issued his own public statement:

The money actually was loaned not by the union but by the Central States and Southwest Area Pension Fund, Bishop Carroll said. The monies contributed to this fund come solely from the owners of truck lines which have contracts with the Teamsters' Union. The fund is administered by a board of six men, three of whom are truck owners and three members of the union. The same fund has lent considerable money to other institutions in Florida. Bishop Carroll described the loan as a simple business proposition and expressed surprise that it had received such prominence in the news. "Much of the money will be used for the establishment of greatly needed old people's homes in the Miami Diocese," said the

Bishop. "I do not know of a better way this pension money could be used."[65]

Carroll then wrote to the apostolic delegate on February 19 in defense of his actions. Carroll pointed out that several bishops had already negotiated loans from union pension funds, although their actions had not been noted in the press. He also indicated that although some bankers had also been controversial figures, Church officials dealt with them regularly. Carroll said that he negotiated the loan because the controversy had made it "increasingly more difficult for the Diocese of Miami to obtain sufficient credit from banks." He concluded his defense with a comment that indicated his confidence and wit. He said that some bishops did not react to his transaction negatively: "In fact, I have before me a letter from the Chancery of another Diocese asking me how to go about borrowing more money from the same source."[66] Although Carroll's letter to the apostolic delegate was meant as a defense of his action, it was not defensive in tone. It reflected the assurance, strength, and daring of its author. The apostolic delegate simply thanked the bishop of Miami for the information and the matter was closed.[67]

Carroll sought money from other sources, including various Pittsburgh banks and wealthy Pittsburgh friends. He also instituted a yearly collection called the Diocesan Development Fund, the precedent for which in both name and concept already existed under Hurley. Although local credit opened up somewhat by March 1962, with the settlement of the loans Hurley had taken out on six Florida parishes in September 1958, property and title hindrances continued to make local loans difficult to obtain.[68]

In addition to finances and property titles, the controversy affected the records of the new diocese. Although some had been promised, many diocesan records were not transferred to the Miami diocese. Records of marriages, priests' files, parish files, and titles were not released freely by the St. Augustine diocese.[69]

Although the Hurley-Carroll controversy officially ended in 1965, suspicion lingered among Florida prelates and clerics who knew of or were involved in it long after the material and jurisdictional issues had been settled. This effect was less tangible but even more devastating than the material considerations of the dispute. The two bishops continued to ignore each other, barely maintaining polite appearances. Carroll promised to support Hurley's wishes in the latter's donation of an altar in memory of his mother at Mercy Hospital in 1960, and he attended the dedication of the restored Cathedral of St. Augustine in 1966. For his part, Hurley attended the fiftieth anniversary of Monsignor Barry at Miami Beach in 1960, but relations between the two prelates were stiffly formal on the few occasions they met.[70]

The controversy affected the priests of Florida more than any other group. In some cases, priests who were formerly coworkers, sometimes in the same rectory or chancery, no longer visited or spoke to one another. Like a military confrontation, the ecclesial controversy created wounds not easily healed. Some of the St. Augustine priests felt that the terms of the settlement had robbed the Diocese of St. Augustine, and one quoted Hurley, "'We are reduced to poverty in all save history.'"[71]

In Miami, on the other hand, the sense of history itself was affected negatively, because the historical legacy of Florida Catholicism was rarely communicated to priests, religious, or laity who came to the diocese after 1958. Bishop Carroll referred only infrequently to the accomplishments of his predecessors, especially Hurley. Miami was forced to be on its own right away, not only materially but historically, unconnected with its mother diocese except by land. At the end of a peninsula, it was making its own history; the present was what was important. Because of the controversy and other circumstances, the Miami diocese took on a day-to-day mentality, rather than rooting its present actions in an understanding of the past. All of this was helpful to Carroll, since attention focused on him and his administration without any comparisons with the past. It was almost as if South Florida Catholicism began in 1958 with Coleman F. Carroll. The historical caesura, the myth of the new, was reinforced by the dramatic events that occurred from 1958 to 1968 in the development of South Florida Catholicism.

6

The Cuban Challenge, 1959–68: Part 1, Cuban Catholics and the Exile

B esides the unfortunate controversy that clouded the first seven years of the history of the Diocese of Miami, Catholicism in South Florida was forced to face another unexpected set of challenges with the influx of refugees from the Cuban revolution. The diocese was two and one-half months old when Fidel Castro entered Havana on January 8, 1959.

Catholicism in Cuba

The Cuban Church in the nineteenth century had been neither strong nor vibrant. In colonial Cuba, as in Spain, church and state formed one inseparable reality. Before independence, Spanish clergymen discouraged native vocations as much for political as ecclesial reasons. Afterward, the Cuban Constitution of 1901 separated church and state. With the rise of Cuban nationalism, which was influenced among the educated classes by Freemasonry and liberalism, patriots were anticlerical and anti-ecclesial, a mentality that continued in Cuba through the 1920s. American Protestant missions were also established there in the twentieth century. In the 1950s and early 1960s millions of dollars and hundreds of Protestant ministers (mostly Puerto Ricans) poured into Cuba, but their efforts never had significant impact.[1]

Religious, especially Americans, had been active in founding educational institutions in Cuba since 1900. For example, the Oblate Sisters of Providence, composed of black women religious, arrived in Cuba in November 1900 and started Our Lady of Charity School in Havana for black and mulatto Cuban children. As early as 1901, the Oblates had their first Cuban postulant. From 1900 to 1940, the Oblate Sisters operated five different schools in Cuba.

Meanwhile, the Cuban Catholic hierarchy applied for and received permission from Rome in 1916 to proclaim Our Lady of Charity the patroness of Cuba. Popular devotion to the Virgin under this title, which had its origin in seventeenth-century Cuba, was deeply ingrained in the religious consciousness of the Cuban people. Bishop González Estrada, Cuba's first native Cuban bishop, encouraged native vocations. In January 1929, the *Caballeros Católicos* were established as a laymen's organization as a defense against Freemasonry. In the 1930s, Catholic Action began to take hold in Cuba.[2]

However, it was not until native-born Manuel Arteaga was named archbishop of Havana in December 1941 that the Cuban Church grew in strength and influence. Catholic Action groups, including the Caballeros Católicos, Damas Católicos, and Juventud Católica, were organized under his auspices. In sixteen years Arteaga ordained forty-five native priests, and in 1945 established Good Shepherd Diocesan Seminary on the outskirts of Havana. He encouraged the growth of the educational apostolate by religious, including the establishment of Villanueva University by the American Augustinians in 1946. Named cardinal in 1945, Arteaga supported a national pilgrimage to celebrate the fifty years of the Cuban Republic in 1952 and to renew the popular devotion of Our Lady of Charity, whose statue was carried in procession throughout the country on the occasion.[3]

On the eve of the revolution, Cuban Catholicism had reached its zenith under Cardinal Arteaga. But that did not mean it had reached its full potential. Religious priests outnumbered diocesan clergy by more than two to one. The number of native vocations was still small. Most priests in Cuba were from Spain, with a good representation from the United States and Canada, but even so there were not enough priests. At its peak in September 1959, the Cuban Church had 229 diocesan priests and 561 religious priests serving 6.5 million people in 671 churches—one priest per 8,000 Catholics. Approximately 90 percent of Cubans were baptized Catholics, but only about 10 percent were practicing.[4] As one Cuban prelate explained: "Perhaps hundreds of thousands of Cubans have rarely if ever seen a priest . . . . In Havana alone there are some parishes with more than 100,000 population."[5]

Dedicated laity played an important role in the Cuban Church after World War II. Catholic Action, initiated by the Christian Brothers and organized under Cardinal Arteaga, and Agrupación Universitaria, university students under Jesuit leadership, were important in teaching religion to the poor, operating dispensaries for the needy, sponsoring radio and television programs, and publishing information booklets.[6] Although the number of these active, dedicated laity was small, their effect was disproportionate to their numbers.

Catholic schools were an important aspect of Cuban Catholicism. Cuban middle- and upper-class parents sent their children to private, Catholic schools run by religious; the Cuban public schools were predominantly populated by the poorer classes. Catholic schools were never numerous enough or financially within the reach of the poorer agrarian classes who needed them.[7]

In spite of the Protestant evangelizers, in spite of the lack of priests, in spite of the small number of lay apostles, the vast majority of Cuban people of all classes considered themselves Catholic, though most were nonpracticing. Catholicism was woven into the social and cultural fabric of Cuban life, legitimizing and organizing the communal existence of most of the people. Most had their children baptized; most children received First Communion; most upper- and middle-class Cubans were married and buried in the Church. As one commentator put it, "The Cuban is naturally religious in spite of his great ignorance of solid doctrine."[8] To be a Cuban meant to be sensitive to the sacred, to be religious, to be a Catholic.

The political, social, and economic revolution inspired by Fidel Castro had important effects on Cuban Catholicism. The deterioration of the government's relations with the Church can be seen in five stages. The first, in 1959, was characterized by caution on both sides. When Castro came out of the mountains and entered Havana on January 8, 1959, he was welcomed by an overwhelming majority of the people, including Church leaders, reacting to the excesses and negligence of the Batista regime his forces had overthrown. Idolized by the masses, Castro revealed himself to be a talented politician, an eloquent speaker, and a charismatic leader who used his three- or four-hour television speeches on social justice to capture the imagination of the Cuban people. Castro met early on with the Cuban hierarchy and appeared friendly to Church leaders.[9]

From January 9 through July 1959, Castro enacted a series of laws designed to stabilize his position and implement the ideals of the revolution. Constitutional rights were revoked; unions were not permitted to strike; agrarian reform was begun (May 19). Legislation that directly affected the Church included the prohibition of Mass at army posts or in prisons, the disallowance of shrines in hospitals, the supervision by the government of all education, and the sale by the state of all textbooks and school supplies.[10]

Church leaders did not speak out against the legislation, perceiving Castro to be correcting the abuses of Batista. Catholic commentators, especially those in Catholic Action, saw agrarian reform as complementary to papal social justice encyclicals and the Christian humanism of Jacques Maritain.[11] To commemorate the 26 of July Movement pushed by the Castro government, Mass was offered by the papal nuncio of Cuba at the cathedral in Havana with top officials of the army and government (including Castro) in attendance.[12] While Cuban Church officials were trying to coexist with the new regime, Richard Cardinal Cushing of Boston began to attack it in November. Labeling Castro a Communist, Cushing called the Cuban Church the "silent Church," a phrase used previously in the cold war to describe Catholicism under Communism. In response to the American prelate's accusations, Bishop Evelio Díaz y Cía, apostolic administrator of Havana, stated on behalf of the Cuban hierarchy, "There has been no interference whatsoever on the part of the government in Church activities."[13] Díaz's statement, cautious in tone and defensive in posture, was not altogether accurate.

The second stage of Cuban church-state relations under Castro, marked by increasing friction, occurred in January–August 1960. By the beginning of 1960, the Cuban people were still unclear about Castro's intentions or political philosophy. As more Communists were observed in the government, the counterrevolutionary movement began. In February, when the first deputy premier of the USSR, Anastas Mikoyan, visited Cuba, students of the Catholic University of Villanueva organized an anti-Communist rally that became a riot. Father Eduardo Boza Masvidal, chancellor of Villanueva, later denied inciting the demonstration, but he defended the students' right to demonstrate. Government spokesmen said that whoever was anti-Communist was a traitor to the revolution. Threats were made against Catholic Action by the president of the Popular Socialist party. Cuba's Catholic Action groups protested this verbal assault in a joint statement affirming their adherence to the principles of social justice, national sovereignty, and public morality, which had inspired the Cuban Revolution, but their rejection of atheistic, totalitarian Communism.[14]

Archbishop Enrique Pérez Serantes of Santiago de Cuba, who had saved Castro's life in 1953 by persuading him to surrender to Batista forces, supported the social program of the revolution. However, on May 17, 1960, he warned of the "enemy within," referring to the clear signs of Communism in the Castro government. In June, both Pérez Serantes and Boza Masvidal gave speeches at Villanueva denouncing the unjust confiscation of property by the state. In mid-July in a televised speech, Castro labeled Catholic priests "Facists."[15] Friction between the Cuban Church and the Castro government was exacerbated by a Pastoral Letter signed by every Cuban prelate and read in all the churches on the island on August 7. In the letter, the bishops praised the reforms but said human rights had been violated; among other things, agents of the Castro government had attacked worshippers as they were leaving church. The prelates called the Cuban Church the "Church of Silence." The battle lines had now been clearly drawn; the Church would be silent no longer, but its voice had little effect.[16]

The issuance of the Pastoral marks the transition to the third stage of the Church's relations with the revolutionary government. The months September–December 1960 were characterized by increasing government rhetorical abuse and harassment. At this time, relations between Cuba and the United States were deteriorating seriously. In October the State Department advised American sisters in Cuba to leave the island, and some communities of women did.[17] In the same month, Archbishop Pérez Serantes accused the Castro regime of trying to destroy the Church and replace it with Communism. Instigators disturbed church services; religious radio and television programs were suppressed; Catholic schools were forced to use Marxist texts; three Havana churches were burned. In early December, Cuban bishops published another Pastoral Letter accusing the government of attempting to create a national church and a nationwide antireligious drive. Castro skillfully used the television as a medium for the "rhetoric of sensation," encouraging the Cuban masses to see the Church as an enemy of the revolution. In a nationally televised speech, he called priests "counterrevolutionary 'henchmen in cassocks'" who took bribes from American sugar companies. He called Cardinal Arteaga a "Judas" who had supported the "bloody dictator" Batista. In an attempt to divide the presbyterate, he distinguished between real Cuban priests and "Fascist" priests.[18]

The fourth stage in the erosion of relations between the Castro government and the Church, from January to March 1961, saw the occupation and seizure of some Church property. Although the Pastoral of December had forced Castro to retaliate with more concrete action against the Church, the severing of diplomatic relations by the United States on January 3, 1961, further eroded the Church's position. All American religious were ordered out of Cuba by their superiors. In early January, Castro's forces occupied several Catholic churches and schools and the headquarters of three lay groups, Agrupación Universitaria, the Knights of Columbus, and the Union of Christian Workers. All three Cuban seminaries were also occupied.[19] Connecting the Cuban Church with the United States, Cuban President Osvaldo Dorticós said that Catholic opposition to the revolution was closely connected to President Kennedy's aid to Cuban refugees. He went on to attack the Catholic schools and announced their nationalization in early February 1961.[20]

The fifth stage in the deteriorating relations between the Church and the Castro regime immediately preceded the coming of the Cuban exiles to Miami. It was closely related to the ill-fated Bay of Pigs invasion, which was a disaster for the Cuban Church as well as a political and military fiasco. On the day of the battle (April 17,

1961), Bishop Eduardo Boza Masvidal was arrested, along with 100 priests. Approximately 250,000 people, including many foreigners, were put under arrest.[21] On May 1, Premier Castro in a televised speech told all foreign priests to pack their bags since they soon would be expelled. Shortly thereafter, government officials gave foreign priests and some Cuban priests two or three days to leave the country. The papal nuncio advised these priests to remain; some stayed and were not expelled, others left the country. By May 1, all Catholic schools were in the process of being nationalized, 173 in the Havana Archdiocese. Catholic lay leaders were either in jail or in hiding. Catholic Action was destroyed. Three Cuban bishops were placed under house arrest. Sisters were forbidden to leave their convents; two cloistered communities were ordered to resume civilian attire and return to their families. Neither priests nor laity were permitted to evangelize the unchurched outside of the church building. Some churches were desecrated by the militia.[22]

In September 1961, the Castro government made its boldest move against the Church. Militia organized armed raids on most of the churches in all six Cuban provinces.[23] Father Agustín Román, a priest of the Diocese of Matanzas, recalls the events leading up to that September. On the day of the Bay of Pigs invasion, he remembers, Castro incarcerated all of the priests of Cuba; none were executed. Román was imprisoned with twelve other priests from April 17 to May 2. When he returned to his church, he found militia dressed in liturgical vestments and all the sacred vessels missing. That summer, government soldiers came at night and took ten priests of the Diocese of Matanzas. To combat further disappearances, fourteen priests of the municipio Cardinas stayed at one central place during the evenings.

On September 13, 1961, Father Román was conducting a retreat at Colón in the Matanzas diocese. After he had heard confessions, two men approached him, saying that they were to take him before a judge. Román had no idea what the escort and summons were about since he had never preached on any political topic. He took with him his breviary, one other book (*Mary and Dogma*), and two handkerchiefs (one of which was soon to be lost), plus the cassock and shoes he had on. His escorts let him go to his parish, where he consumed the hosts in the tabernacle, then took him to prison in Matanzas. The next morning he was in Havana, incarcerated with 131 other priests and brothers, including 46 Cuban-born priests. With Boza Masvidal as their leader, the group was put on the underprovisioned *Covadonga*, a Spanish passenger ship bound for Spain, without trial or specific charges. The priests and religious did not stay in Spain long but returned to the New World.[24]

The ejection of the priests and brothers on the *Covadonga* represented the final stage of deterioration in the relationship of Castroism and Catholicism. It illustrates the effects of tensions created when Communism and Catholicism are found in the same polity. Yet this process had some aspects that were specific to Cuba and not precisely reflective of Communism and the Church as seen in Eastern Bloc countries or China. The work of Catholic Action from the 1930s among the poor prepared the way by means of rhetoric and action for dissatisfaction with the Batista regime and the desire for social justice articulated by Castro. The final takeover of the Cuban government by revolutionary forces was remarkably bloodless. Castro rode into Havana in January 1959 virtually unopposed. Although 960 political prisoners had been killed by his firing squads by October 1961, not one priest or religious had been put to death.[25] Castro's view of the Church and his actions against it seem integrated with his perception of threat from the United States. He identified antirevolution sentiment and anti-Communism with American imperialism and Cuban Catholicism. Moreover, the Cuban Church was silent for too long. When it did voice itself through its official leaders, it lacked the power to grapple with the government. Although at the peak of its long history, the Cuban Church had neither internal cohesion nor the loyalty of the masses, who were too far from Church leaders to be informed and to act in concert when challenged. Through threats, intimidation, some short-term imprisonment, and the physical expulsion of 132 priests and brothers, as well as several uncontested laws of limitation, the Cuban Church was nipped before it blossomed. With over 66 percent of its clergy religious, with almost 90 percent of its people unchurched, with a vestigal benefice system, with only the beginnings of native personnel, the Church was simply not strong enough to do battle with the power of Castro's charisma, social reform, and Marxism.

The Cuban Catholic Exodus

As the true nature of Castro and the revolution surfaced and as the social, economic, and political effects of the revolution began to touch individuals, some Cubans decided to leave their homeland. For priests and religious of Cuba, the year 1961 was a watershed.

Religious women left even before Castro's May 1 speech warning foreign priests to pack their bags. The Dominican Sisters of St. Catherine de Ricci began withdrawing in stages in September 1960, until the last of the original twenty-four sisters left in January 1961, after the break in U.S. diplomatic relations with Cuba. After the May 1 speech and the confiscation of Catholic schools, religious women, whose primary task was education, left Cuba en masse, inundating South Florida with a cosmopolitan mix of sisters from France, Canada, America, Holland, Spain, and Cuba. By July 1961, 600 sisters had disembarked in South Florida from Cuba. Some Miami women religious granted hospitality to the Cuban sisters until the latter could make connections to their motherhouses or other institutions outside the United States.[26] Several communities were invited to remain in the Diocese of Miami, including the Oblate Sisters of Providence, who left Cuba not because Castro wanted them to but because they refused to teach from Marxist texts and wear secular dress.[27]

Along with the women religious, some diocesan priests and hundreds of religious priests and brothers left Cuba before the general expulsion in September 1961. Of the 125 priests from Cuba listed in Miami as of July, 36 were diocesan priests, although most did not stay in the Miami area for long. Other Cuban diocesan priests in exile emigrated to Spain, Canada, and Mexico. By November 1962, 30 of the 74 priests emigrating from Cuba were working in the Miami diocese. The Extension Society helped in 1962 by providing stipends for priests from Cuba.[28] Two OCSHA priests (*Obra de Cooperación Sacerdotal Hispano América*, an organization of Spanish diocesan priest missionaries) were among those in Miami before May 1, 1961. By 1964, eleven of the seventeen OCSHA priests in the Miami diocese were from Cuba.[29]

The day after the Bay of Pigs invasion, April 18, 1961, Villanueva University, run by the American Augustinians, was closed. After incarceration, house arrest, release, then house arrest again, the Augustinians were ordered to leave Cuba. Six of them arrived in Miami at the end of May 1961. Around the same time, with the closing of Catholic schools, the entire Cuban province of 104 Christian Brothers who operated 14 institutions in Cuba was ordered off the island by the provincial. Not all of these men were foreign born; in fact the Christian Brothers were among the most successful in attracting native Cuban vocations. Most of the Christian Brothers went to Central and South America; 18 were asked by Bishop Carroll to remain in Miami. In May, 182 Marist Brothers left Cuba for Miami along with several Jesuit priests. By the middle of the month, 500 religious priests had fled the country. In July, one charter flight to Miami carried 50 priests and 108 religious brothers and sisters. At that time, 89 of the 125 priests from Cuba in the Miami diocese were religious, including Augustinians, Dominicans, Vincentians, Franciscans, Jesuits, Capuchins, and Piarists.[30]

The abortive invasion at the Bay of Pigs, which triggered Castro's retaliatory response against the Church, also forced the Cuban bishops' decision to withdraw their seminarians from Cuba. Monsignor Arcadio Marinas, vicar general of the Archdiocese of Havana, went on two begging trips to the United States to seek funds and support for the Cuban bishops' plans. During the summer of 1961, Marinas coordinated the removal of diocesan seminarians from Cuba with the help of the National Catholic Welfare Conference (NCWC) Immigration Bureau, its Spanish American Bureau, and Bishop Carroll of Miami. That summer, thirty-five Cuban seminarians were housed at St. John Vianney Seminary, where they took English classes.[31] Having been advised by the archbishop of Havana not to return to Cuba, Marinas made the American Augustinians in New York his headquarters for the care of Cuban seminarians in exile. By March 1962, eighty-four major seminarians and thirty-four minor seminarians were out of Cuba under Marinas's care. They were educated free of charge in Europe, South America, the United States, and Canada, supplemented by funds that Marinas was able to solicit. The first of the Cuban seminarians ordained in exile were sent back to Cuba by Marinas. One of these, who had been ordained in Miami, made the naïve blunder of writing his bishop about his being an agent of the Central Intelligence Agency. The Castro government intercepted the letter, summarily expelled the priest, and barred future Cuban priests in exile from returning to their homeland.[32]

The inundation of priests and religious from Cuba had subsided considerably by the fall of 1961. After October 1962, the number of ecclesiastical personnel arriving in Miami from Cuba dropped to a few a year, those often coming via another country, such as Spain or Mexico, to which they had gone after leaving Cuba. By the beginning of 1968, the flow of diocesan priests, religious priests, and religious brothers and sisters from Cuba had stopped. The exodus of ecclesial personnel from Cuba, mostly through intimidation and the governmental control of schools, was devastating to the Cuban Church. Of the 2,000 religious women who had staffed more than 350 Catholic institutions on the island, only 100 remained. Where previously there had been 45 Jesuits on the island, only 18 remained in mid-1961. Only 100 priests were left on the island where there had recently been more than 700.[33] The Castro government had managed, without protest, bloodshed, or mass arrests, to force Catholic schools to shut down and priests to minister only within a church building. Once foreign religious superiors were assured of Castro's political leanings, they ordered their personnel out. Once the schools were under state control, religious who depended on those institutions for their self-definition and for their income felt impelled to leave. Most were not forced to choose between leaving and being expelled. They were free to leave and did, thus further weakening the position of the Cuban Church.

Although the shackling of the institutional Church by the Castro government impelled ecclesiastical personnel to leave the island, the exodus of approximately 10 percent of Cuba's population was inspired less by religious motivations than by political, social, and economic considerations.

The place where most Cuban refugees came was not an area bereft of Hispanic influence. Miami had long been called the "Gateway to Latin America" because South American tourists made it their favorite North American vacation spot. Barry College had 50 students from Latin America in 1959, and there were 230 at the University of Miami, 52 of them from Cuba. Twenty-five South American airlines flew into the city and employed their own nationals at Miami International Airport, where Spanish and English were routinely used in announcing arrivals and departures. Several South American consular offices were located in Miami, and the city's economy was closely linked to South America by air and sea transport. *Diario Las Americas*, a Miami-based newspaper founded in 1953, served twenty-one South American capitals. Because of its closeness to their homeland, Cubans were even better acquainted with Miami than were other Latin Americans.[34]

The Hispanic connection had made itself felt in the Church of South Florida before the Cuban exile. In 1951, Mercy Hospital introduced nurses' training for Spanish speakers; by 1959, Mercy had twenty physicians with Spanish surnames. Archbishop Hurley had already asked his younger priests to study Spanish in 1951, as he foresaw more and more connections between South Florida and South America. In 1956, a children's religion class was taught in Spanish by a group at Gesu Parish who called themselves "The Cenacle." By early 1959, St. Michael's Parish had 550 families who spoke Spanish, some of whom had resided at St. Michael's a generation or more. By 1959, one-fourth of the children of St. Michael's School were Spanish-speaking. Before March 1959, confession and sermons in Spanish were offered at three Miami parishes, Gesu, Corpus Christi, and St. Michael's.[35]

Sociologist Juan Clark divides the Cuban exodus of 1959–74 into four stages:[36]

	Number	Percent
1. Early departures, January 1, 1959–October 22, 1962	248,070	38.8
2. Post–missile crisis lull, October 22, 1962–September 28, 1965	55,916	8.7
3. Family reunion period, September 28, 1965–December 31, 1971	297,318	46.4
4. Wane of the exodus, January 1972–December 1974	38,903	6.1
Total	640,207	100.0

In the first several months of the Castro regime, those closely linked with the Batista regime fled. These were few, and most of them moved away from the Miami area for fear of reprisals. With the agrarian reform of May 1959, plantation owners, ranchers, and businessmen fled Cuba, many settling in Palm Beach County. At the end of 1960, the seizure of businesses increased and the urban housing reform was implemented, both causing some upper- and middle-class Cubans to flee their homeland. From the summer of 1961 to October 22, 1962, the Cuban economy continued to deteriorate, political persecution increased, and food rationing began, all of which spurred middle- and lower-class Cubans to leave.[37]

Clark demonstrates that, contrary to popular belief, by the mid-1960s the majority of Cuban exiles were working-class people. The boat escapees are even more representative of the Cuban population as a whole, he maintains. Early refugees tended to be highly overrepresentative of Havana, but later arrivals showed a wider geographical distribution. Lower-income people and blacks were underrepresented among the refugees in the beginning, but that gap was closing by the end of the exodus.[38]

Miami was the main point of entry, the "Ellis Island," for Cuban exiles coming to the United States. Most arrived by airplane, a much smaller number by boat.[39] They soon formed the largest single Hispanic group in South Florida, but at no time during the 1960s did they constitute a majority of the Latin American population in Dade County:[40]

	Cuban	Non-Cuban Hispanic	Percent Cuban
1960	24,000	50,000	32.4
1970	217,892	299,217	42.1

A great deal of the literature concerning the Cuban exodus has stressed the political motivation that pushed Cubans to leave their homeland.[41] The political explanation was necessary if the Cuban exiles were to be accepted into the United States as "political refugees"; otherwise U.S. immigration quotas would not have allowed so many Cubans to enter the country in so short a time. The political explanation was also important to ease American acceptance of the immigrant Cubans as freedom-loving people fleeing the evils of Communist-totalitarianism. Beyond doubt, many Cubans left their homeland for strictly political reasons; but the political rationale does not adequately explain the Cuban exodus. One of the expectations of the Cuban people when Castro took power was that life would be better for them than under the Batista regime. Not just the lure of political freedom but the failure of

Castro to improve economic, social, and personal realities pushed approximately 10 percent of the Cuban population to Miami.

Despite the corruption, the political intolerance, and the opposition of most Cubans to the Batista regime, the economy had improved under Batista; the standard of living had risen and jobs were available. After only four months of Castro, one-third of Cuba's labor force either was unemployed or had only part-time jobs, and this at the time of the sugar harvest, when employment should have been at its highest. Sixty-two percent of the working class was earning less than $75 per month at a time when food costs for a small family were $42 per month. Castro undertook not only a political revolution but a social and economic restructuring of Cuba according to Marxist ideology. But it did not work out well. In 1961 and 1962, the economy deteriorated even more, and medical supplies, consumer goods, and food all became scarce. Forced labor was initiated in 1963.[42]

Conditions such as these caused the exodus. The Castro government initiated no massive persecutions, threatened no physical destruction of property or personal dislocation. People came to the United States because of intolerable and disillusioning personal experiences.[43] Upon arrival, they did not sit and brood about their fate; they began immediately to build new lives. Neither brooders nor beggars, Cubans were workers. Contemporary newspaper and magazine accounts lauded Cuban industriousness and success in America, and, for the most part, did not exaggerate.[44]

One aspect of the Cuban exodus that sets it apart from other immigrant arrivals was the significant role of the U.S. government in the Cubans' reception. The National Origins Quota Act of 1924, which limited immigration to the United States, was amended during the cold war to allow flexibility for "political refugees." From 1954 through 1968, a total of 446,326 political refugees were admitted into the United States, 119,474 of whom (21.1 percent) were Cubans.[45] The federal government paid for the commercial airline trips ("Freedom Flights") twice a day, five days a week, between December 1, 1965, and February 1, 1970, at a cost of $50 million a year.[46]

Besides creating laws to ease Cuban exiles' entry, the federal government aided them materially. The Migration and Refugee Assistance Act of 1962 made federal funds available to assist state and local agencies in providing services to Cuban exiles. By 1974,

TABLE 6.1. Cuban Refugee Program, 1961–69

Year	Registrations[a]	Resettlements	Refugees Receiving Federal Financial Aid in Florida	
			Cases	Persons
1961	78,236	16,954	–	–
1962	77,613	35,753	30,960	64,011
1963	14,134	19,869	21,473	44,595
1964	5,396	13,075	11,347	20,782
1965	11,050	11,905	8,077	13,671
1966	42,376	37,389	9,323	15,760
1967	42,212	36,929	11,666	18,966
1968	38,258	34,020	13,334	20,911
1969	46,919	29,949	14,939	23,234
Total	356,194	235,843	121,119	221,930

SOURCE: U.S. Bureau of the Census, *Statistical Abstract of the U.S.: 1970*, p. 95.
a. At Cuban Refugee Center, Miami

some $935 million had been spent under this arrangement for health and education services, special training, income supplements, and other social programs.[47]

The federal government was also heavily involved in resettling Cuban exiles out of South Florida, which had reached its saturation point (table 6.1). In January 1961, approximately 1,300 Cubans were coming weekly to Miami. The federal government ascertained which were willing to resettle (59 percent), paid their traveling expenses, and helped them get jobs in some other part of the country. By the end of 1968, 39.9 percent of the Cuban exiles had been resettled outside of South Florida. This resettlement was also aided by the efforts of Catholic Relief Services with the cooperation of one hundred American archdioceses and dioceses.[48]

Though many originally intended to return as soon as Castro was overthrown, Cuban exiles settled in Miami in residential patterns that became permanent as time passed. Because of the Castro government's prohibition on exporting material possessions and the ban on taking more than five dollars in cash off the island, most exiles settled in low-rent neighborhoods in Miami, close to shopping and transportation facilities. Initially, the immigrants lived in the numerous low-rent apartments in downtown Miami and the southwest area. Hialeah was another popular early settlement because of the low cost of housing and availability of blue-collar employment. In time, more diffusion took place within the Cuban exile community in Miami.[49] As a demonstration of the growth of Cuban and Hispanic elements in Miami, as well as the development of their economic base, there were 45 Spanish grocery stores in Dade County in 1960, 127 in 1968, and 224 by 1976.[50]

Although not indicated in Clark's "Four Stages of the Cuban Exodus," the year 1968 is a watershed in the history of the Cuban Catholic exodus. By 1968, priests and religious virtually ceased emigrating from Cuba. It was also at that time that diocesan authorities began to realize that more Spanish-speaking personnel might increase the apostolate among the Hispanics of the diocese. By the end of 1968 the diocese had seventy-five Spanish-speaking priests. Also in 1968 an immigration law placed Cuban immigrants on a quota basis like other Latin Americans. (In May 1970, the Cuban government stopped accepting exit applications, thus halting the "Freedom Flights.") In 1968, the number of boat escapees declined, beginning a trend that continued into the 1970s and that was directly related to the nationalization of all ships and boats by the Cuban government in 1968. By the beginning of that year, there were 122,628 Cubans in Dade County and 136,244 in the entire state of Florida; 26 percent of the population of the City of Miami was Cuban, 21 percent of the City of Hialeah. Of the Cubans in Dade County, 66 percent lived in the City of Miami, 14 percent in Hialeah.[51]

7

The Cuban Challenge, 1959–68: Part 2, Responding to a New Situation

Cuban Catholics who left their native island in the 1960s brought with them to Miami their own cultural expression of Catholicism. When they arrived, they found another.

The American Catholic Response in Miami

The federal government was not the only agency to aid the incoming exiles. The local Church (the Diocese of Miami) also played an important role in welcoming and situating the new arrivals. At the beginning of 1959, the Diocese of Miami had sixty-three priests, six of whom were Spanish diocesan priest missionaries from Obra de Cooperación Sacerdotal Hispano América (OCSHA). Of this number, twenty could hear confessions in Spanish, eighteen could speak it adequately, and sixteen could preach in it. There were at the time 392 sisters in 16 different communities, none Hispanic. Nine Sisters of St. Joseph ministered to Hispanic migrants. Only three parishes regularly provided confessions and sermons in Spanish. In general, the diocese was far from adequately supplied with Spanish-speaking personnel to deal with the Cuban inundation to come.[1]

Social service institutions of the Diocese of Miami were likewise unprepared. Catholic Charities had not kept up with the rapid growth in population in South Florida in the 1950s, and the few services offered were understaffed and underfunded. In 1959, the Catholic Charities Bureau was mostly a child welfare agency, with four programs, two offices, and a budget of a little over $135,000, almost half of which went to salaries.[2]

More than a year and a half elapsed after Castro's takeover before the numbers of disaffected Cuban exiles began to have an impact on South Florida. By the fall of 1960 the refugee population had become so large and the tempo of entry had increased so greatly that Miami could not respond without outside help. A committee of Miami citizens, including Catholics, petitioned the president of the United States for aid in employment, immigration status, counseling, social service, and funds. In November 1960, President Eisenhower released $1 million which, earmarked predominantly for the resettlement of exiles outside of South Florida, provided only a safety valve. The emergency funds offered no direct help to the community, the Church, or the Cuban exiles themselves.[3]

Until March 1, 1961, the Diocese of Miami, aided by national Catholic organizations, was the major source of social service for Cuban exiles in Miami. No direct help was available to them from any public agency, except for emergency hospital care. In two months (December 1960 and January 1961), the diocese contributed goods and services to the Cuban exiles amounting to more than $300,000. In late December, the Catholic Relief Services and the National Catholic Welfare Conference opened a Cuban Refugee Emergency Relief Center in Miami. In February 1961, priests from Catholic Charities agencies throughout the United States organized the National Resettlement Conference for Cuban Refugees to facilitate Eisenhower's program.[4]

Finally, on March 1, 1961, the Kennedy administration funded the Florida State Department of Public Welfare in order to get financial aid for exiles in need. But federal aid was not sufficient to cover all refugees' needs. From March 1 to October 31, 1961, the

Diocese of Miami rendered another $561,243.81 in goods and services which did not duplicate existing government programs. In the eleven months from December 1, 1960, to October 31, 1961, the diocese contributed $875,149.97 in goods and services to the Cuban exiles, a remarkable contribution considering the paucity of diocesan personnel and the financial difficulties surrounding the Hurley-Carroll controversy. Because more federal help was needed, Bishop Carroll testified on December 6, 1961, before a subcommittee of the U.S. Senate.[5]

The diocese also sought outside help through the solicitation of private contributions. In July 1961, when diocesan officials publicized the plight of Miami's Cuban exiles, contributions began to come from individuals and American corporations, including Texaco and the Ford Foundation; but by November 1962, private contributions had "fallen off almost altogether."[6]

In late 1962, the Diocese of Miami was pressed financially to serve the needs of the exiles, in spite of federal aid available in the area. During 1962, the diocese contributed $498,136.38 in goods and services for the welfare of Cuban exiles, none of which was ever reimbursed by the U.S. government.[7]

The Diocese of Miami and the Catholic Service Bureau were able to respond to the unexpected challenge of the Cubans because of administrative and institutional flexibility. Bishop Carroll relished a challenge, and his leadership style lent itself to ad hoc responses. All diocesan decisions ultimately were approved by him; all information flowed through him. Diocesan agencies could move quickly and decisively at the command of the ordinary. In addition, because diocesan structure was small and without any long-established or vested interests, it was adaptable.[8] Examples of such flexibility can be found in two programs sponsored for Cuban exiles, Centro Hispano Católico and the Unaccompanied Children's Program.

The need for a social service agency to serve the particular needs of the Spanish-speaking population of Miami was recognized by Archbishop Hurley, who had made plans to establish a Hispanic center. However, it was not until October 15, 1959, that Centro Hispano Católico was opened in a remodeled wing of Gesu Parochial School in downtown Miami.[9] Father Hugh Flynn was appointed diocesan director of the center, and its administrator, Sister Miriam Strong, OP, had served for six years in Havana before coming to Miami. Besides these two, the original staff consisted of three other St. Catherine de Ricci Dominican Sisters and two Spanish Dominican priests. Sister Miriam and the other sisters at Centro, although untrained in social work, had numerous contacts among the exiles, and word spread quickly in the Miami Cuban community about their work, although the first clients (about one hundred per month) were primarily Colombians and other South Americans.[10] Bishop Carroll was proud of the center which he had established and supported it strongly, visiting it often after the exiles began to pour in. He once told Sister Miriam: "Spend what money you have, but don't let anyone go hungry. When you have no more, you know where to come."[11] The purpose of Centro was "to provide for cultural, social, and spiritual needs of the Latin American Community . . . to provide for the orientation of the Latin American, to give him a better understanding of, and appreciation for, the American way of life." Services offered by Centro from 1959 through early 1961 included English classes, a day nursery, an outpatient clinic, a dental clinic, and a high school for the Spanish-speaking. The staff coordinated its activities with those of other Miami Catholic agencies and institutions.[12]

In January 1961, Centro cared for one hundred cases a day. From February, the daily caseload tripled, since at the time about 1,700 Cubans were arriving weekly in Miami. In 1962, the total number of cases Centro cared for was 12,964, of which 12,567 were Cuban, 182 Colombian, 77 Puerto Rican, and 21 Peruvian. The dollar value of services rendered in 1962 was almost $445,000, the next year almost $300,000.[13]

In February 1964, the slackening of exile arrivals caused Centro to reorganize. Father Frederick Waas was named director of Centro, and a new board of directors was chosen.[14] With the lull and the change in personnel, the project began to grow stale. In June, Centro Hispano Católico was redefined with reference specifically to Cuban exiles. The agency was to help with acculturation but with a sensitivity to Hispanic culture: "The chief purpose of the Centro Hispano Católico is to help the new arrival to bridge the gap between his old way of life and the new. It seeks to prevent personal and social disorganization. It tries to interpret American Culture for him through understanding, bi-lingual personnel who know and appreciate *his* customs, culture, morals, values and lan-

guage." Although services were expanded, they were simply varia-
tions of the assistance offered originally.[15] From October 1959 to
June 1968, Centro Hispano Católico handled 450,015 cases. With
the waning of Cuban immigration from 1972 to 1974, and the self-
sufficiency of the exile population, Centro's caseload lessened, although it continued to serve those in need in the Miami Cuban
and Hispanic community. In July 1982, Gesu School, which housed
Centro Hispano Católico, was slated to be razed for a church park-
ing lot. However, at the last minute the building was spared; plans
now call for a $2.3 million renovation project to turn Gesu School
into an office building.[16]

The second major program sponsored by the Diocese of Miami
to meet the exiles' needs was the Unaccompanied Children's Program. By the end of 1960 in Cuba, rumors were rife that Castro
was planning to send more than a thousand young people to work
on farms in the USSR. Many Cuban parents feared this proposed
indoctrination of their children and the breakup of their families.
Later in 1961, rumors spread of another indoctrination plan to have
children ages three to ten live in state-run dormitories, seeing their
parents for only two days a month. Some children were actually
sent to the USSR, and, although the state children's dormitories
were never fully implemented, some Cuban parents began sending their children to Miami to avoid these two possibilities. The
fact that unaccompanied children in Miami could apply for a visa
waiver permitting their parents to join them also had encouraged
Cubans to send their children on ahead of them with the hope of
entering the United States soon themselves.[17]

The diocese began to concern itself with unaccompanied Cuban
children in mid-November 1960, when Monsignor Bryan Walsh,
director of the Catholic Welfare Bureau, came across a fourteen-
year-old boy, Pedro Menéndez, who had spent a month in Miami
being passed from one family to another since his parents were
still in Cuba. Walsh quickly discovered many more children in the
same situation. The Eisenhower administration promised Walsh
that some of its $1 million allocation could be used to care for un-
accompanied Cuban children. Next, Walsh was contacted by a
group of American businessmen who wanted to get their children
out of Cuba. Just before Christmas 1960, the State Department
asked Walsh to accept two hundred unaccompanied children from
Cuba. Walsh had no idea where the money was to come from,

when the children would come, or where they would be housed. The first group of twelve children, arriving December 26, 1960, at Miami airport, were lodged in a house across from Assumption Academy. Word spread quickly in Cuba that a priest in Miami was accepting children, and many more were sent. On January 9, 1961, Walsh was given authority by the State Department to issue letters to any child in Cuba between six to sixteen stating that the visa requirement for entrance into the United States was to be waived. Later these visa waivers were also granted by the Swiss embassy in Havana. When the children arrived in Miami, the Catholic Welfare Bureau was their de facto guardian since it was a licensed child welfare agency. The federal government sent the Diocese of Miami its first check ($75,000) for the program in mid-January 1961.[18]

The Unaccompanied Children Program mushroomed so unexpectedly that the Diocese could not care for all the children entering the country. A plan for the resettlement of the children was worked out in January 1961, with government officials and Catholic Relief Services, which eventually involved one hundred dioceses in more than thirty states. In the first eleven months of its operation, expenditures for the program totaled almost $1.5 million. The program peaked in October 1962, with the Cuban missile crisis. Even with the resettlement program, during peak periods in 1961 and 1962 upwards of 2,000 children were housed in five different centers in the diocese: Camp Matecumbe, Kendall, Florida City, Jesuit Boys' Home, and St. Raphael's Hall. The U.S. government gave the diocese $6.50 per diem per child for institutional care and $5.50 per diem per child for foster family care. The average cost per child of diocesan care was $6.58 per diem per child. In the summer, a sixth center for unaccompanied children was opened by the diocese at Opa-Locka Naval Air Base barracks. The Catholic Welfare Bureau had to rent these six sites since the diocese had no large institution for group child care.[19]

As of September 1963, the Unaccompanied Children Program, known journalistically as "Operation Pedro Pan," listed 14,156 Cuban youths. From April 1962, to August 1963, between 7 percent and 13 percent of the children in the program were cared for in South Florida; the rest were either united with parents or relatives or cared for outside of the diocese. But every child who stepped off the plane unaccompanied in Miami was under the care of the diocese until he or she reached majority or was united with family. And the last Cuban children's home in the Archdiocese of Miami was not closed until mid-1981.[20]

This program had a number of unusual features. After World War II, the United States accepted unaccompanied orphaned refugee children from Europe under the Displaced Persons Act of 1948, but only 375 children were cared for by the Catholic Committee of Refugees. Operation Pedro Pan handled over 14,000 children who were not orphans but had families in Cuba.[21] Another unique aspect of the program was that the Diocese of Miami had no institutions to care for so many children, so facilities were rented (except for Camp Matecumbe). The children's accommodations were deinstitutionalized by using house parents and cottages whenever possible. Larger metropolitan dioceses with huge child-care institutions were least able to participate in the Cuban Children Program, disqualified by their own overwhelming child-care problems and their institutional inflexibility in adapting to the children's Hispanic culture.[22] The flexibility of the Miami Catholic Welfare Bureau was another unique characteristic which made it possible for the diocese to respond to the unexpected challenge of the Cuban children.

Besides the Centro Hispano Católico and the Unaccompanied Children's Program, the ordinary and his executive administrators formulated an ad hoc policy for dealing with the Cuban priests, religious, and laity who suddenly swelled Catholic ranks in South Florida. Never formally drawn up or promulgated, this policy can be inferred from the concrete actions of diocesan administrators. The ecclesial unity of the diocese under the ordinary was Bishop Carroll's primary concern. It required attention to practical problems with Cuban lay organizations, national parishes, assimilation, and the reaction of American Catholics to the exiles.

The first aspect of the diocesan policy was to welcome the exiles and make available to them the resources of the Miami Church. In his public actions toward the Cuban exiles, Carroll was also concerned about setting the proper example for his fellow American Catholics. He used the diocesan newspaper, the *Voice*, to present the exiles in a positive light and to urge Miami Catholics to welcome the new arrivals with generosity, and he was quick to defend Cubans publicly when they were criticized. In June 1962, Carroll also organized a clergy conference on the problems and challenges of the concentration of Hispanic Catholics in the diocese in which priests were encouraged to "be real missionaries" among the Cuban exiles.[23]

A second problem that diocesan policy addressed was Cuban lay organizations, beginning with a consultative committee meeting on October 10, 1961, to discuss the possibility of organizing various Cuban and Hispanic groups. The members of the committee suggested that each Cuban organization in Miami "have the complete approval of the Bishop and each officer be recommended by the pastor of the parish in which he lives." The lay organizations, said the committee, should stress that they were "Latin rather than Cuban," adding, "However, we should recognize the vast number of Cubans and other Latins among us, and because it will take a long time to absorb them into parish societies, there is no reason why we should not recognize their own particular emotions and let them celebrate their patronal feasts, etc."[24] This meeting evidenced both the American penchant for organization and a naïveté about Cuban culture and American immigrant history. Cuban Catholics were accustomed neither to direct discipline under the ordinary nor to the American diocesan and parochial form of organization. Not surprisingly, these early attempts at diocesan control were unsuccessful. Only after 1968 were Cuban Catholic lay groups organized under diocesan auspices.

In practice, policy was carried out on the parochial rather than the diocesan level. Carroll had first-hand experience with national parishes and ethnic subgroups among clergy, religious, and laity from his home diocese of Pittsburgh (see chapter 5). As a result, he did not favor the idea of national parishes at all and did everything in his power to combat the concept and its implementation in Miami. Carroll wanted the diocese to be unified under his aegis.[25] However, his policy against national parishes was not simply a personal eccentricity; the 1918 revised code of canon law strongly discouraged their establishment, prescribing that every diocese be divided into "distinct territorial parts" with specific boundaries and an assigned church and pastor for the population of each territory. The code went on to state that national parishes "cannot be created without special Apostolic indult; as regards to parishes already in existence, no change is to be made without consulting the Holy See."[26] Carroll could also find precedent in the actions of twentieth-century American bishops (such as George Mundelein of Chicago) and papal pronouncements (such as the 1952 "Norms for the Spiritual Care of Emigrants").[27]

Although Carroll was under pressure from Cuban priests and people within the diocese to create national parishes, he did not establish them in the technical or legal sense.[28] Instead of creating national parishes, "which incidentally would be most unfortunate," Carroll preferred "that a priest be named Auxiliary Bishop," someone who would devote himself to Hispanic concerns.[29]

At the same time, Bishop Carroll tried to effect the rapid assimilation of the exiles into the diocese. He, along with many of his associates up to 1968, wanted to integrate Cubans into the American-style territorial parish, although the Cuban Catholic's identifications were personal and particular, not legal, territorial, or formally organizational. Nevertheless, on every front, the diocese sought integration, assimilation, and unity, which was equated with a sameness of religio–cultural expression. Liturgical changes were introduced at the same pace for Spanish and English liturgies in the diocese. The use of semipublic oratories by religious, a common practice in Cuba, was discouraged since it drew people away from their parishes. Cuban religious such as the Piarists, the Marists, and the Christian Brothers were assigned to teach in high schools with American religious and with student bodies mostly American in composition. Eleven Discalced Carmelite Sisters were sent to Ft. Myers, where the Cuban population was negligible, to begin a cloistered convent there.[30] The Spanish Sisters of St. Philip Neri opened a novitiate near Vero Beach, far away from Cuban population centers, on land donated by the diocese. The reception ceremony of St. Philip Neri postulants in 1964 was to be in English with commentary in Spanish for those who "do not understand English."[31] As for the numbers of Cuban and Spanish priests who arrived in 1961, Carroll encouraged their rapid assimilation: "It is hoped that they will learn the language and within six months or so be of some service to the Diocese."[32] As an organizational link to the Spanish-speaking, the "Latin American Chancery" was set up in February 1962 under Monsignor John Fitzpatrick at Centro Hispano Católico. Father Eugenio Del Busto, a native Cuban, was assistant chancellor with Fitzpatrick as chancellor of the entire diocese in 1964 when the Latin American Chancery was disbanded and integrated as part of one diocesan chancery. All courses in the

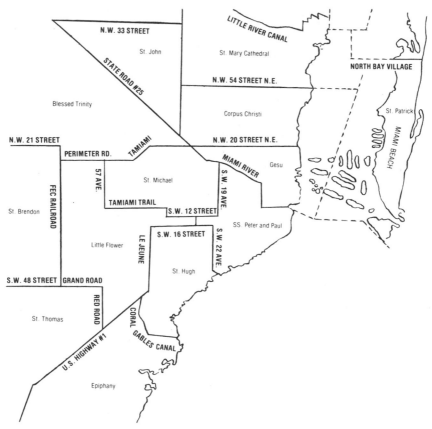

Map 4. Miami parishes with large percentages of Hispanics and Cubans, about 1962. Source: *Voice,* March 30, 1962.

Catholic diocesan schools continued to be taught in English, except Spanish language and literature courses.[33]

The pre-1968 diocesan policy of rapid integration and assimilation into the American Church community was not successful in practice. In 1965, Del Busto told Fitzpatrick that, although much progress had been made, the hoped-for "rapid assimilation" was not taking place. Thousands of Cubans and Hispanics were not attending church or receiving the sacraments or religious instructions; efforts to incorporate them into parish life had been unsuccessful because too close an adherence to American patterns was expected. The fact was, said Del Busto, that many Hispanic priests did not know sufficient English to be incorporated into English-speaking parishes, and Hispanic youths were not joining American parish organizations because of differences in language, social life, and culture. Although the policy of "rapid assimilation" did defuse the dangers of disunity caused by national parishes, and also fit current American cultural expectations when racial integration was seen as the model in the area of civil rights, the diocese lost many opportunities for evangelization among Cubans and Hispanics as a result of the policy. Although the attempt to make North American Catholics out of Hispanics could be dictated, the results could not. A reassessment of the diocesan assimilation policy began in April 1967, with a committee formed for that purpose. A different approach was adopted in 1968 when Monsignor Fitzpatrick became auxiliary bishop and when Monsignor Bryan O. Walsh was named vicar for the Spanish-speaking.[34]

But even under the rapid assimilation policy, more flexible pastoral accommodations were being implemented on the parish level. Sermons were given and confessions were heard in Spanish at parishes with significant numbers of Cuban exiles (see map 4). By mid-1967, after the liturgical changes of Vatican II, thirty Spanish Masses were being said weekly in fourteen Dade County parishes. Also, Cuban children were matriculating, albeit in English, in Greater Miami parochial and diocesan high schools.[35]

Besides sermons, confessions, Masses, and education for the Spanish-speaking, two specific positive pastoral responses to the Cuban influx during the period 1959–68 were the creation of St. John Bosco Mission and the Shrine of Our Lady of Charity.

Although not specifically designated a national parish, St. John Bosco Mission served as one. It was established as a mission of SS. Peter and Paul Church on February 3, 1963, under the leadership of Father Francisco Ibarra. Mass was said at the Tivoli Theater on Flagler Street. In June 1963, Father Emilio Vallina, a native Cuban, was named administrator of the mission. Mass continued at the Tivoli from June 1963 through December 1963, while Vallina lived at SS. Peter and Paul Rectory. Meanwhile, through Monsignor James Nelan, Bishop Carroll had purchased the three-story Waco Motors building at 1301 West Flagler Street in the heart of Little Havana. Vallina said the first Mass there on December 29, 1963. By January 1964, St. John Bosco had six Masses on Sunday, five of which were in Spanish, as well as an assistant pastor and three Cuban Christian Brothers who helped with catechetical instruction. At about the same time, the Misioneras Catequistas Guadalupanas Sisters from Mexico were invited to the diocese to help with the religious education of public school children, initially at St. John Bosco. The Guadalupanas were still working at St. John Bosco in 1968.[36]

The renovation of the first floor of the three-story structure for use as a church was completed in 1965 and dedicated by Bishops Carroll and Boza Masvidal. To support the renovation of the church building, Vallina organized the first parish tombola, a festival; a Ford Falcon was raffled off amid refreshments and other games of chance. Since the parishioners were of lower and lower-middle income and were not used to contributing through the envelope system, the tombola was a way of raising necessary funds from churched and nonchurched parishioners. Through such fund-raising events and other projects, building renovation and parish activities were made possible.[37]

From the beginning, St. John Bosco Mission, which became a parish in 1968, was a unique place. Although technically a territorial parish, it had regular parishioners from outside its boundaries—it was, in effect, a national parish for Cubans. Phones rang constantly from 7 AM until about 11:30 PM. Lay involvement was considerable, necessitating meetings at the church late into the evening. People rarely called ahead for an appointment; they simply showed up at the parish wanting to see a priest. Instead of a parochial school, St. John Bosco opened the Escuela Cívico-Religiosa on November 6, 1967, in the new classrooms and hall on the second floor. Religion, Spanish, Cuban history and geography, and Cuban culture were taught daily in Spanish to elementary and high school students after public school classes were over. By not establishing a parochial school subject to diocesan regulations, St. John Bosco parents had the opportunity of having their children attend classes in Spanish on Cuban Catholicism and culture. As an indication of the size of St. John Bosco, the number of baptisms climbed from 307 in 1963 to 592 by 1968. The number of funerals celebrated by priests of the parish in those years was much higher than in the average Miami parish, partly because of St. John Bosco's large percentage of elderly poor. Another reason was that Cubans wanted to have the funerals of their loved ones performed at the Cuban parish by a Cuban priest. According to sacramental indicators, St. John Bosco was at its peak of numerical strength and activity in 1968.[38]

A second positive pastoral solution to the Cuban influx was the establishment by the Diocese of Miami of the *Ermita*, a shrine to Our Lady of Charity, the patroness of Cuba. The idea for the Ermita was proposed by Carroll at the annual Mass in honor of Our Lady of Charity on September 8, 1966. He donated land on Biscayne Bay near Mercy Hospital for the shrine and appointed a committee of prominent Cuban lay persons to organize its financing and construction. However, the project floundered until the appointment of a newly arrived Cuban-born priest, Father Agustín Román, as director of the shrine in September 1967.[39] The story of the Ermita's development is one aspect of the Cuban Catholic response in Miami.

The Cuban Catholic Response in Miami

Speaking of earlier immigrants to the United States, Oscar Handlin wrote: "The more thorough the separation from the other aspects of the old life, the greater was the hold of the religion that alone survived the transfer. Struggling against heavy odds to save something of the old ways, the immigrants directed into their faith the whole weight of their longing to be connected with the past."[40] Although the situation of Cuban exiles in the 1960s differed from that of, for example, the Irish in the 1840s or the Germans in the 1850s, the importance of religion as a link with the past, a way of coping with the present, and a hope for the future remained. The Cubans not only found a different culture in Miami; they also found a different expression of Catholicism. They arrived at a time when Catholicism in South Florida, as throughout the world, was becoming more localized in its expression. The liturgical and conceptual changes created by Vatican Council II had given prominence to the character and culture of the local Church (a diocese). American Catholicism was rocked by social forces in the 1960s. In many ways, Cuban Catholics did not find the same Church in South Florida that they had left in pre–Vatican II Cuba.

Priest immigrants from Cuba had a particularly difficult time dealing with their dual uprootedness, first from Cuban Catholicism and, second, from pre–Vatican II Catholicism. They had difficulty interpreting what had happened in their own lives, let alone what had happened to their people. Since national parishes were not formally established, Cuban priests with little or no English were sent to live in rectories with Irish-born or American-born pastors. Language, expectations, and customs were all different from what they had known in Cuba. There were duty days, punctual Masses, appointments, schedules, terse instructions from pastors. These were difficult to adjust to, even though Cuban assistant pastors were usually given a free hand to develop contacts among their own people within and without the parish. The liturgical changes of Vatican II were particularly threatening to priests from Cuba since the Latin liturgy was their sacramental link with the past.[41]

Because of their need for fraternal support and protection in a strange environment, the priests from Cuba formed their own organization, as had immigrant priests of other nationalities in the past. The seeds of the Spanish Priests' Association were planted by the Spanish Priests' Retreat and the organization of OCSHA priests. The first of the retreats took place in October 1962, organized under the initiative of Monsignor Fitzpatrick, head of the Latin American Chancery. The OCSHA priests had gathered occasionally, particularly after the split of the Diocese of St. Augustine, along with their fellow OCSHA priests from throughout the state, thirty-four in 1967.[42] The Spanish Priests' Association was a logical development of those two gatherings.

At the October 1966 Spanish-speaking Priests' Retreat at Our Lady of Florida Monastery, those in attendance began discussing the necessity for a Spanish Priests' Association. On October 25, at St. Ann's Mission, Naranja, twenty-nine priests met, elected as president Father J. Bez Chabebe (a Cuban), as secretary Father J. De la Paz (a Spaniard), and as treasurer Father I. Pertika (a Basque). Its stated purposes were to promote priestly fellowship, to study and solve actual priestly problems, to apply the norms of Vatican II, to unify the application of conciliar reforms for the Spanish-speaking, to make a census of the activities of Protestant Hispanics in the Miami area, to collaborate with the erection of the Ermita, to ensure representation in the proposed diocesan senate of priests, and to promote fealty to the bishop.[43]

Subsequent meetings dealt mainly with the relationship of the Spanish-speaking priests to their pastors and to the diocese. Specific concerns were the establishment of a "Casa Sacerdotal" (a meeting place for Hispanic priests), incardination procedures, the diocesan priests' senate, and pastorates. In spite of its many goals, "priestly problems" took most of the group's time and energy, but it did produce one pamphlet on the Liturgy in 1967. By 1968, the group had adopted a more confrontational style, first over the issue of proper representation in the priests' senate and afterwards over other issues that created a strain between the association and the bishop.[44] The association, like its predecessors among ethnic priests in northern dioceses, was organized primarily to protect and preserve the Cuban, Spanish, and Basque priests, who came to feel they were being ignored by the ordinary, overlooked in pastoral appointments, and unfairly treated by their pastors. They wanted a Hispanic auxiliary bishop, and they wanted formally established national parishes.[45] When the diocese eased up on its assimilation drive after 1968, the climate changed. As OCSHA and Cuban priests were made administrators and pastors, and after a Cuban priest was appointed as auxiliary bishop of Miami in 1979, the original purposes of the Spanish Priests' Association faded and so did the organization.

Priestly vocations among Cubans in exile developed quickly, though not in sufficient numbers. The first Cuban ordained in South Florida was Father Daniel Sánchez of the Pinar Del Rio diocese, who had been studying at Montezuma Seminary at Santa Fe. Cardinal Spellman was the ordaining prelate, Bishop Boza Masvidal preached, and an enthusiastic crowd of 12,500 attended the ordination at Miami Beach Convention Hall on September 2, 1962. One thousand attended the banquet that evening at which Archbishop Paul Hallinan and the governor of Florida, C. Farris Bryant, spoke. Earlier that summer, the first Cuban ordained in exile was Father Roberto Soler, ordained by Paul-Emile Cardinal Leger in Montreal for the Diocese of Havana, early in July 1962. Soler said his first Mass at St. Hugh Church, Coconut Grove. The first Cuban exile ordained for the Diocese of Miami was Father Orestes Todd Hevia, a native of Havana, on May 20, 1967; he continued his theological studies in exile at St. Bernard Seminary, Rochester. In July 1964, seven Cuban-born youths were studying in Miami diocesan seminaries; by the fall of 1967, fourteen were studying for the Diocese of Miami.[46]

Religious priests, brothers, and sisters attempted with varying degrees of success to adapt to their new situation as exiles. The Christian Brothers, the Jesuits, and the Sisters of St. Philip Neri illustrate different approaches to adaptation.

The Cuban Christian Brothers failed to adapt to the demands of their new environment. Three of them helped with the young people's religion classes (CCD) at St. John Bosco Mission, while fifteen others took over LaSalle High School which opened in 1961 for Cuban boys. About three hundred Cubans attended the school the first year, along with a few Americans. Immaculata High School, composed mostly of American girls taught by the Sisters of St. Joseph, was already in existence next door. The two schools were separate entities, and communication between them was not always good. The Brothers taught in Spanish, since they had little command of English. Although a few American Christian Brothers were also at LaSalle, the Cuban Brothers did not run the school according to American standards or diocesan school policy. The Cuban Brothers were replaced in 1962 by American brothers and later by diocesan administrators in 1966. In 1962, the Cuban Christian Brothers were sent to help at Camp Matecumbe's Unaccompanied Children Program, where they stayed until 1963.[47]

One of the most successful Cuban transplantations of religious was made by Belen Jesuits of Antilles Province. In 1961, sixteen Jesuits taught two hundred male students at the Colegio de Belén (established 1854) on the outskirts of Havana. They were removed from the school after Castro's speech of May 1, 1961, but they had already made plans to establish a Colegio de Belén in exile. In the summer of 1961 they left Cuba, resettled in Miami, and, that fall, opened Belen High School, using classrooms donated by the Diocese of Miami at Centro Hispano Católico.[48] The 1962–63 school year began in a different building, at 824 Southwest 7th Avenue, formerly a liquor warehouse used by Al Capone. The Catholic Welfare Bureau paid the tuition of 34 of the 166 students in the 1963–64 school year. The diocese also loaned Belen $38,000 in 1965 to help them through a financial pinch. By that time, Belen had 163 pupils in grades seven through twelve, a faculty of fourteen Jesuits and two laymen, and 125 exile alumni. Although the diocese claimed Belen as part of the diocesan school system, this was not the case. The Belen Jesuits from the beginning charted an independent course for their school and apostolate. In early 1969, the Jesuit general in Rome asked Carroll for approval of the bicultural school of Belen, an approval which was very much ex post facto.[49]

From 1959 to 1968, the Diocese of Miami was deficient in

Spanish-speaking religious communities of women. In 1966, the diocese had six such communities, totaling about sixty sisters, which rose to seventy in 1968 with a seventh community.[50]

The Sisters of St. Philip Neri began an ambitious plan to establish a house of formation in South Florida, even though there were only thirty of them in the whole country and only one other house of religious formation in the diocese, the novitiate of the Sisters of St. Joseph at Jensen Beach. The St. Philip Neri Sisters, whose motherhouse was in Barcelona, Spain, opened their novitiate in mid-December 1964 on land donated by the diocese near Vero Beach, and in May 1965 five postulants, all Cubans, took the habit. The Diocese of Miami continued to support the novitiate financially as long as it operated.[51]

The quest for religious vocations among Cuban and Cuban-American women was not new to South Florida. As early as 1875, two Cubans from Key West joined the Sisters of St. Joseph of St. Augustine, and a Cuban-American entered the Sisters of the Holy Name in 1928. However, such vocations were rare, and, after an initial flurry of activity, the Sisters of St. Philip Neri found them equally rare in the late 1960s. Their novitiate closed in 1968.[52]

The adjustment of Cuban laity to the Church in South Florida was not so much an assimilation to American Catholicism as an adaption of Cuban Catholicism to a new environment. The great majority of Cubans were unchurched. In Cuba their Catholicism was supported by Cuban culture, popular religious belief and practice, and family traditions. Since such a milieu did not exist in Miami, unchurched Cubans relied even more heavily than before upon popular religion, especially on what is called *santería*.[53]

Santería, like *candomble* in Brazil, *vaudou* in Haiti, and *shango* in Trinidad, is a syncretistic religion combining West African Yoruban elements with Christian hagiography and symbolism. Santería includes the cult of the gods, ancestor worship, magical practices, and ritual performance. The relatively late importation of African slaves into Cuba in the nineteenth century and the decadence of Church-sponsored slave *cabildos* (mutual aid societies organized along African ethnic lines) after the abolition of slavery in 1868 caused the creation of semiunderground ex-slave African cults called *reglas*, especially in Havana. By the early years of the twentieth century, membership in the reglas was based more on the spiritual path one followed and less on ethnic descent. Membership was by then open to blacks, mulattoes, and whites. Three types of santería cults existed in Cuba: the Lucumi or Regla de Ocha; the Bantu, Mayombe, or Regla de Conga; and the Arara.[54]

The pressures and uprootedness of exile contributed to the practice of santería in Miami, and even increased its popularity. Although the secret dimension of santería was diminished in Miami, where *botanicas* (establishments where santería herbs and accoutrements could be purchased) flourished publicly, santería was a way for the Cuban exile to acquire power and security through magic, ritual, and symbol. It kept him in touch with the sacred in the midst of the secular, technological culture of America. Paradoxically, santería in Miami was not a communal cult but a personal, individual transaction between the *santero* (a shaman) and the devotee, between the devotee and the gods (*orishas*). Although there was a communal dimension to the reglas of Cuba, santería in Miami stressed the liberation of the individual from social forces with which he could not cope without supernatural help.[55]

In Cuba, public festivals, *Carnival*, religious processions, dancing, music, and singing were important religious expressions, especially for the Afro-Cuban, and these practices were encouraged by the Church. The greatest celebration was Epiphany, followed by the Feast of Our Lady of Charity (September 8) and the Feast of St. Barbara (December 4), all of which played an important role in Cuban popular religion. In santería, African orishas and Catholic saints were identified with each other; the most popular are St. Lazarus (*Bablualle*), St. Barbara (*Chango*), and Our Lady of Charity (*Ochun*). It is difficult to separate santería from popular religion and from Catholicism itself in the Cuban religious synthesis.[56]

Our Lady of Charity was the primary devotion of popular religion in Cuba, as was Our Lady of Guadalupe for the Mexicans. The Cuban devotion to Our Lady of Charity, approved as national patroness of Cuba by Rome in 1916, represented the intersection of santería, popular religion, and the Catholicism of the churched. The significance of this feast, held on September 8, was rapidly appropriated by the Diocese of Miami. In 1960, the first annual Our Lady of Charity Mass was celebrated at SS. Peter and Paul Church with 800 in attendance. The next year the Mass was celebrated at Miami Stadium before 25,000. On the fiftieth anniversary of the proclamation of Our Lady of Charity as the Patroness of Cuba, Bishop Carroll invited the Cuban exiles to erect a shrine to their patroness on Biscayne Bay property to be donated by the Diocese.[57]

Father Agustín Román was placed in charge of the project in September 1967. A native of Matanzas educated in the Cuban public schools,[58] he had arrived in Miami in May 1966. He had a special affinity for the unchurched, since he came from their ranks. He once described the qualitative difference between churched and unchurched Cuban Catholics as the difference between two cultures and two languages:

> Even though I was not raised within a liturgical community, at no time did anyone in my family or among those around us manifest that they did not belong to the Catholic Church. In 1944, when I began to be inserted into the liturgical community, I suffered a sort of cultural shock, as if I had been transplanted into a new, totally different cultural setting. I had always communicated with the Lord, but now I had to do it in a different way; I would compare the experience to that of learning a new language and having to take care so as not to use personal peculiarities in speaking and writing. It was hard at the beginning, but since I had been taught to love and admire the Church, I persevered, and overcame the difficulties of assimilation and integration.[59]

Román wasted no time in putting into focus the mandate of Bishop Carroll to "build a shrine." The bishop specified that no Mass was to be said there on Sundays; no funerals, baptisms, or weddings could be performed there; and funds for construction and maintenance had to come from the Cuban people. This episcopal mandate led Román directly into the evangelization of the Cuban unchurched.[60]

On September 8, 1967, the provisional chapel was dedicated by Bishop Carroll.[61] Román was faced with three problems: how to get the people's financial support, how to get them to come to the shrine, and what to do with them once they came. Getting the people to come was pivotal. His first idea, organizing the shrine around the patron saints of each Cuban municipality, proved unworkable: there was a paucity of municipal patron saints, and they were duplicated in unrelated regions. His next idea was to organize the Ermita around the political and physical geography of

Cuba's 126 prerevolutionary *municipios*, political units smaller than American counties, each including a city with its surrounding lands. The Cuban people identified with their municipio, which provided a natural communal unit. Román drew up a yearly schedule of pilgrimages to the shrine, with municipios coming three times a week, and large Sunday gatherings of each of the six provinces of Cuba on six different Sundays of the year. In putting this plan into effect, Román began by calling people randomly to discover who was from which municipio in order to invite them to the shrine on the appointed day. At first the phoning was tedious and time-consuming; eventually he developed a computerized list of people with phone committees for each municipio. During the first year, Román spoke to people gathered at the shrine while he conducted the rosary for them and led a procession around the grounds. The second year he added a Mass to the ceremonies. The unchurched who went to the shrine contributed small change to build a permanent edifice. Román established the Confraternity of Our Lady of Charity, which asked of its members the daily recitation of the "Memorare" (a Marian prayer), participation in the Eucharist on September 8, and the donation of 50 cents each month to the shrine. In 1968, every municipio visited the shrine, pilgrimages that amounted to half a million people. From its inception, the shrine offered courses on the Bible. In 1973, these Bible courses were conducted by mail; in 1976, a taped biblical message was available by telephone. By 1973 sufficient funds had been raised by these methods to permit the dedication of a new chapel on December 2.[62]

The shrine became a success because Román was in touch with the religious sensibilities of his Cuban people and appealed to them in creative ways. Using the devotion to the Blessed Mother, preaching, the rosary, and the Bible, Román reached the unchurched and offset the influences of both Protestantism and santería among them. However, the success of the Ermita did not make up for the general lack of evangelization of the Cuban exiles by priests, religious, and laity of the diocese. Despite the pastoral service offered in parishes, the relative availability of Catholic educational facilities, the annual Our Lady of Charity Mass, and the occasional parochial mission in Spanish, most of the unchurched Cubans in exile remained as untouched by formal Catholicism as they had been in Cuba.[63]

Cuban lay organizations, so important in prerevolutionary Cuba (see chapter 6), also developed in the exile community. In late November 1961, the ordinary attempted to put Cuban lay organizations under diocesan control. At that time seventeen lay groups were represented at an organizational meeting of the "Coordinating Committee of Cuban Catholic Organizations." Among them, the Caballeros de Colón, Movimiento Familiar Cristiano, and Agrupación Católica Universitaria deserve attention. The Knights of Columbus already had a branch in Cuba, but the first Spanish-speaking Council of the Caballeros de Colón was founded in St. Michael Parish in January 1961. The Christian Family Movement (Movimiento Familiar Cristiano) was established in Cuba before the revolution. By early 1963, eleven small CFM groups for Spanish speakers had been organized in as many parishes, the first at St. Agnes at Key Biscayne under Father Antonio Navarrete. The diocese officially approved these groups in February 1963. By mid-1966, Spanish CFM had 450 couples in 45 groups in 20 Dade parishes.[64] Movimiento Familiar Cristiano was an important lay organization for those that it touched since all problems among the exile community were rooted in the family. The Catholic University Group (Agrupación Católica Universitaria), organized by Jesuits in Cuba for promising university students and alumni, was reestablished in Coral Gables in July 1962 by Father Amando Llorente, SJ. Within a month, he had 450 members and a house with seven residents; and all had belonged to the organization in Cuba.[65]

Perhaps the most significant Catholic lay group in exile was the Cursillos de Cristianidad. The Cursillo movement began in Spain in 1949; it was brought both to the United States and to Cuba in 1957. (A Cursillo, an intensive weekend short course on basic Christianity, stresses content and affect and is designed to rekindle faith commitment to Christ and the Church.) The first Cursillo in Miami was in Spanish with twenty-five participants on March 9–11, 1962, at the Dominican Retreat House. It was conducted by Father A. Petro and three men, all from Texas, with the encouragement and assistance of Monsignor Fitzpatrick. By March 1966, twenty-one Cursillos had been conducted for 1,008 Cursillistas. The Cursillo movement was important in Miami because, by reaching the unchurched, it became an effective method of evangelization for both men and women, although the numbers touched were relatively small. Miami Cursillistas got involved with radio and television broadcasting, as well as publishing their own magazine, *Ideal*, all of which reached the churched and the unchurched Catholic Cuban community in exile.[66]

In mid-1968, twelve Spanish-speaking lay groups were officially invited to the installation of Coleman F. Carroll as archbishop of Miami.[67] These were not all of the Hispanic lay groups in the diocese, nor were they of equal importance. The fact is that the Bishop and the chancery were perplexed about these lay groups that had sprung from the grass roots and proliferated, often uncontrolled, uninstigated, and unrecognized by the official Church. Not in 1968, nor in the entire episcopacy of Coleman F. Carroll, were these Cuban lay groups brought under the umbrella of Church officialdom. Yet the groups played important roles in the lives of the churched since they were a way of integrating their new American environment with Cuban life and faith.

Culture Clash: Cuban Catholicism in South Florida

The unexpected influx of Cubans created tensions in South Florida Catholicism which were the results of frustrations and misperceptions. Until 1968, official diocesan policy encouraged the rapid assimilation of Cuban Catholics; this policy was unsuccessful and created ill will among Americans and Cubans alike. Some Irish or American pastors, and some of their parishioners, resented the assignment of a Cuban priest to their parish because of language problems and cultural differences in ministerial style and pastoral approach. For example, Cuban priests were on the phone much more than their Irish or American counterparts, a cultural behavior pattern that was upsetting to pastors. The Cuban priests felt slighted by the chancery and by the priests' senate when they protested what they perceived to be unfair treatment. Some American or Irish pastors were hesitant to allow Spanish-speaking parishioners to organize separate Spanish-speaking parochial organizations. Carroll and several chancery officials failed to understand the meaning and significance of the Cuban lay organizations, regarding them as possible threats to ecclesial order and diocesan authority. American parishioners were upset to see their parishes and neighborhoods change seemingly overnight. In many places, where Americans became a minority in their parish, they complained about having all the financial burdens since Cubans did not support the Church through the regular collection process. The American laity were also annoyed by the Cubans' lack of formality, unpunctuality, and lack of silence during Mass.[68]

As a result of such cultural differences, tensions arose between Americans and Cubans, just as they had earlier between Spanish-speaking and English-speaking groups at Key West (see chapter 3). Neither group understood or appreciated the culture of the other. Hispanics in general have a different sense of the person, of law, of personal communication, of community, of family, of time, and of fiesta than Anglo-Americans. Cubans, unlike Americans, do not hide their faith or feel inhibited in showing it, by a gold chain and medal of Our Lady of Charity around their necks or by touching a statue and lighting a candle during Mass. Cubans love big crowds, and they love to talk in their homes, on the street, in the church, wherever there is a group of people. For them the interpersonal is central; hence they feel a personal responsibility for the aged of their families. Family is not just the nuclear family but a network of relationships in the extended family, reaching at times to those who have no blood relationship. This emphasis on the interpersonal is carried over into their concept of heaven and God, the communion of saints, the Church, and the parish. Because funerals are important social events, the funeral home is expected to be open all night to accommodate family and friends.[69] An example of the difference in cultural perspectives and perceptions of Cubans and Americans is illustrated by an incident:

> One Good Friday not too long ago, Bishop Román saw two fishermen standing by the edge of the water with their lines. One was an American, the other a Cuban. Since it was a special feast day which would draw a good sized crowd to the Shrine, the Bishop was concerned that the men leave before their rather irreverent spectacle was seen by those who came to pray. He went up and asked the American fisherman to leave.
>
> "Why can't I fish here?" the man asked.
>
> "Today is Good Friday and people will be coming here to pray," the Bishop replied. The man shrugged, "So what?"

"Look, sir," the Bishop finally said emphatically, "this is private property. . . ." Before he had time to say anything else the man had picked up his things and left.

The Bishop then went over to the second fisherman, the Cuban. Pleased with the results in the previous case, the Bishop went straight up and said, "Sir, this is private property and you can't fish here."

"But, Father," the Cuban objected, "how can you say a thing like that? Don't you know that God gave us the land and the sea and the sun for all of us to enjoy?"

"Yes, that's true," the Bishop admitted. "But today is Good Friday and people will be coming to pray. . . ."

"Not another word, Father, I'm leaving this minute," the second fisherman replied.[70]

It is still too early to assess the impact of the Cuban exiles upon Catholicism in the Diocese of Miami.[71] Nor is it yet possible to evaluate fully the quality of the diocese's response to the influx of Cuban Catholics, except to say that South Florida Catholicism showed a flexibility and generosity of response in social service not afforded immigrant groups in the past, partly as a result of federal government aid, partly the anti-Communist rhetoric surrounding the refugees. The "organizational revolution" in Catholic social service also played a part, and so did the youthful adaptability and creativity of the Diocese of Miami. The missionary heritage of South Florida Catholicism probably had a beneficial influence on the generally flexible way in which the diocese responded to the Cuban influx. One thing that can be said with confidence is that the Cuban exiles took a great deal of diocesan time, energy, and resources; indeed, the Cuban challenge overshadowed all other diocesan considerations from the years 1959 to 1968. But there were other issues during those years that deserve attention.

8

Building the Kingdom
on Shifting Ground,
1958–68

B esides the Hurley-Carroll controversy and the Cuban exiles, South Florida Catholicism from 1958 to 1968 faced other significant challenges. This was a period of transition, linking the previous decades with new forces that were to reshape the Church's milieu in South Florida.

The Building Up and the Tearing Down

The first decade of the Diocese of Miami provides a complete unit for analysis, like a single wave that gathers momentum until it crashes against the shore and recedes, all in one unbroken motion. Three of the forces that gave the decade its wavelike character were the local Church's concern for progress, the universal Church's concern for renewal, and the tension between Florida Catholicism and American culture.

On the occasion of his fiftieth anniversary as a priest in 1960, Monsignor William Barry, the patriarch of Miami Beach, commented, "The future is limitless. Under the direction of the vigorous and tireless guidance of our good Bishop, the future looks very bright indeed."[1] The leaders of Catholicism in South Florida, especially Bishop Carroll, shared this optimistic confidence in the future. The spirit of the early 1960s in both sacred and secular circles was one of progress, energy, and youthful freshness. Carroll was interested in building up the Kingdom of God, which, according to his episcopal motto, "Primum Regnum Dei," was to be a priority. He saw the task in concrete organizational terms: to provide the money for buildings, personnel, and institutional structures which would offer programs to serve the physical and spiritual needs not only of Catholics but of others in need as well.

In 1959, Bishop Carroll decided to reinstate Archbishop Hurley's Diocesan Development Fund (DDF) in order to fuel his special building plans, chiefly the construction of a minor seminary in Miami for which he needed more than the $700,000 he had already collected from special donors. The need to build and support the seminary inspired the 1960 DDF campaign, the first such drive in the new diocese open publicly to all donors. Like Hurley, Carroll established quotas for each parish in order to reach the goal of $850,000. Unlike Hurley, Carroll instituted special DDF dinners for "selected donors." By April, contributions topped $975,000.[2]

The DDF campaigns were essential in the institutional building up of the new diocese (table 8.1). Unlike Hurley, Carroll publicly announced the specific purposes of the campaigns, an important ingredient in their success even though not all of the purposes were always realized. From 1960 to 1968, a consistent amount of money was collected annually from the three-month-long DDF, making it a reliable source of income. In 1968 the DDF campaign shifted emphasis from building institutions to maintaining them.

In keeping with his Pittsburgh experience, Carroll stressed organization and institutional building. In the first thirty-nine months of his episcopacy, the diocese became an extensive construction site in perpetual motion: $30 million worth of building was done, $13 million for parochial construction and $17 million in diocesan and nondiocesan projects. By March 1962, 32 percent of all non-residential construction done in three years in the sixteen counties of South Florida had been contracted by the Diocese of Miami, placing it in the top ten private builders in the state. This fact is particularly amazing given the financial shackles imposed by the Hurley–Carroll controversy at the same time. From 1958 through

TABLE 8.1. DDF Campaigns, 1959–68

Year	Projects	Goal	Money Received
1959	St. John Vianney Seminary	?	$ 716,621.96
1960[a]	St. John Vianney Seminary		
	Old Age Home		
	Home for Dependent Children	$ 850,000	975,247.35
1961	Home for Dependent Children		
	Men's Retreat House	1,000,000	1,065,347.47
1962	New Dorm for Seminary		
	Additions to Five High Schools		
	Newman Center	1,000,000	1,265,479.74
1963	New Home for Elderly		
	School for Exceptional Youth		
	New St. Vincent Hall		
	Library for Minor Seminary	1,250,000	1,862,000.00
1964	School for Exceptional Youth		
	Care for Aged and Infirm		
	Care for Dependent Children		
	Construction of Newman Centers	1,500,000	1,660,797.00
1965	Homes for Dependent Teens		
	Nursing Home for Aged		
	Schools for Mentally Disturbed		
	Education	1,500,000	1,648,446.00
1966	Three New High Schools		
	Cathedral Renovation		
	Enlargement of Chancery and		
	Catholic Welfare Bureau		
	Property for Church Purposes	1,500,000	1,689,508.00
1967[b]	Eleven Different Projects—		
	Mostly for Seminary and		
	Charitable Institutions	1,500,000	?
1968[c]	Maintenance and Staffing of		
	Existing Facilities	1,500,000	1,597,550.00

SOURCE: *Voice*, January–March 1961–68.

a. This was the first year of the public DDF.

b. No final total was ever announced beyond an incomplete total of $1,553,000 (*Voice*, March 24, 1967).

c. The DDF changed its name to the ABCD, Annual Bishop's Charity Drive. In 1969, it became the Archbishop's Charity Drive, still using ABCD.

1968, Carroll's building program of parishes and other ecclesial institutions included five buildings at St. John Vianney Minor Seminary, fifty-eight new churches (permanent and provisional), eight new mission churches, nine new high schools, seventeen new parish schools, twenty-seven new convents, four diocesan office buildings, sixteen new facilities for dependent persons, and four high school faculty residences.[3]

In early 1959, Bishop Carroll established the Diocesan Building Commission (composed of priests of his choosing), the Diocesan Purchasing Commission, and the Diocesan Maintenance Department, organizational machinery which channeled the DDF money and directed all construction. Another structure aiding the direction of the diocese, the Diocesan Consultors, mandated by canon law, consisted of a consultative body of priests chosen by the ordinary to meet with him periodically. Its agenda was determined by the bishop.[4]

Hurricanes continued to plague South Florida, but their damage did not affect Church property as had the hurricanes of the twenties due to stricter building codes, better warning systems, and an informed public. The most serious, Betsy, in 1965 destroyed $20–$30 million worth of property, including damages to diocesan property exceeding $100,000.[5] But the worst storms to hit the Church in South Florida in the decade were not hurricanes; they were powerful intangible forces, more subtle, more energizing, yet more destructive to the old order and the corporate ecclesial mentality than any physical attack. One came from Rome, the other from secular American culture.

Pope John XXIII surprised the world when he decided to invoke an Ecumenical Council at the Vatican, the first since 1869–70, the second at the Vatican, and the twenty-first in the history of the Roman Catholic Church. On October 11, 1962, Vatican Council II was convened by Pope John XXIII in St. Peter's Basilica, with 2,300 bishops in attendance. Bishop Carroll attended all of the council sessions.[6]

Even before the council began, expectations for change within the Church were raised by journalistic speculation in both the Catholic and non-Catholic media, as well as by speakers who interpreted the council. Such articles appeared in the diocesan newspaper, the *Voice*, as early as July 1959. When Vatican II ended on

December 8, 1965, the *Voice* claimed that the conciliar decrees would "revolutionize the Church of the Twentieth Century."[7]

Vatican II significantly changed American Catholicism ecumenically and liturgically. In the Diocese of Miami, the former effects were limited, the latter more pervasive.

Unlike Hurley, who forbade interfaith activities, Carroll participated in ecumenical activity as early as February 1963, a result not of his experience in Pittsburgh but of the spirit of Vatican II with its dominant theme of Christian unity. Carroll was the first Catholic clergyman to address the Greater Miami Ministerial Association, was the honored guest of the forty-first annual convention of the Episcopal Diocese of South Florida, and was invited to talk before Miami Jewish leaders on the subject of the council, all in 1963. Two years later, Methodist Bishop Frederick P. Carson was invited by Carroll to talk at a dinner for the DDF campaign.[8]

The ecumenical endeavors of the ordinary went beyond tabletalk and an exchange of podiums to more substantive activities such as, by 1967, the practical concerns of racism and social justice for blacks and migrant workers and the establishment of a tri-faith chapel at Miami International Airport (January 1968).[9]

However, with a few exceptions such as the "Man to Man" weekly television program (1967), the Barry College Catholic-Jewish dialogues (1966), and Catholic-Lutheran dialogues (1967), ecumenical gestures were carried out symbolically on high Church levels. Certainly ecumenism in South Florida did not have the impact that it seemed to have on some northern dioceses. One reason for this difference was that, with the close of Vatican II in late 1965, ecumenical dialogue became less appealing to the bishop himself, who became concerned over liturgical abuses that sometimes resulted from ecumenical gestures.[10] As a result, Carroll became more circumspect in his official ecumenical activities. In addition, not only did the Cuban exiles take much of the diocese's attention and energy, but Hispanic priests took a dim view of evangelistic efforts by Protestants among Miami's Hispanics. It was difficult to talk with those who were perceived as attempting to "steal" Hispanic Catholics away from their traditional Catholic heritage. Finally, since South Florida Catholicism had only recently become a force to be reckoned with economically, politically, and numerically, some Protestants felt little inclination toward a dialogue with no significant interests at stake. Race relations proved an exception to the rule.

The most immediate change that resulted from Vatican II was symbolized and realized in the liturgy. For practicing Catholics especially, the liturgy was their weekly contact with the diocese, with the Church universal, and with their Catholic heritage. A change in the liturgy challenged their religious perspective. However, most lay people adjusted more easily than did their bishop, Coleman Carroll, since they had not internalized the theological and aesthetic presuppositions that he had. In Pittsburgh, Carroll had been organist of Holy Rosary Parish and later pastor of the liturgically minded Sacred Heart Parish. Upon arriving in Miami, he set out to make alterations on St. Mary's Cathedral, a project that took six years.[11] Because he was so entrenched in an older Eucharistic theology, a segment of which viewed the liturgy as a forum for artistic, aesthetic presentation, the new concepts presented in *Sacrosanctum concilium* (December 4, 1963) and subsequent Roman documents of liturgical implementation were difficult for him to assimilate.

In October 1963, the council approved the use of the vernacular in the liturgy. The Constitution on the Sacred Liturgy, promulgated December 4, 1963, was implemented in the Diocese of Miami in eight distinct steps over a four-year period that began on February 16, 1964. The first and most significant was that all Masses on Sundays and Holy Days were to include a homily based on the Scriptures of the day. (The *Voice* called the upcoming liturgical changes "revolutionary," although they would take place "gradually." Somehow there was to be a gradual revolution.) A second implementation occurred on April 28, 1964, when the Latin phrase said by the priest while distributing communion was shortened and made dialogic between priest and recipient.[12]

In the third set of liturgical changes in the diocese, the vernacular administration of the Sacraments and Sacramentals was permitted on September 14, 1964. The following changes were initiated in the Mass beginning on the First Sunday of Advent, November 29, 1964: English was to replace Latin in the readings, the propers, and the ordinary; all rites and sacraments would be administered in English; the congregation would be encouraged to sing; male lay lectors and commentators would be used. The extensive use of English was authorized so that the liturgy would lead all people to "full, conscious, and active participation." Although the American bishops had voted for these changes on April 2, 1964, Bishop Carroll not only had delayed their implementation for eight months but also had imposed some limitations: the congregation was to sing approved hymns only; no offertory procession was allowed; the communion rail was to remain in all churches; no church renovation was to take place without chancery permission; Mass facing the people was permitted only twice a week; no Mass was to be said after 1:30 P.M. These prescriptions bespoke legalism and highly cautious gradualism. It was in January 1965 that Carroll expressed his concern over "excesses" taking place in interfaith religious services. Only after hearing of Archbishop Dearden's first Solemn Mass in English in Detroit did Bishop Carroll consent to sing High Mass in English at St. Mary's Cathedral on Easter 1965.[13]

The fourth group of liturgical changes in Miami took place on March 7, 1965, when the prayers at the foot of the altar, the Last Gospel, and the customary prayers after Mass were omitted. In his instruction to his priests, Carroll pointed out, "There is no law requiring Mass to be offered facing the congregation." He also cautioned that music in the vernacular was "still in the experimental stage." The first concelebrated mass in the diocese was celebrated by the Bishop on a specially constructed altar at St. Rose of Lima Church on Holy Thursday, April 15, 1965. As a fifth liturgical change, priests were permitted to concelebrate in their parishes for the Holy Thursday liturgy, and eleven instances where communion was permitted under both species were specified but general permission was not granted.[14]

In October 1965, the *Voice* announced that the U.S. bishops had decided that virtually all parts of the Mass were to be in the vernacular. This sixth major liturgical change went into effect five months later, on March 27, 1966. Immediately after these changes, Carroll issued some "Liturgical and Ecumenical Guidelines": vernacular in the liturgy should be encouraged, although one Latin Mass should be offered "for those disquieted by the changes"; music must be approved; caution should be taken in moving altars facing the people, although all new churches must have the altars so constructed; the altar rail must be retained. These admonitions reveal Carroll's less-than-enthusiastic reaction to the changes. The seventh major change took place on October 22, 1967, when the canon of the Mass was changed from Latin to English. On the First

Sunday of Advent, 1968, three new eucharistic canons in the vernacular were introduced, marking the eighth major liturgical change in four years.[15]

More subtle changes in liturgical practice and general Catholic piety were affecting South Florida Catholicism. The eucharistic fast for priests was changed in January 1964 to a three-hour abstention from food and alcohol, with a one-hour abstention from non-alcoholic drinks. This rule was applied to priests, religious, and laity alike in December 1964. In February 1966, fast and abstinence were in effect only on Ash Wednesday and Good Friday, although abstinence on Fridays was still in effect in the diocese. Carroll added, "Self-denial is still a duty for Catholics." On the First Sunday of Advent, 1966, the U.S. bishops decreed that Catholics were no longer obliged "under pain of sin to abstain from meat on Friday, except during Lent"; however, people were urged to abstain from meat by free choice or take up some other form of penitential practice.[16]

Another sign of the shifting liturgical and devotional landscape was the decline of the Forty Hours Devotion, once a popular form of piety with lay people and a fraternal event for priests. Bishop Carroll continued the practice of Archbishop Hurley of issuing yearly a diocesewide parochial schedule for Forty Hours Devotions for each parish of the diocese. The last such schedule for Forty Hours was sent out in November 1967, for 1968. Participation in Forty Hours declined in the diocese, as it had throughout the United States by the late sixties. Two other less publicized, though significant, changes were the simplification of pontifical rites and insignia for bishops (June 1968) and the restoration of the permanent diaconate (June 1967).[17]

The eight stages in the changes of the liturgy and the alterations in Catholic piety, the results of Vatican II, shifted the spiritual ground of Catholicism in South Florida. The post-Tridentine Catholic synthesis was being eroded, to be replaced by a post–Vatican II formulation just beginning to have concrete liturgical and pietistical effects, the real significance of which were not clearly perceived by 1968. Early on, confident expectations were raised by media and churchmen about the value, purpose, and meaning of ecclesial change. However, confidence in progress was soon to give way to a religious self-questioning that brought with it doubt and skepticism.

Like the initial expectant exultation produced by the news of Vatican II, American Catholics felt positive and optimistic about American government and culture in the early 1960s. The election of a Catholic president in 1960 had given them reason to be proud as citizens who were not generally accepted as part of the American mainstream. With Kennedy's election, Catholics felt that the "religious issue" and anti-Catholicism had been finally laid to rest. By the 1960s, American Catholics had "arrived" economically, politically, and intellectually.[18]

The *Voice* mirrored the patriotic anti-Communism of contemporary America with its coverage of both the aftermath of the Cuban revolution and Khrushchev's visit to the United States. Moreover, Carroll, as a native of Pittsburgh, identified with American labor unionism. Although the union situation was quite different in Miami than in Pittsburgh, Carroll organized the First Annual Labor Day Observance on August 31, 1961, the first public forum for labor in the Miami area. The celebration brought together representatives of labor and management in seminars. The first year's topic was "Labor and Management Oppose Communism." These labor-management seminars continued for six years, with speakers from government, business, and the Church, the last occurring on September 1, 1966.[19]

However, not everything American was embraced uncritically, nor was Catholicism accepted in many instances by the larger American culture. Often Catholic values differed from American secular values. The *Voice* contained articles and editorials on indecent literature and movies. Every year, at least up to 1965, the Legion of Decency pledge was administered to the faithful at all the Masses. In 1967, the proposed liberalization of Florida's abortion law and the increase of drug abuse sparked reaction from the Catholic community.[20]

Catholic Florida's ambiguity in relation to American culture was particularly pointed up by the issues of birth control and the Vietnam war. As early as August 1963, the *Voice* carried a front-page discussion of the birth control pill. In June 1964, Pope Paul VI announced that the Church was in the process of "a major re-evaluation of the question of birth control." In April 1966, it was announced that the Papal Birth Control Commission was expected to report in June, but by November the papal ruling was still delayed. In a media scoop, the *National Catholic Reporter* in

April 1967 published the commission's conclusions. Although the majority of the commission favored a change in the Church's teaching on birth control, a year later (July 29, 1968) the encyclical *Humanae Vitae* reaffirmed the traditional Catholic position. Bishop Carroll praised the encyclical, which was printed in full in the *Voice*. By early August, numerous theologians, priest groups, lay associations, educators, and professionals in the United States had expressed disagreement with *Humanae Vitae*, but the American bishops supported it in their Pastoral, "Human Life in Our Day" (November 15, 1968).[21] Andrew Greeley maintains that the papal encyclical and the negative reaction to it was a crucial turning point in American Catholicism, alienating many Catholics from the Church.[22] The effect of the document upon Catholicism in South Florida has yet to be studied.

The Vietnam war created tension between Florida Catholicism and the national culture. Having received pressure from the military ordinariate, Carroll gave permission for one diocesan priest volunteer, Father Oscar Carlson, to become an army chaplain. In 1966, the *Voice* took a "hawkish" stance supporting the American involvement in the war. In November 1966, it was reported that U.S. bishops saw the U.S. military position as one they could "conscientiously support," but by November 1968 their Pastoral, "Human Life in Our Day," took a more circumspect view toward the Vietnam war, especially regarding its proportionality. They suggested that selective conscientious objection was permissible.[23]

Because of the changes precipitated by Vatican II and the growing uncertainty between Catholicism and Americanism in the years from 1958 to 1968, the spirit of South Florida Catholicism (excluding the Cuban exiles) moved from confident expectation to uneasy disillusionment. By 1968, the wave had crashed and was beginning to recede. Yet the physical progress of the local Church had reached unparalleled heights.

Structuring the Kingdom: Parochial and Extraparochial Planning

Institutional organization, Vatican Council II, and the American cultural scene of the 1960s were all part of the building up and tearing down that occurred in the transitional period 1958–68. If the

Hurley years witnessed the fastest rate of growth in South Florida in its history, then the first ten years of the Carroll episcopacy witnessed the fastest rate of ecclesial development in three areas: parish building, education, and social service.

Parish building continued to follow the basic techniques developed during the Hurley period (see chapter 4). When Carroll came to Miami in 1958, there were fifty parishes in the diocese; within seven months, he established ten new ones. By January 1964, there were eighty-five parishes and thirty missions, by the end of 1968 ninety-five parishes. With the necessary support from his parishioners, the priest who was more often described as administrator than pastor, following the custom of both Pittsburgh and St. Augustine, organized the construction of a provisional church or church/school, later to become a social hall or to be incorporated in the school. The building was put up according to the regulations of the Diocesan Building Commission. One parish, St. Charles Borromeo in South Broward, had a provisional church fifty-one days after it had been erected as a parish, with the church itself constructed in twenty-five days![24]

Two unusual chapels were established as missions of near-by parishes. One, a storefront chapel at Northside Shopping Center (called St. Mary's Chapel), was said to be the first church in the United States located in a shopping center to provide regularly scheduled services. It opened on March 16, 1960, but had closed by 1965. The second was the Miami International Interfaith Chapel, which had a Sunday Mass from 1966 through 1969.[25]

Parish statistics reflected the population growth and demographic shifts of the area from 1958 through 1968. Based on baptismal and marriage records, the incidence of Hispanic surnames rose dramatically in most Miami parishes and Cuban-American marriages increased slightly. Mixed marriages (those between a Protestant and Catholic) were about 50 percent for Americans, a proportion much higher than either Hispanic Catholics in South Florida or American Catholics in northern urban centers and one which had remained constant among South Florida Catholics for seventy years (table 8.2).

Parish building was closely allied with parochial school building, since Bishop Carroll pressed for Catholic schools as a general rule for new parishes. However, some pastors and administrators successfully avoided the pressure. From 1958 to 1968 the diocese

TABLE 8.2. Growth and Hispanic Component of Five Selected Parishes, 1958–68

Parish	Year	Baptisms		Marriages			
		Hispanic	Total	Both Hispanic	One Hispanic	Mixed/ Disparity of Cult	Total
Immaculate Conception	1958	20	379	0	2	18	36
	1960	38	342	4	2	18	47
	1965	208	521	67	8	21	111
	1968	226	409	64	12	30	154
St. Brendan's	1958	18	351	0	2	20	37
	1960	40	442	1	5	25	54
	1965	74	289	13	8	18	51
	1968	82	233	14	15	21	67
St. John Bosco	1958	–	–	–	–	–	–
	1960	–	–	–	–	–	–
	1965	450	463	–	–	4	90
	1968	591	592	–	–	2	95
St. Mary's Cathedral	1958	21	363	4	5	50	105
	1960	31	305	3	6	33	86
	1965	112	254	38	5	28	103
	1968	149	252	63	10	23	152
St. Patrick's	1958	7	72	2	2	9	31
	1960	9	78	13	1	15	34
	1965	25	84	14	3	4	27
	1968	35	73	12	4	7	36

SOURCES: Baptism and marriage registers of the respective Miami parishes.

opened eleven new parish schools and added to twenty-three. Carroll had no intention of phasing out parochial schools, especially when the influx of Cubans and northerners into the area seemed to justify his policy; during his episcopacy not one parochial school was closed. One change did occur in parochial school policy under Carroll: the phasing out of the ninth grade in parochial schools in 1960. Carroll chose to follow the more traditional first-through-eighth, ninth-through-twelfth system found in some northern states.

As in the past, the faculties of parochial schools were more or less equally divided between lay teachers and sisters. St. Brendan's in Miami was a typical larger parochial school of the 1960s. In 1963 it had its first graduating class of students who had gone through the full eight years, and its enrollment reached a peak of 1,027. Eleven Sisters of the Holy Family of Nazareth and twelve lay teachers staffed the school at that time. St. Brendan's School also reflected shifts in the parish population. By the end of 1963, the parish was approximately 60 percent American and 40 percent Cuban; by 1967, 50 percent each; by 1970, approximately 30 percent American and 70 percent Cuban.[26]

The number of diocesan high schools in South Florida more than doubled between 1958 and 1968. When Bishop Carroll arrived, there were five diocesan high schools in operation: Curley and Christopher Columbus, staffed by diocesan priests, and Immaculata, Notre Dame, and St. Thomas Aquinas, staffed by the Sisters of St. Joseph of St. Augustine, the Immaculate Heart of Mary Sisters of Philadelphia, and the Adrian Dominicans, respectively. St. Patrick's in Miami Beach had a parochial high school, the last of its kind, under the sponsorship of Monsignor Barry. During his first five years, Carroll established seven new diocesan high schools. Religious who taught in secondary education were Marist Brothers, Holy Cross Brothers, Marianists, LaSalle brothers, School Sisters of Notre Dame, Adrian Dominicans, Piarists, Sisters of St. Francis of Mary (Joliet, Ill.), Allegheny Franciscans, and Philadelphia Immaculate Heart of Mary Sisters. Unlike Hurley, Carroll sought religious to teach in diocesan high schools. In addition, the Society of the Sacred Heart opened a private school for girls in Coconut Grove, and the Cuban Jesuits began Belen as a private school for boys.[27]

In order to direct the development of the burgeoning diocesan schools, Carroll established a diocesan school board to act as liaison between pastors and principals, to consider financing of school construction and plan staffing, and to offer suggestions to the ordinary. In January 1967, the board was reorganized and redefined, theoretically acquiring more power. Although the new plan looked fine on the organizational chart, the board never had the powers claimed for it on paper. It was merely advisory, and each component in the education system could act autonomously.[28]

Bishop Carroll was interested in promoting CCD, weekly religion classes for public school Catholic children. Shortly after taking over the diocese, he appointed Father Romould E. Philbin director of religious education in South Florida. A month later Carroll mandated a CCD program for every parish by January 1, 1960. Several conferences for priests, sisters, and laity to stress the importance of CCD and the training of lay catechists were held, and the first annual Catechetical Sunday was instituted on May 1, 1960, to emphasize the necessity of CCD and the importance of lay catechists.[29] Three months after Carroll's deadline, however, over half the parishes still lacked a CCD program, a fact that illustrates the limitations of moral persuasion in the exercise of episcopal power. A second deadline of January 1961 likewise failed to produce results.

In 1962, Father Emilio Vallina, a Cuban exile priest, was made assistant CCD director in charge of Spanish-speaking CCD, and Father Joseph Brunner was named assistant CCD director, assignments intended to put the program on a firmer basis. In May 1963, Carroll assigned a committee of three monsignors to find out why the parishes were not implementing CCD. The committee reported four reasons for the delay: lack of interest on the part of some pastors, untrained teaching personnel, multiple changes in pastors, and inefficient executive boards.[30]

In a personnel shuffle characteristic of the bishop's results-oriented management, in 1964 Carroll assigned Philbin as full-time CCD director. However, it was Brunner, not Philbin, who became the moving force of diocesan CCD from 1964 by establishing a system of certificating CCD teachers. Six Victory Noll Sisters gave CCD training courses throughout the diocese in 1964. By November 1966, approximately five hundred laity were being instructed at twenty-two centers. After virtually running the office for three years, Brunner was appointed director of CCD in February 1967.[31]

In the spring of 1968, Brunner developed his most creative idea, the formulation of the position of director of religious education (DRE). This full-time person was to be a priest, sister, or layperson who would be connected with a parish and would have charge of training teachers and creating CCD programs. These directors were to be trained at the proposed Christian Formation Center where, through affiliation with Barry College, an M.A. in religious education would be required. Although the Christian Formation Center was never built, a summer program was established at St. John Vianney Seminary, and courses during the year were given at Barry College to certify the directors. The DRE program was successful because it not only served to staff competent CCD personnel in the parishes but it gave another expression to ministry in South Florida for women religious and laity. Furthermore, the summer program played an important role in post–Vatican II theological renewal for both priests and sisters.[32]

Education in the Diocese of Miami flourished from 1958 to 1968 at all levels. Apart from its central mission as an education center for women religious of South Florida, Barry College offered spiritual conferences, lectures in theology and other disciplines, and cultural events, as well as summer school. In the summer of 1963, for example, 280 sisters representing twenty different communities of the diocese were studying at Barry. In 1964, the college began to apply for and get federal money for its programs. In 1968, it had 1,196 full-time students, 482 of them Floridians. Although the type of student at Barry changed during the 1960s, the college had little campus ferment.[33]

In the midst of the Hurley-Carroll controversy, Bishop Carroll established Biscayne College on land heavily implicated in the dispute, securing the services of the Augustinians, recently exiled from Cuba, to operate the proposed college as well as a parish in Dania. Carroll was to donate fifty acres of land and to contribute $500,000 for the construction of the college buildings. Father Edward McCarthy, OSA, recently stationed at Villanueva University in Havana, was named rector. From September 1962 until January 1963, classes at Biscayne College for men were held on the Barry campus, until its buildings were ready. Like Barry, Biscayne was little touched by campus unrest. Though financing was their biggest problem, the Augustinians began purchasing the Biscayne property from the diocese by 1967 and had an enrollment of over five hundred students by 1968.[34]

A second new college had its beginnings in early 1959. Clarence F. Gaines, a resident of Sherborne, New York, notified Bishop Carroll that he wished to be the patron of a Marymount School in Florida to be run by the Religious of the Sacred Heart of Mary. Gaines had purchased fifty acres of land at University Park, west of Boca Raton, by that May. In the fall of 1961, Religious of the Sacred Heart of Mary came to the diocese, taught at St. Lawrence Parochial School in North Miami Beach, and oversaw developments at Marymount, which was to be a women's junior college. Four buildings costing $1.5 million were opened in the fall of 1963, with facilities for one hundred resident students. Mother de la Croix was named as superior and president of the college, with five other members of her community as the staff. In 1965, the college became coeducational.[35]

From its inception, Marymount emphasized action over academics. Of the Catholic colleges in South Florida, Marymount most clearly reflected American culture of the 1960s, its concern for social problems directly reflecting the influence of the civil rights movement upon a mostly northern, affluent, residential student body and an administration also from the North. In the winter crop season, Palm Beach County, in which Marymount was located, had one of the largest concentrations of migrant farm workers in the United States. Beginning in 1963, Marymount initiated a volunteer program, attracting half of its students, which placed the women as Girl Scout leaders and religion teachers at a nearby migrant mission in Delray Beach. In the fall of 1964, plans were laid for a summer project at Marymount which would include programs for migrant children, teenagers, and adults. The project received $55,000 in government funding, becoming a model for other programs in the diocese; indeed, Marymount was the first college or university to receive a Title III-B grant. Four hundred sixty-nine migrants participated in the program which was staffed by forty-three professionals and thirty volunteers. In 1966, the summer migrant program was expanded with a federal Office of Economic Opportunity (OEO) grant of $252,427, enrolling some one thousand adults and five hundred children in six centers. Seminarians from St. John Vianney and St. Vincent de Paul were employed in the program. In 1968, Marymount still had its summer program though on a more modest scale. In that year, four major seminarians started a spin-off program in the black community of Deerfield Beach for about two hundred nonmigrant black American children.[36]

Marymount was also a center for liberal activism in other ways, in 1964 offering lectures and conferences on ecclesially controversial topics. Robert W. Gleason, SJ, Daniel Berrigan, SJ, Philip Berrigan, SSJ, John L. McKenzie, SJ, and John Courtney Murray, SJ, were among its invited speakers.[37]

After only nine years, in 1972, the Religious of the Sacred Heart of Mary withdrew from Marymount, an action which closed it as a Catholic college.[38] At Marymount, enrollments did not increase; the private junior college concept was not viable in South Florida because of the proliferation of public two-year community colleges; the sisters who were the driving force of Marymount found other interests and their community suffered personnel shortages; in short, activism overpowered academics. A northern idea, supported by northern money, composed of northern sisters and a mostly northern student body, Marymount never took root in the sand of South Florida.

A third new college, an offshoot of the Sisters of St. Joseph Novitiate in Jensen Beach, opened in 1966 as a coeducational two-year junior college. The college also had as its prototype the St. Joseph Teacher's Training Institute run by the St. Joseph Sisters for years.[39]

Education in the diocese also took less formal forms. The diocesan newspaper, the *Voice*, published its first issue March 20, 1959, printing a Spanish language section from the beginning. As had been the custom of Archbishop Hurley with the *Florida Catholic*, Carroll ordered a quota of papers sent to each parish. Unpaid newspaper subscriptions were charged to the pastor, assuring the *Voice* a steady circulation and a steady source of income. The *Voice* experimented unsuccessfully with distribution on secular newsstands in 1959 and again in 1968.[40]

Other informal educational tools of the decade included Newman Clubs at area colleges (1950); marriage instruction sessions sponsored by the Family Life Bureau (1959); radio and television diocesan informational programs (1960); televised Mass for shut-ins (1962); and the diocesan educational television system (established in September 1965). Miami was the first diocese in the country to use a closed-circuit television system in Catholic schools, in 1966 reaching thirty-eight schools in Dade County and seventeen in Broward. Costs were $100,405 by mid-1966. The microwave component was added in 1968, but by then Bishop Carroll had decided to abandon the system because of prohibitive operational expenses.[41]

The Catholic Service Bureau expanded its programs significantly from 1958, not only to absorb the impact of the Cuban influx but also to take advantage of newly available federal funds. Before this innovation, money for the rather limited programs of Catholic Social Services came from the United Fund, the St. Vincent de Paul Society, and the diocese itself.[42]

Other kinds of federal funding, besides the programs for the Cubans, made available housing assistance for the elderly and aid for the poor and disadvantaged. The Housing Act of 1959 offered loans to qualifying groups at 3¼ percent interest. The diocese first availed itself of this offer with the renovation of Lake Court Apartments (Lourdes Residence) in 1960. Later, with a $1.8 million federal loan, it sponsored St. Elizabeth Gardens, its first new home for the aged, with 150 apartments. When President Lyndon Johnson launched his War on Poverty, federal money began to pour in, initiating a period of virtually uncontrolled growth of Catholic Charities. The diocese put unemployed youth to work, sponsored more housing for the poor, and established drug-abuse facilities. Federal money was soon supplying half of the Catholic Charities budget, not only permitting great expansion but also requiring Catholic Charities to extend the scope of its work since federally funded programs could not be restricted to members of any specific religious communion.[43]

Specific concerns of the Welfare Bureau shifted throughout the 1960s. In October 1958, Catholic Charities was basically a child-care and adoption service with a budget of $181,977.26. Its foster home program handled 819 cases. In 1962, the number of adoptions declined, reflecting a national trend, and Catholic Charities became heavily committed to the Cuban Unaccompanied Children's Program. Just when that program was getting smaller, the OEO was offering money for community projects, thus drawing the Catholic Service Bureau into new areas where money and pro-

grams were available. By 1964, the bureau had five regional offices, a child-care and foster home program of 963 cases (not including Cubans), a psychological service department, and four
new facilities, including the Children's Home in Perrine and St.
Vincent Hall for Unwed Mothers. That same year, with the Cuban
programs included, it had the second largest child welfare and care
agency in the United States.[44]

In 1965, Edwin Tucker, formerly of Pittsburgh and head of the
Dade County Urban Renewal Program, resigned his federal post
and was appointed director of the newly created Diocesan Office
of Community Service. He became the diocesan expert in feder-
ally funded programs. In 1967, Ben Sheppard, a medical doctor
and former juvenile and domestic relations judge, was appointed
executive director of the Catholic Welfare Bureau, replacing Monsignor Rowan Rastatter, who had held the position for two years.
A family counseling service opened at the bureau under the direction of Father Roger Radloff and Dr. Thomas Haupt that September, and, at the same time, a medical clinic opened at Holy Redeemer, in the same area where Hurley had opened one in 1956. In
1968, the Catholic Welfare Bureau spent $837,644, with a deficit of
$267,639 supplied by the diocese (deficits had been appearing in
the budgets since 1965). Facilities developed between 1964 and
1968 included Boystown of Florida, the Marian Center for Exceptional Children, St. Joseph's Residence for the Aged, the Maura-
wood Residence for Unwed Mothers, the Bethany Residence for
dependent teenage girls, the Drug Education Center, and Good
Shepherd Day Care Center. Adoptions in the five-year period
were 1,210.[45]

Personnel

Like Florida prelates before him, Bishop Carroll was concerned
about fostering native vocations. During the first year of his episcopacy, he designated April as Vocation Month and sponsored a
variety of activities such as special days of prayer and awards for
altar boys, practices carried on throughout the sixties. He emphasized in 1959: "We do not have sufficient priests in this Diocese and
a continual increase in the Catholic population moving here from
the North and West makes our problem much greater than ever

before. . . . The only solution is for the Diocese of Miami to train its own priests. We can't continue to look to other places for help."[46] All of this preaching, publicity, and rhetoric was not without effect. Where in June 1959 the diocese had 22 major seminarians and 24 minor seminarians, by 1967 it had 65 major seminarians, 180 minor seminarians, and 50 seminarians elsewhere in the United States and Europe, a total of 295.[47]

To provide an institutional and financial foundation for the diocesan vocation drive, Bishop Carroll in 1959 established the Burse Fund and the annual Seminary Collection, both based upon a Florida Catholic precedent going back to 1924. He also founded the Serra Club (lay professionals dedicated to fostering vocations) in Miami in 1960 and subsequently in Ft. Lauderdale, West Palm Beach, and Ft. Pierce.[48] But the most significant institutional support for native vocations was the establishment of two diocesan seminaries within the Diocese of Miami.

In 1873, Bishop Verot had established at St. Augustine a domestic seminary of a type common in the United States in the nineteenth century, but it lasted only a year.[49] Carroll opened St. John Vianney Minor Seminary in September 1959, with fifty-seven seminarians and staffed by five Vincentian priests, with Father John Young, CM, rector. In seven years eight structures were added; the physical plant was completed by 1968 just as enrollments began to fall (table 8.3).[50] The cultural and ecclesial ground had begun to shift. In June 1966, the *Voice* had reported that "the golden age of vocations" to the American priesthood might be coming to an end. By 1967, the Church in Western countries observed a noticeable drop in the number of vocations. On April 9, 1967, Pope Paul VI had called for a World Day of Prayer for Vocations, in which each parish in the Diocese of Miami participated.[51]

St. John Vianney was also affected by the changes in curriculum and style penetrating all American seminaries by the mid-1960s. Seminarians were permitted to leave seminary grounds in 1966 to teach CCD in parishes and to migrant children. Twenty-five college seminarians formed Students Organized for Social Justice (SOS), whose primary purpose was to aid in migrant ministry and social concerns. Administratively, a new board of trustees was organized in 1966, composed of eleven priests and six laymen.[52]

Even as he was beginning St. John Vianney Minor Seminary, Carroll was making plans to acquire enough land to build a major

TABLE 8.3. Seminary Enrollments, 1959–68

Year (fall)	St. John Vianney			St. Vincent de Paul			Ordained
	High School	College	Total	Philos.	Theo.	Total	
1959	60	–	60	–	–	–	–
1960	107	8	115	–	–	–	–
1961	148	34	182	–	–	–	–
1962	155	29	184	–	–	–	–
1963	154	27	181	29	–	29	–
1964	158	46	204	26	11	37	–
1965	138	63	201	23	37	60	–
1966	117	60	177	38	36	74	–
1967	101	35	136	50	41	91	–
1968	82	41	123	36	47	83	14[a]

SOURCES: AVF, "Numerical Progress of Classes, S.J.V., 1959–68" (mimeo); AVF, "S.J.V. Rosters, 1965–72"; FSVDP, "Student Rosters, 1962–68."

a. Not all those ordained were for the Diocese of Miami. Some were for Puerto Rico.

seminary west of Boynton Beach. Part of this land had been purchased earlier by Hurley, but, despite its entanglement in the controversy between the two bishops, Carroll announced the construction of the only major seminary on the east coast south of Baltimore. In October 1961, the property was conveyed finally to the Diocese of Miami by Archbishop Hurley and within the month deeded to the Vincentian Fathers for a token fee of ten dollars. The seminary opened on September 24, 1963, with five Vincentians on the staff and Father Carey J. Leonard, CM, rector. In August 1966, a new rector was named, Father John Gallagher, CM, who implemented many changes in seminary curriculum and life. The first seminarians from Puerto Rico (thirteen of them) were admitted in the fall of 1965, adding a Spanish and Caribbean flavor to the student body (for statistics on student enrollments, see table 8.3).[53]

Although the southern character of the seminary was really never stressed (primarily because the Vincentians were northerners), Vatican II and the contemporary cultural upheaval in American life had more effect on St. Vincent de Paul than on the seminary in Miami. Even before the major seminary was dedicated, plans for the chapel were readjusted during construction to fit new liturgical requirements. Similar to Marymount in nearby Boca Raton, education at St. Vincent de Paul became, over time, more and more education for the social service apostolate. Action and academics were both seen as integral and integrating. From the spring of 1964, seminarians helped to teach CCD to the migrant children of Our Lady Queen of Peace Mission in Delray Beach. Some seminarians aided the Marymount Summer Program by 1966, eventually starting their own summer project in the black community in Deerfield Beach in the summer of 1968. With major changes in seminary rules, curriculum, and life-style beginning in 1967, seminarians became more and more active outside the seminary. At the same time, many different groups were allowed inside the seminary for conferences and activities. Rather than staying within the confines of the seminary, the seminarian was expected to "go out and experience life."[54] The nature of the seminary faculty and the distance of the seminary from the Miami area minimized the influence of Hispanic culture and language upon the non–Hispanic seminarians up to 1968.

The purpose of vocation recruitment and seminary construction was of course to produce priests for the diocese. The first diocesan ordinations took place on June 20, 1959, in the cathedral. Seven men, the first class from the major seminary, were ordained on May 25, 1968. Native vocations and near-native vocations were on the rise.[55]

However, as in the past, native and near-native priests were too few to staff the parishes and institutions of South Florida. Therefore, seminarians born, raised, and educated in the North were recruited, a high proportion from Josephinum Seminary in Ohio.[56] Foreign seminarians were also sought, as in times past. In 1962 four OCSHA priests were ordained to aid Miami. Cuban Ernesto García Rubio (1963) was ordained for the Archdiocese of Havana to work in Miami, and Orestes Todd Hevia (1967) became the first Cuban-born priest ordained for the Diocese of Miami.[57] However, Ireland continued to be by far the most important source of seminarians from outside the diocese. The number of Irish priests ordained for Miami during the period were five in both 1960 and 1961, ten in 1965, eight in 1966, ten in 1967, and six in 1968.

Bishop Carroll put Monsignor Thomas O'Donovan, the Irish recruiter in the Hurley years, in charge of obtaining vocations from Ireland. Like their predecessors, Irish priests continued to have difficulties adjusting to their new environment, especially since they were given little formal preparation. Adjustments were even more acute under the changes of Vatican II and the permutations of American culture in the 1960s.[58] The symbolic passing of an era for Irish priests in South Florida occurred with the death of the patriarch of Miami Beach, the pastor of St. Patrick's, Monsignor William Barry, on November 17, 1967.[59]

Eighty diocesan priests served the Diocese of Miami in 1958. Ten years later there were 308, approximately one for every 1,500 Catholics. Most dioceses in the Northeast or Midwest had proportions of 745 people per priest or less. The St. Augustine diocese had one priest per 746–1,000 Catholics. Sixty priests were ordained for the diocese from 1964 to 1968; there was one defection and one dispensation from priesthood.[60]

Carroll, unlike Hurley, welcomed the introduction of religious priests, brothers, and sisters into the diocese. In 1958, only twenty-one religious priests were working there, Jesuits and Benedictines, and no religious brothers. By January 1964, eleven communities of priests and five communities of brothers served the diocese. Besides secondary education and parish work, the new male religious communities staffed a retreat house (Passionists), two seminaries (Vincentians), black parishes and missions (Josephites), and a shelter and kitchen for needy men (Little Brothers of the Good Shepherd). Religious men's communities received several native and near-native South Floridian vocations from 1958 to 1968.[61]

Bishop Carroll's interest in vocations extended to the recruitment of women religious. Vocation exhibits, vocation month, and publicity in the *Voice* comprised considerable advertisement for the religious vocation of women. Young South Florida women entered several communities, but a larger number of postulants came to the Allegheny Franciscans, the Sisters of St. Joseph of St. Augustine, and the Adrian Dominicans. The Sisters of St. Joseph of St. Augustine had at its peak seven from South Florida in 1964 and again in 1966. The Adrian Dominicans had ten from South Florida enter in 1964.[62] Besides the novitiate in Jensen Beach, which existed before the Diocese of Miami was created, some communities opened novitiates: the Poor Clare Nuns (1961), the Sisters of St. Philip Neri (1964), the Sisters of St. Joseph Benedict Cottolengo (1967), and the Religious of the Apostolate of the Sacred Heart of Jesus (1968). In 1958, nine communities of religious, composed of

392 women, worked in the diocese; in mid-1968, there were 827 sisters in 44 different religious communities, only six of which were Hispanic in origin.[63]

The new sisters' communities that came to the diocese in the decade 1958–68, mostly in the years 1959–63, were mainly dedicated to the teaching apostolate. However, some sisters were involved with other works: retreat houses (the Dominican Sisters of St. Catherine De Ricci and the Cenacle Sisters), a Catholic book and film center (the Pious Society of the Daughters of St. Paul), a refugee center (the Dominican Sisters of St. Catherine De Ricci), nursing homes (the Sisters of the Bon Secours and the Carmelite Sisters of the Aged and Infirm), a hospital (the Mercy Sisters of Pittsburgh), a cloistered monastery (the Poor Clare Sisters), and a center for exceptional children (Sisters of St. Joseph Benedict Cottolengo).[64]

Two other new developments concerning women occurred in the decade: the founding of a new religious community and the introduction of an institute of women who were technically not religious at all. The idea for the new religious community came from outside the diocese. In February 1966, Father Lawrence Lovasik, SVD, stationed at Divine Word Seminary in Girard, Pennsylvania, was in the process of founding a new community of women. With thirty young women interested in the idea, eight of whom spoke Spanish, Lovasik sought to locate the new community in Miami. The group, it was agreed, would be a diocesan community under the jurisdiction of the ordinary. By September 1966, with characteristic rapidity, Carroll had assigned the twenty women of the new community (the Daughters of Mary) to five locations. In 1968, the diocesan community, the first and the only so established, dropped their previous assignments to begin their apostolate at St. Elizabeth Gardens Home in Pompano. The second group introduced, the Teresians, a secular institute of Madrid, Spain, came to the Diocese of Miami in March 1961 to work in education, marking the first foundation of the institute in the United States.[65]

Women's communities that had been in South Florida prior to 1958 continued to work in the area. The second largest group of sisters in the Diocese of Miami from 1958 to 1968, the Sisters of St. Joseph of St. Augustine, a diocesan community, continued to be stretched in many directions, although attempts were made toward consolidation. In South Florida from 1962 to 1968, the Sisters of St. Joseph closed three academies, six elementary schools, the St. Joseph's Catholic Home for Children, Morning Star Schools, and St. Ann's Mission, Naranja. They opened a college, a parochial school, and a home for unwed mothers. In 1966, a year which marked their hundredth anniversary in Florida, Bishop Carroll transferred diocesan ownership of Mercy Hospital to the Sisters of St. Joseph under the title of Mercy Hospital, Incorporated.[66]

As of March 1959, the distribution of the place of origin of the 263 St. Joseph Sisters was 89 from the Diocese of St. Augustine, 66 from the Diocese of Miami, 89 from Ireland, and 19 from other states. In 1968, of a total of 296 sisters, 198 taught, 20 nursed, 15 were in social service or migrant work, and 40 were in formation. In the same year the sisters had 14 houses in the Miami archdiocese out of the 33 in the four dioceses of Florida. The Sisters of St. Joseph reached their zenith of communal strength in 1964 with 324 members.[67]

The Adrian Dominicans were still the largest and the most influential and prestigious community in the diocese from 1958 to 1968. In 1958, there were 127 sisters in the Miami diocese, 124 in education, the others in a home for working girls. In 1968, there were 155 in the diocese, 3 in Casa Francesca and 152 in education, of whom two were diocesan supervisors of education, a new role for sisters in the diocese at the time. The Adrian Dominicans had an all-time membership high of 2,474 in 1968; their peak commitment to the diocese was from 1964 to 1968.[68]

South Florida's oldest women's religious community, the Sisters of the Holy Names, celebrated its hundredth anniversary in Key West on October 27, 1968. The last remains of the old wooden convent, built in 1875 and a military hospital in the 1898 war, were torn down in August, condemned as much by the regulations of the Southern Association of Accreditation as by its age.[69] This event was symbolic of the winds of change that were developing in South Florida Catholicism.

Ministry to Ethnic Groups

Ministry to blacks, a traditional component of Florida Catholicism, took some unexpected directions in the decade 1958–68, influenced by contemporary integration and civil rights activities. Integration became a concern in the whole Miami religious community as early as 1955. Even before Bishop Carroll came to Miami, Mercy Hospital was integrated, at least for private rooms, by order of Hurley, who had pushed for the construction of Mercy Hospital so that blacks might have Catholic hospital care. Hurley also ordered that Curley High School accept black students in September 1958, making it the first school in Florida to be integrated.[70]

Bishop Carroll commissioned a report on the seven black missions and five black schools in the diocese in 1960. At that time there was still segregation in Miami as well as the rest of Florida and the South. As late as July 1963, racial discrimination existed in the employment practices and use of facilities of local governments in Dade County. A year later, black Catholics of St. Francis Xavier Parish still had to hold their parish picnic at Virginia Beach, the "colored beach" in Miami.[71]

Carroll expanded Hurley's integration policies and became a leader in the Miami religious community by encouraging integration in both Catholic and non-Catholic circles. In late 1960, it was recommended that St. Augustine Mission be closed so that the black Catholics there might be integrated with St. Hugh's. Yet not all black Catholics favored "mixed" parishes. Carroll wanted to close down Holy Redeemer and have black Catholics go to Corpus Christi, but Holy Redeemer Catholics collectively and successfully protested the closing of their school and parish. The *Voice* claimed that integration was working out more effectively and swiftly in Miami than anywhere in the "deep South or the deep-freeze North." By June 1963, nineteen of the twenty-four southern dioceses had integrated their Catholic schools. The Diocese of Miami schools had been officially integrated in September 1961.[72]

In Miami, the concern for integration broadened in 1963 to a concern for civil rights, human dignity, and justice, and an interfaith committee on civil rights was formed that year. When it was his turn to chair its meeting, May 31, 1963, Bishop Carroll read a statement that affirmed: "We proclaim as inalienable every man's right to equality without discrimination of any kind in: employment, education, housing, hospitals, labor unions, job training, public accommodations, recreation, political organizations, and worship. We proclaim that racial prejudice, discrimination and segregation are a violation to justice and an affront to the dignity of man." After all those present agreed to the contents of the proclamation, Bishop Carroll asked the twenty-five ministers and rabbis present to sign it and to preach about it in their churches and synagogues. This manifesto was published in local secular papers as well as in the *Voice*, and Carroll sent the statement to all pastors to make it known to their parishioners. Soon thereafter, Carroll went to the county commission and testified on the need for desegregation in Miami, as well as the need for a community human relations board. An eighteen-member Metro County Human Relations Board was soon established, with Carroll serving as president for two years.

In August, Bishop Carroll had the text of the just-issued U.S. bishops' Pastoral, "Bonds of Union," published in the *Voice* and had all his priests preach on the subject. At that time racial tensions in Miami were rising. Lunch counters were being desegregated, but not all establishments cooperated. Restroom facilities for blacks were still limited to the two interstate railroad and bus stations in downtown Miami. Before leaving for Rome for Vatican Council II, Carroll went before the county board of commissioners to encourage them to enact a public accommodations law.[73]

With his return to the diocese, Bishop Carroll set up a diocesan commission on human relations (also called the Diocesan Human Relations Board) with Father John Kiernan, SSJ, pastor of Holy Redeemer, chairman. At the first meeting of the board, February 14, 1964, it stated that its purpose was to eliminate discrimination and segregation in South Florida. The board encouraged Catholics to work with persons of other faiths for civil rights and justice and sponsored conferences for priests, sisters, and lay people. Men's and women's diocesan organizations were encouraged to support civil rights in Miami. As a moving force behind the board, Carroll was named by B'nai B'rith "Dade County Citizen of the Year of 1964" for his civil rights activities. After going through four executive directors in less than two years, in May 1968 members of the board's executive committee were asking themselves how to make the body more effective. With the rise of the Black Power movement, racial relationships were shifting.[74]

Although racial disturbances broke out for two nights in the black communities of West Palm Beach and Riviera Beach in the summer of 1967, Miami and the rest of South Florida did not suffer the kind of riots that were experienced in northern cities such as

Newark, Rochester, Detroit, and Cairo, Illinois that same summer. However, the concern over the possibilities of racial riots did inspire the Catholic Welfare bureau to open a clinic for Negroes at Holy Redeemer Church, near the one set up by Archbishop Hurley in 1956–58. In 1967, only one of the five black churches in the diocese had fulltime resident priests—two Josephites at Holy Redeemer. By December, to demonstrate the diocesan commitment to the black community, Father Oliver Kerr, a diocesan priest, had been made administrator of St. Francis Xavier. Kerr was the second diocesan priest to serve a black parish; the first was Joseph Devaney, who served as founding administrator of Holy Redeemer from 1951 to 1959.[75]

Certain groups and individuals were active in the black apostolate between 1958 and 1968. Bishop Carroll asked the Josephite Fathers to take over Holy Redeemer Parish in the spring of 1959. In July 1961, the Josephites began Christ the King Parish at Richmond Heights, the same year that the Oblate Sisters of Providence, a black community, were invited to the diocese. The Monroe Immaculate Heart of Mary Sisters, who had taught at Holy Redeemer since the school opened in 1951, withdrew from the school so that the Oblates could take it over. Seven Oblates staffed both Holy Redeemer and St. Francis Xavier schools in 1961.[76]

In June 1966, Sister Marie Infanta, an Oblate of Providence, came to live at St. Francis Xavier Convent, not to teach in the school but to be director of the Culmer Day Care Center, after she had organized Head Start in Washington. Paid through the federal Office of Economic Opportunity, she was the first sister in the diocese not to teach, nurse, or administer a Catholic institution. She sparked some controversy since she continued to wear her habit as the director. By 1967, she also ran two other "Child Opportunity Centers," one in Naranja and the other in Goulds. Freed from the shackles of school or hospital schedules, Sister Infanta became rapidly immersed in Miami community and diocesan affairs. Another black Catholic woman, Mrs. Athalie Range, a native of Key West and a businesswoman, sat on the Diocesan Community Relations Board in 1965, chaired the Diocesan Committee of Negro-Cuban Affairs in late 1965, and became even more involved in community affairs as a Miami city commissioner, the second woman to be elected to that body. In 1965, Father John

Wynn, a native black Miamian, was ordained for the Society of the Divine Word at Gesu Church. Only one native Floridian black Catholic had been ordained to the diocesan priesthood in the history of Florida Catholicism up to 1968, namely, Charles Jackson, born in Alachua, Florida, in 1911 and ordained in 1955 for the Diocese of St. Pierre et Fort de France, Martinique. In 1966 he came to minister in the Diocese of Miami for the first time.[77]

Although pastoral concern for the Hispanic community was at an all-time high between 1958 and 1968 primarily because of the Cuban influx, non-Cuban Hispanics were also the subject of apostolic concern. The migrant ministry inaugurated by Archbishop Hurley continued to be supported by Bishop Carroll. In August 1960, plans were announced for establishing four new migrant missions, aided by the Extension Society. Father Hugh Flynn was appointed head of the Migrant Mission Program in September 1960, with a budget of $25,000 and a team of six OCSHA priests and nine St. Joseph Sisters to serve thirty-six camps. With the arrival of sisters from Cuba in 1961, it was thought that they would be able to take over the migrant apostolate, but by September only one Sister of St. Joseph of the original nine, Sister Mary Thomas Aquinas, SSJ, was left in migrant work and supported by the diocese.

In Delray Beach in 1962, Our Lady Queen of Peace Mission was established in a Quonset hut. With the help of seminarians from St. Vincent de Paul, collegians from Marymount, and volunteers from surrounding parishes, Sister Aquinas visited homes and picked up children from the surrounding area for religion class and Mass. To fund the migrant missions, the Diocesan Mission Collection began as an annual appeal in 1963. By that year, there were three missions: St. Ann's, Naranja; Our Lady Queen of Peace, Delray Beach; and Our Lady of Guadalupe, Immokalee.[78]

By 1968, with eight migrant missions and most of the mission system built and staffed, the diocese began to change its approach to migrant work, emphasizing day-care centers and government programs for housing. As the Public Health Department began condemning labor camps toward the end of 1968, and smaller farmers began selling their farms to larger corporations or land developers by 1971, more and more migrant workers started becoming permanent residents, obtaining steady jobs in construction or landscaping. Another shift affecting the migrants evolved from the general reorganization of the diocesan structure of the Spanish-speaking apostolate, of which migrant ministry was a part.[79]

Bishop Carroll also promoted Hispanic affairs at local, national, and international levels, instituting, among other things, the first annual Pan-American Day Mass at Bayfront Park in April 1961. Representatives of local, state and federal governments attended, along with representatives of eighteen South American countries. Monsignor William Barry, who in the 1940s had promoted liaison between South America and Miami, was named honorary chairman. The Pan-American Day Mass became an annual affair; it moved from Bayfront Park to Gesu Church in 1965, the last year that the event was held, since the popularity and purpose of the Mass faded and Cubans in Miami did not participate in it to any significant degree.[80]

In 1962, Bishop Carroll was named a member of the Latin American Committee of the National Catholic Welfare Conference (NCWC). In September 1964, he established the Inter-American Institute of Social Formation to train South American leaders in Catholic social doctrine and leadership in Miami, under the sponsorship of the NCWC. By August 1965, the institute had graduated from its six-week course five groups of agrarian leaders from eight South American countries. In recognition of Miami as the "Gateway to Latin America," Bishop Carroll was appointed in 1967 as acting chairman of the National Catholic Conference of Bishops' Latin American Committee.[81]

It is apparent that not all of the diocese's energies during the years from 1958 to 1968 were focused on responding to the Cuban exiles. Although South Florida Catholicism witnessed the greatest institutional development in its history, changes were taking place that were eroding some of those institutions. The year 1968 was the watershed of this new ecclesial milieu.

9

The Culmination of an Era,
1958-68

During the decade 1958-68, Catholicism in the Diocese of Miami had grown and developed. Yet at the same time that the Church was being built up externally, it was being eroded internally by a wave of ecclesial and cultural change. The year 1968 represents a significant shift in the life of South Florida Catholicism, the end not only of a decade but also of a century of missionary Catholic life.

Characteristics of the Period: Catholicism in Transition

The transitional character of the decade 1958-68 was reflected in the human elements of Florida Catholicism: the episcopacy, the priesthood, religious life, and the laity. Among these, only the office of the episcopacy did not change, because the person who held that office did not change. Coleman F. Carroll, even more than Joseph P. Hurley, colored and channeled South Florida Catholicism.

Carroll was not an intellectual, not a theologian, not a linguist, not a theoretician. He was a politician, an organizer, a leader. Aggressive, impulsive, and energetic, Carroll wanted to be in control, and thus he was extremely sensitive to threats, real or imagined, to his authority. With a keen political sense of timing, he was not averse to using the media to capture a magnanimous gesture.[1] Carroll's autocratic rule created organizational and administrative problems as the diocese grew, although it proved efficient in the earlier years. One problem was that while he enjoyed starting new projects, he often lost interest in the details of implementation and the routine of upkeep. He was concerned with producing immediate, tangible results.

As a builder and organizer, Carroll was unequaled in the history of Florida Catholicism. He even compares favorably to one of the most outstanding builders and organizers in the history of American Catholicism, Philadelphia's Dennis Cardinal Dougherty, who called himself "God's Bricklayer."[2]

Dougherty, 1918–28	Carroll, 1958–68
92 new parishes	45 new parishes
89 new parish schools	17 new parish schools (23 new additions to schools)
48 new churches	58 new churches
3 new diocese high schools	9 new diocese high schools
1 new women's college	3 new colleges
14 new academies	2 new academies
1 minor seminary	2 seminaries, minor and major
25 different women religious communities introduced	35 different women religious communities introduced

Besides the more visible aspects of building, Carroll laid the necessary financial groundwork: a $16 million bond issue in 1960, the Teamster pension fund loan of $1 million that carried the diocese through the financial and legal rigors of the Hurley-Carroll controversy, and the diocesan savings account. This last fund, an idea borrowed from Chicago, acted as an internal diocesan bank so that parishes could be started without paying commercial bank interest. In May 1968 Miami adopted a new and unique pension plan for all priests, religious, and lay employees of the diocese, the first in any American diocese in which these persons were provided benefits under one plan and one trust management.[3]

Carroll was not a creative innovator or a man of vision. Although reluctant to recognize his debt to his predecessors, Carroll borrowed and amplified on the base established for him in Pittsburgh by Father Coakley and in South Florida by Archbishop Hurley.[4] Carroll's personality and leadership style combined to make him highly visible in Miami, where he improved relations between the Roman Catholic Church and the larger Miami community. The Cuban immigration and civil rights issues were just two examples of his use of public issues to gain respectability for Catholicism. Before Carroll came, Catholicism was relatively isolated from the larger Miami community because of the paucity of Catholics and Hurley's discouragement of interfaith activity or media publicity, as well as his physical distance from South Florida.[5]

Carroll was slow to respond to the reforms of Vatican II. He was especially upset by the liturgical changes, and he became more reactionary as time went on. Although he was a leader in responding to the Cuban influx and in integration, civil rights, and social welfare, the anti-authoritarian, anti-institutional element of the 1960s had absolutely no appeal for him.[6]

In 1969, Carroll suffered a heart attack which he admitted slowed him down. After incurring a foot injury while on a trip to Rome in 1975, and refusing to have his leg amputated when complications set in, Coleman F. Carroll died in office on July 26, 1977, at the age of seventy-two.[7]

To the end, Carroll was a churchman who had a keen sense of his duty as ordinary of Miami, as he himself said: "Of course, in carrying out our responsibilities, there are painful duties. To be responsible, to a serious degree, to carry out the material responsibility of all this. . . . You know the Archdiocese of Miami is in debt $18 million right now. . . . How would you like to carry *that* around on your shoulders? . . . You've got to have a sense of humor in this job, otherwise you'd go nuts. . . . I hope the people will say a prayer for me. Someday, I'm going to have to answer to God for my stewardship. I hope I wouldn't have to appear empty-handed. . . . I realize full well the responsibility I have before God."[8] Carroll's accomplishments as a leader by no means left him or South Florida "empty-handed." However, almost from the beginning of his Miami episcopacy, the Church and the world were changing at a pace and in ways to which neither he, nor aspects of the Catholicism he knew, could adjust. In that decade, the Tridentine model of Catholicism was being eroded, and the Vatican II model was promised but not realized.

Although continuities from the Hurley period existed in diocesan priestly life, changes in the first Carroll decade signaled new expressions in diocesan presbyteral life-style. Bishop Carroll inaugurated a monthly day of recollection for priests in October 1959, which, unlike the annual priests' retreats, was voluntary. Sixty priests came for the first day of recollection, but, as priestly life in South Florida became more complex, the leisure time necessary for attendance at days of recollection dwindled. By 1966, the themes pursued at the days of recollection took on a Vatican II flavor, becoming almost indistinguishable from clergy conferences on the new liturgy. By 1967, priestly days of recollection ceased.[9]

In November 1964, the chancery recommended books to priests to assist them in instructing in the new liturgy. Outlines for a series of sermons on liturgical changes were sent to priests in early 1965 and again in early 1966. In many cases the implementation of the liturgical instructions for the people was poorly done, not out of disobedience or disagreement over the changes but because priests often did not understand the new liturgy any more than did the people. Ultimately, both priests and people accepted the liturgical changes out of obedience to and faith in the Church, the Holy Father, and the bishop.[10]

By 1966 Carroll was becoming increasingly concerned about liturgical aberrations, not only because he himself was uneasy about the reformed liturgy but also because he saw unauthorized liturgical innovations as a threat to his authority and the Church's law. The Diocesan Liturgy Commission established in February 1964 was disbanded by the bishop in 1967 and replaced by the Episcopal Vicar for the Implementation of Vatican II (1967–68) in the person of Monsignor John Fitzpatrick, who later pointed out with characteristic frankness that his job was given no description by the ordinary and that it was mostly just a title, "so that we could say we were doing something about Vatican II, but hope that nobody would ask us what!"[11]

The changes induced by Vatican II created a qualitative shift in the way the priest in South Florida perceived himself and the way he was perceived by his people. Now he was required to give not just a sermon but a homily based on the scriptural readings prescribed for the day. Most priests had not been trained in giving such homilies or in the newer developments in biblical studies. The priest was required to say Mass facing the people and at a closer distance than before, and this change in liturgical posture had ramifications for the exercise of priestly ministry. Moreover, the Mass, the sacraments, the rituals of the Church were now in the vernacular. What the priest said, the way he said it, were now understood by the congregation in a way that the Latin mumblings of the past were not. The priest's personality came through more clearly in his liturgical presence and became more important in his ministry. Shifts in Catholic piety such as the change in the Eucharistic fast, the decline of Forty Hours Devotion, the restoration of the diaconate all in time affected priestly life-style.[12]

One indirect offshoot of the council was an increase in the number of meetings that priests had to attend on the diocesan and parochial level. This phenomenon grew out of the implementation of the new liturgy and the emergence of a new role for the priest, as well as the increased complexity of Catholicism in South Florida. Bureaucracy on all levels proliferated to the point that one priest called the diocese a "meeting machine." Priests had less and less time for what had been called "priestly fraternity" or visiting with their people.[13]

Other modifications in priestly life in South Florida resulted from changes in American culture. Rather than set apart from society, the priest was expected to become immersed in it. The role of the priest was increasingly under scrutiny with the publication of such bestsellers as James Kavanaugh's *A Modern Priest Looks at His Outdated Church* (1967). Priests began to wonder who they were and what their role was. A handful of Miami diocesan priests and seminarians sought answers in social activism.[14]

Changes in style of priestly ministry resulted from the rapid growth and development of South Florida Catholicism. Priest transfers under Carroll were even more frequent than during the Hurley period. From 1960 to 1961, five major new assignment announcements affected more than 55 priests, 33 percent of the 165 priests in the diocese in 1961; in 1966–67, six major announced appointments involved more than 158 priests, 36 percent of the 441 priests in the diocese in 1967.[15] Besides parochial responsibilities, many priests had one or more additional diocesan assignments. It was Carroll's policy to give a young priest two or three different parochial assignments before naming him administrator (usually ten years after ordination). For example, from 1960 to 1968, Father John Nevins had eight different pastoral appointments, plus a diocesan assignment. In 1963, Father Thomas Dennehy was chaplain to Marymount, assistant pastor at St. Ambrose in Deerfield Beach, and supervising principal of Cardinal Gibbons High in Ft. Lauderdale. Pressured with putting out the "bonfires" associated with building parishes and institutions, paying off debts, managing budgets and burgeoning parishes, and coping with cultural and linguistic diversity, Miami priests did not have the time or the luxury to consider many theoretical ecclesial problems. They were of necessity pragmatic and practical. The presbyterial horizon rarely extended beyond the parish or the institution; hence Miami priests of the decade were often "parochial" in more ways than one. Up to 1968, those leaving the priesthood were relatively rare; only five Miami diocesan priests were laicized, while two diocesan priests had departed uncanonically.[16]

A final innovation in the priesthood in Miami during the decade 1958–68, a product of both Vatican II and contemporary American life, was the rise of corporate priestly action. The Spanish Priests' Association was established in October 1966. In December, preliminary plans were announced at a clergy conference for the establishment of a Priests' Senate as called for by Vatican II, its purposes "to assist the Bishop in the governing of the Diocese and to promote the overall welfare of the Church."[17] Father Ronald Brohamer was chosen chairman of the constitutional committee of twenty priests. Difficulties soon arose over who had the right to vote, over the lack of Spanish-speaking priests' representation, and over the bishop's right to appoint some members to the senate.[18]

Finally, in September 1967, the Priests' Senate adopted a constitution. Representation comprised twelve elected senators from four age groups, five priests elected from the five deaneries, and four priests appointed by the bishop. Carroll made it clear that the senate was not autonomously authoritative, only advisory. Its first meeting was February 15, 1968; its first officers were elected by March, with Brohamer as president. An immediate offshoot of the Priests' Senate was the five-man personnel committee, which became a separate entity in the 1970s.[19]

The Priests' Senate strove for cohesion in spite of a presbyterate of tremendous diversity: Irishmen (the largest single block), Cubans, Spaniards, Basques, Hungarians, Poles, Lithuanians, Maltese, Englishmen, transplanted northerners, near-native Floridians, native Floridians, religious, and the ordination class of 1968 from St. Vincent de Paul Seminary. Three Miami priests attended a 300-priest convocation in Chicago of representatives from 135 dioceses, the upshot of which was formation of the National Federation of Priests' Councils in May 1968, a body representing 127 councils and 40,000 priests. Miami did not join this federation.[20]

Although the life of sisters in the diocese showed some continuity with the earlier period, at the same time it heralded changes that would blossom after 1968. Of all the groups in the diocese, religious women most clearly reflected the erosion of the Tridentine model of the Church and the transitional character of the decade.

The Diocese of Miami offered to women religious, up to 1965, teachers' institutes, days of recollection, convent visitation, ordinary and extraordinary confessors, and monthly spiritual conferences. From these monthly diocesan spiritual conferences, there evolved talks to the sisters on the Second Vatican Council, a subject which the sisters heard more about than anybody else in the diocese in the years between 1960 and 1966.[21] The same message, the need for renewal of religious life, was repeated again and again not only at numerous diocesan-sponsored conferences but also in popular books such as *The Nun in the World* (1962) by Leon Cardinal Suenens, in secular and sectarian magazines, and eventually in their chapter meetings called as a result of conciliar and postconciliar documents. More than bishops, priests, male religious, or the laity, women religious experienced higher expectations and stronger motivation to "renew" themselves for the "modern Church."[22] The sisters took the challenge of "renewal" more seriously than any other group and felt its effects most acutely.

One of the most visible and most contested examples of the change in religious life for women concerned the habit. Habit modification was adopted in South Florida by the School Sisters of Notre Dame in 1962, by the Religious of the Sacred Heart of Mary in 1963, and by the Philadelphia Sisters of the Immaculate Heart of Mary, the Sisters of St. Joseph of St. Augustine, the Adrian Dominicans, and the Sisters of the Holy Names in 1967. By 1968, habit modification was virtually universal in the Diocese of Miami; no community had as yet abandoned the habit altogether, but the *Voice* in 1965 and in 1967 gave a hint of things to come with pictures of sisters in northern states wearing ordinary street clothes.[23]

Altering their clothing was a superficial reflection of more significant changes in religious life of women from 1958 to 1968. As in the Hurley period, sisters serving the Miami diocese in the early 1960s continued intercommunity socialization; around 1965, this socialization ended, partly because of the tremendous multiplication of women religious in the diocese in only five years. The nine communities composed of 392 religious serving the diocese in 1958 increased to 41 by early 1964, with 856 women religious. There were other reasons for a cessation of intercommunal socialization: the many meetings for sisters on the diocesan and provincial level; the concentration on more graduate education and professionalization; the increased self-consciousness of each community as a result of the soul-searching following Vatican II; and the slightly different timetable and agenda each community had for "renewal," which separated them from one another in ways that were more substantive than the style of their habits.[24]

The sisters' life in South Florida in the early 1960s usually revolved around school and convent, with weekend CCD work. This pre–Vatican II routine was beginning to break up nationally when in 1966 sisters began complaining to the U.S. bishops about salaries, medical care, the need for lay cooks (to free the sisters for professional work), and representation on international, national, diocesan, and parish levels. All of these issues were affected by the shrinkage in the size of religious communities that was beginning to make itself felt.

Also by 1966, the public and personal images of the woman religious were beginning to change. The new superior of the Sisters of the Assumption at Assumption Academy in Miami was twenty-seven years old. Sister Marie Infanta, OSP, came to the Miami diocese to work for the OEO at the Culmer Day Care Center. In 1967, two sisters joined the staff of the Catholic Welfare Bureau, the first time in the history of the diocese that sisters had held such positions. In January 1968, Sister Regina, RSHM, head of Marymount Music Department, sang and played guitar at the Florida Atlantic University Coffee House.[25] The public image and the sisters' self-images were being reshaped, though the ramifications of this transformation were still not apparent in 1968.

Two other examples pointed to shifts in the lives of women religious in the diocese. First, the position of director of religious education was created in 1968 in the diocese, an event that exposed many sisters to an updated theological orientation as well as new expressions of ministry. Second, the Sisters' Senate (Council) was initiated by the diocese in 1967 "to provide a voice that might offer suggestions and recommendations to the Bishop." Sister Marie Carroll Hurley, OP, head of the Barry College Drama Department and raised in St. Ann's Parish, West Palm Beach, chaired the executive committee to organize the council. By March 1968, sisters from six areas of the diocese had elected representatives, one for every forty sisters in an area, plus four sisters elected at large. Sister Marie Carroll, OP, was elected chairwoman of the Sisters' Council, which was to meet every two months and act as an advisory committee to the ordinary in all matters concerning sisters.[26]

Laity flourished under Bishop Carroll partially because he was more a bishop for the laity than was Archbishop Hurley and partially because of the times. Of course Carroll's notion of the role of lay persons was based on Catholic Action's laity "under the guidance of the hierarchy" rather than upon any of the notions of Vatican II.[27] Yet the 1960s showed a tremendous increase in Catholic lay organizations, especially among the Cubans.

As in the previous period, laity gave money for parish building and for institutional building. By the mid-1960s, a few lay persons were invited as consultants on parochial and institutional planning. Because Bishop Carroll had a special affinity for the affluent and powerful, he encouraged several elite organizations new to South Florida such as the Catholic Lawyers' Guild (1959), the Serra Club (1959), the Knights of St. Gregory (1962), and auxiliaries for women for the Marian Center and St. Vincent Hall (1961).[28] Lay benefactors continued to be important. Frank J. Lewis, his wife, Julia, and the Lewis Foundation supported parish construction, diocesan high schools, and Catholic colleges and seminaries. Mrs. Mary Lou Maytag McCahill, a convert of Bishop Carroll's from Pittsburgh, was the single most outstanding benefactor of the period. Among her many benefactions to the diocese were several buildings at St. John Vianney Seminary, the chancery building, homes for unwed mothers and exceptional children, and contributions to the Burse Fund and the Diocesan Development Fund.[29]

More egalitarian lay organizations for women also developed in the period, including the Diocesan Council of Catholic Women (1958), the Diocesan Council of Catholic Nurses (1959), and the Legion of Mary (1958).[30] Similar Catholic men's organizations seemed to lack the vitality and pervasiveness of the women's groups. The Diocesan Council of Catholic Men (DCCM), chartered in 1959, had all but faded out of existence by 1968. In between, an ambiguous relationship grew up between the DCCM and the nearly defunct Holy Name Society. Men from the two groups held separate annual conventions during the decade. Feverish attempts were made to boost Holy Name membership, revive vitality, and redefine objectives, but to little avail. Two men's groups that existed before the creation of the Diocese of Miami expanded their quiet work in the 1960s, the St. Vincent de Paul Society and the Knights of Columbus.[31]

The first of the new corporate movements for laity that began in the decade was really not new but took new directions in the 1960s. Before the Diocese of Miami was created, lay retreats were offered irregularly for South Floridians because no retreat facilities existed. In the late 1950s, Archbishop Hurley made plans to establish a diocesan retreat house run by diocesan priests. Under Carroll young Irish-born Father Noel Fogarty was put in charge of lay retreats in January 1959; they were held at the Golden Strand Hotel, Miami Beach, during the summers of 1959 and 1960. In 1961, men and women's retreats were held at the newly established Passionist Retreat House, the Cenacle, and the Golden Strand Hotel. Kendall Retreat House was opened for women in the summer of 1962. In 1963, the College Building at St. John Vianney Seminary housed summer retreats of the Knights of Columbus of Dade and Broward counties. A shift in lay retreats began with the first English-speaking retreat conducted in the diocese for married couples (November 4–5, 1967), held at the Dominican Retreat House, Kendall. The new phenomenon of couple retreats was soon introduced at the Cenacle (April 1968) and at the Passionist Retreat House (June 1968).[32]

Other lay movements of the period were initiated from the grass roots, especially within the Cuban and Hispanic community (see chapter 7). One of the Hispanic movements, the Cursillo, was first introduced in English into the diocese by a team of Cursillistas from the Dioceses of Lafayette and Kansas City. As a gesture of solidarity, the Hispanic Cursillistas of Miami paid the expenses of the first English-speaking Cursillo, held at the Opa-Locka Airport barracks March 17–20, 1966. The first Spanish-speaking Cursillo in the diocese had been in 1962, and by 1966 the movement had over 2,000 Cursillistas.[33]

Monsignor Robert Schiefen, pastor of Holy Family Parish (1958–68) and head of the Diocesan Family Life Bureau (while chancellor and vicar general), had experimented with the Christian Family

Movement (CFM) with 120 families of his parish. Mr. and Mrs. Pat Crowley, CFM leaders from Chicago, visited Holy Family Parish in September 1966 and by May 1967 about 150 couples from Dade, Broward, and Palm Beach counties attended the First Diocesan Convention of CFM (English-speaking) at Boystown. Schiefen was the diocesan chaplain. CFM had begun among some Cuban families by 1961. When the first Marriage Encounter Weekend in English took place at the Cenacle Retreat House in January 1968, all twelve couples attending were CFM couples.[34]

The first parish council of the diocese was at SS. Peter and Paul Parish in January 1966. Affected by the traumatic impact of the Cuban influx, plus rising costs, the Parish Coordinating Council was formed. The first parish council properly so-called was founded in Sacred Heart Parish in January 1967 and was composed of two priests, two sisters, six women, and ten men who met to discuss the spiritual, educational, and financial aspects of the parish. In April 1967, Carroll asked pastors to implement councils in every parish in the diocese as encouraged by Vatican II. The concept of parish councils was slow to take effect, however, because many reluctant pastors saw it as a threat to their authority, and implementation had barely begun in 1968.[35]

Some liturgical and devotional transformations associated with Vatican II were initiated by Church leaders. Dramatic liturgical alterations in the Mass, for example, mandated by Rome, the U.S. bishops, and the local ordinary, took place in less than four years. In general, the laity adapted to the new liturgy with flexibility; yet the Tridentine model of spirituality was taken away and replaced in many instances with nothing. For example, devotional statues were removed from many parishes by individual parish priests with little or no explanation. The style of prayer at Mass shifted from silently praying in the back of the Church, fingering rosary beads, and following along with one's head in the Missal to responses in English and congregational singing. One change built on another with such rapidity that, by 1968, many Catholics often felt an inexplicable void, an unidentifiable sense of having been cast adrift. Concomitantly, some laity became more active in liturgical and ecclesial affairs during the decade. By 1965, members of the laity were lectors and commentators at Mass. After 1965, laity served on diocesan commissions, on boards of directors for seminaries and colleges, and as directors of diocesan departments.[36]

By 1970, approximately one-third of Florida's population lived

TABLE 9.1. General Population of South Florida Cities, 1960–70

City	Year	Population	Percentage of Increase
Ft. Lauderdale	1960	83,648	130.3
	1970	139,590	66.9
Ft. Myers	1960	22,523	70.7
	1970	27,351	21.4
Ft. Pierce	1960	25,256	87.1
	1970	29,721	17.1
Hialeah	1960	66,972	240.4
	1970	102,297	52.7
Key West	1960	33,956	28.5
	1970	27,563	−18.8
Miami	1960	291,688	17.0
	1970	334,859	14.8
Miami Beach	1960	63,145	36.4
	1970	87,072	37.9
North Miami	1960	28,708	167.4
	1970	34,767	21.1
West Palm Beach	1960	56,208	30.2
	1970	57,375	2.1

SOURCE: U.S. Bureau of the Census, *Population, 1970*, 1:11-56–59.

TABLE 9.2. Percentage of Florida's Population 65 Years or Over, 1960–70

	1960	1970
South Florida Metropolitan Areas		
Ft. Lauderdale/Hollywood	11.4	17.9
Ft. Myers	12.7	18.8
Miami	10.1	13.6
West Palm Beach/Boca Raton	12.7	17.3
Non–South Florida Metropolitan Areas		
Daytona Beach	19.7	22.3
Sarasota	18.4	28.6
Tampa/St. Petersburg	17.3	21.1
National Average	9.2	9.9
Florida Average	11.2	14.6

SOURCES: AFAM, Archbishop's Private Files, First Research Corp., "The Florida Economy, Part I," p. 55; U.S. Bureau of the Census, *Population, 1960*, 1:11-27; U.S. Bureau of the Census, *Population, 1970*, 1:1-270, 11-55.

TABLE 9.3. Diocese of Miami, 1958–77

	1958	1964	1968	1977
Diocesan priests	63	142	177	253
Religious priests	21	154	159	186
Religious women	392	115ᵃ	827	661
Parish schools	44	60ᵇ	55ᶜ	63
Churches	53	92	94	129
Missions	24	22	8	3
Stations	5	10	6	26
Total baptisms	6,084	9,383	9,084	10,905
Total marriages	1,212	2,590	3,397	3,628
Mixed marriages	492	866	1,181	955
Catholic population	185,000	426,000	400,000	771,600

SOURCES: OCD-1959, p. 529; OCD-1965, pp. 591–92; OCD-1969, p. 463; OCD-1978, p. 511.

a. The OCD figure is a misprint; the number of sisters in 1964 was 821. AFAM, Archivist's Office, "Five Year Report, 1964–68."

b. This figure is inaccurate. The *Voice* (January 17, 1964) reported 13 new schools from 1958 to 1964; thus the total for 1964 is 57.

c. This figure is inaccurate. Four new schools were reported from 1964 to 1968; thus the total for 1968 is 61. AFAM, Archivist's Office, "Five Year Report, 1964–68."

in Dade, Palm Beach, and Broward counties (table 9.1). In that year, Cubans made up approximately 22 percent of the population of Dade County. All those who came to South Florida in the 1960s found employment in (listed in order of economic importance) tourism, agriculture, aluminum fabrication, the garment industry, printing and publishing, plastics, precision electronics, aircraft maintenance, and seaport industries.[37] Although South Florida's population of those over sixty-five years of age was slightly above the national average from 1960 to 1970, the Cuban influx gave Miami one of the lowest percentages of retired persons of any Florida metropolitan area, as well as the highest cost of living on the southeast coast (table 9.2).

As in the Hurley period, the Catholic population grew apace. Statistics point to considerable growth in personnel and parochial institutions. From 1958 to 1968, the number of marriages increased by 180 percent, baptisms by 49 percent, diocesan priests by 181 percent, religious women by 111 percent, parishes by 77 percent, and parochial schools by 38 percent (table 9.3).

The result of the weight of numbers was in many cases anomie, or the individual's feeling uprooted without any connections or responsibilities, a feeling not found just among Cuban exiles but as likely to occur among Americans moving down from the North. This feeling resulted in challenges for the Church. Building a sense of community in the parish was increasingly difficult not only because of transplanted persons but also because of ethnic diversity and the newness of many South Florida subdivisions. On the other hand, as in the past, parish building and parish fund drives cemented people for a common purpose with tangible results, and building projects were numerous enough in the decade to provide common bonds for people who otherwise lacked a sense of unity.[38]

The people of South Florida were highly mobile, with thousands moving into the area monthly from Cuba and the northern United States. In 1960, Dade County had 2.4 cars per person, one of the highest ratios in the country. From 1960 to 1968, Ft. Lauderdale's population increased by 57.5 percent, Miami's by 22.9 percent. Such high rates of migration and immigration affected family life. In 1967, Ft. Lauderdale's marriage rate was 9.5 per thousand and the divorce rate 4.4 per thousand; Miami's marriage rate was 9.9 per thousand, the divorce rate 4.8 per thousand. Mixed marriages began dropping from 50 percent of the total Catholic marriages, as was the case in earlier periods (table 9.3). Ecclesial marriage cases were often complicated not only by the number of mixed marriages or the number of Cubans whose ecclesial records were difficult to retrieve from Cuba but also by northern transplants sometimes leaving marriage problems they had at home in order to find a fresh start in South Florida. Family advice columns in the *Voice* up to 1967 reflected upon husband-wife relationships, but by late November 1967 articles began to highlight teenage problems such as the generation gap and drug abuse problems.[39]

Catholicism in South Florida became extremely unstable under the influences of Vatican II, the tumultuousness of American culture in the 1960s, and the demographic shifts. Yet this instability also created a freshness, a flexibility, an energy that manifested itself in a missionary spirit. In a continuation of its missionary past, South Florida Catholicism continued to ask for money from the Extension Society. In early January 1959, Extension allotted $10,000 to the Diocese of Miami. Following the tradition of past

Florida bishops, Carroll begged for more money from Extension yearly. In addition to helping with Mass stipends for some Spanish-speaking priests, by 1965 Extension had assisted financially in the construction of twelve mission chapels throughout the diocese. By September 1967, the amount of Extension grants for chapel construction totaled $170,000. As late as February 1971, Extension was still sending stipends to the diocese for those working in the diocesan missions.[40]

From 1958 to 1968, South Florida was still perceived by many as missionary, especially by those northern religious coming to tropical Florida. In 1959, Bishop Carroll himself referred to Miami as "a struggling missionary diocese."[41] Five years later, he cited the instability of the missionary situation in South Florida: "Breaking up a parish works a hardship on priests. . . . It's also been difficult for some church members. I know of cases where a family has found itself in three different parishes in a year because of boundary changes, and that isn't good. But they'll just have to bear with me until we get the diocese straightened out."[42] As late as 1969, priests writing to religious in the North still referred to the situation in South Florida as missionary. If commentators did not use the word "missionary" to describe South Florida between 1958 and 1968, they often characterized the Diocese of Miami as "different" from what they had been used to in the North.[43]

Rapid growth and development, or "progress," was not without its price. The Hurley-Carroll controversy cut off South Florida Catholics from their past; many transplanted northerners wanted to leave their pasts; changes that came from Vatican II were described as "revolutionary," implying a break with the past. The rapid "progress" of South Florida Catholicism from 1958 to 1968 only fed this growing identity crisis, this sense of being on a boat with no sails, rudder, or helmsman.

Priests of the period were often doing too many jobs and were being moved too many times. With an emphasis on building and fund raising, priests' worries often were more financial than pastoral. As the old devotionalism faded, so did the older form of priestly fraternity. However, the pressures clergy felt in the period, which sometimes affected their health, were not the result of an unrelenting ordinary but rather of the "weight of numbers," as well as of the cultural tensions produced by an ethnically diverse presbyterate and laity.[44]

The laity too were constantly pressured to build churches and schools and to give more money, so that the energies of both priests and people were directed toward institutional building while other concerns were put aside. In addition, resentments grew between Catholics in Broward and Palm Beach counties and on the west coast, and those in Dade, where most of the nonparochial institutional buildup was occurring.[45]

The decade was a period of transition in which South Florida Catholicism moved from a missionary situation to a more institutionally established situation. Although it was a time of tremendous progress, an undercurrent of instability threatened to become an eroding force.

The Watershed of 1968

There occurred a kind of watershed between the early Carroll years and the post-1968 period, indeed between the whole hundred-year history of Catholicism in South Florida and the contemporary epoch.[46]

The principal external events that made 1968 a watershed were the shifts in American culture and the effects of the implementation of Vatican II. A decade earlier, Americans had a feeling of invincibility and an anticipation of even greater things to come. At that time Americans held what Arthur M. Schlesinger, Sr., once approvingly called "the profound conviction that nothing in the world is beyond its [America's] power to accomplish."[47] Irish-Catholic President Kennedy ushered in the New Frontier, an era of confidence and optimism. Martin Luther King, Jr., raised the consciousness of Americans about segregation, civil rights, and racism, issues Americans seemed confident they could act rightly on. Even more important, President Johnson stepped up the war in Vietnam to eliminate the Communist threat, at the same time using federal action to eliminate the causes of poverty in America. All of this optimism, all of these heightened expectations soon began to sour. President Kennedy was assassinated; the Vietnam War bogged down, its morality in question; civil rights turned into Black Power; poverty persisted; and summer riots broke out in American cities in the years 1965–68. Robert Kennedy and Martin Luther King, Jr., were assassinated in 1968. After tumultuous conventions, Democrats in Chicago and Republicans in Miami Beach, Richard Nixon was elected president. High expectations degenerated into radical doubt.[48]

The confidence and optimism that existed in American culture were reflected in American Catholicism in the early 1960s, reinforced by the high expectations generated by news of Vatican II. But by 1968, it had become clear that Vatican II had also raised some specters, for example, the relation of the sacred and secular (liturgical changes) and the relation of freedom and authority (*Humanae Vitae*). Around 1968, the norms regarding the celebration of the liturgy had solidified. *The 1967 Instruction on Eucharistic Worship* had been promulgated; *The General Instruction on the Roman Missal* (April 3, 1969) was also published. These liturgical changes were beginning to effect changes, particularly in music and in interpretation of celebrative style by certain presiders.[49]

Yet not all changes in South Florida Catholicism were directly related to American cultural shifts or Vatican II. One such example was the creation of the Archdiocese of Miami and the installation of Coleman F. Carroll as the first archbishop of Miami in 1968. Miami had in 1962 been moved from the Province of Baltimore to the newly created Province of Atlanta under Archbishop Paul J. Hallinan, metropolitan. Soon after the settlement of the Hurley-Carroll controversy, Carroll began to lay the groundwork with the apostolic delegate for the creation of two new dioceses for Orlando and St. Petersburg. As early as 1963, the apostolic delegate had asked Carroll to review his diocesan boundaries. The way was paved for the creation of two new Florida dioceses and the Metropolitan See of Miami with the deaths of Archbishops Hurley (October 30, 1967) and Hallinan (April 1, 1968). In December 1967, Carroll wrote the apostolic delegate requesting two auxiliary bishops, one for Hispanics and one for non-Hispanics.[50] Bishop Paul Tanner of the NCWC, an old associate of Carroll's, was installed as bishop of St. Augustine on March 27, 1968. Carroll was invested as archbishop of Miami on June 13; Charles McLaughlin (Raleigh, North Carolina) was installed as ordinary of St. Petersburg on June 17; and William Borders (Baton Rouge, Louisiana) was ordained bishop of Orlando on June 18, 1968. Carroll was given one auxiliary, John Fitzpatrick, a Miami priest, ordained a bishop August 28, 1968. Unlike previous splits in Florida dioceses, the ecclesial divisions of 1968 caused no disputes or controversies.

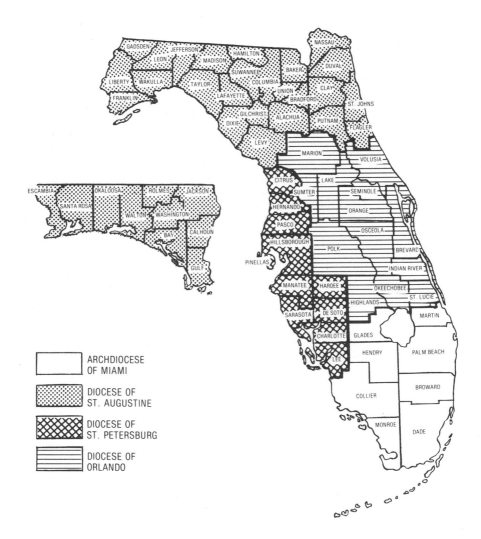

Map 5. Dioceses of Florida, 1968.

ARCHDIOCESE
OF MIAMI

DIOCESE OF
ST. AUGUSTINE

DIOCESE OF
ST. PETERSBURG

DIOCESE OF
ORLANDO

The transfer of deeds, the splitting of Irish and American seminarians took place in a smooth and orderly fashion. As a result of the divisions, Florida now had four dioceses. The Diocese of St. Augustine received the Florida Panhandle from the Diocese of Mobile; the Dioceses of Orlando and St. Petersburg were created from territory of the Dioceses of St. Augustine and Miami, which shrank from sixteen counties to eight (map 5).[51]

With the creation of the archdiocese, Carroll wasted no time reorganizing his chancery structure. He appointed Auxiliary Bishop Fitzpatrick as director of education and vicar of the clergy, Father Ronald Pusak as tribunal officialis, Father Rene Gracida as chancellor, Father Charles Zinn as assistant chancellor, and Monsignor Bryan Walsh as director of the Spanish-speaking apostolate. As an expression of unity in Florida Catholicism that had not existed between 1958 and 1968, Carroll organized with the other Florida bishops the Florida Catholic Conference, headquartered in Tallahassee, to be the legislative watchdog for the Catholic bishops of Florida.[52]

Local concerns of diocesan planning shifted about 1968. Parish building between 1968 and 1977 slowed slightly from its 1958–68 rate. The first decade saw an increase of forty-one parishes; between 1968 and 1977, thirty-five were erected. However, according to baptism and marriage statistics, the diocese had increased by 33 percent and 64 percent, respectively, from 1958 to 1968, but only by 17 percent and 6 percent from 1968 to 1977. Using marriage statistics from five selected Miami parishes (table 8.2), all five showed significant increases during the former decade, whereas, in the latter, increases, if any, were slight. At St. John Bosco, at St. Mary's Cathedral, and to some extent at Immaculate Conception, the year 1968 was a peak sacramental year in parish history.[53]

Changes in parochial life reflected the changes in the life of the laity. The most obvious difference in the life of the Catholic laity after 1968 was that the liturgy was completely in English (or Spanish) and completely revised, producing a shift in spirituality and piety. After 1968, not only did the laity generally cease going to Forty Hours and cease abstaining from meat on Friday, but they also dropped the practice of confession, and some stopped going to Mass altogether. Around 1970, experienced South Florida parish missioners like Father Charles Mallen, CSSR, began a home-Mass mission designed to readapt the traditional parish mission and also to act as a forum for introducing the revised liturgy. The nineteenth-century parish mission formulas were not working any more.[54]

Three more indicators of a change in the Catholic laity showed up in more civil cases directed against the archdiocese, more marriage tribunal cases, and the rise of the Charismatic Movement. With the Civil Rights Act of 1964, the beginnings of class action suits around 1966, and the introduction of implied warranty cases around 1970, civil litigation increased in general in South Florida. From 1900 to 1958, only six cases were reported against the Diocese of St. Augustine. From 1958 to 1960, only two or three cases involved the Diocese of Miami. After 1968, litigation involving the archdiocese grew at a record rate. By 1981, twenty to twenty-five litigated cases per year involved the archdiocese, and an equal number did not find their way to court.

Ecclesiastical courts were also much busier after 1968. Before then, marriage cases were mostly routine and simple, but they became more complicated and numerous. Liberalization of the annulment process had been in effect in the United States and Australia since 1970, and annulments in 1981 were almost 77 times those of 1968 (448 cases in 1968, 34,484 cases in 1980). In Miami, the marriage tribunal processed a growing number of cases in the seventies: 7 cases in 1972, 17 in 1973, 40 in 1974, 27 in 1975, 99 in 1976, and 153 in 1977.[55]

Finally, the Charismatic Movement, a sign of a new lay spirituality in South Florida, began in late 1969 at Chaminade High under the local leadership of Father Daniel Doyle, SM. In 1969, national Charismatic leaders Kevin Ranaghan and Steve Clark came to Chaminade High to address South Florida Charismatic Catholics.[56]

The pace of expansion of Catholic education slowed after 1968, although not one Catholic elementary parochial school was closed from 1958 to 1977. From 1958 to 1968, the diocese added seventeen parochial schools, seven diocesan high schools, and three Catholic colleges. From 1968 to 1977, the archdiocese added two parochial elementary schools, but no diocesan high schools, and closed two colleges. By 1968, Catholic education in America was under attack and was undergoing swift transformations.[57] As a result of changes in religious life, after 1968 fewer women religious were teaching. From 1968 on, the concept of the DRE was implemented in parishes, which affected expressions of ministry and parish CCD education.

Catholic Social Service was expanding into new areas by 1968. Doctor Ben Sheppard, a layman, became executive director of the Catholic Welfare Bureau. The first day-care center administered by the diocese (Good Shepherd Day-Care Center, Perrine) was opened in 1968. Programs were established for the dependent: St. Luke Methadone Clinic (1970); Sheppard Medical Clinic (1970), a nonresident clinic especially for unwed mothers; Genesis, a residence for drug addicts (1971); Ozanam, a halfway home for ex-offenders (1971); Bethesda, a halfway house for alcoholics (1970); Miami Bridge, a home for runaway teenagers (1974). New directions for archdiocesan Catholic Services also began in 1968 with the opening of St. Elizabeth's residence for the elderly under the U.S. government's 202 Program. From 1972 to 1981, four other such residences were erected by the archdiocese. The programs of the Catholic Welfare Bureau mushroomed after 1968, becoming more entwined with governmental funding, more diverse and complex, more bureaucratic than ever before. In addition, with the creation of the Florida Catholic Conference in early 1969, as well as affiliations with national associations such as the National Conference of Catholic Charities and the Child Welfare League, Miami Catholic Social Services became active in social advocacy on state and national levels.[58]

The year 1968 was also important for the Miami diocesan presbyterate: in that year the first class of locally formed and trained young men from the two Miami seminaries was ordained for the priesthood. For the first time in the history of Catholicism in South Florida, the institutional machinery for local education of native and near-native priests was bearing fruit. Yet 1968 also marked rising tensions between pastors and the archbishop against the Vincentian faculty at the major seminary over its manner of education and life-style. In Holy Week of 1969, one of the priests on the staff of St. Vincent de Paul had an open confrontation with the archbishop before a number of other priests. From that point on, Carroll turned against the Vincentians at St. Vincent de Paul and sought to have them removed. More turmoil was created when, in 1970 and 1971, five Vincentians, half the staff of the major seminary, left the priesthood, including the rector, the dean of students, and the academic dean. This wholesale departure was demoralizing to seminarians, priests of the archdiocese, the archbishop, and the Vincentians themselves. To add insult to injury, in the fall of 1970 a liturgical aberration at the seminary became the subject of conversation in clerical circles not only in Florida but up and down the east coast. These events, added to the growing antipathy between the seminary staff and chancery, caused the Vincentians to withdraw from the major seminary in the spring of 1971, citing as a reason the shortage of qualified personnel in their community. Archbishop Carroll, determined to keep the seminary open, staffed it in 1971 with a few qualified diocesan priests and volunteers from religious communities and other dioceses. In 1975 the Vincentians also had to withdraw from St. John Vianney Minor Seminary due to personnel shortages and enrollment problems. As mandated by the archbishop, St. John Vianney was staffed by a small number of diocesan priests in the fall of 1975 and supplemented by a teaching staff recruited from local colleges.[59]

The death of Monsignor William Barry on November 17, 1967, corresponded with the end of an era for Irish priests in South Florida. Ireland no longer provided sufficient vocations for export because the seminary situation had changed there as it was changing throughout the world. Irish seminary rectors and faculty were less cooperative, and the number of seminarians available for the missions diminished rapidly due to vocation shortages.[60]

Corporate action after 1968 became important for the Spanish Priests' Association and the Priests' Senate. Confrontations increased beween these groups and the ordinary, as well as between the archbishop and individual priests. The most dramatic evidence of change, of course, was the sharp increase in the number of priests leaving the priesthood. Between 1964 and 1968, only one Miami priest was laicized and one defected (left the priesthood without applying for laicization); between 1968 and 1977, thirty-three priests left the priesthood (no distinction is available between those who were laicized and those who defected). Of the original seven men ordained for the Diocese of Miami in May 1968 from St. Vincent de Paul Seminary, only two remained in the active ministry in 1983.[61]

Religious life changed dramatically after 1968. Two examples of this in male communities in the diocese were the Holy Cross Brothers at Curley High and the Christian Brothers at LaSalle High. By

1970, the Holy Cross Brothers were making individual contracts with schools. Due to problems within the Holy Cross community in Miami, a diocesan priest was assigned as acting principal of Curley in 1970, and the Holy Cross Brothers withdrew from the school in 1973. When in 1969 the Christian Brothers could no longer provide a principal for LaSalle High, the Archdiocese decided to merge Immaculata and LaSalle into one coeducational school with a diocesan priest as principal. From 1969 to 1974, the number of brothers decreased at LaSalle because of personnel shortages, open placement, and personality differences among the brothers, and because Miami was considered an "undesirable outpost." In 1974, the brothers withdrew from LaSalle.[62]

Religious women underwent the most noticeable changes beginning around 1968. In response to the mandates of Vatican II, communities serving South Florida went through "General Chapters of Renewal": the Adrian Dominicans (1968), the Sisters of the Holy Names (1967), the Catherine de Ricci Dominicans (1970), the Allegheny Franciscans (1968), the Philadelphia Immaculate Heart of Mary Sisters (1970), and the Sisters of the Holy Family of Nazareth (1968). "Renewal Chapters" might be too antiseptic a phrase to describe those often painful, long-lasting deliberations, whose effects would change the character of many religious communities in unexpected ways. To illustrate the complexity of the renewal negotiations, the Adrian Dominican archives have one file drawer containing materials dealing with the General Chapters of 1924, 1933, 1939, 1945, 1951, 1957, 1962; one and one-half file drawers cover part of 1962 and all of the 1968 Chapters; two full file drawers are required for the 1974 Chapter.[63]

Not all communities changed at the same pace or in the same way, but after 1968 significant alterations took place in the life and image of religious women. In general, the Renewal Chapters sought a redefinition of the role of religious women in the Church. With the decline of Catholic schools in many places in the North, sisters desired to break the traditional educational mold in which they found themselves. The traditional vows of poverty, chastity, and obedience were reexamined and redefined. With the stress on individual responsibility over conformity to the corporate institution, diversity was sometimes expressed at the expense of unity. As one religious put it, "The person became more important than the work." A variety of apostolates were now offered and encour-

aged. At the same time that more emphasis was placed on professionalization and social awareness, the clarity of the corporate
apostolate and image was blurred. This democratization of religious life, this shift in self-understanding, had specific effects in
South Florida.

The modification of the habit had occurred in most communities in the 1960s. After 1968 almost all communities had undergone
some habit modification, and by the 1970s some began to wear no
religious habit at all. In some convents (houses), to wear the habit
or not became a source of painful division. In 1972, 42 percent of
the Allegheny Franciscans felt that the habit change was a response
to the influence of social factors upon religious.[64] But beyond the
issue of religious dress, decision making was decentralized and
more emphasis placed on individual choice and responsibility.
After 1968, most sisters reverted to their baptismal names; the title
"Mother" for generals, provincials, novice mistresses, and local
superiors was changed in egalitarian fashion to simply "Sister."
Older titles for community positions of authority were replaced
with bureaucratic jargon—area co-ordinators, administrative directors, provincial team, facilitators. One of the most significant
organizational developments after 1968 was the implementation of
"open placement," allowing individuals to select their own apostolates, emphasizing individual choice and responsibility over communal mandates or institutional presence.[65]

The renewal of religious life of women had the effect of diver-
sifying the ministerial roles of religious women in South Florida.
After 1968, some sisters became DRE's, worked for the chancery,
assisted the Catholic Service Bureau, served as campus ministers,
aided the migrants. Sisters moved from nursing and education
only into areas of social service, diocesan administration, and pastoral work. In South Florida, Sister Joyce LaVoy was musical su-
pervisor for diocesan schools, 1969–73, and chairwoman of the
Liturgical Music Department of the Office of Worship, 1973–76;
Sr. Marie Infanta, OSP, was assistant superintendent of diocesan
schools, 1970–72; Sr. Joseph Ellen Raffin, IHM, was assistant superintendent of schools, 1970–75. Even communities whose renewal followed different patterns found themselves in new ministries. For example, Sister Josephine, CSFN, became the first in her
community to become a DRE (St. Brendan's, 1971–76). Sister
Carol Coston, OP, an Adrian Dominican and near-native Florid-

ian, became one of the founders of "Network," a group of religious women Washington lobbyists whose first organizational meeting was held in December 1971.[66]

Concomitant with the diversification of roles for women religious was the sharp decline of their numbers in education, especially at the primary levels. One reason for this was the appeal of other ministerial expressions now available, especially with the open placement system. Contributory factors also included the falling off of vocations from the standards of the 1950s and early 1960s, as well as the rapidly increasing numbers leaving their communities. The 1950s and 1960s saw a greater demand for sisters in education and therefore more communal commitments that simply could not be met with the decline of personnel, let alone the shift in the self-image of many sisters. Statistics for women religious in South Florida demonstrate that the period of stability and growth gave way to one of instability and decline around 1968 (tables 9.4 and 9.5). This phenomenon was caused by changes created by relogous renewal, as well as changes in American culture.[67]

After 1968, the ministry to blacks changed rapidly. Ironically, at the time the archdiocese was addressing the social and cultural causes of discrimination through community action, when several diocesan priests had been assigned to black parishes, when Miami was integrating and civil rights becoming a legal reality, a traditional component of Catholic ministry to blacks, black Catholic education, was being deemphasized. By the late 1960s and early 1970s, blacks were becoming conscious of their Afro-American heritage, yet after 1968 only two black Catholic schools remained in the archdiocese. Although black Catholic schools were a product of segregation and racial prejudice, they also served as ethnic schools, similar in many ways to Polish or German schools in the North. Black Catholics lost their ethnic schools, and the Church lost an important presence in the black community.

Although the Archdiocese of Miami participated in many more government programs after 1968—programs open to all races and creeds, touching more blacks than the older black missions and schools had—these projects were more secularized. Their specifically Catholic religious dimension was less defined, especially when diluted by myriad governmental regulations. In addition, such programs disbanded when government funding dried up. A flurry of jointly sponsored government Church programs for

TABLE 9.4. Selected Women's Communities in South Florida, Provincial Statistics, 1958–77

	Total Professed							Professed Departures						
Year	SNJM	SSJ	OP[a]	OSF	SSND	CSFN	IHM[b]	SNJM	SSJ	OP[a]	OSF	SSND	CSFN	IHM[b]
1958	234	263	c	847	966	c	1,984	1	2		5	4		5
1959	238	274	c	845	1,010	328	1,961	1	2		7	4	3	2
1960	235	276	283	860	1,000	329	1,990	2	3		3	4		3
1961	262	286	296	880	1,009	329	2,017	2	3	1	10	5	2	4
1962	259	289	296	886	1,021	331	2,060	2	0		10	5	3	3
1963	267	304	300	910	1,042	334	2,112	1	0		11	6		4
1964	268	324	318	928	1,055	341	2,139	6	3	3	12	9		6
1965	275	317	301	926	1,063	345	2,163	4	10	1	13	12	3	8
1966	271	313	301	910	1,064	345	2,227		14		8	16	4	5
1967	279	306	301	913	1,059	349	2,257	4	8	1	15	22	4	16
1968	277	297	296	932	1,042	347	2,293	6	8	1	18	22	3	25
1969	271	248	294	904	991	336	2,296	5	24		20	32	10	42
1970	253	207	293	882	950	336	2,281	11	16	2	22	54	8	41
1971	242	202	307	860	931	327	2,231	8	18		22	20	7	48
1972	230	191	293	832	898	325	2,206	4	7	4	16	24	2	21
1973	222	188	280	813	854	321	2,174	9	1		9	19	2	23
1974	212	188	278	796	812	318	2,132	10	5	2	10	26	3	28
1975	209	187	277	784	785	310	2,104	5	2	2	10	13	5	19
1976	203	182	256	771	758	303	2,063	3	6	11	13	13	5	25
1977	199	178	255	778	730	294	2,029	7	1	1	12	12	4	24

SOURCES: ASHN, ASSJ, AADS, ASSF, ASSND, ACSFN, AIHM.

a. Adrian Dominicans
b. Philadelphia's IHM's
c. Information presently unavailable

TABLE 9.5. Selected Women's Communities in South Florida, Diocesan Statistics, 1958–77

	Total Professed in S. Florida							Professed Departures While in S. Florida						
Year	SNJM	SSJ	OP[a]	OSF	SSND	CSFN	IHM[b]	SNJM	SSJ	OP[a,c]	OSF	SSND	CSFN	IHM[b]
1958	36	103	111	55	4	c	10		0		1			
1959	36	101	110	57	9	10	21		0					
1960	35	104	137	66	11	14	21	1	1					
1961	34	104	146	c	15	15	23	1	1					
1962	33	106	152	62	18	16	24		0		1			
1963	34	108	152	57	20	17	25		0					
1964	34	109	160	58	21	18	27	2	0					
1965	34	107	162	55	23	18	29		4					
1966	30	106	160	54	25	17	31		4		1	2		
1967	31	105	162	55	25	17	32		3		1			
1968	30	106	157	49	25	17	35	1	6		2			
1969	27	95	151	45	23	17	34		11			3		
1970	27	81	154	52	21	16	36	1	6			4	1	
1971	22	72	155	45	20	16	34	1	10		1	1		
1972	16	68	150	46	24	16	33	1	3					
1973	16	65	140	54	19	15	33	2	0			1		
1974	9	64	138	54	28	15	34		1		1			
1975	9	62	141	55	26	15	35		1				1	
1976	12	59	141	46	24	13	33		1			3		
1977	9	54	127	37	24	15	31		1		1	1		

SOURCES: ASHN, ASSJ, AADS, AADS, ASSF, ASSND, ACSFN, AIHM.

a. Adrian Dominicans

b. Philadelphia IHM's

c. Information presently unavailable

blacks in the late 1960s and early 1970s quickly faded for either by lack of funding or lack of interest.

From 1968, Catholic missions to blacks were reduced to three churches, St. Philip's (diocesan), Holy Redeemer (Josephites), and St. Francis Xavier (diocesan). Christ the King Parish became an integrated parish with a white majority. St. Francis Xavier Parish went through a series of upsets in the 1970s, with the pastor leaving the priesthood (1971) and fewer sisters teaching in the school (1975). Another change in the black Catholic situation was apparent by 1980 when the influx of Haitians (beginning in 1972) and Mariel Cubans (those who came in the Cuban boatlift of 1980) dramatically raised the number of black Catholics in South Florida, and their presence presented cultural and linguistic challenges for ministry to blacks.[68]

Hispanic ministry in the diocese began to change. Soon after 1968, Cubans became the majority among Miami's Hispanics. In 1968, Monsignor Bryan O. Walsh was appointed director for the Spanish-speaking apostolate. His appointment shifted diocesan policy, since he pushed for more Hispanic parish administrators, the support of Hispanic lay movements, Hispanic vocations and a bilingual major seminary, the introduction of more Hispanic religious communities, and the end of the unofficial policy of assimilation.[69] In addition, by 1968, no more diocesan priests or religious immigrated to South Florida from Cuba. When the 1968 Immigration Law placed Cubans entering the United States on a quota basis, the number of boat escapees from Cuba declined and, in 1970, the "Freedom Flights" ended. Hispanic pastoral innovations introduced around 1968 included Father Román's evangelization technique at the *Ermita* and the change of St. John Bosco from a mission to a parish. Protestant evangelization, always perceived as a threat, stepped up its efforts among Hispanics after 1968, and ten years later Miami had the largest number of Baptist baptisms of any city in the world, an increase of 225 percent since 1967. Miami also became the center of Baptist evangelization for South and Central America. Yet Catholic sacramental indices (baptisms and marriages) in five selected Miami parishes showed an increase after 1968 in the number of Spanish surnames, as well as in the number of culturally mixed marriages.[70]

The creation of the Archdiocese of Miami in mid-1968 signified not only a juridical and structural change of the Diocese of Miami but also the end of an era. The year 1968 separated the formative years of Catholicism in South Florida from a new era, yet to be identified. By 1968, the missionary character of South Florida had disappeared, for the most part. No longer, it seemed, would the concerns of South Florida Catholicism revolve around too little money and too few Catholics, institutions, structures, and personnel. As Bishop Fitzpatrick said in 1968 upon his ordination as the first auxiliary bishop of Miami, the future tasks of South Florida Catholicism would center on two basic issues: the implementation of Vatican II and the attempt to build a Christian community (not just buildings, institutions, or structures) out of a divergent and diverse people.[71]

In 1968, the razing of the remains of the Convent of Mary Immaculate in Key West symbolized the end of a decade and the end of a century of Catholicism in South Florida. The cross that Menéndez de Avilés planted on the shores of Biscayne Bay in 1567 now gleamed in the tropical sun for all to see, yet the power of that image was still to be realized.

Conclusion

That Catholicism in South Florida grew and developed between 1868 and 1968 is a fact that may be measured by statistical evidence and organizational structures. That Catholicism developed from a frontier church to an archdiocesan Church is also demonstrable by examining the episcopacy, the diocesan priesthood, religious, laity, and parochial and extraparochial organizations. What is impossible to measure is the quality of that growth and development, how well it achieved the purpose for which the external quantitative elements exist—deepening the faith life of believers. Any human science, history included, can measure only the measurable. Intangibles such as the level of faith can only be perceived indirectly, "through a glass darkly" by means of tangibles.

Identity is another intangible, and the story of the growth and development of Catholicism in South Florida from 1868 to 1968 deals with the evolution of an identity, a particular kind described by Vatican II as the "local or particular Church" (*Lumen gentium*, 23; *Christus Dominus*, 11; *Ad gentes divinitus*, 19–20). Catholicism is never found in the abstract, except in theology books. As Pope Paul VI wrote in his Apostolic Exhortation, *Evangelii nuntiandi*:

Nevertheless, this universal Church is in practice incarnate in the individual Churches made up of such and such an actual

226

part of mankind, speaking such and such a language, heirs to
a cultural patrimony, of a vision of the world, of an historical
past, of a particular human substratum. . . . In the mind of
the Lord, the Church is universal by vocation and mission,
but when she puts down her roots in a variety of cultural, social and human terrains, she takes on different external expression and appearances in each part of the world.[1]

Identity can be discovered by comparison, by connection, by
similarities and differences, by continuity and discontinuity. This
study was not meant to be comparative, even though points of
comparison were often made. The history of Catholicism in South
Florida is uniquely its own, although it shares in the history of
American Catholicism and universal Catholicism. In the one hundred years studied, each period had its own characteristics: frontier
Catholicism (1565–1870), pioneer Catholicism (1868–1914), Catholicism under nativism and the tropical depression (1914–40),
Catholicism of vision and pragmatic implementation (1940–58),
Catholicism of Cuban exiles, institutional development and transition (1958–68). Yet threads of continuity ran through all the
periods: the influence of South Florida's geography (peninsular
and subtropical); the influence of Hispanic and southern culture,
direct and indirect; and the influence of poverty upon the local
Church.

What characterized the life of the local Church in South Florida
over the century 1868–1968 was its missionary quality. Although
there is no universally applicable definition of the word *missionary*
in Roman Catholic usage, in the context of South Florida the term
may be broadly defined as a place where the Church had not been
established. The Church in this region was missionary primarily
in that it was poor, unestablished in the full sense, and unable to
sustain itself during most of the century under study. South Florida Catholicism lacked money, personnel, institutions, organizational structures, native vocations, and adherents. Only in the last
ten years of that century did poverty, in all of its broad aspects,
cease to be an immediate preoccupation. The Church was also
missionary in light of the increasingly intense migration and immigration throughout that century. American blacks moved in
with the growth of the railroad and other work opportunities;
American whites moved in from the North and Midwest, espe-

cially after World War II. Hispanics from Cuba settled in numbers at Key West after 1868, Hispanics from South America, Mexico, and Puerto Rico from World War II on, and Hispanics from Cuba again as exiles from 1959. This gradual change in Catholic population reached a crescendo after World War II, and the challenges it posed formed the character of the local Church.

These developments created instability and a lack of roots on many levels yet also required flexibility in problem solving. Priests, religious, and laity coming to serve in South Florida soon discovered the uniqueness of the local Church. That which was imported without regard for the environment generally did not last. That which was transplanted to South Florida soil usually grew, rooting itself in its new environment to become part of the local landscape.

In such a missionary situation the importance of leadership is undisputed. The missionary bishops of Florida were indispensable in channeling and increasing the meager resources of a nascent Church. Their leadership, vision, and pastoral energies gave Catholicism its direction, its purpose, its goals, and to some extent its identity. The ordinary was the connection of South Florida Catholicism with Rome and universal Catholicism, past and present. But other individuals also made an impact on the character and direction of the local Church: the selfless dedication of multitudes of priests, religious, and lay people during the century under study contributed to the eventual flourishing of the Church of Miami.

When Pedro Menéndez de Avilés planted the cross on the shores of Key Biscayne, all indications pointed to the futility of such an endeavor. His action was motivated not simply by immediate military considerations but by a nationalistic and religious confidence. Although the Spanish mission on Key Biscayne was short lived, the missionary cross was picked up almost three centuries later by Bishop Verot and his successors, Bishop Carroll, Mother Alice, OSF, Mother Gerald, OP, Sr. Aquinas, SSJ, Monsignor William Barry, Bishop Román, Mr. Edward R. Bradley. In spite of a continual poverty of resources, it was confidence in the Church, in the power of the message of the Gospel and the Cross, that motivated bishops, diocesan priests, religious men and women, and laity not just to preserve the Catholic faith but to assist in its development.

Around 1968, the missionary situation of South Florida altered, and so did the underlying confidence that had hitherto provided the impetus to missioners and faithful. As Americans, Catholics were affected by the anti-authoritarianism and corporate self-doubt created by the racial crisis and the Vietnam War. At the same time, ecclesial authority was brought into question by the birth control issue; rapid changes in the liturgy, in piety, and in the image of priests and sisters eroded the former Tridentine model of devotional Catholicism, reinforcing the sense of change and unsettledness.

The disillusionment created by the "spiritual earthquake" of the post–Vatican II era has been the most serious change in South Florida Catholicism in the last one hundred years. It is a crisis of confidence that is still acting itself out. Sir Kenneth Clark, in his perceptive work *Civilisation*, has some thoughts pertinent to this Catholic identity crisis with regard to modernity. You do not have to be young to dislike institutions or want to abolish them, he says, "but the dreary fact remains that, even in the darkest ages, it was institutions that made society work." The Church as an institution is at the core of Western civilization. The Church, as well as other institutions, must be made to work if civilization is to survive. As Clark comments, "I said in the beginning that it is a lack of confidence, more than anything else, that kills a civilization. We can destroy ourselves by cynicism and disillusion, just as effectively as by bombs."[2]

It is not that good people do not have convictions but rather that they have too many of them. An infinite number of choices and questions has left us reeling—uprooted, unfocused, with no center. How American Catholicism and Catholicism in South Florida ultimately deal with the erosion of confidence will determine the future of Catholicism in South Florida. Knowing what challenges our predecessors met and overcame, we can be optimistic, yet the prospect before us is sobering.

Abbreviations in the Notes
and Bibliography

AAB	Archives of the Archdiocese of Baltimore
AADS	Archives of the Adrian Dominican Sisters (Adrian, Mich.)
AAP	Archives of the Archdiocese of Philadelphia
ACC	Archives of Carlow College (Pittsburgh, Pa.)
ACSA	Archives of the Carmelite Sisters for the Aged and Infirm (New York City)
ACSFN	Archives of the Sisters of the Holy Family of Nazareth (Torresdale, Pa.)
ACSFND	Archives of the Sisters of the Holy Family of Nazareth (Des Plaines, Ill.)
ACUA	Archives of the Catholic University of America (Washington, D.C.)
ADP	Archives of the Diocese of Pittsburgh
ADSA	Archives of the Diocese of St. Augustine (St. Augustine, Fla.)
ADSCR	Archives of the Dominican Sisters of St. Catherine de Ricci (Elkins Park, Pa.)
ADU	Archives of Duquesne University (Pittsburgh, Pa.)
AFAM	Archives and Files of the Archdiocese of Miami
AFM	Archives of the Henry Morrison Flagler Museum (Palm Beach, Fla.)

AFSC	Archives of the Christian Brothers (Lockport, Ill.)
AIHM	Archives of the Sisters, Servants of the Immaculate Heart of Mary (Immaculata, Pa.)
AIHMM	Archives of the Sisters, Servants of the Immaculate Heart of Mary (Monroe, Mich.)
AJF	Archives of the Josephite Fathers (Baltimore, Md.)
AOSP	Archives of the Oblate Sisters of Providence (Baltimore, Md.)
APF	Archbishop's Private Files (Miami, Fla.)
ARA	Archives of the Religious of the Assumption (Philadelphia, Pa.)
ASB	Archives of the Sisters of Social Service (Buffalo, N.Y.)
ASC	Archives of the Sisters of Charity of St. Elizabeth (Convent Station, N.J.)
ASHN	Archives of the Sisters of the Holy Names of Jesus and Mary (Albany, N.Y.)
ASM	Archives of the Sisters of Mercy (Enniskillen, Northern Ireland)
ASSF	Archives of the Sisters of St. Francis (Allegheny, N.Y.)
ASSFJ	Archives of the Sisters of St. Francis (Joliet, Ill.)
ASSJ	Archives of the Sisters of St. Joseph of St. Augustine (St. Augustine, Fla.)
ASSND	Archives of the School Sisters of Notre Dame (Baltimore, Md.)
ASVA	Archives of St. Vincent Archabbey (Latrobe, Pa.)
AVF	Archives of the Vincentian Fathers (Jamaica Plains, N.Y.)
CCD	Confraternity of Christian Doctrine
CO	Chancellor's Office
CUA	The Catholic University of America
DCCM	Diocesan Council of Catholic Men
DCCW	Diocesan Council of Catholic Women
FSVDP	Files of St. Vincent de Paul Regional Seminary (Boynton Beach, Fla.)
NCCB	National Catholic Conference of Bishops
NCWC	National Catholic Welfare Conference
OBRA	Obra de Cooperación Sacerdotal Hispano
OCD	Official Catholic Directory
OCSHA	Obra de Cooperación Sacerdotal Hispano

SBCC   St. Brendan Convent Chronicles of the Sisters of the
         Holy Family of Nazareth (Miami, Fla.)
SJV–SC   St. John Vianney College Seminary Library, Special
         Collections (Miami, Fla.)
USBC   United States Bureau of the Census

Notes

Chapter 1

[1] Eugene Lyon, *The Enterprise of Florida*, pp. 49, 43–44; Michael V. Gannon, *Cross in the Sand*, pp. 20–31. St. Augustine was founded forty years before Jamestown. Santiago de Cuba was the only diocese in nearby Cuba at the time. From the beginning, St. Augustine had close political, social, economic, and ecclesial ties with Cuba. For a partial list of all priests who were assigned to St. Augustine from 1565, see *Los Cumpleaños de San Augustin* (1940), pp. 15–16. Extant parish records in St. Augustine date from 1594. ADSA, *Baptisms, Marriages, Burials*, 1:1594–1638.

[2] Jesuits first came to Florida in 1566. Gannon, *Cross in the Sand*, pp. 29, 32.

[3] Félix Zubillaga, S.J., *La Florida*, pp. 296–97. Most of the pertinent documents can be found in Félix Zubillaga, ed., *Monumenta Antiquae Floridae, 1566–72*. For more recent works on Menéndez and the Jesuit missions, see Lyon, *The Enterprise of Florida*; Robert Allen Matter, "Defense of Spanish Florida."

[4] Zubillaga, *La Florida*, pp. 301–2, 350. For more on the Tequesta, see John M. Goggin, "Tekesta Indians of South Florida." The Jesuits were pulled completely out of Florida in 1572. For some more recent anthropological studies on Miami, see Bert Mowers, Wilma Williams, Mark Green, and Wesley Coleman, "The Arch Creek Site"; Wesley Coleman, "Site DA-141, Dade Co., Fla."; and D. D. Laxton, "The Dupont Plaza Site."

[5] *The Jesuits in Florida*, p. 9; Michael Kenny, CSSR, *The Romance of the Floridas*, pp. 337–38.

[6] Florida had a mission system for American Indians as did Spanish colonial Texas, Arizona–New Mexico, and California. For more on the Florida Franciscan missions, see Gannon, *Cross in the Sand*, pp. 49–83; Zelia Sweet and Mary H.

Sheppy, *The Spanish Missions of Florida*; Maynard Gieger, OFM, *The Franciscan Conquest of Florida*; Mark F. Boyd, Hale G. Smith, and John W. Griffin, *Here They Once Stood*. Some more recent studies include Robert A. Matter, "The Spanish Mission of Florida"; B. Calvin Jones, "Col. James Moore"; Robert A. Matter, "Seventeenth-Century Florida Missions"; Fred Lamar Pearson, Jr., "Spanish-Indian Relations in Florida."

[7] Gannon, *Cross in the Sand*, p. 83. This fact says as much about the British as it does about the Spanish. The British took the position that Church property in fact belonged to the Spanish crown (*patronato real*) and therefore could be conveyed to the British government. For more on the fate of Catholics during the British period, see pp. 86–90; also Jane Quinn, *Minorcans in Florida*.

[8] Don Juan McQueen, *Letters*, pp. 64–65, 81; Charlton Tebeau, *A History of Florida*, pp. 114–15.

[9] Tebeau, *A History of Florida*, pp. 162–70, 193–95; the war left one hundred to three hundred Indians in the southern Everglades (p. 170). For more on the Second Seminole War, see Kenneth Wiggins Porter, "Florida Slaves"; and John K. Mahon, *Second Seminole War*. For drawings and descriptions of the Florida Cracker cowboy in the latter part of the nineteenth century, see Frederic Remington, *Crooked Trails*, pp. 116–26.

[10] ADSA, Verot Papers: 1(x)-A-28, Decree of Pius IX creating the Vicariate Apostolic of Florida, January 9, 1857; 1(x)-A-31, Papal Bull of Appointment to the Florida Vicariate, December 11, 1857. See also Michael V. Gannon, *Rebel Bishop*, p. 25; Gannon, *Cross in the Sand*, pp. 49–162.

[11] AAB, Spalding Papers, 36-G-7, Verot to Spalding, May 24, 1866. For a review of Verot at Vatican Council I, see Gannon, *Rebel Bishop*, pp. 192–227.

[12] ADSA, Verot Papers, 1(x)-G-9, Papal Bull, Pius IX, erecting the Diocese of St. Augustine, March 11, 1870. On that same date the Pope issued a directive transferring the Bishop of Savannah (Verot) to the See of St. Augustine (ibid., 1(x)-G-10). See also USBC, *Abstract, 1970*, pp. 165–66, 176–86; *Rand McNally Road Atlas*, p. 20; *OCD-1950*, p. 517.

[13] USBC, *Historical Census*, pp. 12–13; *Sadlier's Catholic Directory–1877*, p. 369.

[14] ADSA, Verot Papers: 1-B-20, Persico to Verot, October 31, 1871; 1-C-1, Persico to Verot, November 9, 1871; 1-D-19, Verot to Secretary of Propaganda (draft in Latin), July 27, 1875. The SSJs in Georgia were designated a diocesan community for Savannah in 1874 (ASSJ, "Women Religious Archives Survey," Exhibit C).

Chapter 2

[1] Gannon, *Rebel Bishop*, pp. 1–25, 63–64, 228–32, 247.

[2] Ibid., pp. 20–21; the quote is taken from a letter of Verot to Très Honoré Père, February 4, 1858, found in the Archives of the Society of St. Sulpice in Paris. See also ADSA, Verot Papers: 1(x)-B-4, Fr. Carrier, Superior of St. Sulpice, Paris, to Bp. Purcell of Cincinnati, April 1, 1858; 1(x)-A-29, Arch. Francis P. Kenrick of Baltimore to Verot, May 5, 1857.

[3] Henri P. Clavreul, "The Late Bishop Vero."

[4] Ibid.

[5] Gannon, *Rebel Bishop*, p. 25. For a description of St. Augustine c. 1856, see George R. Fairbanks, *History and Antiques of St. Augustine.*

[6] AAB, Kenrick Papers, 32-D-2, Verot to Kenrick, October 23, 1858. Four hundred dollars had been collected (ibid., 32-D-5, Verot to Kenrick, September 18, 1860).

[7] Gannon, *Rebel Bishop*, pp. 31–164. Verot offers prayers of thanks for Confederate victories (ADSA, Verot Papers, 1(x)-C-30, *Savannah Morning News* (photostat), September [no day] 1862); he defends the Church's role in the war (ADSA, Verot Papers, 1(y)-C-19, *St. Augustine Examiner* (photostat), 20 April 1867); Verot decorates the graves of the Confederate dead making mention of the "Lost Cause" (ADSA, Verot Papers, 1(x)-H-20, *Daily News and Herald* (photostat), Savannah, April 27, 1868). Verot once again wished to decline in 1861 the episcopal office (Gannon, *Rebel Bishop*, pp. 63–64).

[8] Tebeau, *A History of Florida*, pp. 203, 209, 212–238.

[9] Ibid., pp. 208–18. In 1860, there were 77,747 whites and 61,745 blacks in Florida: Ira Berlin, *Slaves Without Masters*, pp. 398–99; Thomas Wentworth Higginson, *Army Life in a Black Regiment*, pp. 54, 200–208. For more on the War between the States, see Emory M. Thomas, *The Confederate Nation*; John E. Johns, *Florida During the Civil War*; John B. Heffernan, "Blockade of the Southern Confederacy"; Ovid L. Futch, *History of Andersonville Prison*; George Robbins, ed., *Diary of Rev. H. Clavreul.*

[10] Tebeau, *History of Florida*, pp. 252, 264. The decline of property values was due more to wear and neglect than to property destruction by invasion (pp. 257–58). See also Jerrell H. Shofner, *Nor Is It Over Yet*; Berlin, *Slaves Without Masters*; C. Vann Woodward, *Strange Career of Jim Crow*; Leon F. Litwack, *In the Storm So Long.*

[11] Tebeau, *History of Florida*, pp. 257, 271–72.

[12] AAB, Spalding Papers, 36-G-6, Verot to Spalding, January 30, 1866; ADSA, Verot Papers: 1(x)-E-3, Verot to Spalding (copy), February 27, 1866; 1(y)-B-16, Verot to Patrick Lynch, Bishop of Charleston, (copy), April 16, 1866. See also Gannon, *Rebel Bishop*, p. 147.

[13] Gannon, *Rebel Bishop*, p. 17.

[14] This sermon was delivered January 4, 1861. Bp. Verot sent the manuscript to Baltimore for publication. See Rt. Rev. Augustin Verot, *A Tract for the Times*; Gannon, *Rebel Bishop*, pp. 31–55; Michael V. Gannon, "Verot and Slavery," pp. 67–69. Verot explains to Arch. Kenrick of Baltimore that his sermon is in the context of the formation of the Southern Confederacy and the plight of black Americans: "It would do a great service to the negroes and to religion in general, if some social, moral, and religious improvement were obtained for our poor slaves of our plantations." Verot mentions that he is particularly concerned about fostering conditions for the possibility of stable black marriages and disallowing the breakup of families through sale. Verot submitted a proof copy of his manuscript to his metropolitan, Kenrick, for approval (AAB, Kenrick Papers, 32-D-6, Verot to Kenrick, January 18, 1861).

[15] ADSA, Verot Papers, 1(y)-C-11, *St. Augustine Examiner* (photostat), January 26, 1867. See Section XII of the Pastoral Letter of 1866 in Peter Guilday, ed., *National Pastorals*, pp. 220–21.

[16] Gannon, "Verot and Slavery," p. 69; Gannon, *Rebel Bishop*, p. 136.

[17] Tebeau, *History of Florida*, pp. 264–65. See also Bruce Rosen, "Negro Education in Florida."

[18] Bp. Verot was the ordinary of Savannah at the time: ADSA, Verot Papers, 1(y)-B-14, Verot to Bp. Le Breton (copy), September 3, 1866.

[19] Gannon, "Verot and Slavery," p. 69.

[20] AAB, Spalding Papers, 39B-G-23, Verot to Spalding, October 13, 1865; ADSA, Verot Papers, 1(x)-E-25, Verot to Lynch (copy), October 1, 1868.

[21] ADSA, Verot Papers, 1(y)-D-4, *St. Augustine Examiner* (photostat), February 22, 1868. Another article from a contemporary Catholic newspaper mentions that Protestants attended the mission and twenty became Catholics. The CSSRs also gave a mission in Jacksonville (Verot Papers, 1(y)-D-19, *The Morning Star and Catholic Messenger*, New Orleans [photostat], May 24, 1868). For more on Catholic parish missions in the nineteenth century, see Jay P. Dolan, *Catholic Revivalism*. The CSSRs gave missions throughout the South during the postwar period. Bp. Verot praised the 1868 CSSR mission: "We cannot enumerate the solid and substantial good that has been accomplished by the mission. God alone knows the number of sinners that have been reconciled. . . . Many invalid and dubious marriages have been rehabilitated." Bp. Verot's Pastoral Letter, April 5, 1868, quoted in Vincent McMurry, "The Catholic Church During Reconstruction," p. 105.

[22] David Page, ed., *Peregrini Pro Christo*, p. 5. Moore was deeply concerned with the "Germanization" of the American Church: AAB, Gibbons Papers: 79-O-11, Moore to Gibbons, July 15, 1885; 79-S-2, Moore and Gilmour to Gibbons, October 3, 1885; 82-G-8, Gilmour to Moore, December 10, 1886; 82-H-6, Moore to Gibbons, December 19, 1886. For his opinions on the McGlynn case, see ibid.: 82-L-10, Moore to Gibbons, January 15, 1882; 83-J-8, Burtsell to Moore, August 31, 1887; 83-K-2, Moore to Gibbons, September 2, 1887; 83-K-4, Burtsell to Moore, September 3, 1887.

[23] AAB, Gibbons Papers: 83-G-12, Moore to Gibbons, August 17, 1887; 85-K-4, Moore to Gibbons, December 3, 1888; ADSA, Moore Papers: 2-N-17, Moore to Pace, May 11, 1887; 2-P-13, James Renwick, architect, to W. T. Cotter, builder (copy), September 10, 1888.

[24] AAB, Gibbons Papers, 77-I-2, Moore to Gibbons, July 5, 1883.

[25] Ibid., 75-M-2, Moore to Gibbons, November 2, 1880; ACUA, Pace Papers, Edward Pace, "Program for a Series of Lectures on 'The Origin of Human Rights,'" January 20, 1920; Benedict Roth, OSB, ed., *History of the Diocese*, Fr. Clavreul's "Diary," January 11, 1866, p. 60; ACUA, Pace Papers, Pace to Benedict Roth (copy), January 7, 1923 (actually 1924). For more details on Pace's family and early boyhood in Starke, see Pace Papers, "Commemorative Booklet of the 25th Anniversary of the Death of Edward A. Pace—1963," pp. 1–13; 19–22; ACUA, Moore to O'Connell (copy from Diocese of Richmond Archives), October 30, 1886; ADSA, Moore Papers, 2-N-15, Moore to Pace, April 25, 1887.

[26] ACUA, Pace Papers, Moore to O'Connell (copy from Richmond Archives), February 22, 1888.

[27] Pace's 73-page doctoral dissertation was titled: "Das Relativitätsprincip in Herbert Spencer's psychologischer Entwicklungslehre" (Leipzig, 1891): ACUA,

Pace Papers: Henry J. Browne, "Pioneer Days, Part II"; "Commemorative of the Death of Pace," pp. 27–28; Patrick H. Ahern, *Catholic University*.

[28] Walter J. Smith, "Msgr. Pace and Scientific Psychology," pp. 31–33. In the United States, the study of psychology as a science began at Harvard in 1874 and Johns Hopkins in 1883. The Catholic University of America began teaching psychology in 1891 and had the only Department of Psychology in any American Catholic institution of learning for many years.

[29] ACUA, Pace Papers, Pace to Gibbons (copy), January 27, 1919. Pace wrote the section on education (ibid., Pace to O'Connell (copy), December 19, 1919). For the complete Pastoral, see Guilday, *National Pastorals*, pp. 266–340.

[30] ACUA, Pace Papers: Ernest Laplace, M.D., of Philadelphia, to Pace, July 23, 1920; Gibbons to Pace, August 25, 1920; Pace to Fr. Mike [?] (copy), June 14, 1935; Maurice S. Sheehy, "Last Days of Msgr. Pace." No book-length biography of Pace has been published, but two unpublished works exist: ACUA, Pace Papers, J. K. Ryan, "Unpublished Notes"; William P. Braun, "Pace."

[31] Extern priests provided a steady, though unstable, supplement of personnel (ADSA, Moore Papers, 2-P-17, Moore to Pace, May 10, 1889).

[32] Most of the Italian priests stayed for brief periods, but Fr. Felix Ghione served in Florida in 1871–97, and Fr. Dominique A. G. Battalaccio served in 1876–1920 (Roth, "History of the Diocese," pp. 109–10). See also *Sadlier's Catholic Directory—1871*, pp. 281–82; *Sadlier's Catholic Directory—1878*, pp. 376–79.

[33] Gannon, *Cross in the Sand*, p. 45; Page, *Peregrini Pro Christo*, pp. 2–3. Before 1858, fifteen Irish-born priests had served in Florida, the first, Richard Arthur, from 1598 to 1606. Fr. William Hamilton was at Immaculate Conception Church in Jacksonville when Verot arrived in 1858 (Page, pp. 3–4). Bp. Kenny praised six priests of his diocese who were Mungret alumnae, attending there in the 1890s (ADSA, Kenny Papers, 3-G-13, Kenny to E. Cahill, Director of the Apostolic School, Mungret College (copy), November 28, 1905; OCD-1902, pp. 494–98).

[34] This event took place November 23, 1899 (*Living Waters*, p. 10). Needless to say, this rupture created a tremendous crisis within the community, with some sisters deciding to return to Le Puy (Jane Quinn, *The Story of a Nun*, p. 83).

[35] Jurisdiction of St. Leo's in San Antonio, Florida, shifted from St. Vincent's to Belmont Abbey, N.C., in 1889 (Jeremiah O'Mahoney, ed., *Fides*, p. 47). Bp. Moore gave permission for the Benedictines to reside in San Antonio *in perpetuum* for the care of souls (ADSA, Moore Papers, 2-A-9, Boniface Wimmer, Abbot, St. Vincent Abbey, to Moore, March 21, 1887). There was already a settlement at San Antonio from 1883; see Edmund F. Dunne, *Our American Sicily*; George E. Pozzetta, "Foreigners in Florida."

[36] SJV-SC: Moore to O'Shanahan, Provincial of the New Orleans Province of the Society of Jesus (copy), April 15, 1889; Contract (copy), Moore and O'Shanahan, July 31, 1889.

[37] SJV-SC: Moore to Cardinal Simeoni, Cardinal Prefect of Propaganda Fidei in Rome (copies), July 31, October 15, 1889; Simeoni to Moore (copy), August 30, 1889; Contract (copy), Moore and O'Shanahan, September 3, 1891.

[38] McMurry, "The Catholic Church During Reconstruction," pp. 130–38; AAB, Gibbons Papers: 73-F-8, Moore to Gibbons, October 9, 1877; 73-I-7, Moore to Gibbons, November 20, 1877; 85-K-4, Moore to Gibbons, December 3, 1888;

ADSA, Moore Papers, 2-P-16, James Renwick of New York City, to Moore, November 3, 1888; *The Jesuits in Florida*, pp. 11–13; Edward Reynolds, *Jesuits for the Negro*, p. 181; *Hoffman's Catholic Directory—1889*, p. 373.

[39] ADSA, Moore Papers, 2-P-17, Moore to Pace, May 10, 1889. When Bp. Moore initially asked the Jesuits for help, he specifically asked for a Spanish-speaking priest (*The Jesuits in Florida*, pp. 12–13).

[40] SJV-SC, Moore to Rev. Fr. Provincial of the Jesuits, Castile, Spain (copy), March 31, 1891.

[41] SJV-SC, Fr. De Carriere, SJ, to Moore (copy), April 14, 1893.

[42] Joseph B. Code, *Dictionary of the American Hierarchy*, pp. 180–81; ADSA, Moore Papers, 1(y)-D-7, Kenny to Moore, January 1, 1885.

[43] ADSA, Kenny Papers: 3(x)-R-2, Kenny to all parish rectors, February 7, 1905; 3(z)-C-19, Rev. J. S. Budds, Diocese of Charleston, to Kenny, January 27, 1909; 3(z)-D-5, Kenny to all priests, January 22, 1913.

[44] ADSA, Kenny Papers: 3-C-1, Drexel to Kenny, April 20, 1903; 3-R-12, Report, Kenny to Dyer, October 1, 1911; 3(x)-R-6, Rev. Francis Kelly, President, to Kenny, June 17, 1909. Kenny sued, in the name of the diocese and as corporate sole, for damages to Immaculate Conception Church during the War between the States in 1864. He also sued for claims on the former Franciscan Monastery. He was not successful with either suit (ibid.: 3(y)-B-2, Kenny to James Hayday, Attorney, Washington, D.C. [copy], August 6, 1906; 3(y)-D-19, Kenny to Rev. M. P. Foley, February 25, 1909).

[45] Ibid.: 3(z)-D-11, J. Butler, OFM, to Kenny, September 15, 1903; 3(z)-M-7, Butler to Kenny, May 13, 1907; 3-B-6, Rev. J. McQuirk, St. Paul's Rectory, N.Y.C., Pres. and Treas. of Henry McCalden, Jr. Fund for the Education of Candidates for Roman Catholic Priesthood in Poorer Diocese in the U.S., to Kenny, August 5, 1902.

[46] Interview, Msgr. Thomas O'Donovan.

[47] ADSA, Kenny Papers: 3-G-12, Cahill to Kenny, November 16, 1905; 3(z)-E-25, Cahill to Kenny, October 26, 1912; 3(z)-G-13, Curley to Kenny, February 4, 1903; 3(z)-D-16, St. Mary's Seminary to Kenny, June 21, 1906; 3(z)-H-5, St. Mary's Seminary to Kenny, November 7, 1911. William Turner, Michael Curley, and Patrick Barry were Irish priests of the diocese who became bishops. The latter two served as Florida bishops, while Turner became the bishop of Buffalo, 1919–36 (Code, *Dictionary of American Hierarchy*, pp. 342–43). Bp. Kenny praised his Irish priests in 1905 (Kenny Papers, 3-G-13, Kenny to Cahill [copy], November 28, 1905).

[48] ADSA, 3(a)-N-8, Sr. Euphemia, SSJ, superior of the SSJs presently at Mercy Convent, Kilbereen, Ireland, to Kenny, August 14, 1904.

[49] ADSA, Kenny Papers, 3-C-1, Mother Drexel to Kenny, April 20, 1903. The SSJs taught black children in a house on their property before St. Benedict the Moor School opened in 1890 (Roth, *History of the Diocese*, pp. 26–27). Members of the black Catholic community in St. Augustine had their roots in Spanish Colonial times. They had been assigned special seats in the cathedral but preferred their own church (ADSA, Kenny Papers: 3(z)-B-5, E. R. Dyer, Secretary of the Commission of Catholic Missions among Colored People and Indians, to Kenny, October 6, 1903; 3-M-5. Fr. Augustine, OSB, to Kenny, April 17, 1907; *The Georgia Bulletin*, May 7, 1932). The SSJs taught in five of the black schools; the

Holy Names taught in two, one being in Key West (Kenny Papers, 3-R-12, Report, Kenny to E. R. Dyer [copy], October 1, 1911).

⁵⁰Fr. Walter Elliott, CSP, promoted the crusade to "win America for Christ" by urging bishops to organize their own mission bands. By 1900, twenty-five dioceses had such groups. The Apostolic Mission House was opened in 1904, at Catholic University. As Jay Dolan states, "By the turn of the century the non-Catholic mission was emerging as a prominent feature of American Catholicism" (*Catholic Revivalism*, pp. 51–52). ADSA, Kenny Papers: 3(z)-G-21, Bresnahan to Kenny, December 19, 1903: 3(x)-P-16, booklet, "The Apostolic Mission House and Its Course of Study."

⁵¹P. J. Bresnahan, *Seeing Florida with a Priest*, p. 9; ADSA, Kenny Papers, 3-E-10, Abbot Carl, OSB, to Kenny, September 9, 1905. Fr. Aloysius was ordained in May, 1903 (ibid., 3-C-6, Abbot Mohr to Kenny, May 25, 1903).

⁵²ADSA, Kenny Papers: 3(z)-G-23, Bresnahan to Kenny, November 26, 1904, and 41 letters, November 26, 1904, through June 16, 1910.

⁵³Ibid., 3-M-17, Bresnahan to Kenny, February 19, 1908; Bresnahan, *Seeing Florida With a Priest*, p. 76.

⁵⁴ADSA, Kenny Papers, 3-H-2, Bresnahan to Kenny, January 12, 1906.

⁵⁵Ibid., 3-M-22, Doyle to Kenny, May 13, 1908.

⁵⁶Bresnahan, *Seeing Florida with a Priest*, pp. 61–64.

⁵⁷Tebeau, *A History of Florida*, pp. 147–48; Roth, *History of the Diocese*, p. 29; *Rand McNally Road Atlas*, p. 20; USBC: *Population, 1950, Vol. I*, p. 10-18; *Historical*, pp. 12–13, 66.

⁵⁸In four years (November 1852–56) six Savannah priests were assigned to Key West; Bp. John Barry of Savannah confirmed there in 1857 (Roth, *History of the Diocese*, pp. 28–31).

⁵⁹Ibid., p. 172; ASHN, Introduction to the Key West Chronicles (translation), Verot to Bp. Bouget of Montreal (quoted), February 27, 1868. Since the sisters were at this time a diocesan community and remained so until 1877, Bp. Verot needed to get permission and made arrangements for the sisters to come through the ordinary of Montreal. Also, Fr. Allard acted as the novice master at the founding of the sisters' community on November 1, 1843 (L. S. Flintham, *The Key West Convent-Hospital*, pp. 6–8; ASHN, Key West Chronicles [translation], October 15, 1868).

⁶⁰The sisters had stayed in New York City before traveling by boat to Key West, thus enhancing the contrast of cities (ASHN, Introduction to the Key West Chronicles [translation], October 24, 1868).

⁶¹On December 8, 1868, Mallory deeded the barracks and land to Bp. Verot who in turn deeded it to the sisters (ASHN, Key West Chronicles [translation], October 24, 1868; August 18, 1868—Synoptical Table). For more on Stephen Mallory, see Tebeau, *A History of Florida*, pp. 218–19; Joseph T. Durkin, *Stephen R. Mallory*.

⁶²Jan Kippers Black et al., *Area Handbook for Cuba*, pp. 36–37; Flintham, *Convent-Hospital*, p. 8. See also Gerald E. Poyo, "Cuban Revolutionaries"; Gerald E. Poyo, "Cuban Ten Years War."

⁶³Roth, *History of the Diocese*, p. 31; ADSA, Verot Papers: 1-D-13, La Rocque to Verot, May 24, 1876; 1(x)-H-14, *Morning Star and Catholic Messenger*, New Orleans (photostat), June 20, 1875.

[64] Flintham, *Convent-Hospital*, pp. 11–14.

[65] Roth, *History of the Diocese*, p. 110; Fr. Flaget to [?], May 18, 1898, quoted in *Jesuits in Florida*, p. 33; ADSA, Moore Papers, 2(y)-C-23, Ghione in Gorrino, Italy, to Moore, December 20, 1897.

[66] *Jesuits in Florida*, p. 36; Roth, *History of the Diocese*, p. 31. ADSA, Kenny Papers: 3(z)-N-23, "Monthly Collections and Pew Rents of Catholics of Key West from October 1, 1901, to July 10, 1905"; 3(z)-N-25, Friend to Kenny, January 8, 1906. The financial arrangements must have been particularly salutary because by January 1911, Fr. Friend reported to the Bishop that the parish had deposits and bank notes totaling $24,000, approximating then the cost of construction and furnishing the church (ibid., 3(z)-P-9, notitiae, January 1, 1911).

[67] ADSA, Kenny Papers, 3-K-5, Friend to Kenny, September 1, 1906.

[68] ADSA, Verot Papers, 1-G-5, La Rocque to Verot, September 24, 1876; ADSA, Kenny Papers, Fr. Clinger, SJ, to Kenny, June 8, 1908.

[69] The Apostleship of Prayer was started by a Jesuit in France in 1844 as a spiritual association. There were three "dues and duties" of membership: daily offering of all their works and joys to the Sacred Heart of Jesus, Mass and communion at least once a month, and daily recitation of the rosary.

[70] ADSA, Verot Papers, 1(y)-N-10, *St. Augustine Examiner* (photostat), February 17, 1872. "Fr. Dufau is gone to the Indians out of the pale of civilization," wrote Bp. Verot (ibid., 1(x)-H-4, Verot to Gibbons [copy] February 12, 1872). See also *The Florida Catholic*, August 2, 1963; Gannon, *Rebel Bishop*, pp. 238–40; Roth, *History of the Diocese*, pp. 265, 177; Verot Papers, 1(x)-H-2, Clavreul to Members of the Council of the Propagation of the Faith, Lyon, France, August 19, 1872. For more about the Miami of the period, see Arva Moore Parks, "Miami in 1876"; Harry A. Kersey, Jr., *Pelts, Plumes, and Hides*. The Wagner chapel remained on the family property until 1894, when after nineteen years a fire destroyed the structure (Roth, *History of the Diocese*, pp. 165–66; ADSA, Moore Papers, 2-N-11, Moore to Propaganda, September 3, 1886). For more on the Wagners, see Margot Ammidown, "The Wagner Family."

[71] Tebeau, *History of Florida*, pp. 191–92, 230–35, 271, 281–82, 295. See also Edward C. Williamson, *Florida Politics*.

[72] Tebeau, *History of Florida*, pp. 283–84, 87. See also Sidney W. Martin, *Florida's Flagler*; Edward N. Akin, "Sly Foxes." For a primary account of Palm Beach County before Flagler, see Charles W. Pierce, *Pioneer Life*.

[73] Tebeau, *History of Florida*, p. 287. See also Henry S. Marks, "Labor Problems"; Paul S. George, "Passage to the New Eden," p. 443.

[74] Tebeau, *History of Florida*, pp. 314, 320–26. See also Donna Thomas, "Camp Hell"; Thelma Peters, *Lemon City*; William J. Schellings, "The Role of Florida"; Roth, *History of the Diocese*, pp. 261–65, 268; *Jesuits in Florida*, pp. 26–27; ADSA, Moore Papers, 2(a)-P-8, *Lake Worth News* (photostat), March 26, 1896.

[75] Roth, *History of the Diocese*, pp. 266–69; *Jesuits in Florida*, pp. 28–29; ADSA: Moore Papers, 2(a)-T-3, notitiae, Holy Name, January 1, 1901; Kenny Papers: 3-G-7, Sr. Mary Euphemia, Superior of St. Catherine's Convent, to Kenny, September 13, 1905; 3-G-8, Kennedy to Kenny, September 14, 1905; 3-K-18, Kennedy to Kenny, February 21, 1907; 3-K-17, M. D. Barry to John Crimmons of N.Y.C., to Kenny, February 9, 1907.

[76] ADSA: Kenny Papers: 3(a)-G-2, notitiae, St. Ann, January 1, 1902, 1905, 1907; 3(b)-A-1, notitiae, Holy Name, January 1, 1906; Curley Papers: 4(c)-C-1, notitiae, St. Ann, January 1, 1915; 4(c)-C-2, notitiae, Holy Name, January 1, 1915.

[77] AAB, Gibbons Papers, 80-P-4, Moore to Gibbons, March 12, 1886. For another contemporary account of nineteenth century Cuban Catholicism, see Antonio María Clarét, *Escritos Autobiográficos y Espirituales*. See also Rafael Estenger, *Sincera Historia de Cuba*; Hugh Thomas, *Cuba*; Jaime Suchlicki, *Cuba*.

[78] ADSA, Verot Papers, 1(x)-H-14, *Morning Star and Catholic Messenger* (photostat), June 20, 1875.

[79] *Jesuits of Florida*, pp. 33–35; Gerald E. Royo, "Cuban Patriots in Key West," p. 29. For a description of the Cuban community in Ybor City in 1893 and the clergy's attempt to reach them, see ADSA, Moore Papers, 2(a)-M-11, William Tyrrell, SJ, to Moore, January 9, 1893.

[80] *Jesuits of Florida*, p. 35.

[81] ASHN, Key West Chronicles (translation), February 14, 1869; McMurry, "The Catholic Church During Reconstruction," p. 106.

[82] ADSA, Verot Papers, 1-A-2, La Rocque to Verot, March 29, 1875.

[83] ASHN, Key West Chronicles (translation), October 3, 1873.

[84] ADSA, Verot Papers, 1-A-2, La Rocque to Verot, March 29, 1875.

[85] ADSA, Moore Papers, 2(y)-D-1, Sisters of the Holy Names to Moore, June 1877.

[86] ASHN, Key West Chronicles (translation), September 2, 1878.

[87] ADSA, Kenny Papers, 3(z)-N-16, Friend to Kenny, March 28, 1904.

[88] ADSA: Verot Papers: 1(x)-H-14, *Morning Star and Catholic Messenger* (photostat), June 20, 1875; 1-D-13, La Rocque to Verot, May 24, 1876; Moore Papers: 2(y)-B-13, Ghione to Moore, September 29, 1879; 2(y)-C-21, notitiae, Key West, January 1, 1896.

[89] ADSA, Kenny Papers, 3(z)-N-19, Friend to Kenny, April 22, 1904.

[90] ASHN, Key West Chronicles (translation), March 7, 1870, September 30, 1875, September 4, 1876, January 1, 1877, August 27, 1962.

[91] ADSA, Kenny Papers, 3(z)-T-6, Friend to Kenny, November 18, 1904.

[92] For more, see Woodward, *Strange Career of Jim Crow*.

[93] AAB, Gibbons Papers, 77-A-3, Moore to Gibbons, January 4, 1883.

[94] Sr. T. J. McGoldrick, "The Contributions of the Sisters of St. Joseph of St. Augustine to Education, 1866–1960"; Sr. Mary Roselina O'Neill, "Sisters of the Holy Names"; ASHN, "Inventory of Materials from Mary Immaculate Convent," April, 1981.

[95] *Jesuits in Florida*, p. 31; ADSA: Kenny Papers, 3(z)-W-22, notitiae, St. Anastasia, January 1, 1913; Curley Papers: 4(c)-C-1, notitiae, St. Ann, January 1, 1915; 4(c)-C-2, notitiae, Holy Name, January 1, 1915.

Chapter 3

[1] USBC, *Historical Census*, pp. 12–13; USBC, *Abstract, 1970*, pp. 20–21. Key West long before World War I lost its two major industries—cigar-making to Tampa and sponge-fishing to Tarpon Springs. The boom left Key West relatively

untouched. By 1933, the city was $5 million in debt. In July 1934, the governor declared Key West in a state of emergency in order that it might be turned over to the FERA, who undertook to rehabilitate the city. The Labor Day hurricane of 1935 wiped out the overseas railroad originally constructed by Flagler. It was decided not to rebuild the railroad; instead, the overseas highway was built, completed in 1938. It took the economy of World War II to revive the island city. See Charlton W. Tebeau, *A History of Florida*, p. 404; Durwood Long, "Key West and the New Deal."

[2] Code, *Dictionary of the American Hierarchy*, p. 67; ADSA: interview, Msgr. William Barry; Kenny Papers, 3(b)-M-18, Minutes of Diocesan Consultors, October 25, 1913; Curley Papers, 4-A-10, Bonzano to O'Brien, April 3, 1914.

[3] AAB, Gibbons Papers, 139-J-4, Curley to Gibbons, January 29, 1921.

[4] ADSA: interviews, Msgr. William Barry and Msgr. John Tracy Ellis; Curley Papers, 4(d)-B-1, Report to Apostolic Delegate (copy), n.d. [c. 1914].

[5] AAB, Curley Papers, W-770, Curley to Wiesel (copy), January 6, 1943.

[6] Ibid., H-1697, Curley to Hurley (copy), March 31, 1944.

[7] Edward Cuddy, "Revival of Anti-Catholicism," p. 236.

[8] John Higham, *Strangers in the Land*, pp. 81, 178–79; Cuddy, "Revival of Anti-Catholicism"; Woodward, *Tom Watson*, p. 49; Page, "Curley and Nativism," p. 106.

[9] ADSA, Curley Papers, 4(x)-A-4, Curley to Pastors, January 28, 1915.

[10] Ibid.

[11] ADSA, Curley Papers, 4-G-22, Kittredge, Richards, Clark to R. E. Hall (copy), July 17, 1915. At this time Ft. Lauderdale and Miami were both in the Dade County school system; Broward County was not formed until late 1915.

[12] *Miami Daily Metropolis*, August 27, 1915.

[13] ADSA, Curley Papers, 4-H-12, Fr. James McLaughlin, SJ, to Curley, August 25, 1915; *Miami Herald*, August 26, 1915.

[14] McLaughlin bought 250 copies of that edition for distribution. ADSA, Curley Papers, 4-H-13, McLaughlin to Curley, August 28, 1915; *Miami Daily Metropolis*, letter to the editor by P. Disch, September 10, 1915.

[15] Page, "Curley and Nativism," pp. 109–10.

[16] ADSA, Curley Papers, 4(c)-B-34, Callahan to Abbot Mohr (copy), December 18, 1914. In fact, Catholic fisherman voted for Catts because of his anticonservation stand! Wayne Flynt, *Cracker Messiah*, pp. 57–61; Tebeau, *History of Florida*, pp. 362–63. Catts was born in Alabama in 1863 and moved to De Funiak Springs, Fl., in 1911, as pastor of the First Baptist Church. See also Page, "Curley and Nativism," pp. 112–17. For more detail on Catts and his political career, see Flynt, *Cracker Messiah*; Wayne Flynt, "Sidney J. Catts."

[17] *Miami Herald*, October 25, 1915.

[18] Bresnahan, *Seeing Florida with a Priest*, pp. 73–74.

[19] Tebeau, *History of Florida*, pp. 364–65.

[20] Chapter 6490 of the *Laws of Florida* (1913) reads: "*Section 1*. From and after the passage of this Act it shall be unlawful in the State for White teachers to teach negroes in negro schools, and for negro teachers to teach in White schools. *Section 2*. Any person, or persons, violating the provisions of this Act shall be punished by a fine not to exceed five hundred ($500.00) dollars or by imprisonment

in the County jail not exceeding six (6) months. *Section 3.* This Act shall take effect upon and after its passage and approval by the Governor. Approved: June 7, 1913." Quoted in the opinion by Judge George Cooper Gibbs, *Ex Parte Sister Mary Thomasine*, Docket #3, p. 44, Law #778, Circuit Court, St. John's County, St. Augustine, Florida, May 20, 1916. The 1913 law was not the first of this sort. An 1895 law forbade black and white students to be taught in the same school: *Compiled General Laws of Florida, 1927*, Article 31, Violation of School Laws, Section 8107 (5866), Chap. 4335, (paragraphs 1 & 2 [1895]).

²¹ Vincent de Paul Fitzpatrick, *Life of Curley*, p. 33; *St. Augustine Record*, April 24, 1916; *St. Augustine Meteor*, April 28, 1916; *Florida v. Ex Parte Sister Mary Thomasine*, Docket #3, p. 44, Law #778, Circuit Court, St. John's County, St. Augustine, Florida, May 20, 1916; *Morning Star*, June 3, 1916; ADSA, Curley Papers, 4-K-9, Giovanni Bonzano, Apostolic Delegate to Curley, August 25, 1916; Page, "Curley and Nativism," pp. 110–112.

²² AAB, Gibbons Papers, 116-Q-11, Curley to Gibbons, January 19, 1916.

²³ Tebeau, *History of Florida*, pp. 369–70.

²⁴ ADSA, Curley Papers: 4(b)-T-10, Report: McLaughlin to Curley, April (n.d.) 1918; 4(b)-P-11, Holy Name War Council Report, August (n.d.) 1918; 4(b)-S-6, Marguerite Denicke, Miami Daughters of Isabella, to Curley, September 15, 1918; 4(b)-T-12, Rev. Wm. Power, SJ, to Curley, October 22, 1918.

²⁵ ADSA, 4-D-5, *Florida Times-Union*, Jacksonville (photostat), July 29, 1915.

²⁶ ADSA, Curley Papers: 4(x)-B-26, Gibbons to Curley, April 22, 1918; 4(y)-H-13, Chancellor to All Pastors (copy), April 22, 1918; 4(b)-T-13, Rodgers to Curley, November 5, 1918; 4(b)-S-9, F. P. Fleming, Chairman of Speaker's Committee, to Curley, September 21, 1918 (Bp. Curley spoke in Miami on September 28, 1918); 4(b)-S-20, J. M. Braxton, engineer of the U.S. War Department, to Curley, October 2, 1918 (permission was scribbled on the letter by Bp. Curley); 4(b)-W-19, Maj. H. P. McCain, Camp Devens, Ma., to Curley, April 1, 1919.

²⁷ SJV-SC, Curley to Bonzano (copy), n.d. [c. 1919].

²⁸ SJV-SC: Emile Mattern, provincial of New Orleans Jesuits, to Curley, June 12, 1919; Curley to Mattern (copy), June 17, 1919, January 13, August 1, 1920; Curley to Bonzano (copy), December 16, 1920; Agreement Between the Jesuits and Curley, August 7, 1920.

²⁹ SJV-SC, Curley to Bonzano (copy), December 16, 1920.

³⁰ SJV-SC: Agreement Between Curley and Mattern (copy) June 20, 1921; Sacred Congregation of Religious to Curley (copy), October 7, 1921.

³¹ SJV-SC: Curley to Apostolic Delegate (copy), n.d. [c. 1919]; Curley to Mattern (copy), January 30, 1920. See also John P. Marschall, "Diocesan and Religious Clergy"; SJV-SC, Curley to Mattern (copy), June 17, 1919.

³² Code, *Dictionary of the American Hierarchy*, p. 12; AADS, Correspondence of Mother Gerald, Fr. John F. Conoley to Mother Gerald, October 4, 1940; AAB, Curley Papers, B-334, Barry to Curley, January 15, 1923; B-358, Barry to Curley, February 18, 1926; B-379, Curley to Barry (copy), April 29, 1930.

³³ AADS, Bp. Gerald P. O'Hara, bishop of Savannah-Atlanta, to Sr. Mary Philip Ryan, February 7, 1941; AADS, Correspondence of Mother Gerald, Barry to Sr. Gerald, May 6, 1932, Barry to Mother Gerald, April 16, 1940.

³⁴ AADS, Correspondence of Mother Gerald, Wm. Barry to Mother Gerald,

March 19, May 5, 1937, March 3, 1939, September 4, 1940; ADSA, interview, Msgr. Barry.

[35] *Msgr. William Barry*, pp. 17–32; St. Patrick Church, Rectory Files, Minutes of the Men's and Women's Guild of St. Paul's, Jacksonville (copy), May 10, 1926; AAB, Curley Papers: B-408, Curley to Wm. Barry (copy), November 10, 1923; B-402, Wm. Barry to Curley, March 5, 1923.

[36] AADS, Annals and Mission Files, St. Ann's; ADSA, Barry Papers, 19-R-10, Bitting to Mother Gerald (copy), July 8, 1933.

[37] More study is needed on the apparent paucity of Ku Klux Klan anti-Catholicism in South Florida in the 1920s.

[38] Tebeau, *History of Florida*, pp. 348–51. See also Baynard Kendrick, *Florida Trails to Turnpikes*. The railroad extended to Okeechobee (1915), Moore Haven (1918), Clewiston (1922), and Belle Glade (1926). A private toll road for autos was opened from 25 Mile Bend, west of West Palm Beach, to and around Lake Okeechobee in 1924.

[39] George, "Passage to the New Eden," pp. 449–50; Jeanne Bellamy, "Marketing of Miami." See also Charles E. Herner, *Florida Promoters*.

[40] Gene Burnett, "'Binder Boys,'" pp. 155–57. See also T. H. Weigall, *Boom in Paradise; Florida—"The East Coast," Its Builders, Resources, Industries, Town and City Developments*; Kenneth Ballinger, *Miami Millions*.

[41] AAB, Curley Papers, B-348, Barry to Curley, November 26, 1925. The $550,000 in 1925 would have been worth $2,096,875 in 1980 dollars (Economic Statistics Bureau, *Handbook*, pp. 99–101).

[42] Tebeau, *History of Florida*, pp. 385–87; Burnett, "'Binder Boys,'" pp. 158–59.

[43] "'Binder Boys,'" p. 159; Tebeau, *History of Florida*, p. 387; *Miami News*, September 19, 1926; American National Red Cross, *The Florida Hurricane*. Interesting first-person accounts of Adrian Dominicans who lived through the hurricane at St. Patrick's Parish, Miami Beach, are available in AADS: Sr. Francis Margaret Grix to Mother Camila, September 26, 1926; Sr. M. Blanca to Mother Camila, n.d. [c. September 1926]; account of Sr. Marie Raphael Dunigan, August 5, 1975; ADSA: Barry Papers, Memo Notes, 23-E-7, n.d. [c. 1926]; Memo Notes, 23-E-5, n.d. [c. 1925]; AAB, Curley Papers, B-363, September 26, 1926.

[44] AAB, Curley Papers, B-367, Barry to Curley, December 2, 1926. It seems that Bp. Barry exaggerated the value of the Miami property, whose purchase price was actually $200,000. No evidence exists that any of these properties were in fact foreclosed since the diocese was able to keep up the payments. Notre Dame Academy for Girls, most recently redesignated as the Pierre Toussaint Haitian Catholic Center, was built on the Miami parcel in 1954 (ADSA, Barry Papers, 6-E-16, Affidavit [undated copy], [c. 1928]; 6-E-17, Affidavit [undated copy], [c. May 1928]; 11-D-5, "Properties," April 7, 1931). For monographs on the depression and Catholicism in the South and South Florida, see David O'Brien, *Catholics and Social Reform*; Paul E. Mertz, *New Deal Policy*; Alexander R. Stoesen, "Road from Receivership"; Long, "New Deal."

[45] AADS, Correspondence of Mother Gerald, Bp. Barry to Sr. Gerald, December 16, 1927.

[46] *Palm Beach Post*, September 26, 1928; American National Red Cross, *The West*

Indies Hurricane Disaster; Laurence E. Will, *Okeechobee Hurricane*; ADSA, Barry Papers: 28-G-20, Fr. William Nachtrab to Barry, December 18, 1928; 28-G-18, A. D. Doherty, SJ, pastor of St. Ann's, to Barry, December 16, 1928; AADS: Correspondence of Mother Gerald, Doherty to Sr. Barry, n.d. [c. September 1928]; St. Ann's on the Lake Annals, September 1928.

[47] AADS, Correspondence of Mother Gerald, Wm. Barry to Bp. Barry, September 18, 1928. For more first-person accounts of the hurricane, see ibid.: Sr. Jane Francis Woekers to Sr. Gerald, September 25, 1928; Sr. Rose Dominic to Mother Augustine, September 18, 1928; Sr. Mary Leona, to Sr. Gerald, September 25, 1928.

[48] ADSA, Barry Papers: 12-D-21, Barry to Merrick (copy), April 22, 1924; 12-G-15, Liguori H. Matheson to Barry, January 5, 1925; 6-E-21, Barry to Mrs. Mary Kerr, New Brunswick, N.J. (copy), July 19, 1928; 6-K-16, George Beck, Buffalo, N.Y., to Barry, October 12, 1930.

[49] ADSA, Barry Papers: 6-E-12, E. R. Bradley, Idle Hour Farms, Lexington, Ky., to Barry, April 24, 1928; 12-S-21, Bradley to Barry, April 18, 1927; 28-G-8, List of Donations, St. Edward Church, n.d. [c. April 1928]; 18-X-21, Bradley to Barry, April 10, 1929. AAB, Curley Papers: B-1397, Curley to Bradley (copy), May 9, 1922; B-1403, Bradley to Curley, May 21, 1944. There was another reason for Bradley's style of exclusive generosity: He was the proprietor of America's most exclusive gambling casino, the Beach Club of Palm Beach. Known for the fairness and honesty of its owner, this gambling and dining establishment was open during the winter season (virtually unmolested by law enforcement authorities) from 1898 to Bradley's death in 1946 (*Palm Beach Post*, Supplement, April 3, 1983).

[50] ADSA, Barry papers, 22-X-19, McNicholas to McGill, Administrator of the Diocese of St. Augustine, August 21, 1940. Arch. McNicholas, as part of his master plan for "The Athenaeum of Ohio," sought and obtained property in Palm Beach County for the *Institutum Divi Thomae*, "a place for research and training of a small but select number of workers to be trained for scientific research." McNicholas also had constructed a bungalow for himself on ocean frontage, one mile north of Seminole Golf Club (ibid., 22-G-17, McNicholas to Barry, March 7, 1936). As ordinary, Bp. Barry granted McNicholas permission to conduct the *Institutum* in Palm Beach in March 1936, since no bishop is allowed to conduct affairs in another bishop's diocese without express permission (ibid., 22-G-18, McNicholas to Barry, March 19, 1936).

[51] ADSA, Barry Papers: 25-D-7, Barry to Curley (copy), December 2, 1926; 25-D-9, Barry to Mundelein (copy), December 3, 1926; 12-R-11, Mundelein to Barry, December 13, 1926; 12-R-12, Curley to Barry, December 17, 1926; 23-G-5, Speech (copy), n.d. [c. 1932]; 23-G-3, n.d. [c. 1939 or 1940].

[52] ADSA, Barry Papers, 5-X-15, Bitting to P. J. McGill, June 20, 1927. The collateral for the loans were bonds held by the diocese at the American Trust Company of St. Louis (ibid., 5-X-24, Barry to American Trust Company [copy], July 26, 1927).

[53] ADSA, Barry Papers, 18-S-13, Confidential Memo, Bitting to Barry, August 1, 1927.

[54] ADSA, Barry Papers: 6-C-3, Bitting to Barry, October 22, 1927; 18-T-19, Bitting to Barry, May 8, 1928; 6-E-3, Bitting to Barry, March 6, 1928; 18-T-22, Bitting to Barry, June 27, 1928.

[55] ADSA, Barry Papers: 6-E-3, Bitting to Barry, March 6, 1928; 13-C-21, Mary A. Mulcahy, Sec. to Bitting, to Barry, March 2, 1931; AADS, Correspondence of Mother Gerald, Bp. Barry to Sr. Gerald, September 16, 1930, November 5, 1931. Bitting was received into the Roman Catholic Church in 1943 (AADS, Correspondence of Mother Gerald, Wm. Barry to Mother Gerald, October 20, 1943).

[56] ADSA, Barry Papers: 7-B-19, Bitting to Fr. J. Nunan, V. G., June 10, 1932; 6-R-3, Bitting to Barry, June 1, 1931.

[57] Bitting had trouble collecting from the bishop of Cleveland. ADSA, Barry Papers, 19-R-5, Bitting to Barry, March 30, 1933. Bitting took the bishop of Mobile to court for nonpayment of a loan (ibid., 13-G-20, Bitting to Barry, April 8, 1933).

[58] Gesu in Miami, St. Patrick's in Miami Beach, and St. Anthony's in Ft. Lauderdale were three South Florida examples. ADSA, Barry Papers, Bitting to Fr. Michael McNally, SJ, pastor of Gesu, October 15, 1931; AADS, Correspondence of Mother Gerald, Barry to Sr. Gerald, August 22, September 16, 1930; AAB, Curley Papers, B-377, Barry to Curley, October 6, 1930.

[59] AAB, Curley Papers, B-377, Barry to Curley, October 6, 1930.

[60] ADSA, Barry Papers: 7-H-6, Bitting to Barry, April 29, 1933; 7-K-2, Bitting to Barry, July 7, 1933; 7-K-15, Bitting to Barry, August 8, 1933. The bishop of St. Augustine had become the "corporation sole" by force of common law in court by 1927. ADSA, Kenny Papers, 3(b)-M-9, copy of Florida bill, February 25, 1913; Hurley papers, Folder-151-F, Correspondence to and from Geo. Rockett, Chancellor, 1941–1946, "Affidavit—Reid vs. Barry, April 14, 1927" (copy). See also Ambrose DePaoli, *Property Laws*, pp. 59–66.

[61] ADSA, Barry Papers, 6-N-20, Bitting to Barry, n.d. [c. 1931]. This amounted to over $5 million in 1980 dollars (Economic Statistics Bureau, *Handbook*, pp. 99–101).

[62] AADS, Correspondence of Mother Gerald, Barry to Mother Gerald, February 29, 1940.

[63] ADSA, Curley Papers: 4-C-7, Card. Farley, N.Y.C., to Curley, October 7, 1914; 4(c)-H-4, John T. Smith, Smith & Bros., candy manufacturers, N.Y.C., to Curley, January 1, 1917; 4(y)-K-6, Rev. Edward Cahill, Mungret College, to Curley, February 16, 1915.

[64] ADSA, Curley Papers: 4(z)-A-11, Rev. J. F. Goggin, rector of St. Bernard Seminary, to Curley, October 19, 1914; 4-E-12, Rev. James Bennett, Aurora, Il., to Fr. Wilde, Tallahassee, February 13, 1915.

[65] ADSA, Curley Papers: 4(y)-K-6, Cahill to Curley, February 16, 1915; 4-B-16, Mt. Mellery Seminary to Curley, July 31, 1914; 4(x)-A-16, Carlow College to Curley, Report—1917; 4(y)-K-19, St. Patrick's, Carlow, to Curley, April 4, 1918; 4-D-19, St. Mary's Seminary to Curley, Report—1915; 4-K-4, St. Mary's, Emmitsburg, to Curley, Report—1916; 4-D-1, Friburgh to Curley, April 1, 1919; 49(b)-Y-10, North American College to Curley, September 1, 1921.

[66] AADS, Rev. Jeremiah O'Mahoney to Sr. Mary Philip Ryan, OP, May 5, 1942; interview, Rev. John F. McKeown; ADSA, Barry Papers, Arch. Pietro Fumasoni-Biondi, apostolic delegate, to Barry, June 1, 1928.

[67] ADSA, Barry Papers: 12-H-3, Dr. Joseph Och, rector of Josephinum, to Barry, March 20, 1925; 9-E-15, Rev. Lawrence D. Flanagan, Bronx, N.Y., to Barry, May 28, 1940; 5-K-3, Lawrence J. Flynn, Philadelphia, to Curley (copy), October 10, 1925; 5-D-2, Rev. James Veale, Brooklyn, to Barry, January 7, 1924; AAB, Curley Papers: B-352, Curley to Barry (copy), December 16, 1924; B-414, Curley to Wm. Barry (copy), February 5, 1927. Among those from Josephinum were Romould E. Philbin, George Rockett, James Nelan and Rowan Rastatter.

[68] AAB, Curley Papers: B-348, Barry to Curley, November 26, 1925; B-358, Barry to Curley, February 18, 1926.

[69] Roth, *History of the Diocese*, p. 44; ADSA, Barry Papers: 7-B-21, Bitting to Barry, June 10, 1932; 18-C-13, Barry to U.S. Consul (copy), July 1, 1931; 18-A-6, Rev. W. C. Byrne to Barry, January 19, 1927; 10-E-13, James F. Enright to Barry, September 25, 1926; 25-Y-23, St. Mary Seminary, Baltimore, to Barry, September 8, 1927; 18-K-12, St. Patrick College, Tipperary, to Barry, November 17, 1938; 22-H-9, Irish College to Barry, Report, 1935–36; 25-W-16, Patrick Keogh to Barry, August 30, 1932; 18-T-17, Barry to O'Mahoney (copy), April 13, 1928. Among these Irish recruits were Timothy Geary, Peter Reilly, James Enright, John O'Looney, Dominic Barry, Patrick Donohoe, Patrick Keogh, and Jeremiah O'Mahoney.

[70] ADSA, Barry Papers: 12-B-16, Memo, October 22, 1922; 12-E-6, To All Pastors (draft), May 27, 1924; 12-H-16, To All Pastors, May 26, 1925; 20-B-14, Memo, March 17, 1935; 20-C-3, Memo, March 20, 1938; 20-E-3, Memo, March 17, 1940.

[71] For a brief history of their European roots and their growth in America, see Sr. Mary Philip Ryan, *Amid the Alien Corn*. This work was based mostly on oral sources, which the author began collecting in 1934.

[72] ADSA, Curley Papers, 4-D-9, Fr. Patrick Barry to Curley, January 6, 1915; Ryan, *Amid the Alien Corn*, pp. 312–13. In the 1923–24 school year, the sisters taught seventy-nine Catholic and fifteen non-Catholic students (AADS, Annals and Mission Files, St. Ann's). They taught in the wood-frame church until 1925 (Roth, *History of the Diocese*, p. 152).

[73] AADS: Annals and Mission Files, Rosarian; Annals and Mission Files, St. Ann's; ADSA, Barry Papers, 12-E-2, T. F. Hynes, Miami contractor, to Rev. M. A. Grace, SJ, pastor of St. Ann's (copy), May 27, 1924.

[74] AADS: Barry to Mother Augustine, December 23, 1925; Rev. M. Mullaly to Mother Augustine, June 14, 1926; Annals and Mission Files, St. Anthony's; Annals and Mission Files, St. Anastasia's; Correspondence of Mother Gerald: Wm. Barry to Sr. Gerald, September 16, 1931, April 13, 1937, March 30, September 18, 1939; Bp. Barry to Mother Gerald, February 29, 1940.

[75] ADSA, Curley Papers, 4-G-20, Fr. M. O. Semmes, SJ, pastor of St. Mary's, Star of the Sea, to Curley, July 8, 1915.

[76] *St. Francis Hospital*, pp. 19–23; ASSF, Summary of Mission Book, St. Francis Hospital. See also Polly Redford, *Billion Dollar Sandbar*.

[77] *Palm Beach Post*, January 20, 1939. For additional material on the foundation of St. Mary's Hospital, see ASSF: Summary of Mission Book, St. Mary's Hospital; Sr. M. Andre Phillips, OSF, "Closing Decades," pp. 11–13; Summary of Mission Book, St. Francis Xavier School, Ft. Myers.

[78] *Souvenir of the Silver Jubilee of Rev. Thomas Comber*, AAB, Curley Papers, B-330, Barry to Curley, December 19, 1922. Gesu was dedicated February 1, 1925, by the apostolic delegate, Pietro Fumasoni-Biondi. The new church could seat 1,400 in the nave, 200 more in the choir loft, and 1,200 in the basement auditorium (Roth, *History of the Diocese*, pp. 272–74). For more detailed accounts of the history of Gesu and St. Anthony's, see *Voice*, October 2, June 12, 1959. A parallel might be the feeling Chicago Catholics had at the 1926 Eucharistic Congress, as interpreted by William S. Halsey, *Survival of American Innocence*, p. 61.

[79] Former missions and stations which became parishes during the period included St. Edward's, Palm Beach (1928), Little Flower, Hollywood (1929), St. Joseph's, Stuart (1928), St. Mary's, Little River—Miami (1930), St. Margaret's, Clewiston (1930), Sacred Heart, Homestead (1929), and SS. Peter and Paul, Miami (1939).

[80] Roth, *History of the Diocese*, pp. 200–201.

[81] Baptism Register, St. Patrick's, vol. 1, March 28, 1926–May 8, 1932 (the first baptismal entry by Fr. O'Leary is dated April 8, 1926; previous entries in O'Leary's hand are prefatory to the records); ADSA, Barry Papers: 12-M-25, O'Leary to Barry, March 30, 1926; 12-N-1, O'Leary to Barry, April 12, 1926; 12-N-10, Sr. Mary Ruardo, College of Misericordia, Dallas, Pa. to O'Leary, April 29, 1926; 12-N-12, O'Leary to Barry, May 4, 1926.

[82] The material on Wm. Barry's pastorate in 1926–40 was gleaned from several sources, including: (1) AADS, Annals and Mission Files, St. Patrick's; (2) AADS, Correspondence of Mother Gerald: Wm. Barry to Mother Gerald, January 4, 1929; Barry to Sr. Gerald, March 21, May 5, 1929; telegram, Barry to Mother Gerald, May 15, 1937; telegram, Srs. of St. Dominic to Msgr. Barry (copy), October 17, 1939; (3) *Msgr. William Barry*, pp. 32–34, 39, 44–47, 50; (4) ASSF, Summary of Mission Book, St. Francis Hospital; (5) ADSA, Barry Papers: 6-C-25, Bitting to Barry, January 9, 1928; 19-P-2, Wm. Barry to Bitting (copy), October 14, 1932; 19-P-3, Wm. Barry to Bitting (copy), October 21, 1932; (5) *St. Patrick's Patrician Club*; (6) *Florida Catholic*, December 1, 1939; (7) St. Patrick's Rectory Files, "Sunday Announcement" Notebooks, vols. 1–11, 1926–62.

[83] ADSA, interview, Msgr. William Barry. See also Tebeau, *Synagogue in the Central City*; *Msgr. William Barry*, pp. 36, 64–65.

[84] AADS, Correspondence of Mother Gerald, Wm. Barry to Mother Gerald, September 14, 1938.

[85] AADS, Correspondence of Mother Gerald, Wm. Barry to Mother Gerald, September 7, 1936. Barry established St. Francis de Sales Mission on Miami Beach, January 1941; built St. Joseph's Mission on Miami Beach, 1942; erected Casa Francesca, 1942, the first Catholic residence for women in South Florida (it was staffed by Adrians); negotiated the opening of Catholic University in the Dominican Republic in 1944; received an honorary LL.D. from the University of Notre Dame, June 30, 1946. In 1953, Barry was named protonotary apostolic for

his contributions to the Church. *Msgr. William Barry*, pp. 36–38, 52–55; *25th Anniversary of St. Patrick's*.

[86] Baptism and marriage statistics for St. Patrick's:

Year	Baptisms	Mixed/Disp. of Cult	Total Marriages
1926	9	4	10
1930	22	11	18
1935	38	7	12
1940	33	21	28

Source: St. Patrick's Baptismal and Marriage Records.

Baptism and marriage statistics for St. Mary's:

Year	Baptisms	Mixed/Disp. of Cult	Total Marriages
1930	4	1	1
1935	60	16	18
1940	125	21	40

Source: St. Mary's Baptismal and Marriage Records.

Obviously, St. Mary's was a more active and populous parish.

[87] ADSA, Barry Papers: 27-D-16, M. Teresa McKenna to Barry, October 17, 1923; 9-G-8, Annette Reynard Rike to Barry, July 30, 1940.

[88] ADSA, Barry Papers: 18-P-4, Parishioners of Seabreeze to Mullaly (copy), December 15, 1924; 5-T-9, St. Anthony's Men's Club to Barry, March 28, 1927; 12-S-6, R. P. McAdams to Barry, March 17, 1927; 18-X-20 and 18-C-18, Mullaly to Barry, April 3, May 24, 1929; 19-O-21, Members of St. Helen's to Mullaly (copy), December 4, 1929; AAB, Curley Papers, M-2093, Curley to Mullaly (copy), March 14, 1927.

[89] ADSA, Barry Papers: 9-G-8, Annette R. Rike to Barry, July 30, 1940; 22-K-9, Petition of the Catholics of Delray, February 10, 1937; 22-W-22, Petition of the Catholics of Coconut Grove, n.d.; 12-N-8, A. Merrill, Chairman of St. Anthony Building Committee, to Barry, April 16, 1926; AADS, Annals, St. Patrick's.

[90] ADSA, Barry Papers: 26-W-9, Report, Mrs. Cora Bain to Barry, April, 1922; 12-C-16, T. F. Hynes, Faithful Navigator, to Barry, October n.d. [c. 1923]; Miami Charter, Knights of Columbus, Council #1726, March 29, 1914; *Voice*, May 8, 1959, April 10, 1964, November 20, 1981; *Catholic Service Bureau Golden Anniversary*, p. 7.

[91] ADSA, Barry Papers: 8-T-18, Barry to Pius XII (copy), October 15, 1937, and 18-T-2, Program, First Annual Convention of Holy Name Society, January 8, 1928; O'Mahoney, *Fides* (1934), p. 51; Roth, *History of the Diocese*, pp. 142–43.

[92] For more on this idea, see O'Brien, *Catholics and Social Reform* and "The American Priest," pp. 423–70.

[93] ADSA, Curley Papers: 4-H-5, Memo, July, 1913; 4-C-10, Curley to St. Joseph's Society of the Sacred Heart, Baltimore (copy), August 12, 1914; 4-C-12,

E. R. Dyer, Sec. of Commission for the Negro Missions, to Curley, November 25, 1914; *History of Nuestra de la Leche y Buen Parto and St. Augustine*, p. 23.

[94] ADSA, Curley Papers, 4-H-2, McLaughlin to Curley, July 21, 1915.

[95] The committee of six was composed of Malaliah Bethel, chairman, William Scavella, Gerald Johnson, Fontanei Lalame, Joseph Parell, and Louis McKinon. The Sunday School classes met first in the homes of Mrs. George Lowe and Mrs. D. J. Ryan, then later in the home of Mrs. Ellen Kelly. *Voice*, October 9, 1959; Curtis Washington, "Miami Mission"; Reynolds, *Jesuits for the Negro*, pp. 185–86; ADSA, Barry Papers, 19-G-15, McNally to Barry, September 28, 1930; AADS, Correspondence of Mother Gerald, Barry to Sr. Gerald, April 17, 1932; *Regnum Regis*, p. 15. For more on blacks in Miami, see Paul S. George, "Policing Miami's Black Community."

[96] The reasons given for closing the chapel were that Fr. Maureau, the Jesuit in charge, was too old for the active apostolate and was transferred; with the increase of servicemen in Key West, chaplains were needed to serve them; and some blacks were leaving Key West because the military was buying up their property, and there was a consequent lack of housing for blacks. ASHN, "History of the Chapel of St. Francis Xavier"; AADS, Annals and Mission Files, Blessed Martin Mission, Mrs. F. Agnes Dillon to Sr. Mary, June 8, 1940.

[97] AADS, Correspondence of Mother Gerald, Mother Gerald to Bp. Barry (copy), February 24, 1936.

[98] *Voice*, October 16, 1959; Reynolds, *Jesuits for the Negro*, p. 185; AADS: photo album, Blessed Martin Mission; Correspondence of Mother Gerald, Mother Gerald to Bp. Barry (copy), October 24, 1938; photo album, St. Martin de Porres Mission, Mission Files, St. Martin School.

[99] *Georgia Bulletin*, May 7, 1932.

[100] OCD-1915, pp. 678–80; OCD-1923, pp. 589–92; OCD-1941, pp. 563–66.

[101] ADSA: Curley Papers, 4(y)-H-12, Rescript, Sacred Consistoral Congregation to Curley, April 25, 1921; Barry Papers: 6-B-8, Rescript, Sacred Consistoral Congregation to Barry, October 4, 1927, and 23-K-22, Rescript, Sacred Consistoral Congregation to Barry, July 4, 1935.

[102] ADSA, Barry Papers: 23-G-3, copy of speech, n.d.; 25-A-1, copy of speech, June 18, 1936.

[103] AADS, Correspondence of Mother Gerald, Barry to Sr. Gerald, March 6, 1930.

Chapter 4

[1] *Boston Daily Globe*, November 26, 1945; ADSA, Hurley Papers: 145-H, various photos, 1933–41; 145-C-2, Hurley to Mooney (copy), July 25, 1940; 145-F-5, Mooney to Hurley, July 16, 1941; 145-G-6, Hurley to Walter Carroll (copy), October 17, 1941.

[2] ADSA, Hurley Papers: 147-B-24, J. A. Groh, M. D., Cleveland, to Hurley, August 2, 1945; 147-D-2, Frank Doran, M.D., Cleveland, to Hurley, October 13, 1945; 51-F-4, X. L. Pellicer, St. Augustine National Bank, to Msgr. P. J. McGill, April 18, 1941; 51-F-21, Fitzpatrick, Director of La Leche Shrine, to All Pastors

(circular), February 2, 1944; 101-A, material on shrine; interviews, Fr. John Mc-
Keown and Msgr. John McNulty. The Mestrovic works, completed in 1958, were
"Bust of Arch. Hurley" (St. Augustine), "Fr. Lopez Memorial" (St. Augustine),
"Pieta" (Miami), six bas-reliefs of bishop-martyrs to communism (Miami), and
"Crucifix" (Corpus Christi Church, Miami) (Lawrence Schmeckebier, *Ivan Mes-
trovic*, p. 66). Hurley also had several churches built to reflect Florida's Spanish
heritage, among them, San Pedro and St. Juliana's. His interest in Florida Church
history culminated in his sponsoring the 400th Birthday of Our Lady of Leche
Shrine in October of 1966 (ADSA, tapes of historical symposium, October 1966;
interview, Bp. John Fitzpatrick).

[3] The composite characterization of Hurley was drawn from interviews: ADSA,
interviews, Msgr. William Barry, Fr. Roberts, Msgr. O'Donovan, Msgr. Reilly,
Msgr. Dominic Barry, Fr. Genovar, Msgr. Nelan, Msgr. James Walsh, Mrs. Fillyaw Donohue, Msgr. McNulty, Msgr. Schiefen, Judge Atkins, Msgr. O'Dowd,
Msgr. Bryan O. Walsh, Fr. McKeown, Mr. Kindelan, Sr. Mary Albert, SSJ, and
Bp. Fitzpatrick. See also AIHM, Sr. Maria Pacis to Mother Maria Alma, August
30, November 8, 1953; ADSA, Hurley Papers: 149-F-5, Hurley to All Priests (circular), December 31, 1952; 123-K, Love to Hurley, May 31, 1955 (with a scribbled
reply by Hurley at the bottom).

[4] Interview, Msgr. Harold Jordan. It took Msgr. George Rockett almost five
years to straighten out the financial accounts (ADSA, Hurley Papers, 151-F, Correspondence of Rockett, Chancellor, and Barry Family, 1941–January 11, 1944).

[5] ADSA, Hurley Papers: 56-A-4, Hurley to Rev. Thomas Mitchell, Dean of
Faculty of Social Work, CUA (copy), June 1, 1941; 53-H-2, Retreat Schedule—
List of Priests and Regulations, June 16–20, 1941; 56-G-16, Hurley to William D.
O'Brien (copy), September 3, 1941; 56-G-17, Hurley to O'Brien (copy), Septem-
ber 3, 1941; 56-G-31, Hurley to O'Brien (copy), March 17, 1942; 135-A-1, Alpha-
betical List of Priests of St. Augustine, November 14, 1941; George A. Kelly,
Practice of the Faith.

[6] ADSA, Hurley Papers, 50-I-1, Hurley to Wm. Barry (copy), December 15,
1941.

[7] ADSA, Hurley Papers: 52-A-1, Hurley to Pastors, November 7, 1942; 52-
F-18, Hurley to Deans, n.d. [c. June 1943]; 52-F-23, Map, n.d. [c. late 1943]; 96-
G, Chancery Correspondence, Forty Hours Schedules, 1945–58.

[8] Tebeau, *A History of Florida*, pp. 416–17.

[9] ADSA, Hurley Papers, 46-D-1, Hurley to Bishops (copy), December 10,
1942. The letter was sent to the ordinaries of Baltimore, Cleveland, Albany,
Brooklyn, Fall River, Newark, Chicago, Springfield, Boston, Providence, and
Hartford.

[10] ADSA, Hurley Papers, 146-E-13, Hurley to Feory (copy), May 5, 1943.

[11] Interview, Msgr. Peter Reilly. For more on German war prisoners in Florida,
see Robert D. Billinger, "Wehrmacht in Florida."

[12] *Florida Catholic*, June 7, 1940; St. Patrick Rectory, Msgr. Wm. Barry, Files and
Notebooks, "Sunday Announcement Notebook," vol. 3, June 23, 1940; *Florida
Catholic*, June 4, November 12, 1943, January 28, 1944; interview, Msgr. John
O'Dowd.

[13] ADSA, Hurley Papers: 146-E-4, Diocesan Board Meeting, National Council

of Catholic Women, December 5, 1944; 143-F, Chancery Correspondence, United Catholic Charities Campaign, January 1945; 143-K, List of Materials—United Charities Drive, 1945; 80-D-1, Correspondence Concerning the Deering Mortgage, June 4, 1945–February 24, 1947; AAP, Dougherty Papers, Mother Ann Elizabeth, RA, Assumption Academy, to Card. Dougherty, Philadelphia, December 26, 1944; Dougherty to Mother Ann Elizabeth (copy), June 9, 1945; interview, Msgr. McNulty. The operational costs for three orphanages (one in Miami), three homes for the aged (one in Miami), a Social Work Scholarship Fund, a mobile chapel, two catechetical camps, a working girls' home (Miami Beach), and the Shrine of Our Lady of Leche totaled $650,000.

[14] AAP, Dougherty Papers, Mother Ann Elizabeth to Dougherty, November 28, 1945; ADSA, Hurley Papers, 148-D-23, Memo, McDonough to Hurley, Belgrade, June 23, 1949; *Miami Daily News*, October 28, 1945; *Around Mercy* 5 (December 1980).

[15] AAP, Dougherty Papers, Mother Ann Elizabeth to Dougherty, December 11, 1945; ADSA, Hurley Papers, 147-D-16, *Boston Daily Globe*, November 26, 1945. Hurley indicated publicly that he thought the assignment would be for a few months (*Miami Daily News*, October 28, 1945).

[16] *Around Mercy* 5 (December 1980); AFAM, Archbishop's Office, Mildred Geary, "History of Mercy Hospital" (mimeo); ADSA, Hurley Papers: 80-F-1, Correspondence Concerning Mercy Hospital Gifts, June 3, 1945–December 13, 1950; 81-B, Correspondence Concerning Financing and Public Relations of Mercy Hospital, October 28, 1946–March 10, 1950; 81-I, Mercy Hospital Building Funds Campaign Plans, August 24, 1945–September 6, 1945; interviews, Judge C. Clyde Atkins; Mrs. Marjorie Fillyaw Donohue, Mr. James Kindelan, and Fr. Lamar Genovar.

[17] Interviews, Fr. Genovar, Msgr. James J. Walsh, Msgr. O'Dowd, and Msgr. McNulty; AFAM, Archbishop's Office, Geary, "Mercy Hospital"; ASSJ, Memo, Sisters of St. Joseph to Bp. McDonough (copy), April 11, 1949; *Around Mercy*, 5 (December 1980).

[18] ADSA, Hurley Papers, 148-D-23, Memo, McDonough to Hurley, June 23, 1949.

[19] *Around Mercy* 5 (December 1980); AFAM, Archbishop's Office, Geary, "Mercy Hospital." Mercy Hospital still needed funds to pay off a $1 million debt and loans from the diocese, and early in 1951 money was collected from Miami parishes for it. Fr. Rowan Rastatter was now in charge of hospital affairs. The Annual Charity Ball began April 14, 1952, at the Surf Club.

[20] Tebeau, *A History of Florida*, pp. 415, 417, 422; interview, Msgr. William McKeever. See also Aurora E. Davis, "Major Commercial Airlines"; William C. Lazarus, *Wings in the Sun*; George and Jane Dusenbury, *How to Retire in Florida*. Corpus Christi could not be dedicated as planned in October 1947, due to the shortage of building materials. *Silver Jubilee, Corpus Christi School*; ADSA, Hurley Papers, 136-J, Rev. John Love, Vice-Chancellor, to Rev. F. J. Finnegan (copy), September 29, 1947.

[21] *Voice*, June 26, July 10, September 4, 1959; ADSA, Hurley Papers: 148-D-9, Memo, Hurley to McDonough (copy), February 12, 1949; 148-D-23, Memo, McDonough to Hurley, June 23, 1949.

[22] Interview, Msgr. McNulty.

[23] ADSA, Hurley Papers: 47-A-1, Hurley to Pastors (circular), December 23, 1943; 91-A, Hurley to O'Donovan (copy), December 27, 1952; 91-A, Archbishop's Correspondence on Missionary Burse Fund; 93-C-3, Correspondence of Missionary Burse Fund, 1953–58; interviews, Msgr. James J. Walsh, Msgr. O'Dowd, and Msgr. McNulty. St. Theresa's, Coral Gables, had an assessment of $525,000 (interview, Msgr. Reilly).

[24] Interview, Msgr. McNulty.

[25] Approximately 90 percent of parochial and institutional building during the Carroll period was on Hurley land; interviews, Msgr. O'Dowd, Msgr. James F. Nelan, and Msgr. Rowan Rastatter.

[26] Interviews, Msgr. Reilly, Msgr. O'Dowd, Fr. William Balfe, and Fr. Genovar; USBC, *Population, 1960, vol. 1*, pp. 11-9, 11-10; *Voice*, May 8, 15, July 24, September 18, 1959; *Florida Catholic*, February 3, 1956; ADSA, Hurley Papers, 135-G, Chancery Correspondence, St. Mark's, 1952–58; AFAM, CO, Parish Files.

[27] Interviews, Msgr. Thomas O'Donovan, Mr. Kindelan, and Msgr. Nelan. The diocesan banks were Manufacturer's Hanover of New York and Florida National for short-term money, Connecticut Mutual for long-term money.

[28] ADSA, Hurley Papers: 94-B, Vincent de Vivo to McDonough, May 31, 1948; 94-B, Marjorie L. Fillyaw to McDonough, May 19, 1948; interview, Fr. Genovar.

[29] ADSA, Hurley Papers: 119-S, Polish Roman Catholics of Miami to McDonough, June 4, 1947; 119-S, Mr. and Mrs. John Hulak to McDonough, April 27, 1948; 119-S, Mrs. Peligia Lukaszewska to Hurley, April 16, October 24, 1950; interview, Mrs. Fillyaw Donohue; *Florida Catholic*, February 19, 1954.

[30] ADSA, Hurley Papers: 147-B-19, Frank J. Lewis to Hurley, June 2, 1945; 148-D-23, McDonough to Hurley, June 23, 1949; *Florida Catholic*, April 12, 1957. St. Juliana's Church was named in honor of Julia, the wife of Mr. Frank Lewis (interview, Senator Philip Lewis).

[31] ADSA, Hurley Papers, 98-L, Chancery Correspondence, Holy Name Society, January 3, 1946–April 19, 1958; interviews, Mr. Joseph Fitzgerald, Msgr. Dominic Barry, and Judge Atkins; OCD-1956, p. 595; OCD-1957, p. 608; OCD-1958, p. 628.

[32] Interview, Mrs. Fillyaw Donohue; AIHM, Sr. Maria Pacis to Mother Maria Alma, November 22, 1953; Kelly, *Practice of the Faith*, p. 96.

[33] Interview, Fr. Charles Mallen; Msgr. Wm. Barry, "Sunday Announcement Books," vol. 4, October 12, 1941; ADSA, Hurley Papers, 121-Mc, 122-C, Chancery Correspondence, Lay Retreats, 1943–58.

[34] AADS, Correspondence of Mother Gerald, Philbin to Mother Gerald, May 23, 1942, December 5, 1947; ADSA, Hurley Papers: 151-E, Supt. of Schools Correspondence, 1940–44; 118-O, Chancery Correspondence, Newman Club, 1945–54; OCD-1950, p. 519.

[35] Interviews, Msgr. McKeever and Fr. Louis Roberts. In the summer of 1958, Hurley had 22 of a total of 155 diocesan priests studying at Catholic University of America, University of Notre Dame, and Seton Hall. ADSA, Hurley Papers, 153-B, University Appointments List, n.d. [c. Spring 1958]; interview, Msgr. Bryan O. Walsh.

[36] Interview, Msgr. McKeever; AADS, Correspondence of Mother Gerald, McKeever to Mother Gerald, n.d. [c. 1952].

[37] *Palm Beach Post*, September 16, 1956; *Voice*, June 5, 1959; AIHM, McKeever to

Mother Maria Alma, April 22, 1953. This was the begging letter that persuaded the IHMs of Philadelphia to come to South Florida.

[38] *Catholic Service Bureau Golden Anniversary; Florida Catholic,* July 13, 1941, June 4, July 16, November 12, 1943; ADSA, Hurley Papers: 146-F-16, Manning to Hurley, December 28, 1944; 147-A-5, Manning to Hurley, January 3, 1945.

[39] Interview, Msgr. Bryan O. Walsh; *Catholic Service Bureau.*

[40] Interviews, Msgr. O'Dowd and Msgr. O'Donovan. The six Irish seminaries were St. Patrick's, Carlow; St. John's, Waterford; St. Kiernan, Kilkenny; Mungret, Limerick; All Hallows, Dublin; St. Patrick's, Thurles (ADSA, Hurley Papers, 148-C-24, List of College Seminaries, 1948–49).

[41] ADSA, Hurley Papers: 148-C-24, List of College Seminaries, 1948–49; 148-D-2, McDonough to Hurley, Belgrade, January 6, 1949; 148-D-15, McDonough to McNulty, Belgrade, March 21, 1949; 148-D-17, McDonough to McNulty, Belgrade, May 12, 1949; 149-Q-2, Love to "To Whom it may Concern," June 5, 1950; 149-A-16, Memo, McNulty, July, 1950; interview, Msgr. McNulty.

[42] ADSA, Hurley Papers: 149-C-1, Hurley to European Bishops (draft in French), October 3, 1950; 153-K, List of Loans to the Diocese, September 21, 1957; interviews, Msgr. Dominic Barry and James Walsh.

[43] Interview, Msgr. McNulty; ADSA, Hurley Papers, 52-C-20, Memo, Rev. Martin Gilligan, Sec. to the Bishop, to Mr. E. A. Durn, ed. of the *Florida Catholic* (copy), n.d. [c. April 1942]. Fr. Coleman F. Carroll was studying canon law at CUA. He conducted a retreat for the students of St. Mary's High School, Miami, March 26–29, 1944. ADSA, Hurley Papers: 122-C, Chancery Correspondence, List Sent March, 1944—High School Retreats; 52-A-6, Fitzpatrick to McDonough, February 22, 1944.

[44] Heffernan was born in Miami, July 15, 1918. ADSA, Hurley Papers, 119-E, F, G, H, I, Chancery Correspondence, Miami Ordinations, 1945–58; AFAM, CO, Priests' File; interview, Msgr. Jordan.

[45] AAB, Curley Papers, H-1695, Hurley to Curley, September 22, 1943; interviews, Msgr. O'Dowd, Msgr. Bryan O. Walsh, Msgr. Dominic Barry, Msgr. McNulty, and Msgr. Nelan; AFAM, CO, Priests' File.

[46] A weekly Sunday night social gathering of Irish priests was held at Immaculate Conception Rectory during the pastorate of Msgr. Dominic Barry (1956–71). Interviews, Msgr. Reilly, Msgr. O'Dowd, Msgr. Dominic Barry, Mr. Fitzgerald, Msgr. Rastatter, Msgr. Robert Schiefen, and Msgr. McKeever.

[47] Interviews, Msgr. Dominic Barry and Msgr. Reilly. Forty Hours Devotions were the exposition of the Blessed Sacrament for forty consecutive hours to facilitate silent prayer and adoration before the Eucharistic presence. ADSA, Hurley Papers: 153-I, "Ecclesiastici," n.d. [c. 1953]; 153-J, Seniority List—Diocesan Priests, April 17, 1957; 98-J-26, Cicognani to Hurley, June 4, 1958.

[48] ADSA, Hurley Papers, 153-L, Augustinian Priests; interviews, Msgr. McNulty, Fr. McKeown, Msgr. McKeever, Msgr. Robert Schiefen, and Fr. Cyril Burke. See also Richard Pattee, *Cardinal Stepinac;* Fr. Terry Steib, SVD, Provincial Superior, Southern Province, to author, December 30, 1981.

[49] Interview, Fr. Mallen, CSSR. See also Joseph Wissel, *The Redemptorist;* Dolan, *Catholic Revivalism,* pp. 67, 70.

[50] OCD-1958, pp. 631–32; ADSA, Hurley Papers, 132-E-2, Vicar of Religious

Correspondence, 1942–47; interview, Msgr. McKeever; AADS, Correspondence of Mother Gerald: Brush to Mother Gerald, January 8, 1956; Mother Gerald to Hurley (copy), June 13, 1956, November 24, 1957; Hurley to Mother Gerald, June 23, 1956. One Pastor was refused sisters forty-eight times!

[51] AIHMM, Domestic Affairs, St. Michael's; AIHMM, Mission Affairs, Holy Redeemer; *Florida Catholic*, September 9, 1955; SBCC; AIHM, Epiphany Annals; ASM, "His Mercy Endures Forever" (mimeo), n.d. [c. 1981]; ASSND, *Directory, 1957–58*. The School Sisters of Notre Dame were first established in Florida at Tampa in 1944.

[52] ACSAI, Summary of Annals and Chronicles, Florida; AAP, Dougherty Papers, Correspondence of Dougherty to Mother Elizabeth Ann, Superior of Assumption, April 1942–June 1947; interview, Sr. Sheila Flynn, RA.

[53] ASHN, "Service of the Sisters of the Holy Name to Key West, Florida, 1941–80." The Sisters of the Holy Name also served at St. Mel's (1955–77) and St. Pablo's (1958–66). Sr. Lorean Whiteman, SNJM, to author, October 9, 1981; ASHN, "Vocations from Key West and Miami, 1879–1959"; Statistics, 1958–77.

[54] ASSF: Summary of St. Francis Xavier Chronicles; Summary of Corpus Christi Chronicles; Summary of Sacred Heart Chronicles; Summary of Holy Name Chronicles; Summary of St. Mary's Hospital Chronicles; Statistics, 1958–77.

[55] AADS: Photo Album, South Florida Foundations; "Listing of Annual Appointments"; ASSF, *Regnum Regis*, 2 (October 1940), 34; SBBC, September 26, 1956; interview, Fr. Burke, OP; AADS, Correspondence of Mother Gerald, Mother Gerald to Hurley (copies), November 24, 1957, April 14, 1958; ASSJ, Mother Anna Joseph to Hurley (copy), May 11, 1953; AIHM, McKeever to Mother Maria Alma, March 27, 1953.

[56] AADS, Correspondence of Mother Gerald: Hurley to Mother Gerald, July 7, September 22, 1944, September 23, 1945; Mother Gerald to Hurley (copy), July 13, 1944 (copy), September 29, 1945; Hurley to Fr. John F. Monroe, OP, April 18, 1958.

[57] Interviews, Msgr. McKeever, Fr. Genovar, and Sr. Mary Albert Lussier, SSJ.

[58] ASSJ: "Chronicles of 1953–62—Superior General, Mother Anna"; Mother Anna Maria to Hurley (copy), April 7, 1957; Love to Mother Anna Maria, April 23, 1957; Quinquennial Report, January 1, 1956–December 31, 1960.

[59] Interviews, Sr. Mary Aquinas O'Shaughnessy, SSJ, and Sr. Mary Albert, SSJ; ASSJ: Love to Mother Anna Joseph, January 13, 1949, and Mother Anna Maria to Hurley (copy), May 27, 1956. The first Irish-born SSJ was Sr. Mary Ann Hoare, originally a Sister of Mercy who had come to St. Augustine with the Mercy Sisters in 1859. When the Sisters of Mercy left St. Augustine during the war, she stayed on to nurse in Florida and Georgia. With the arrival of the SSJs after the war, she joined them and started St. Mary's Home for Orphans in 1886 in Jacksonville. She was called the "Angel of Jacksonville" by both Catholics and Protestants because of her charity and concern for the poor (David P. Page, ed., *Peregrini Pro Christo*, p. 42; ASSJ, Sr. Mary Edith, SSJ, Asst. Superior General, to Love [copy], December 16, 1957).

[60] Interviews, Sr. Kathleen Reilly, SSND, and Sr. Rita Gleason, OP; SBCC, August 18, 1956; ASSF, Sr. Marie Bernard (Sr. Clair McMaster) to Sr. Joan

Wheeler, September n.d., 1956; AIHM: Epiphany Annals, June 6, 1955, and Sr. Mary Ivo to Mother Maria Alma, October 20, 1953.

[61] Interviews, Sr. Kathleen Reilly, SSND, and Sr. Joyce LaVoy, OP; ASSF, Sr. Marie Bernard (Sr. Clair McMaster) to Sr. Marie Wheeler, September 1956. The quotation is from AIHM, Epiphany Annals, August 23, 1953. See also SBCC, September 11, 1955. One group received lighter habits from the motherhouse due to the heat (AIHM, Sr. Mary Ivo to Mother Maria Alma, September 8, 1953).

[62] AIHM, Epiphany Annals, June 6, 1955; interview, Sr. Kathleen Reilly, SSND.

[63] Interviews, Sr. Kathleen Reilly, SSND, and Sr. Joyce LaVoy, Op; AIHM: Epiphany Annals, December 30, 1955, February 1, 1957, and Sr. Mary Ivo to Mother Maria Alma, October 20, 1953; SBCC, September 10, 18, October 30, 1955.

[64] AADS, Correspondence of Mother Gerald, Mother Gerald to Sr. Mary (copy), April 9, 1941; George Wilson, "Convention of Colored Catholics"; AADS, Photo Album, Second Annual Diocesan Convention for Negro Catholics, May 17, 1942; ADSA, Hurley Papers, 52-B-1, Study of the Negro Apostolate, January 13–14, 1942.

[65] ADSA, Hurley Papers, 118-M, Fr. Francis Dunleavy, St. Patrick's, to Hurley, October 15, 1945; Tebeau, A History of Florida, p. 441. See also Thomas Ray Wagy, "A South to Save"; Joseph A. Tomberlin, "Florida Whites"; Joseph A. Tomberlin, "School Desegregation Issue."

[66] ADSA, Hurley Papers, 118-M, Chancery Correspondence, Negro Catechetical Centers, 1945.

[67] ADSA, Hurley Papers, 51-I-8, Hurley to Rev. M. J. Ahern, SJ, Boston (copy), December 5, 1944.

[68] AADS, Annals of Blessed Martin Mission, 1937–52; AADS, Photo Album, Blessed Martin Mission, 1943–45. From South Florida's black Catholic schools came fifteen to twenty black leaders of Miami in the 1970s and the 1980s; the influence of these schools was out of proportion to the small percentage of blacks who attended them (Interview, Msgr. Bryan O. Walsh).

[69] AADS, Annals and Mission Files, St. Martin Mission, 1940–62; interview, Sr. Joyce LaVoy, OP.

[70] AAF, Summary Notes on Pine Ridge Hospital.

[71] AADS, Mission Files, St. Martin School; OCD-1952, p. 546; Florida Catholic, January 13, 1956, March 22, 1957.

[72] Curtis Washington, a native of Coconut Grove, was born in 1917 and ordained for the Society of the Divine Word, February 24, 1949, at St. Augustine's, Bay St. Louis, Mississippi. After ordination, he was assigned as a missionary to Ghana, where he was still stationed in 1982 (Steib to author, December 30, 1981). However, Washington was not the first native black Floridian to enter religious life: George Miller of Dade City received the Benedictine habit in February 1908 at St. Leo's Abbey but was not ordained. Both Miller and Washington were converts (ADSA, Kenny Papers, 3-M-15, Mohr to Kenny, February 18, 1908).

[73] Voice, December 2, 1966; Notre Dame Alumnus Magazine 24 (August 1946): 11; AAP, Dougherty Correspondence, Mother Anne Elizabeth to Dougherty, August 27, 1945.

[74] Baptism and Marriage Records at St. Brendan Church, Miami, Immaculate Conception Church, Hialeah, St. Patrick Church, Miami Beach, and St. Mary

Cathedral, Miami; ADSA, Hurley Papers, 123-C, Chancery Correspondence, Spanish Language to be studied by Priests, June 2, 1951.

[75] AIHM, Sr. Mary Ivo to Mother Maria Alma, September 3, 1953.

[76] ADSA, Hurley Papers, 149-G-6, McKeever to Pastors of the Miami Area (circular), August 17, 1954; interview, Fr. Antonio Navarrete. The Spanish-speaking woman hired was Gladys Garcia, MSW, of Puerto Rican descent who was still on the staff of the Catholic Service Bureau in 1982 (*Catholic Service Bureau*).

[77] ADSA, Hurley Papers: 146-F-5, Rev. Manuel Almazen, Barcelona, to Hurley, December 10, 1944; 142-F, McNulty to Msgr. Love, Chancellor, August 14, 1953; interviews, Msgr. McKeever and Fr. Navarrete; *Voice*, July 3, 1959.

[78] The first six OCSHA priests: Luis Altonaga, St. Margaret's, Clewiston; Antonio Navarrete, Corpus Christi, Miami; Colombiano Virseda, St. Joseph's, Miami Beach; Estaban Soy, Sacred Heart, Homestead; Miguel Goñi, Corpus Christi, Miami; Xavier Morras, St. Michael's, Miami (*Voice*, July 3, 1959). Fr. José Paniagua came after. Msgr. Juaristi, Frs. De la Calle, Paz, and Ordax were OCSHA priests working in Cuba who left there after the revolution (interview, Fr. Navarrete).

[79] Interviews, Sr. Mary Albert, SSJ, and Sr. Mary Aquinas, SSJ; ASSJ: Msgr. James Enright, Vicar of Religious, to Mother Anna Maria, SSJ, December 2, 1960; Rev. Joseph H. DeVaney, Pastor of St. Francis Xavier, Ft. Myers, to Mother Anna Maria, May 19, 1961.

[80] USBC, *Historical Census*, pp. 12–13; Tebeau, *A History of Florida*, p. 431; USBC, *Population, 1960, Vol. I*, pp. 11-7, 11-11; USBC, *Abstract, 1970*, pp. 20–21.

[81] OCD-1941, p. 566, and General Summary; OCD-1958, p. 632 and General Summary.

[82] Kelly, *Practice of the Faith*, pp. 194–95, 204; interviews, Sr. Kathleen Reilly, SSND, Mr. Kindelan, Msgr. Nelan, and Bp. Keith Symons; AIHM, Sr. Maria Pacis to Mother Alma, August 30, 1953; AAP, Mother Anne Elizabeth to Card. Dougherty, July 22, 1944.

Chapter 5

[1] ADSA, Hurley Papers: 153-J, Seniority List of Diocesan Priests, April 17, 1957; 153-K, Priests on Loan to the Diocese, September 21, 1957.

[2] Interviews, Msgr. Bryan O. Walsh, Msgr. James J. Walsh, Msgr. John McNulty, Msgr. John O'Dowd, and Bp. Keith Symons.

[3] Interviews, Msgr. Robert Schiefen, Msgr. Thomas O'Donovan, Msgr. Rowan Rastatter, Msgr. McNulty, Msgr. Bryan O. Walsh, Bp. Symons, and Msgr. O'Dowd.

[4] AADS, Correspondence of Mother Gerald, Wm. Barry to Mother Gerald, August 19, 1958.

[5] Interviews, Msgr. Dominic Barry, Msgr. Peter Reilly, Msgr. Wm. Keever, Mrs. Marjorie Fillyaw Donohue, Msgr. Rastatter, and Msgr. James J. Walsh.

[6] AADS, Correspondence of Mother Gerald, Mother Gerald to Wm. Barry (copy), August 25, 1958.

[7] Interviews, Fr. Charles Mallen, CSSR, and Sr. Kathleen Reilly, SSND.

[8] Interviews, Mr. Joseph Fitzgerald, Mr. James Kindelan, and Mr. and Mrs. Ben Benjamin.

[9] Interviews, Bp. Vincent Leonard and Fr. Joseph Girdis; Gerald V. Carroll, Rochester, N.Y., to author, July 10, 1981; ADP, Application for Admission as a Diocesan Seminarian, Coleman F. Carroll, June 10, 1926, and Application for Admission as a Diocesan Seminarian, Howard Joseph Carroll, June (n.d.) 1921; ACUA, Pace Papers: Rev. Donald J. Malady to Rev. Edward Pace, October 15, 1921; Pace to Malady (copy), March 28, 1922.

[10] Interviews, Fr. Girdis, Fr. Robert M. Murphy, and Fr. Larry O'Connell.

[11] Interviews, Sr. Isabel Concannon, CSJ, Bp. Leonard, Fr. John Unger, John Cardinal Dearden, Fr. Murphy, and Fr. O'Connell; Carroll to author, July 10, 1981; ADP, Application for Admission as a Diocesan Seminarian, Coleman F. Carroll, June 10, 1926; ADP, "Installation Commemorative of Coleman F. Carroll, Aux. Bp. of Pittsburgh, November 10, 1953."

[12] Interview, Sr. Isabel Concannon, CSJ; ADU, Registrar's Office; ADP, Application for Admission as a Diocesan Seminarian, Howard Joseph Carroll, June (n.d.) 1921; ASVA, Record Book, Rector's Office, St. Vincent Seminary, Howard Joseph Carroll; ADP, Howard Carroll File: Boyle to Fr. A. M. Wildenberg, OP, Rector of the Albertinum (copy), September 17, 1923; Boyle to Howard Carroll (copy), September 17, 1923; Lonergan to Boyle, August 14, 1923.

[13] ADP, Howard Carroll File: Howard Carroll to Boyle, December 11, 1926, March 2, 1927; Wildenberg to Boyle, January 12, 1928; Boyle to Howard Carroll (copy), February 11, 1928; Howard Carroll to J. A. Reeves, Seton Hall College (copy), May 29, 1931; Howard Carroll to Boyle, May 29, 1931; Boyle to Howard Carroll, December 1, 1930; Vicar General and Chancellor to Howard Carroll, May 18, 1932; ADU, *Duquesne University Bulletin, 1932–33*, 21 (October 1932): 8; *Duquesne University Bulletin, 1933–34*, 22 (October 1933): 9; ACC, Faculty Files. Mt. Mercy College is now called Carlow College.

[14] ADP, Howard Carroll File: Msgr. Michael J. Ready to Howard Carroll, May 28, 1938; Arch. Edward Mooney to Howard Carroll, May 31, 1938; Ready to Boyle, June 1, 1938; Cicognani to Boyle, August 6, 1942, October 20, 1943. Arch. Mooney, later Cardinal Mooney, played an important part in the lives of the Carroll brothers. For more on Mooney, see James Hennesey, *American Catholics*, pp. 263–64, 268, 275–77, 285, 302, 313; OCD-1977, p. 43.

[15] ADU, Registrar's Office, Walter Sharpe Carroll File; ADP, Application for Admission as a Diocesan Seminarian, Walter Sharpe Carroll; ADP, Walter Carroll File: A. Freller, Rector of the Albertinum, to Boyle, July 28, 1933; Walter Carroll to Boyle, December 9, 1933, July 3, November 9, 1936; Chancellor to Walter Carroll (copy), December 14, 1936; Robert L. Hayes, Rector of the North American College, to Boyle, January 17, 1940; Boyle to Walter Carroll (copy), March 28, 1940; Cicognani to Boyle, September 27, 1940; Hurley to Boyle, April 14, 1940; Hurley to Carroll, August 12, 1940. Carroll to author, July 10, 1981.

[16] ADP, Walter Carroll File, Synopsis of the Life of Walter Carroll, NCWC News Service, May 27, 1951. See also AFAM, Walter Carroll Papers.

[17] ADSA, Hurley Papers, 148-F-14, Rev. Joseph McGeough, Secretariate of State, Vatican City, to Hurley, March 31, 1950; ADP, Walter Carroll File: Synopsis of the Life of Walter Carroll, NCWC News Service, May 27, 1951, and Death

Card of Walter Carroll; interview, John Cardinal Dearden; Carroll to author, July 10, 1981.

[18] ADP, Coleman Carroll File, Application for Admission as a Diocesan Seminarian, Coleman F. Carroll; ADU, Registrar's Office, Coleman F. Carroll; ASVA, Record Book Rector's Office, vol. 3; interviews, Fr. O'Connell, Fr. Murphy, Bp. Leonard, and Sr. Isabel Concannon, CSJ.

[19] ASVA, *Seminarist's Symposium, 1929–30*, 12, pp. 91, 147, 159.

[20] ADP, Coleman Carroll File, Official Appointments Card; ACC, Faculty Files; ADU, *Duquesne University Bulletin, 1945–46*, 33 (May 1945): 12; interview, Fr. Unger.

[21] Interviews, Fr. O'Connell, Fr. Unger, and Fr. Girdis; ADP, Coleman Carroll File, Carroll to Diocese (invoice), January 26, 1943; ACUA, Registrar's Office, Coleman F. Carroll.

[22] Interviews, Fr. Unger and Fr. Girdis; ADP, Coleman Carroll File, Fr. E. D. Fusseneggar, pastor of St. Basil's, to Boyle, November 10, 1945.

[23] ADP, Coleman Carroll File, Boyle to Carroll (copy), November 17, 1945.

[24] Ibid., Carroll to Boyle, November 21, 1945.

[25] Ibid.: Carroll to Boyle, May 6, 1949, and Official Appointments Card; ADP, Parish Files, St. Maurice; interviews, Fr. Unger, Fr. Girdis, Fr. Murphy, Sr. Isabel Concannon, CSJ, and Fr. O'Connell.

[26] Interview, Card. Dearden.

[27] Maria Thecla Hisrich, *Sacred Heart*, pp. 17–45, 51–54; interviews, Fr. Girdis, Fr. O'Connell, and Fr. Unger.

[28] Hisrich, *Sacred Heart*, p. 51; interviews, Card. Dearden, Sr. Isabel Concannon, CSJ, and Fr. Murphy.

[29] Interviews, Bp. Leonard, Fr. O'Connell, Fr. Murphy, Fr. Girdis, and Fr. Unger.

[30] ADP, Coleman Carroll File: Dearden to Carroll (copy), July 2, September 5, 1952, December 4, 1956; Papal Bull, Pius XII to Carroll, August 25, 1953; interview, Fr. Unger.

[31] Interviews, Fr. Girdis and Fr. O'Connell; ADP, Vicar of Religious Office, Carroll to Mother Mary Hyacinth, CSFN (copies) September 3, 1953, May 28, 1957.

[32] ADP, Vicar of Religious Office, Correspondence; interviews, Fr. Girdis, Sr. Isabel Concannon, CSJ, and Fr. Unger.

[33] OCD-1958, p. 564; interviews, Fr. Murphy, Fr. Unger, Fr. Girdis, Fr. O'Connell, and Card. Dearden.

[34] Interviews, Fr. Girdis, Card. Dearden, Fr. Unger, and Fr. O'Connell.

[35] Interviews, Card. Dearden and Fr. Unger; Walter Romig, ed. *The American Catholic Who's Who—1952–53*, p. 100; ADP, Coleman Carroll File, Dearden to Carroll (copy), June 8, 1955.

[36] Interviews, Card. Dearden, Fr. Girdis, Fr. Unger, and Fr. Murphy.

[37] Interviews, Msgr. McNulty, Bp. Leonard, Msgr. James J. Walsh, Card. Dearden, Fr. Murphy, and Fr. Unger; ADSA, Hurley Papers: 122-C, "List of Priests Giving High School Retreats," March 1944; 145-C-3, Walter Carroll to Hurley, January 13, 1941; 145-G-21, Walter Carroll to Hurley, November 17, 1941; ADP, Coleman Carroll File, Carroll to Dearden (copy), January 17, 1951.

[38] Interviews, Fr. Unger and Fr. O'Connell; ADP, Vicar General's Office, To Priests, Religious and Seculars of the Diocese of Pittsburgh (circular), August 19, 1958.

[39] ADP, Coleman Carroll File, Commemorative Booklet of the Installation of Coleman F. Carroll (1958); AFAM, CO, Circular Letters, 1958–64: engraved invitation to the installation; Fr. Robert Schiefen, Acting Chancellor, to Priests (circular), October 16, 1958; Statement of Bp. Carroll on the Occasion of the Death of the Holy Father, October 8, 1958. Films were made of the installation highlights.

[40] Interviews, Fr. Unger, Fr. Girdis, Fr. O'Connell, Bp. Anthony G. Bosco, Fr. Murphy, and Sr. Isabel Concannon, CSJ; Hisrich, *Sacred Heart*, p. 17.

[41] Felician Foy, OFM, ed., *The 1960 National Catholic Almanac*, p. 473.

[42] Interview, Card. Dearden.

[43] Interviews, Msgr. Schiefen and Mr. Fitzgerald.

[44] John A. Abbo and Jerome D. Hannan, *Sacred Canons*, p. 711.

[45] Lawrence Cardinal Shehan, "Memoir," p. 247. Many thanks to Miss Ann Rice of Notre Dame Press for letting me see the manuscript, as well as to Cardinal Shehan who was kind enough to duplicate the section of his manuscript dealing with the Hurley-Carroll controversy. The pagination referred to is from the Notre Dame manuscript. Shehan's manuscript has since been published as *A Blessing of Years: The Memoirs of Lawrence Cardinal Shehan*; pp. 163–68 of that text refer to the Hurley-Carroll controversy. AFAM, APF, Votum of Bp. James H. Griffiths to Arch. Egidio Vagnozzi, Apostolic Delegate (copy), September 2, 1963.

[46] AFAM, APF, Miami–St. Augustine Dispute. Msgr. Schiefen was of the opinion that the opening meeting set a bad tone for subsequent negotiations. Msgr. Love, who would have been the most informed in regards to the disputed properties, had died. Bp. Carroll gave Msgrs. O'Donoghue, Nelan, and Schiefen a free hand in the negotiations (interview, Msgr. Schiefen).

[47] AFAM, APF, Miami–St. Augustine Dispute. As a lawyer, Mr. Fitzgerald felt there was a lack of proper legal procedure at the six meetings; for example, positions were not filed with opponents (interview, Mr. Fitzgerald). Msgr. Schiefen held that there was a complete lack of cooperation by those on the commission from St. Augustine with those from Miami (interview, Msgr. Schiefen).

[48] Shehan, "Memoir," p. 248; AFAM, APF: Vagnozzi to Carroll, August 5, 1959, and Votum of Griffiths to Vagnozzi, September 2, 1963.

[49] AFAM, APF: Carroll to Griffiths (copy), April 8, 1960, and Vagnozzi to Carroll, May 27, 1960; interview, Msgr. James Nelan.

[50] AFAM, CO, Carroll to Sylvester A. Taggart, CM, Provincial of the Vincentians, July 7, 1961.

[51] AFAM, APF: Daniel A. Naughton, attorney, Jacksonville, to C. Clyde Atkins, attorney, Miami, August 16, 1961; James Pichowski, Highland Realty, to Mr. R. F. Cook, Director of the Dade Co. Building and Zoning Dept. (copy), August 15, 1961; Fr. Neil Sager, Acting Chancellor of the Diocese of St. Augustine, to Schiefen, Chancellor of the Diocese of Miami, August 16, 1961; Schiefen to Sager (copy), August 18, 1961; Votum of Griffiths to Vagnozzi, September 2, 1963.

[52] *Miami Herald*, October 29, 1961.

[53] AFAM, APF, Votum of Griffiths to Vagnozzi, September 2, 1963.

[54] Shehan, "Memoir," p. 248.

[55] AFAM, APF: Vagnozzi to Carroll, February 21, 1962, and Carroll to Vagnozzi (copy), March 2, 1962.

[56] AFAM, APF: Votum of Griffiths to Vagnozzi, September 2, 1963; Carroll to Vagnozzi (copy), January 29, 1964; Carroll to Shehan (copy), February 8, 1964.

[57] Shehan, "Memoir," pp. 248–50; AFAM, APF, Vagnozzi to Carroll, March 2, 1964.

[58] Shehan, "Memoir," p. 250.

[59] Ibid., pp. 251–54; Abbo and Hannan, *Sacred Canons*, p. 866; interviews, Judge C. Clyde Atkins and Msgr. Nelan.

[60] Interview, Sr. Mary Albert Lussier, SSJ; ASSJ, Fr. John Burns, Chancellor, to Mother Anna Maria, SSJ, October 30, 1958.

[61] *Miami News*, February 5, 1960; *New York Times*, February 7, 1960. See also *Miami Herald*, February 4, 1960; *Detroit News*, February 4, 1960.

[62] *New York Times*, February 5, 1960.

[63] AFAM, APF, Vagnozzi to Carroll, February 6, 1960.

[64] As an example, see *New York Times*, February 16, 1960.

[65] AFAM, APF, Press Statement, n.d. [c. mid-February 1960].

[66] AFAM, APF, Carroll to Vagnozzi (copy), February 19, 1960.

[67] AFAM, APF, Vagnozzi to Carroll, February 20, 1960.

[68] Interviews, Msgr. James J. Walsh and Mr. Fitzgerald; AFAM, APF, Carroll to Vagnozzi (copy), March 2, 1962.

[69] Interviews, Msgr. Schiefen and Msgr. O'Donovan.

[70] AFAM, APF, Carroll to Hurley (copy), March 8, 1960; AFAM, CO, Msgr. John Fitzpatrick to Msgr. John P. Burns, March 11, 1966; *Msgr. William Barry*; interview, Msgr. Schiefen.

[71] Interview, Msgr. McNulty.

Chapter 6

[1] *Voice*, September 11, 1959; interview, Msgr. Arcadio Marinas; Black et al., *Area Handbook for Cuba*, p. 124. For some general histories of Cuba, see Calixto C. Masó, *Historia de Cuba*; Emeritorio S. Sanovenia and Raul M. Shelton, *Cuba y Su Historia*; Suchlicki, *Cuba*; Thomas, *Cuba*; Eric Williams, *From Columbus to Castro*. For a history of the Catholic Church in Cuba, see Justo L. Gonzales, *Development of Christianity*; Ismael Testé, *Historia Eclesiástica de Cuba*. Interview, Bp. Agustín Román, September 11, 1981.

[2] Agustín Román, "La Piedad Popular," p. 11; interviews, Fr. Emilio Vallina (October 26, 1981), Msgr. Marinas, and Fr. Edward McCarthy, OSA; AOSP, Cuban File, "A Short Sketch of the Foundation of the Oblate Sisters of Providence in Havana, Cuba," n.d. [c. 1905].

[3] AFAM, CO, Cuban File, "Notas Biográficos de Su Eminencia Cardinal Arteaga," n.d.; interviews, Bp. Román (September 11, 1981), Fr. Vallina (September 12, 1981), and Fr. McCarthy, OSA.

[4] Sr. Miriam Strong, OP, "Of Fish and Freedom," pp. 132–33; interviews, Sr. Mary Bernadette Scheer, OP, Fr. McCarthy, OSA, and Bp. Román (September 11, 1981); *Voice*, September 11, 1959.

[5] *Voice*, September 11, 1959. The reason parishes were so populous in Havana was that the city had only nine parishes. Since parishes were operated on the benefice system, other churches which might be built within the boundaries of a constituted parish were not named as a parish since they had no benefice or any specific parochial territory (interview, Fr. McCarthy, OSA).

[6] Interview, Sr. Mary Bernadette Scheer, OP; AFAM, CO, Agrupación Católica Universitaria File.

[7] Strong, "Of Fish and Freedom," pp. 11–12; interview, Bp. Román, September 11, 1981. See also Lowry Nelson, *Rural Cuba*.

[8] Quoted from Strong, "Of Fish and Freedom," p. 12. See also Joseph Murphy, "Cuban Santeria," pp. 218–20.

[9] Interviews, Fr. McCarthy, OSA, and Msgr. Marinas. For more on Castro and the revolution, see Edward Gonzalez, *Cuba under Castro*; Herbert L. Matthews, *Fidel Castro*; Mario Llerena, *Unsuspected Revolution*; Fidel Castro, *Revolutionary Struggle*; Lowry Nelson, *Cuba: Measure of a Revolution*.

[10] Strong, "Of Fish and Freedom," pp. 92–96.

[11] *Voice*, April 10, June 5, 12, 1959.

[12] *Voice*, July 31, 1959. The 26th of July movement, organized by Castro, was one of many anti-Batista groups in Cuba. The movement took its name from the ill-fated raid on Moncada Barracks in Oriente Province on July 26, 1953, which first brought Castro into the public eye (Black et al., *Area Handbook for Cuba*, pp. 50–51).

[13] *Voice*, November 27, December 4, 1959.

[14] Interview, Bp. Román, September 11, 1981; *Voice*, January 8, February 19, April 15, 1960.

[15] *Voice*, September 11, 1959, May 20, 27, June 17, July 22, 1960.

[16] The promulgation of the Pastoral followed a national procession of one million members of the Confraternity of Our Lady of Charity (interviews, Bp. Román, September 11, 1981, and Fr. Vallina, September 12, 1981; *Voice*, August 12, 1960). The text of the Cuban Bishops' Pastoral was printed in Spanish in *Voice*, August 19, 1960.

[17] *Voice*, October 7, 1960. For more details on Cuban-American relations of the period, see Kevin B. Tierney, "American Cuban Relations."

[18] *Voice*, October 7, 14, December 16, 23, 1960; interviews, Fr. Vallina, September 12, 1981, and Bp. Román, September 11, 1981.

[19] *Voice*, January 13, 1961. Good Shepherd Seminary was formally confiscated by the Castro regime in 1966 (*Voice*, July 29, 1966).

[20] *Voice*, February 10, 1961.

[21] *Voice*, April 21, 1961; interview, Fr. McCarthy, OSA. In Miami, on the day of the Bay of Pigs invasion, 15,000 Cubans came to Centro Hispano Católico and to Bayfront Park to pray (*Voice*, April 28, 1961). For more on the Bay of Pigs, see Peter Wyden, *Bay of Pigs*.

[22] *Voice*, May 5, June 30, 1961; Strong, "Of Fish and Freedom," p. 124; interview, Bp. Román, September 11, 1981.

[23] Strong, "Of Fish and Freedom," pp. 125–26; *Voice*, September 22, October 6, 1961.

[24] Román went to Chile for four years working as a spiritual director of a high school and than pastor of a rural parish with fourteen tribes of Indians as his parishioners. In 1965, he came to Miami to work with his own people with the encouragement of his bishop in Chile (interview, Bp. Román, September 11, 1981).

[25] *Voice*, October 27, 1961. For some reflections on the social roots of the Cuban revolution, as well as the relation of the Church and state, see James O'Connor, *Origins of Secularism in Cuba*, and Leslie Deward, *Christianity and Revolution*.

[26] *Voice*, October 7, 1960, May 12, 19, 26, July 28, 1961; interview, Sr. Mary Bernadette Scheer, OP; AIHM: Epiphany Annals, May 12–20, 1961; Notre Dame Annals, October 13, 1960, May 1961.

[27] *Voice*, June 2, 16, July 28, 1961; AFAM, CO, Circular Letter File (1958–64), Schiefen to Priests (circular), January 31, 1962; interview, Sr. Mary Henrietta Luaces, OSP.

[28] Interview, Msgr. Marinas; AFAM, CO, Spanish-Speaking Apostolate File: "Number of Priests from Cuba," July 24, 1961; "Directory of Spanish-Speaking Apostolate File," November 1962; Extension File, June 20, July 16, 1962. The *Voice* reported seventy-five Cuban clergy in South Florida in July 1961 (*Voice*, July 28, 1961).

[29] AFAM, CO, OBRA File: McKeever to Schiefen (memo), March 9, 1961; "List of OCSHA Priests," September 6, 1961; "OBRA Priests Working in the Diocese of Miami," n.d. [c. September 1964].

[30] *Voice*, May 12, 26, June 2, July 21, 1961; interviews, Fr. McCarthy, OSA, Br. Patrick Ellis, FSC, Br. Martin Thomas, FMA; AFAM, CO, Spanish-Speaking Apostolate File, "Number of Priests from Cuba," July 24, 1961.

[31] AFAM, CO, Spanish-Speaking Apostolate File, "The Plight of Cuban Seminarians," March, 1962; interviews, Msgr. Marinas and Fr. Vallina (September 12, 1981); *Voice*, August 11, 1961.

[32] Interview, Msgr. Marinas; AFAM, CO, Spanish-Speaking Apostolate File: "The Plight of Cuban Seminarians," March 1962, and Marinas to Carroll, April 12, 1962. Cuban seminarians in the United States were at Kenrick Seminary, St. Meinrad's, St. Paul College (Washington, D.C.), and Mt. St. Mary's (Cincinnati) (*Voice*, August 11, 1961).

[33] AFAM, CO, Religious Communities File, Fr. Eugenio Del Busto, Asst. Chancellor, to Rev. Kenneth J. Smith, Worcester, Ma. (copy), October 31, 1967; *Voice*, September 11, 1959, June 16, 1961.

[34] *Voice*, July 3, 1959, June 19, 1964; interview, Fr. Vallina, September 12, 1981; AFAM, CO, Spanish-Speaking Apostolate File, Copy of Congressional Record from Dante Fascell, June 24, 1963.

[35] *Voice*, March 27, April 10, July 3, 1959; ADSA, Hurley Papers, 123-C, Chancery Correspondence, "Spanish Language to be Studied by Priests," June 2, 1951; AFAM, CO, Religious Education File (1959–70), Fr. J. H. Sweeney, SJ, pastor of Gesu, to Fr. Charles Ward, Asst. Chancellor, January 15, 1964.

[36] Juan M. Clark, "Exodus from Revolutionary Cuba," p. 75. This dissertation was published as Clark, *The Cuban Exodus: Background, Evolution, Impact*. See also Cecilios Morales, *Shrine*, p. 9.

[37] Marino Lopez-Blanco, Pedro A. Montiel, and Luishi Suarez, "Attitudes of Cuban Refugees," pp. 3–6. See also Nelson, *Cuba: Measure of a Revolution.*

[38] Clark, "Exodus from Revolutionary Cuba," pp. 249–50. See also Richard R. Fagan and Richard A. Brody. *Cubans in Exile: A Demographic Analysis*; Richard R. Fagan, Richard A. Brody, and Thomas J. O'Leary, *Cubans in Exile: Disaffection.*

[39] *Voice*, September 18, 1964; Dominick Joseph Adessa, "Unaccompanied Children," pp. 5, 50–55.

[40] Kimball D. Woodbury, "Diffusion of the Cuban Community," p. 10.

[41] "Flight of the Cuban Refugee," p. 777; *Miami Herald*, June 26, 1960. Articles in the *Voice* on the Cuban exiles in 1959–68 stressed the political, anti-Communist nature of the exodus. See also Strong, "Of Fish and Freedom"; Clark, "Exodus from Revolutionary Cuba"; Silvia Pedraza-Bailey, "Political and Economic Immigrants."

[42] Interview, Fr. McCarthy, OSA; *Voice*, May 22, 1959; Strong, "Of Fish and Freedom," pp. 3, 11–12; Lopez-Blanco, Montiel, Suarez, "Attitudes of Cuban Refugees," pp. 3–6; *New York Herald Tribune*, November 23, 1963.

[43] Lopez-Blanco, Montiel, and Suarez, "Attitudes of Cuban Refugees," p. 17. See also Fagan, Brody, and O'Leary, *Cubans in Exile: Disaffection.*

[44] *Miami Herald*, April 9, 1967; *New York Times*, October 1, 1967; Bryan O. Walsh, "Cubans in Miami"; Edward J. Linehan, "Cuba's Exiles."

[45] USBC, *Abstract*, 1970, pp. 89–94; *Voice*, November 4, 1960, October 28, 1966.

[46] *Voice*, November 12, December 3, 1965, December 9, 1966; Tebeau, *A History of Florida*, p. 434; *Miami Herald*, April 9, 1967. See also E. M. Martin, "U.S. Outlines Policy"; Rafael J. Prohias, *Cuban Minority in the United States.*

[47] U.S. Congress, Senate, *Migration and Refugee Assistance Act of 1962*, 87th Cong., 1st sess., P.L. 87-510 (1962). Clark, "Exodus from Revolutionary Cuba," p. 114, gives the yearly and cumulative costs of the Cuban Refugee program in table 10, p. 130.

[48] *Voice*, February 3, 1961, April 13, May 18, 1962; USBC, *Abstract*, 1970, p. 95.

[49] Interview, Bp. Román, September 11, 1981; Woodbury, "Diffusion of the Cuban Community," pp. 2, 30–33, 37, 61. See also Fagan and Brody, *Cubans in Exile: A Demographic Analysis*; B. E. Aguirre, Kent P. Schwiran, and Anthony J. La Greca, "Residential Patterning."

[50] Woodbury, "Diffusion of the Cuban Community," p. 28. See also Kenneth L. Wilson and Alejandro Portes, "Immigrant Enclaves."

[51] AFAM, CO: Religious Communities File, Del Busto to Rev. Kenneth J. Smith (copy), October 31, 1967; Extension File, Schiefen to Fr. Joseph Cusack, Extension Society (copy), July 12, 1967; Clark, "Exodus from Revolutionary Cuba," pp. 97–98, 150, 163; *Miami Herald*, April 9, 1967; Lopez-Blanco, Montiel, Suarez, "Attitudes of Cuban Refugees," p. 57; OCD-1969, pp. 458–62.

Chapter 7

[1] OCD-1959, p. 529; *Voice*, March 18, 1960; AFAM, CO, OBRA General File, McKeever to Carroll (memo), January 25, 1960.

[2] *Catholic Service Bureau Golden Anniversary*, pp. 11–12; AFAM, CO, Catholic Service Bureau File: B. O. Walsh to Carroll (memo), November 14, 1958; B. O. Walsh to Nelan (memo), February 16, 1959; Adessa, "Unaccompanied Children," pp. 22–23, 43–49.

[3] The Resolution of the Cuban Refugee Committee of Dade County is quoted in Adessa, "Unaccompanied Children," pp. 170–73; see also *Voice*, December 9, 23, 1960, and Strong, "Of Fish and Freedom," p. 68.

[4] To receive financial aid from Dade County at the time one had to have had one year's residence in the county; to receive state aid, a five-year residence was required (Strong, "Of Fish and Freedom," pp. 68, 165). AFAM, CO, Centro Hispano Católico File (1960–63), B. O. Walsh to Carroll (report), February 9, 1961; Adessa, "Unaccompanied Children," p. 30.

[5] *Voice*, February 3, December 8, 15, 1961; AFAM, CO, Centro Hispano Católico File (1960–63), Fitzpatrick to Mark Fosters (copy), July 5, 1961; Strong, "Of Fish and Freedom," p. 88; U.S. Congress, Senate, 87th Cong., 1st sess., Subcommittee on Refugees and Escapees, Cuban Refugee Problem Hearings, Testimony of Bp. Coleman F. Carroll, December 6, 1961.

[6] AFAM, CO, Centro Hispano Católico File (1960–63): Fitzpatrick to Mr. Lawton M. Calhoun, President, Savannah Sugar Corp. (copy), November 26, 1962; Fitzpatrick to Borden's Dairy, Miami (copy), December 6, 1962; Carroll to Mr. Aloysius Little, St. Vincent de Paul Society, Philadelphia (copy), May 12, 1961; *Voice*, December 9, 1960; Strong, "Of Fish and Freedom," pp. 24, 26.

[7] AFAM, CO, Centro Hispano Católico File (1960–63), "Report by Sr. Mary William, OP, of Centro Hispano Católico for January 1, 1962 to December 31, 1962," February 19, 1963; Adessa, "Unaccompanied Children," p. 68.

[8] See also Adessa, "Unaccompanied Children," pp. 6, 23–24; Strong, "Of Fish and Freedom," pp. 5–6.

[9] *Catholic Service Bureau Golden Anniversary*, pp. 11–12; AFAM, CO, Catholic Service Bureau File, B. O. Walsh to Carroll (memo), November 14, 1958; Adessa "Unaccompanied Children," pp. 22–25; *Voice*, September 25, 1959.

[10] *Voice*, September 25, 1959. Centro was formally blessed and inaugurated January 31, 1960 (Strong, "Of Fish and Freedom," pp. 7, 9, 19, 23, 69, 99). Carroll offered the Dominican Sisters land in Kendall for a retreat house if they would help at Centro (ADSCR, Centro Hispano Católico File; *Voice*, October 23, 1959). Sr. Miriam Strong, OP, was named by the *Miami News* "Outstanding Woman of 1960" (*Voice*, January 6, 1961). She was transferred from Miami in September 1961 (*Voice*, September 8, 15, 1961).

[11] Strong, "Of Fish and Freedom," p. 5.

[12] AFAM, CO, Centro Hispano Católico File (1960–63), "The History and Purpose of Centro," March 22, 1962. The outpatient clinic was set up by Dr. Edward Lauth, president of the Catholic Physician's Guild of Miami, and staffed two days a week by volunteer Miami Catholic doctors. During its second year, a hundred patients were seen daily (Strong, "Of Fish and Freedom," pp. 29, 39–42).

[13] *Voice*, August 18, 1961; AFAM, CO, Centro Hispano Católico File (1960–63): "History and Report," March 1963; "Report for 1963," n.d. [c. February 1964].

[14] AFAM, CO, Centro Hispano Católico File (1960–63): Fitzpatrick to B. O.

Walsh (memo), February 13, 1964; Carroll to Fitzpatrick (memo), April 17, 1964; "Revamping Centro," April 28, 1964.

[15] AFAM, CO, Census File (1959–70), "Centro Hispano Católico Statement," June 18, 1964.

[16] AFAM, CO, Social Apostolate File, "Dato Sobre las Actividades de Su Excellencia Monseñor Coleman F. Carroll con Referencia a Latino América," July 9, 1968; *Voice*, March 12, 1982; *Miami Herald*, April 12, 1983.

[17] Strong, "Of Fish and Freedom," pp. 78, 83–84; Adessa, "Unaccompanied Children," pp. 34–39, 50–52, 60; "Cuba—And Now the Children," p. 41; *Voice*, January 27, 1959.

[18] Adessa, "Unaccompanied Children," pp. 44–48, 55–58. The house across the street from Assumption Academy was offered by its owner, Maurice Ferré, a Puerto Rican businessman who is presently mayor of Miami (interview, Msgr. Bryan O. Walsh).

[19] Adessa, "Unaccompanied Children," pp. 68–73, 81–83, 102–4; *Voice*, February 3, 1961, March 9, June 15, 1962; interview, Msgr. Bryan Walsh; AFAM, CO, Catholic Service Bureau File (1961–66), Walsh to Carroll (memo), January 3, 1962; Strong, "Of Fish and Freedom," pp. 82–83.

[20] Adessa, "Unaccompanied Children," pp. 32–33, 120, 124. The unaccompanied children stopped coming out of Cuba in the Cuban missile crisis of October 1962. "Report to the Florida State Dept. of Public Welfare on the Costs of Administration of the Cuban Children's Program, 1963," quoted in Adessa, "Unaccompanied Children," p. 69; *Voice*, July 22, 1966; interview, Msgr. Bryan Walsh.

[21] Adessa, "Unaccompanied Children," pp. 10–11. See also Alexander Stanley Joksina, "Orphaned and Unaccompanied Children"; Thomas Leonard Moroski, "Resettlement of Unaccompanied Children."

[22] Adessa, "Unaccompanied Children," pp. 77, 109–11, 166. For summary articles on the Cuban unaccompanied children, see Bryan O. Walsh, "Cuban Refugee Children"; "More About Refugee Cuban Children," pp. 497–98; *Miami Herald*, March 12, 1962.

[23] Interviews, Mr. Joseph Fitzgerald and Msgr. Arcadio Marinas; *Voice*, October 15, November 26, 1965; AFAM, CO, Circular Letters File (1958–64), Schiefen to Priests (circular), June 7, 1962.

[24] AFAM, CO, Spanish Apostolate File, Chancellor (memo), n.d. [c. October 10, 1961].

[25] Interviews, Bp. Vincent Leonard, Msgr. James Nelan, and John Cardinal Dearden.

[26] Canon 216, paragraphs 1 and 4 are cited in T. Lincoln Bouscaren, SJ, and Adam C. Ellis, SJ, *Canon Law*, p. 149.

[27] Charles Shanabruch, *Chicago's Catholics*, pp. 181–85. "Norms for the Spiritual Care of Emigrants" by Pius XII, August 1, 1952, can be found in Latin as "De Spirituali Emigrantum Cura." The document calls ministry to foreigners "missionary."

[28] Interview, Bp. John J. Fitzpatrick.

[29] AFAM, Private Episcopal Files of Coleman F. Carroll, Episcopal Candidates

File, Carroll to Arch. Luigi Raimondi, Apostolic Delegate (copy), December 6, 1967.

[30] Interviews, Msgr. Robert Schiefen, Msgr. Bryan Walsh, and Mrs. Marjorie Fillyaw Donohue; AFAM: CO, Circular Letters File (1965–68), Carroll to Priests (circular), February 1, 1968; Private Episcopal Files of Coleman F. Carroll: Carroll to Fitzpatrick (copy), November 19, 1964; Vagnozzi to Arch. Boyle, NCWC (copy), November 27, 1964; CO, Agrupacion Católica Universitaria File, Fitzpatrick to Schiefen (memo), October 9, 1962; *Voice*, July 28, August 25, 1961.

[31] AFAM, CO, St. Philip Neri Sisters File, Carroll to Fitzpatrick (memo), December 7, 1964.

[32] AFAM, CO, Extension File, Carroll to Cusack (copy), July 27, 1961.

[33] *Voice*, February 9, 1962. Fr. Eugenio Del Busto was made assistant chancellor to the Latin American Chancery officially in 1964, though he had been working at that office since its inception in 1962 (OCD-1965, p. 578). In 1965, after Msgr. Fitzpatrick was named chancellor of the diocese and the Latin American Chancery was dissolved, Del Busto was made assistant chancellor of the Diocese (OCD-1966, p. 587; interview, Msgr. William McKeever).

[34] AFAM, CO, Spanish Apostolate File: Del Busto to Fitzpatrick (memo), May 5, 1965; "Minutes, Parish Reassessment Committee, April 14, 1967"; interview, Msgr. B. Walsh.

[35] *Voice*, March 18, 1960, March 30, 1962, July 28, 1967. The percentage of Spanish-speaking children in the following parochial schools in December 1960, was Gesu, 83; Corpus Christi, 50; SS. Peter and Paul, 35; St. Patrick's, 34; St. Michael's, 29; St. Joseph's, 26; St. John the Apostle, 21; St. Theresa of the Little Flower, 13; Immaculate Conception, 10 (*Voice*, December 9, 1960; AFAM, CO, Spanish Apostolate File, "Spanish Masses in Dade County Parishes," April 1966).

[36] Interview, Fr. Vallina, September 12, 1981; *Voice*, January 10, 1964, February 9, 1968; St. John Bosco Church, Baptismal Register, February 3, 1963; AFAM, CO, Religious Education File (1959–70): Fitzpatrick to Brunner (copy), December 20, 1963; "CCD–Monthly Assessments," n.d. [c. fall 1965].

[37] *Voice*, August 27, 1965, December 16, 1966; interview, Fr. Vallina, October 26, 1981; St. John Bosco Church Files, Vallina to Parishioners (circular), December 2, 1979.

[38] Interviews, Fr. Vallina (October 26, 1981) and Msgr. Schiefen; OCD-1969, p. 458. The school was taught by the Mexican Guadalupanas Sisters and by priests and laity of the parish (*Voice*, October 6, 1967) and was blessed by Bp. Carroll in February 1968 (*Voice*, February 9, 1968; St. John Bosco Church, Baptismal and Marriage Registers, 1963–68).

[39] *Voice*, September 16, 30, 1966; AFAM, CO, Shrine of Our Lady of Charity File (1966–73), Carroll to Román (copy), September 6, 1967.

[40] Oscar Handlin, *The Uprooted*, pp. 105–6.

[41] Interviews, Fr. Vallina, October 26, 1981, and Bp. Agustín Román, October 17, 1981.

[42] Interview, Fr. Vallina, October 26, 1981. Eighteen OCSHA priests were in the Diocese of Miami at the time (*Voice*, April 7, 1967). See also AFAM, CO,

OBRA General File: Fr. Xavier Morras to Fitzpatrick, August 20, 1963; Morras to Priests (circular), November 30, 1966.

[43] St. John Bosco Pastor's Office, Spanish Priests' Association File, Minutes, October 25, 1966.

[44] Ibid.: Minutes, November 22, December 18, 20, 1966, n.d. [c. January 24], April 18, n.d. [c. March 27], 1967; "Protest Against Priests' Senate," n.d. [c. March 27, 1967]. In time, certain individual priests claimed to speak for the association but did not in fact; these individuals went to the secular press and media with matters of complaint (interview, Bp. Román, October 17, 1981).

[45] Interviews, Fr. Vallina (October 26, 1981), Fr. Antonio Navarrete, Msgr. Schiefen, and Bp. Fitzpatrick. For a comparison with other immigrant priests' associations, see Shanabruch, *Chicago's Catholics*, pp. 96–102, 216–19; Anthony J. Kuzniewski, *Faith and The Fatherland.*

[46] *Voice*, July 6, 27, August 3, September 7, 1962, July 17, 1964, May 19, 1967; AFAM, CO: Circular Letters File (1958–64), Carroll to Priests (circular), August 27, 1962; Seminary General File (1959–73), "List of Cuban Seminarians, 1967–68," n.d. Of those fourteen, the first ordained for the Archdiocese of Miami were Frs. Juan Sosa and Orlando Espín in 1972.

[47] *Voice*, January 10, 1964; interviews, Fr. Louis Roberts, Br. Patrick Ellis, FSC, and Bp. Román (October 17, 1981); AFAM, CO, Camp Matecumbe File: Schiefen to B. O. Walsh (copy), September 21, 1962, and B. O. Walsh to Fitzpatrick, November 15, 1963.

[48] *Voice*, August 4, 1961; *Washington Post*, August 4, 1981; AFAM, CO, Jesuits—Cubans File: Carroll to Rev. Richard C. Chisholm, SJ (copy), November 10, 1960, and Rev. J. A. Sweeny, SJ, to Schiefen, July 14, 1961. Bp. Carroll gave permission for the Jesuits to establish Belen, saying that it was to be an American school taught in English. Carroll offered a 20-acre site in South Miami to the Jesuits; they refused the offer since they wanted a site closer to the center of the Cuban population (AFAM, CO, Jesuits—Cubans File, Carroll to Fr. Román Calvo, SJ [copy], August 29, 1961).

[49] *Washington Post*, August 4, 1981; AFAM, CO: Jesuits—Cubans File, Fitzpatrick to Schiefen (memo), October 24, 1962; Belen High School File, Latin American Advisory Committee to Carroll (memo), n.d. [c. September, 1963]; Schiefen to Rev. Ceferino Ruíz, SJ (copy), October 25, 1965; Schiefen to Ruíz (copy), December 20, 1965; Fitzpatrick to Mr. Frank J. Lojacona, Asst. Manager, Better Business Bureau of Greater Miami (copy), September 27, 1965; Fr. Pedro Arrupe, SJ, Jesuit General, Rome, to Carroll, February 12, 1969; Ruíz to Del Busto, December 17, 1965.

[50] OCD-1967, pp. 608–9; OCD-1969, pp. 462–63.

[51] AFAM, CO, Sisters of St. Philip Neri File: Nelan to Carroll (memo), August 9, 1963; B. O. Walsh to Schiefen, September 23, 1963; Fr. Giovanni Verdelli, Sacred Cong. of Religious, to Carroll, January 1, 1965; "Report of the Vicar of Religious on the Novitiate," May 19, 1965; Fitzpatrick to Enright (memo), April 5, 1966; Enright to Carroll (memo), January 16, 1967. See also *Voice*, December 18, 1964. The Novitiate was canonically erected on July 1, 1965.

[52] ASHN, Key West Annals, "Vocations," n.d. [c. 1959]; Roth, *History of the*

Diocese, "Records of the Episcopal Acts of the Rt. Rev. Augustin Verot," November 11, 1875, p. 178; OCD-1969, p. 462.

[53] Fr. Juan Sosa feels that santería was on the increase in Miami as of 1972 ("La Santería," p. 103). See also *Miami Herald*, August 29, 1971.

[54] Albert J. Raboteau, *Slave Religion*, pp. 16–42; Murphy, "Cuban Santería," pp. 150, 190–93, 205–22; William Bascom, "The Focus of Cuban Santería," pp. 520–27. For a description of the essential aspects of Cuban santería, see Sosa, "La Santería," pp. 64–96. See also Kenneth F. Kiple, *Blacks in Colonial Cuba*; Sandra T. Barnes, *Ogun*; Agustín Román, "La Piedad Del Pueblo Cubano," p. 36; Carlos Canét, *Lucumi*; Agún Efundé, *Los Secretos de la Santería*; Migene Gonzáles-Wippler, *Santería*.

[55] Some of these ideas are found in Sosa, "La Santería," pp. 102–38.

[56] Murphy, "Cuban Santería," pp. 198–207; Román, "La Piedad Del Pueblo Cubano," p. 79. For a list of *orisha*-Saint correspondence, see Román, "La Piedad Del Pueblo Cubano," pp. 37–40; Sosa, "La Santería," pp. 159–60; Murphy, "Cuban Santería," pp. 363–64.

[57] Román, "La Piedad Del Pueblo Cubano," pp. 76–79. For a brief account of the origins of the devotion of our Lady of Charity, see Morales, *Shrine*, p. 13; *Voice*, September 16, 1960, September 15, 1961. In 1966, the Mass was held on September 11 (*Voice*, September 16, 1966). A copy of Bp. Carroll's speech on the occasion can be found at AFAM, CO, Shrine of Our Lady of Charity File (1966–73), "Speech," September 11, 1966.

[58] AFAM, CO, Shrine of Our Lady of Charity File (1966–73), Carroll to Román (copy), September 6, 1967; interview, Bp. Román, September 11, 1981.

[59] Román, "La Piedad Del Pueblo Cubano," pp. 1–2 (my translation).

[60] Ibid.; interview, Bp. Román, October 17, 1981. For more on the evangelization of the unchurched, see Wladyslaw Rubin, "Religiosidad Popular y Evangelización Missionera"; Pope Paul VI, *Evangelii nuntiandi*.

[61] *Voice*, September 1, 1967.

[62] Interviews, Bp. Román; Morales, *Shrine*, pp. 16–19.

[63] *Concentracion Religiosa* was planned for January 24–26, 1962, at eight parishes (*Voice*, January 19, 1962). The Franciscans ran a mission at Immaculate Conception January 24–28, 1966 (*Voice*, January 14, 1966).

[64] AFAM, CO: Spanish-speaking Apostolate File (1960–75), "Minutes—Organizations Meeting of the Co-ordinating Committee of the Cuban Catholic Organizations," November 16, 1961; Christian Family Movements File, Fitzpatrick to Schiefen (memo), February 7, 1963, Fitzpatrick to Dr. Humberto Lopez, Key Biscayne, February 19, 1963, Del Busto to Fitzpatrick (memo), June 2, 1966; *Voice*, January 13, 1961.

[65] Interview, Bp. Román, October 17, 1981; AFAM, CO, Bishop's Consecration File, "Official Invitation List," July 17, 1968. In 1979, *Movimiento Familiar Cristiano* had approximately 500 members. AFAM, CO: Christian Family Movements File, José and Nancy Díaz to Fr. G. LaCerra, chancellor, August 2, 1982; Agrupacion Catolica Universitaria File, Fr. Vincent Sheehy, Diocesan Building Commission, to Schiefen, July 9, 1962, Llorente to Fitzpatrick, August 2, 1962.

[66] *Voice*, January 15, 1982; interview, Bp. Román, October 17, 1981; AFAM,

CO, Cursillo File: Fitzpatrick to Fr. John A. Wagner, Exec. Secretary of the Bishop's Committee for Spanish-Speaking (copy), January 5, 1962; Fr. Primitivo Santamaría, OP, to Carroll, March 16, 1962; Fitzpatrick to Santamaría (copy), March 14, 1966.

[67] AFAM, CO, Bishop's Consecration File, "Official Invitation List," July 17, 1968.

[68] Interviews, Msgr. Schiefen, Fr. Vallina (September 12, 1981), and Bp. Román (October 17, 1981); AFAM, CO, Spanish-Speaking Apostolate (1960–75), Fitzpatrick to Pastors (circular), November 23, 1962; *Voice*, September 22, 1967.

[69] Frank Ponce, "The U.S. Church's Hispanic Catholics," pp. 199–201; *Voice*: January 8, 1965, September 22, 1967; interview, Bp. Román, October 17, 1981.

[70] Quoted in Morales, *Shrine*, p. 4. See also Juan Sosa, "An Anglo-Hispanic Dilemma."

[71] An attempt has been made to assess the impact of Cubans upon South Florida Catholicism; see *Voice*, July 18, 1975, and Walsh, "Cubans in Miami," p. 41.

Chapter 8

[1] *Voice*, March 11, 1960.

[2] AFAM, CO, Diocese of St. Augustine File, Hurley to Priests (circular), January 3, 1956; *Voice*, January 15, February 19, March 18, April 8, 1960.

[3] *Voice*, January 12, March 16, December 28, 1962, January 17, 1964; AFAM, Archivist's Office, "Five Year Report, 1964–68."

[4] AFAM, CO: Building Commission File, McKeever to Carroll (memo), January 20, 1959, "Agenda for Meeting," September 28, 1960, and Schiefen to Carroll (memo), August 3, 1964; Consultors' Files, January 1959–January 1968.

[5] AIHM, Notre Dame Annals, September 9, 1960; *Voice*, September 4, 1964, September 17, 1965; SBCC, September 7–8, 1965.

[6] Xavier Rynne, pseud., *Vatican Council II*, p. 25; *Voice*, October 12, December 14, 1962.

[7] *Voice*, July 10, 1959, February 2, 1962, December 10, 1965.

[8] *Voice*, June 10, 1960, February 22, May 10, 17, December 20, 1963, February 12, 1965; interview, Fr. John Unger.

[9] AFAM, CO, Ecumenical File, 1958–72: Carroll to Enright (memo), May 24, 1966; Pierce to Carroll, November 30, 1967; Carroll to Fr. Ronald Pusak (memo), February 5, 1968; Carroll to Fr. Frederick Waas (memo), August 29, 1968; Fitzpatrick to B. O. Walsh (memo), October 23, 1964; Fr. Martin Walsh, Chairman, Interfaith Agency for Social Issues (memo), n.d. [c. April 1967]; *Miami Herald*, August 15, 1967.

[10] AFAM, CO, Ecumenical File, 1958–72: Fitzpatrick to Carroll (memo), March 31, 1967; Ecumenical Commission Meeting Minutes, October 3, 1967; Carroll to Fitzpatrick (memo), January 27, 1965; *Voice*, December 9, 1966; for a comparison of ecumenism in a northern diocese, see *Boston Pilot*, January 9, 16, 20, May 1, 1965.

[11] AFAM, CO, Circular Letters File, 1958–64, Carroll to Clergy, Religious and Faithful (circular) November 30, 1960; *Voice*, April 9, 1965.

[12] *Voice*, October 11, 1963, February 28, March 6, 1964; Austin Flannery, gen. ed., *Vatican Council II*, p. 1; AFAM, CO, Circular Letters File, 1958–64, Carroll to Priests (circular), February 7, 1964. The idea that the liturgical reforms were to be "gradual" was also stressed by Rome and the U.S. Bishops: AFAM, APF, Liturgy Report File, E. Vagnozzi to Card. Spellman (copy), March 31, 1964; CO, Circular Letters File, 1958–64, Fitzpatrick to Priests (circular), April 28, 1964; *Voice*, May 1, 1964.

[13] *Voice*, May 22, 1964; AFAM, APF: Liturgy Reforms (1964) File, Carroll to Fitzpatrick (memo), November 2, 1964, and Vernacular Liturgy File, Carroll to Liturgical Music Commission (copy), January 27, 1965; CO, Circular Letters File, 1958–64, Fitzpatrick to Priests, September 11, 1964; N. C. News Service, January 22, 1965; Liturgy-Sacred Congregation of Rites File, Carroll to Giacomo Cardinal Lercero (copy), January 25, 1965.

[14] AFAM, CO, Circular Letters File, 1965–68: Fitzpatrick to Priests (circular), April 5, 1965; Carroll to Priests (circular), March 5, 1965; AOSP, St. Francis Xavier Annals, March 6, 7, 1965; AFAM, APF, Liturgical Reforms (1965) File, Carroll "For the Record" (memo), April 5, 1965; *Voice*, April 2, 1965.

[15] *Voice*, October 29, 1965, March 18, 1966, October 6, 1967, June 21, 1968; AFAM, CO, Circular Letters File, 1965–68, Carroll to Priests (circular), March 30, 1966.

[16] AFAM, CO, Circular Letters File, 1958–64, Fitzpatrick to Priests (circular), January 17, 1964; *Voice*, December 11, 1964, February 18, 25, November 25, 1966.

[17] AFAM, CO: Circular Letters File, 1958–64, Schiefen to Priests (circular), November 20, 1958; Forty Hours Devotion File, Fr. Ronald Pusak, Acting Chancellor, to Pastors (circular), November 6, 1967; N.C. News Service, February 19, 1968; Carroll to Priests (circular), October 22, 1969; Bishop-Liturgy File, "Simplification of Pontifical Rites and Insignia," June 21, 1968; *Sacrum diaconatus ordinem*, June 18, 1967, *Acta Apostolicae Sedis*, 59 (1967), pp. 697–704.

[18] *Voice*, June–August 1960, November 18, 1960; Andrew M. Greeley, *American Catholic*, pp. 50–89. For an analysis of the relation of Catholicism to American culture, see also Philip Gleason, "Catholicism and Cultural Change."

[19] *Voice*, September 11, 1959, August 4, September 1, 1961, June 29, 1962, August 23, 1963, August 7, 1964, August 20, 1965, August 19, 1966; *Davenport Messenger*, May 1, 1958; *Miami News*, August 25, 1961.

[20] *Voice*, July 10, 1959, December 23, 1960, October 6, December 22, 1967; AFAM, CO, Circular Letters File, 1965–68: Fitzpatrick to Priests (circular), November 30, 1965; Carroll to Priests (circular), April 12, 1967; Pusak to Catholic Organizations (circular), April 14, 1967.

[21] *Voice*, August 30, September 6, 1963, May 15, June 26, November 20, 1964, April 2, 1965, April 15, November 4, 1966, August 2, 9, November 22, 1968; *National Catholic Reporter*, April 19, 1967.

[22] Greeley, *American Catholic*, p. 143.

[23] AFAM, CO, Military Ordinariate File, Fitzpatrick to Carlson (copy), August 22, 1966; *Voice*, February 25, September 9, 1966, February 17, April 14, 1967, March 15, November 22, 1968.

[24] *Voice*, June 12, July 24, 1959, February 26, March 4, August 12, 1960, Janu-

ary 17, 1964; AFAM, Archivist's Office, "Five Year Report, 1964–68"; OCD-1969, p. 463.

[25] *Voice*, February 5, March 11, July 22, 29, 1960; OCD-1965, p. 579; OCD-1966, p. 588; AFAM, CO, Miami Airport Chapel File, Zinn to Gracida (memo), November 17, 1969.

[26] *Voice*, August 5, 1960, November 15, 1963, January 17, 1964; AFAM, Archivist's Office, "Five Year Report, 1964–68"; OCD-1959, pp. 527–29; OCD-1969, p. 463; OCD-1978, pp. 505–11; AIHM, Notre Dame Annals, September 6, 1960; SBCC, June 5, August 14, 1963; ACSFN, "Self-Study Report of St. Brendan School, November, 1974"; interviews, Fr. Lamar Genovar and Msgr. Rowan Rastatter.

[27] *Voice*, January 17, 1964; OCD–1965, pp. 581–82; AIHM, Lourdes Annals, August 20, 31, 1964.

[28] Interview, Msgr. Dominic Barry; AFAM, CO, Education—School Board Minutes File, Diocesan School Board Minutes, February 6, 1964, June 3, 1966, February 5, November 9, 1967.

[29] AFAM, CO: Rel. Ed. File, 1959–70, Philbin to Carroll, September 27, 1959, Carroll to Priests (circular), November 17, 1959; Circular Letters File, 1958–64, Carroll to Pastors (circular) October 12, 1959; SBCC, October 23, 1959; Philbin to Schiefen, February 14, 1960.

[30] AFAM, CO: Circular Letters File, 1958–64, Carroll to Priests (circular), September 19, 1962; Rel. Ed. File, 1959–70, Carroll to Brunner (copy), October 2, 1962; CCD Committee Report, n.d. [c. May 1963].

[31] AFAM, CO: Rel. Ed. File, 1959–70, Carroll to Philbin (copy), January 30, 1964, Fitzpatrick to Priests (circular), October 2, 1964, Carroll to Brunner (copy), February 21, 1967; Circular Letters File, 1965–68, Fitzpatrick to Priests (circular), November 15, 1966; ADSCR, Sr. Collette, OP, to Mother Emmanuel, OP, March 30, 1964.

[32] AFAM, CO, Rel. Ed. File, 1959–70, McKeever and Brunner to Carroll (memo), June 5, 1968; interviews, Bp. Román (October 17, 1981), and Fr. Charles Mallen, CSSR.

[33] AFAM, CO, Spiritual Conference File, Sr. Mary Alice, OP, to Carroll, August 23, 1960; *Voice,* July 1, 1960, July 19, 1963, April 9, 1965, March 8, 1968; SBCC, December 10, 1966, February 21, 1968; interview, Fr. Cyril Burke, OP.

[34] AFAM, CO, Biscayne File: Carroll to Fr. James A. Dunnellen, OSA, Prior Provincial (copy), November 29, 1961; Agreement—Carroll and OSAs, March 25, 1962; Schiefen to Fr. Robert M. Sullivan, Biscayne Prior (copy), August 8, 1967. *Voice*, June 16, 1961; interview, Fr. Edward McCarthy, OSA. Biscayne College changed its name to St. Thomas of Villanova University on February 1, 1984.

[35] AFAM, CO, Marymount File: Clarence F. Gaines to Carroll, March 16, May 11, 1959; Bureau of Information Release, June 6, 1962; "Progress Report on Marymount College, Vol. 1, #2," Fall 1963; *Voice*, November 24, 1961, March 19, 1965.

[36] AFAM, CO, Marymount File: "Project Reports," July 6, 1965, and "Final Report—Marymount Self-Help Project," summer, 1965; *Voice*, April 30, May 28, 1965, July 1, 1966, August 18, 1967, July 12, 1968.

[37] AFAM, CO, Marymount File: Fitzpatrick to Mother de la Croix, RSHM (copy), February 4, 1964, and Fr. Charles Ward, Vice-Chancellor, to Mother de la Croix, RSHM (copy), February 2, 1965; *Voice*, March 27, 1964, January 15, September 17, 1965.

[38] AFAM, CO, Marymount File: Bp. Rene Gracida, Aux. Bp. of Miami, to Fr. Paul Manning, Pastor of St. Joan of Arc (copy), March 10, 1972, and Fr. Noel Fogarty, Chancellor, to Carroll (memo), February 14, 1973; OCD-1972, p. 478; OCD-1973, p. 476.

[39] *Living Waters*, pp. 26-30.

[40] *Voice*, March 20, June 5, 26, 1959, January 12, 1968; AFAM, CO, Circular Letters File, 1958-64, Carroll to Priests (circular), March 10, 1959.

[41] *Voice*, April 10, December 4, 1959, January 12, 1962, December 25, 1964, October 29, 1965; AFAM, CO, Radio and T.V. File, 1958-71: Fr. Louis Roberts to Fr. Joseph McLaughlin, December 10, 1959; Fr. Donald F. X. Connolly, Sec. to the Bishop, to Fr. David Heffernan, Chairman of the Diocesan Radio and T.V., July 11, 1961; Fr. Joseph O'Shea, Director of Radio and T.V., to Carroll (memo), June 15, 1965; O'Shea to Schiefen (memo), September 20, 1965, August 24, 1966, July 24, 1968; *Boston Pilot*, November 6, 1965.

[42] Interview, Bp. John Nevins.

[43] AFAM, CO, Catholic Service Bureau File, 1958-60, William R. Consedine, Dir., Legal Dept., NCWC, to Carroll, September 24, 1959; *Voice*, February 19, 1960, February 12, April 9, 1965, November 4, 1966, March 24, 1967, February 2, March 24, 1968; interview, Msgr. B. O. Walsh; *Catholic Service Bureau Golden Anniversary*, pp. 17-19.

[44] Interview, Msgr. B. O. Walsh; AFAM, CO: Catholic Service Bureau File, 1958-60, "Report on Catholic Charities of the Diocese of Miami," October 7, 1958; Catholic Service Bureau File, 1961-66, General Board of Directors' Minutes, July 5, 1962, September 5, 1963, February 11, 1964; B. O. Walsh to Carroll (memo), February 9, 1965; Diocesan Board Minutes, December 10, 1963; *Voice*, January 10, 1964, January 17, 1965.

[45] *Voice*, August 26, 1960, June 25, 1965, June 23, 30, August 25, 1967; AFAM, CO: Catholic Service Bureau File, 1961-66, Minutes of the Ad Hoc Committee on Catholic Charities Deficits, n.d. [c. July 1965], and General Board of Directors' Minutes, February 16, 1965; Catholic Service Bureau File, 1967-74, "Comparative Data—Budget 1969 (Actual 1968)," n.d. [c. December 1968]; AFAM, Archivist's Office, "Five Year Report, 1964-68"; interview, Msgr. B. O. Walsh.

[46] *Voice*, July 31, 1959.

[47] AFAM, CO: Seminarians, General File, 1959-73; "Seminarians for the Diocese of Miami," June 15, 1959; Circular Letters File, 1965-68, Carroll to Priests, Religious and Faithful (circular), November 29, 1966.

[48] AFAM, CO: Circular Letters File, 1958-64, Carroll to Priests (circulars), March 2, July 24, 1959; Circular Letters File, 1965-68, Pusak to Pastors (circular), December 1, 1967; interview, Msgr. James Walsh; *Voice*, January 15, February 19, 1960, January 17, 1964.

[49] "Record of the Episcopal Acts of Rt. Rev. Augustin Verot," in Roth, *History of the Diocese*, p. 176.

[50] *Voice*, May 29, September 4, 11, 1959, May 26, 1967; AIHM, Notre Dame

Annals, Sr. Marie Jane, IHM, to Mother Maria Pacis, IHM, September 7, 1959; AVF: Fr. John Young, CM, "My Recollections of the Early Days in Miami," August 31, 1981, "SJV–1962 Statement on Enrollments," and *SJV Catalogue, 1968–69*; *Dedication Booklet—St. Raphael Chapel, St. John Vianney Minor Seminary, January 16, 1966*; AFAM, CO, Circular Letters File, 1965–68, Carroll to Priests (circular), February 14, 1967.

[51] *Voice*, June 24, 1966, March 31, 1967; AFAM, CO, Circular Letters File, 1965–68, Carroll to Priests (circular), March 30, 1967.

[52] *Voice*, April 29, 1966, April 21, 1967, March 15, 1968; AFAM, CO, Seminary Board File, Minutes, May 27, 1966.

[53] AFAM, CO, SVDP, 1959–71: Mr. Edward Duffy to Msgr. James Nelan, May 14, 1959, Fr. Irvine Nugent, Chancellor of St. Augustine, to Fitzpatrick, January 17, 1966, and Carroll to Seminary of St. Vincent de Paul, Inc. (indenture—copy), October 30, 1961; *Voice*, February 12, 1960, July 12, September 20, 1963, October 8, 1965. The diocese also gave to the Vincentians in 1963, $25,000 for the Seminary Building Fund Drive: AFAM, CO, SVDP, 1959–71, Fr. Sylvester Taggert, CM, Provincial, to Carroll (copy), April 5, 1963.

[54] AVF, "Dedication Speech for St. Vincent de Paul Seminary" by Arch. Paul Hallinan, January 25, 1966; interview, Sr. Aquinas O'Shaughnessy, SSJ; AFAM, CO, Black Catholics File, Fitzpatrick to Carroll (memo), June 21, 1968; *Voice*; January 28, September 23, 1966, March 17, April 28, 1967, March 29, 1968.

[55] *Voice*, June 19, 26, 1959; AFAM, CO, Circular Letters File, 1965–68, Pusak to Priests (circular), May 22, 1968. Frederick Waas and Lawrence Conway were ordained in June, 1959. Native vocations of the period included Frederick Waas (1959), Charles Clements (1962), and Vernon Langford (1968). Near-natives included John Neff (1960), John Glorie (1960), William Gunther (1960), William Hennessy (1962), Ambrose DePaoli (1962), John Block (1962), Michael Sullivan (1966), James Briggs (1967), James Fletcher (1968), and John McCormick (1968) (AFAM, CO, Priests' Files).

[56] Included among these northern recruits were Lawrence Conway (1959), Ronald Brohamer (1960), Donald Ireland (1963), Gary Steibel (1963), Martin Walsh (1964), Roger Radloff (1965), John McMahon (1966), and David Punch (1968) (AFAM, CO, Priests' Files).

[57] AFAM, CO, OBRA General File: Fr. Antonio Garrigos Meseguer, Sec. Gen. of OCSHA, to Carroll (memo), May 16, 1959; McKeever to Meseguer (copy), April 13, 1960; Fitzpatrick to Fr. Manuel G. Fernandez (copy), July 8, 1964; *Voice*, May 24, 1963, May 19, 1967. Fr. Daniel Sánchez was ordained on Miami Beach, September 2, 1962 but with the intention of working in the Pinar Del Rio Diocese, Cuba (*Voice*, August 3, September 7, 1962).

[58] Interviews, Msgr. Thomas O'Donovan and Msgr. Noel Fogarty.

[59] *Voice*, September 9, 1960, September 8, 1961, June 11, 1965, June 24, December 2, 1966, June 16, 1967, June 21, 1968. AFAM, CO: Seminarians—General File, 1959–73, "Seminarians in Ireland as of 1958–59," n.d. [c. November 1958], and "Major Seminarians, 1964–65," September 22, 1964; Priests' File, William Barry.

[60] AFAM: CO, "Priest Statistics," n.d. [c. October 1981]; Archivist's Office, "Five Year Report, 1964–68"; *Voice*, September 1, 1967.

[61] OCD-1959, p. 529; *Voice*, June 1, 1962, January 17, February 21, 1964, June 25, 1965.

[62] *Voice*, July 10, 1959, February 5, March 4, July 29, 1960, August 16, 1963, August 14, 1964, July 9, September 24, 1965, July 1, 15, 1966, May 12, July 7, 14, 1967; AIHM, Notre Dame Annals, 1959; interview, Sr. Kathleen Reilly, SSND.

[63] *Voice*, February 11, 1961, January 20, 1967; OCD-1959, p. 529; AFAM, CO: "Vicar of Religious, Convents as of September, 1968," September 1968; Consultor's File, Consultor's Meeting Minutes, January 22, 1968; Rel. Communities—General File, Msgr. David Bushey, Vicar of Religious, to Carroll (memo), October 29, 1968. The Sisters of Mercy Novitiate was opened in the summer of 1970: AFAM, CO, Sisters of Mercy File, Gracida to Carroll (memo), October 9, 1970.

[64] *Voice*, July 10, September 18, October 23, 1959, January 15, 1960, December 1, 1961, October 25, 1963, February 9, 1968; AFAM, CO, Cenacle File, Carroll to Mr. James C. Downey, attorney (copy), June 26, 1961; ADSCR: Morning Star School File, Mother Emmanuel, OP, Provincial, to Carroll (copy), June 13, 1963; St. Mary's Mission School File, Thomas and Kathryn Jenkins to Carroll (copy), March 28, 1961; Christ the King Monastery File, Contract—Carroll and Poor Clares, October 4, 1960.

[65] *Voice*, March 10, 1961; AFAM, CO, Daughters of Mary File: Del Busto to Carroll (memo), February 18, 1966; Fitzpatrick to Enright (copy), April 12, 1966; "Proposed Diocesan Community of Sisters," April 16, 1966; Carroll to Schiefen (memo), August 12, 1966; "Brochure on the Daughters of Mary," n.d. [c. 1973].

[66] ASSJ: Quinquennial Reports, January 1, 1956–December 31, 1960, and January 1, 1961–December 31, 1965; "Status of the Congregation Reports—1968," n.d.

[67] ASSJ: "Place of Origin of SSJs," March 28, 1959; "Status of the Congregation Reports—1968," n.d.

[68] AADS, Statistics; OCD-1959, p. 529; AFAM, CO, Vicar of Religious File, Bushey to Carroll (memo), October 29, 1968. Msgr. Bushey counted 166 Adrian Dominicans in the diocese in 1968.

[69] ASHN, Key West Chronicles, April 14, 1964, August 24, October 27, 1968.

[70] ADSA, Hurley Papers, 104-H, Questionnaire of A. C. Taft, *Miami Herald* Religion Editor, n.d. [c. Summer 1955]; interviews, Msgr. B. O. Walsh and Msgr. William McKeever.

[71] In 1960 the diocese had five black schools: Blessed Martin de Porres, Ft. Pierce; Holy Redeemer, Miami; St. Augustine's, Coconut Grove; St. Francis Xavier, Key West; St. Francis Xavier, Miami. Seven separate black missions were open: St. Philip's, Bunche Park; St. Mary of the Missions (St. Francis Xavier), Miami; Annunciation Mission, Ft. Lauderdale; Blessed Martin de Porres, West Palm Beach; Liberia Mission, Hollywood; St. Augustine Mission, Coconut Grove; Holy Redeemer Church, Miami. AFAM, CO, Black Catholic File, "Report on the Colored Mission," n.d. [c. September 1960]; "Report on Catholic Colored Schools," n.d. [c. September 1960]; *Voice*, July 26, 1963; AOSP, St. Francis Xavier Annals, June 14, 1964.

[72] AFAM, CO, Consultor's File, Consultor's Meeting Minutes, December 6, 1960; interview, Msgr. McKeever; *Voice*, June 2, 1961, June 28, 1963; AJF, Kiernan Papers, Fr. John Kiernan, SSJ, to Fr. George F. O'Dea, SSJ, Superior General, May 30, 1961.

[73] AFAM, CO: Circular Letters File, 1958–64, Schiefen to Priests (circulars), August 22, November 19, 1963; Human Relations Board File, Schiefen to Priests (circular), June 6, 1963; *Miami Herald*, June 1, 1963; *Miami News*, June 2, 1963;

interviews, Msgr. B. O. Walsh, Msgr. James Walsh, and Msgr. McKeever; *Voice*, June 7, 21, November 22, 1963; AJF, Kiernan Papers, Kiernan to O'Dea, October 10, 1963.

[74] AJF, Kiernan Papers, Kiernan to O'Dea, April 17, 1963, February 5, May 8, 1964; *Voice*, April 24, May 1, 1964, April 30, 1965; *Miami Herald*, July 4, 1964; AFAM, CO, Human Relations Board File, Executive Committee of the Diocesan Human Relations Board Minutes, May 8, 1968.

[75] Miami did erupt in a racial riot in 1968. *Voice*, July 21, August 4, 25, December 8, 1967; interview, Msgr. B. O. Walsh; OCD-1952, p. 546; Foy, *The 1969 National Catholic Almanac*, p. 576; AOSP, St. Francis Xavier Files, "Harmony: The Path to Religion and Education."

[76] AJF, Diocese of Miami File: Rev. Thomas P. McNamara, SSJ, Superior General, to Carroll (copy), April 29, 1959, Carroll to McNamara, May 11, 1959, Rev. Oscar Carlson, Asst. Chancellor, to O'Shea, July 10, 1961; AIHMM: Congregation Council Minutes, July 29, 1961, Mother Anna Marie, IHM, to Carroll (copy), n.d. [c. August 15, 1961]; AOSP: St. Francis Xavier Annals, August 31, December 25, 1961; St. Francis Xavier File, "Harmony: The Path to Religion and Education."

[77] *Miami Herald*, June 20, 1966; *Voice*, February 26, November 5, 1965, June 24, 1966, June 26, 1967; interview, Fr. John Kiernan, SSJ; OCD-1966, p. 1411; AFAM, CO, Priests' Files.

[78] Interview, Sr. Aquinas, SSJ; *Voice*, August 26, September 23, 1960; AFAM, CO: Spanish-speaking Apostolate File, Schiefen to Carroll (memo), September 20, 1960; Circular Letters File, 1958–64, Carroll to Faithful (circular), April 11, 1963.

[79] OCD-1969, p. 463; *Voice*, November 15, 1963, April 29, 1966, January 27, 1967; AFAM, CO, Circular Letters File, 1958–64, Carroll to Priests (circular), January 28, 1960; interviews, Msgr. B. O. Walsh and Sr. Aquinas, SSJ.

[80] *Voice*, April 7, 14, 1961, April 9, 1965.

[81] AFAM, APF: Latin American Episcopal Committee File, Tanner to Carroll, May 2, 1962; "Proposal Made by Bp. Carroll at the NCWC Board Meeting" (copy), April 1, 1964; *Voice*, August 20, 1965; AFAM, CO: Spanish-Speaking Apostolate File, Del Busto to Carroll (memo), November 8, 1967; Circular Letters File, 1965–68, Fr. David Russell, Director of Latin American Co-operation Week, to Priests (circular), November 17, 1967.

Chapter 9

[1] Interviews, Fr. Lamar Genovar, Mr. and Mrs. Ben Benjamin, Msgr. Brian O. Walsh, and Fr. Cyril Burke, OP. Although Bp. Carroll was sometimes compared to a chairman of the board, his leadership style was more like the political style of an Irish city boss as seen in Boston, New York, and Chicago in the nineteenth and twentieth centuries.

[2] Hugh J. Nolan, "The Native Son," p. 380; OCD-1959, p. 529; OCD-1969, p. 463; AFAM: Archivist's Office, "Five Year Report, 1964–68"; CO, Rel. Communities—General File, Msgr. David Bushey, Vicar of Religious, to Carroll (memo), October 29, 1968.

³Interviews, Msgr. James Nelan and Msgr. Schiefen; *Voice*, May 17, 1968.

⁴The composite portrait of Arch. Carroll was suggested from interviews with Msgr. Bryan O. Walsh, Bp. John Nevins, Mr. Joseph Fitzgerald, Msgr. James Nelan, and Fr. Edward McCarthy, OSA.

⁵Interviews, Senator Philip Lewis, Mr. and Mrs. Benjamin, and Bp. Nevins.

⁶Interviews, Fr. Louis Roberts, Mrs. Marjorie Fillyaw Donohue, and Msgr. Schiefen.

⁷Interview, Bp. Nevins; *Voice*, August 5, 1977.

⁸ *Miami Herald*, February 9, 1971.

⁹AFAM, CO: Circular Letters File, 1958–64, Carroll to Priests (circular), October 14, 1959; Circular Letters File, 1965–68, James Walsh to Priests (circular), April 12, 1966; *Voice*, November 6, 1959, February 18, 1966.

¹⁰AFAM, CO: Circular Letters File, 1958–64, Fitzpatrick to Priests (circular), November 11, 1964; Circular Letters File, 1965–68: Carroll to Priests (circulars), March 9, 1965, and February 24, 1966, Fitzpatrick to Priests (circular), March 17, 1966; Ecumenical File, 1968–72, Carroll to Fitzpatrick (memo), January 27, 1965; interview, Bp. John Fitzpatrick.

¹¹Interviews, Msgr. Peter Reilly and Bp. Fitzpatrick; *Voice*, January 31, 1964; AFAM, CO, Circular Letters File, 1958–64, Fitzpatrick to Priests, March 2, 1964.

¹²For a history of Catholic preaching in the United States see Robert F. McNamara, *Catholic Sunday Preaching*.

¹³Interviews, Mr. James Kindelan and Msgr. Dominic Barry.

¹⁴Interview, Mr. James Kindelan; James Kavanaugh, *A Modern Priest*; *Voice*, June 30, September 22, 1967, March 1, 1968.

¹⁵ *Voice*, June 10, November 4, 1960, May 5, July 28, September 8, 1961, February 4, June 17, August 26, 1966, June 16, August 18, December 1, 1967; AFAM, CO, Priests' Senate File, 1966–70, Fr. Angel Vizcarra, OP, to Fitzpatrick, February 17, 1967.

¹⁶Interviews, Fr. Roberts, Bp. Fitzpatrick, Bp. Nevins; Br. Patrick Ellis, FSC, Msgr. Rowan Rastatter, and Msgr. John O'Dowd; AFAM, CO: Marymount File, Carroll to Dennehy (copy), September 20, 1963; Vatican Reports File, "Basic Questionnaire for 1968," n.d. [c. early 1969].

¹⁷St. John Bosco Pastor's Office, Spanish Priests' Association File, Minutes, October 25, 1966; *Voice*, December 2, 1966.

¹⁸AFAM, CO, Priests' Senate File, 1966–70: Fitzpatrick to Carroll (memo), December 19, 1966; Pusak to Carroll (memo), May 22, 1967; Minutes of the Meeting of Bp. Carroll with the Senate Constitutional Committee, June 5, 1967; St. John Bosco Pastor's Office, Spanish Priests' Association File, "Protest Against Priests' Senate," n.d. [c. March 27, 1967].

¹⁹ *Voice*, September 15, 1967, February 9, March 1, 8, 29, 1968; AFAM, CO, Priests' Senate File, 1966–70: Fitzpatrick to Pusak (memo), February 26, 1968; Carroll to (unnamed) (memo), March 21, 1968; Pusak to Brohamer (copy), April 18, 1968; Brohamer to Carroll, May 14, 1968.

²⁰There were eighty-one Irish-born priests in the diocese at the end of 1966. AFAM, CO, Priests—Misc. Matters File, Fitzpatrick to Bp. James P. Shannon, Aux. Bp. of St. Paul, December 1, 1966; *Voice*, February 16, May 24, 1968.

²¹AFAM, CO: Circular Letters File, 1958–64, Waas to Sisters (circular), August 22, 1960; Vicar for Religious File, Fr. Angel Vizcarra, OP, Asst. Vicar

for Religious, to Sisters (circular), August 21, 1964; *Voice*, September 1, 1961, July 27, 1962, August 26, 1966; AOSP, St. Francis Xavier Annals, October 16, 1962.

²² SBCC, September (n.d.) 1966; Leon Cardinal Suenens, *The Nun in the World*; Austin Flannery, OP, gen. ed., *Vatican Council II*, pp. 611–33. Helen Ebaugh describes the Vatican II mandates to religious as twofold: a return to the sources of Christian life and the original inspiration of a given community, and a modernization (*Out of the Cloister*, p. 7).

²³ Interview, Sr. Kathleen Riley, SSND; *Voice*, January 18, 1963, March 26, 1965, September 1, 8, December 15, 1967; AIHM: Notre Dame Annals, September 3, 1967, and Epiphany Annals, June–July (n.d.) 1959, December 30, 1959, September (n.d.) 1962, February 28, 1965, September 26, 1969; ASHN, Key West Chronicles, April 16, 1967; SBCC, December 13, 28, 1960, September 7, 1963, February 29, November (n.d.) 1964, February (n.d.) 1967; AOSP, St. Francis Xavier Annals, March 17, 1962, March 17, April 15, June 1, 1963.

²⁴ OCD-1959, p. 529; OCD-1964, p. 574; SBCC, October 6, 1962; *Voice*, July 3, 1959.

²⁵ Interview, Sr. Kathleen Reilly, SSND; AFAM, CO: Vicar of Religious File, Notes from the Bishop's Liaison Committee to Major Superiors, Chicago, May 26, 1966; Assumption Academy File, Fitzpatrick to Carroll (memo), August 24, 1966; *Miami Herald*, June 20, 1966; *Voice*, September 4, 1959, June 24, October 21, 1966, May 12, September 29, 1967, January 5, 1968.

²⁶ AFAM, CO, Rel. Ed. File, 1959–70, McKeever and Brunner to Carroll (memo), June 5, 1968. The quote is taken from *Voice*, September 22, 1967. For material on the Sisters' Senate (Council), see *Voice*, September 18, 1959, September 22, 1967, March 15, 1968; SBCC, October 1, October 25, 1967.

²⁷ *Voice*, March 20, 1959, October 16, 1964; Flannery, *Vatican Council II*, pp. 766–98, 903–1001.

²⁸ OCD-1966, p. 587; *Voice*, August 28, October 2, 1959, October 5, 1962, January 17, June 19, 1964, January 22, February 12, 1965; ADSA, Hurley Papers, 122-L, 1952–54; interview, Mr. and Mrs. Benjamin.

²⁹ *Voice*, December 23, 1960, September 11, December 11, 25, 1964, January 7, December 30, 1966, May 17, 1968; AFAM, CO: SVDP File, 1959–71, Schiefen to Leonard, CM (copy), June 13, 1966; Barry File, Philip Lewis, to Sr. M. Dorothy, OP (copy), March 29, 1966; interviews, Fr. John Kiernan, SSJ, Mr. and Mrs. Benjamin, and Mr. Fitzgerald.

³⁰ AFAM, CO: DCCW File, Margaret Mealy, Exec. Sec. of the NCCW, to Carroll, October 21, 1958; Schiefen to Heffernan (copy), October 31, 1958; "General Information Bulletin," May 3, 4, 5, 1959; Legion of Mary File, "The 1961 Report of the Legion of Mary," March 17, 1962; Mr. George Robinson, St. Juliana's, to Carroll, June 25, 1959; *Voice*, October 2, 1959.

³¹ *Voice*, May 1, August 14, October 9, November 27, 1959, January 17, March 4, 1960, October 13, 1961, January 17, April 2, 1964, September 1, 15, 1967; AFAM, CO: Circular Letters File 1958–64, Annual Convention of the DCCM, May 23–24, 1964.

³² AFAM, CO, Lay Retreats File: Carroll to Priests, Religious, and Laity (circular), February 23, 1959, and "Report on Activities of Lay Retreat Movement in

the Diocese," November 9, 1958; interview, Msgr. Noel Fogarty; *Voice*, March 11, July 8, 1960, April 7, 1961, June 8, 1962, June 28, 1963, November 10, 1967.

[33] In 1966 Cursillos were in eighty-five dioceses in thirty-six states. *Voice*, March 11, 25, 1966; AFAM, CO, Cursillo File: Fitzpatrick to Fr. Santamaría, OP, Chiapas, Mexico (copy), March 14, 1966; Mr. J. R. Garrigo, Pres. of the Cursillos of the Diocese of Miami, to Fitzpatrick, April 21, 1966.

[34] AFAM, CO: Spanish-Speaking Apostolate File, 1960–75, "Minutes—Organizations Meeting of the Coordinating Committee of the Cuban Catholic Organizations," November 16, 1961; Christian Family Movements File, Fitzpatrick to Dr. Humberto López, Key Biscayne (copy), February 19, 1963; interview, Msgr. Schiefen; *Voice*, September 9, 1966, May 12, 1967, January 19, 1968.

[35] *Voice*, January 20, March 31, 1967; AFAM, CO: Circular Letters File, 1965–68, Carroll to Priests (circular), April 5, 1967; Parish Councils File, Fr. William Sweeney, CM, pastor of St. Vincent De Paul Parish, to Fitzpatrick, May 3, 1971.

[36] Interviews, Bp. Nevins and Msgr. O'Dowd; *Voice*, May 22, 1959, September 29, 1961, December 4, 1964, June 25, 1965, June 23, August 25, 1967; interview, Mr. Kindelan; *St. Rose of Lima Parish—25th Anniversary, 1948–73*; AFAM, CO, Seminary Board File, Minutes, May 27, 1966.

[37] Tebeau, *A History of Florida*, p. 434; AFAM, APF, Statistics—Miami File, First Research Corp., "The Florida Economy, 1960–65, Part I," n.d., p. 128; William W. Jenna, Jr., *Metropolitan Miami*, pp. 44–68.

[38] AFAM, CO, Catholic Service Bureau File, Minutes, Gen. Board of Catholic Welfare, May 2, 1963; interview, Msgr. O'Dowd.

[39] AFAM, APF, Statistics—Miami File, First Research Corp., "Florida Business Letter," vol. 9, #8, n.d. [c. 1960]; USBC, *1970, Abstract*, pp. 856–57; interview, Br. Patrick Ellis, FSC; *Voice*, November 10, 1967.

[40] Interviews, Fr. McCarthy, OSA, and Msgr. David Bushey; AFAM, CO, Extension File: Bp. William O'Brien, President of Extension, to Carroll, January 8, 1959; O'Brien to Carroll, January 16, 1959; Carroll to O'Brien (copy), January 21, 1959; 1959–68 Correspondence, Del Busto to Mr. Armando López (memo), February 22, 1971.

[41] Interviews, Bp. Nevins and Sr. Kathleen Reilly, SSND; AFAM, CO, Extension File, Carroll to O'Brien (copy), January 21, 1959.

[42] Quoted in *Miami Herald*, July 5, 1964.

[43] ASSND, Diocese of Miami File: Fr. Walter Dockerill, pastor of Visitation, to Mother Mary Maurice, SSND, May 23, 1969; McKeever to Mother Mary Alice, SSND, September 23, 1969; interviews, Sr. Kathleen Reilly, SSND, Msgr. O'Dowd, Fr. Kiernan, SSJ, and Bp. Nevins.

[44] Interviews, Fr. Roberts, Fr. Genovar, Msgr. Thomas O'Donovan, Msgr. James Walsh, Bp. Keith Symons, Msgr. Schiefen, Senator Lewis, Msgr. Dominic Barry, Msgr. O'Dowd, Msgr. Bryan O. Walsh, and Bp. Fitzpatrick.

[45] Interviews, Bp. Keith Symons, Mrs. Fillyaw Donohue, Msgr. Fogarty, Fr. Roberts, Bp. Nevins, Msgr. James Walsh, Msgr. Schiefen, and Msgr. O'Dowd.

[46] Of the data that follow, those previously footnoted will not be annotated again.

[47] Quoted in C. Vann Woodward, *The Burden of Southern History*, pp. 213–14.

[48] Theodore Sorensen, *Kennedy*, p. 757. See also Martin Luther King, Jr., *Why*

We Can't Wait; Coretta King, *Life with Martin Luther King*; William L. O'Neill, *Coming Apart*; William E. Leuchtenburg, *A Troubled Feast*; Theodore H. White, "Summing Up," pp. 32 ff.

[49] Gabe Huck, ed., *The Liturgy Documents*, pp. 37–161; interviews, Sr. Joyce LaVoy, OP, and Msgr. Bushey.

[50] AFAM, CO, Archdiocese of Miami File, "Program of Installation," June 13, 1968; *Voice*, February 23, 1962, November 3, 1967, March 29, 1968; interviews, Msgr. Nelan and Msgr. Schiefen; AFAM, APF: Terna File, Tanner to Carroll, November 30, 1963; Candidates for the Episcopacy File, Carroll to Raimondi (copy), December 6, 1967; ASSND, Chronicles of Good Shepherd, Orlando, October 30, 1967.

[51] AFAM, CO: Archdiocese of Miami File, Gracida to Del Busto (memo), July 18, 1968; Synod File, Minutes of Unofficial Provincial Bishop's Meeting, July 12, 1968; *Voice*, March 29, May 10, May 17, June 21, July 5, August 30, 1968.

[52] *Voice*, August 9, 1968; AFAM, CO, Florida Catholic Conference File, 1969–74, Gracida to Fitzgerald (copy), February 24, 1969.

[53] OCD-1959, p. 529; OCD-1969, p. 463; OCD-1978, p. 511; Baptism and Marriage Registers of Immaculate Conception, St. Brendan's, St. John Bosco, St. Mary's, and St. Patrick's.

[54] Interview, Fr. Charles Mallen, CSSR.

[55] Interviews, Mr. Fitzpatrick, Judge C. Clyde Atkins, and Msgr. Dominic Barry; Fitzgerald to author, January 6, 1982; *Palm Beach Post*, January 13, 1982; AFAM, Marriage Tribunal, Tribunal Staff to Fr. Andrew Anderson (memo), October 5, 1981.

[56] Interview, Msgr. William McKeever; AFAM, CO, Charismatic Movement File, Press Release, December 10, 1969.

[57] OCD-1959, p. 529; OCD-1969, p. 463; OCD-1978, p. 511; AFAM, Archivist's Office, "Five Year Report, 1964–68." For an example of this attack, see Mary Perkins Ryan, *Are Parochial Schools the Answer?*

[58] *Catholic Service Bureau Golden Anniversary*, pp. 18–21; interviews, Msgr. Bryan O. Walsh and Bp. Nevins; AFAM, APF, Vatican Reports File, Annual Statistical Questionnaire, 1976 (copy), n.d. [c. early 1977].

[59] *Voice*, June 21, 1968; interview, Msgr. Noel Fogarty; FSVDP, "Teaching Faculty," 1969–70, 1970–71; AFAM, CO, SVDP File, 1959–71: Fr. Thomas Hoar, CM, Rector to Gracida, November 16, 1970, Fitzpatrick to Carroll (memo), December 16, 1970; AVF: "Official Announcement of the Closing of SVDP," Hoar to Friends of the Seminary, February 2, 1971, and "Archbishop Carroll's Statement," February 2, 1971.

[60] *Voice*, November 24, 1967; interview, Msgr. Fogarty.

[61] Interview, Msgr. Fogarty; AFAM: CO, Statistics and Spanish Priests' Association File, "Petition for a Latin Bishop," May 10, 1971; Archivist's Office, "Five Year Report, 1964–68" and "Five Year Report, 1968–74."

[62] AFAM, CO, Miami File: Br. Michael Dudley, CSC, to Carroll, May 16, 1970; Gracida to Carroll (memo), April 9, 1970; Carroll to Gracida (memo), May 25, 1970; Barthel to Br. Brast, CSC (copy), February 14, 1962. Interview, Br. Ellis, FSC; Br. Richard Grzeskiewicz, FSC, to author, July 5, 1981.

[63] Interviews, Sr. Rita Gleason, OP, and Sr. M. Neomisea, CSFN; ASHN, Key

West Chronicles, March 7, 1967; ADSCR, Miami File, Sr. Carolyn Krebs, OP, Sec. to Special Chapter, to Carroll (copy), June 24, 1970; ASSF, 1968 Chapter Files; AIHM, Epiphany Annals, February 23, 1971; AADS, Records Storage Room.

[64] Interviews, Sr. M. Neomisea, CSFN, Fr. Cyril Burke, OP, and Sr. Mary Albert Lussier, SSJ; ASSF, Sr. Ann Cannon, OSF, and Sr. Maria Vianney Donovan, OSF, "Allegheny Franciscan Study—1972" (unpublished mimeo), 1972; ASHN, Key West Chronicles, April 16, November 24, 1967; AIHM, Epiphany Annals, February 23, 1971; AADS, Photographs, 1968–69, and Msgr. O'Looney, pastor of St. Anthony's, to Mother Rosemary Furgeson, OP, July (n.d.) 1970. For a more detailed account of the process, see Ebaugh, *Out of the Cloister*, pp. 32–38.

[65] ASHN, Key West Chronicles, June 26, 1967; AIHM, Epiphany Annals, January 15, 1970; Sr. Lorean Whiteman, SNJM, Administrative Director, to author, October 9, 1981; AOSP, St. Francis Xavier Chronicles, February (n.d.) 1972; ASSF, Cannon and Donovan, "Allegheny Study—1972."

[66] Interviews, Sr. Mary Bernadette Scheer, OP, Sr. M. Neomisea, CSFN, and Sr. Joyce LaVoy, OP; *Voice*, October 9, 1970; AIHMM, Sr. Loyola Engleman, OP, "Sr. Joseph Ellen Raffin, 1931–75" (unpublished), n.d.; *Palm Beach Post*, December 26, 1981.

[67] Interview, Msgr. Bushey. See also ASSF, "Number of Sisters Professed—Graph," n.d. [c. 1976], and Cannon and Donovan, "Allegheny Study—1972"; ASSND, Diocese of Miami File; ADSCR, Sr. Mary Bernadette Scheer, OP, to Bryan O. Walsh, October 27, 1970; AADS, "Statistical Summary of Adrian Dominican Foundations in Florida," n.d. [c. 1981]; OCD-1959, pp. 527–29; OCD-1969, pp. 458–63; OCD-1978, pp. 505–11. See also Ebaugh, *Out of the Cloister*, pp. 75–88, 122–25.

[68] AOSP, St. Francis Xavier Chronicles, August 29, 1971–January 11, 1972; interview, Msgr. B. O. Walsh.

[69] Interview, Msgr. B. O. Walsh. By 1977, nine different women's communities were working in the Diocese (OCD-1978, pp. 509, 511).

[70] USBC *Population, 1970*, p. 11–290, shows Cubans as 66 percent of Miami's Hispanic population; in Ft. Lauderdale, Cubans made up 23 percent of the Hispanic population (p. 11-259) and in West Palm Beach, 35 percent (p. 11-161; *Miami Herald*, October 24, 1978). For related information, see *National Catholic Reporter*, March 21, 1980; *Origins*, September 11, 1980; Baptism and Marriage Registers of Immaculate Conception, St. Brendan's, St. John Bosco, St. Mary's, and St. Patrick's.

[71] *Voice*, July 12, 1968.

Conclusion

[1] Pope Paul VI, *Evangelii nuntiandi*, paragraph 62, p. 45.
[2] Sir Kenneth Clark, *Civilisation*, pp. 346–47.

Bibliography

Records And Manuscript Sources

Archives and Files of the Archdiocese of Miami, Miami, Fla.
Archives of the Archdiocese of Baltimore, Baltimore, Md.
Archives of the Archdiocese of Philadelphia, Philadelphia, Pa.
Archives of Carlow College, Pittsburgh, Pa.
Archives of the Carmelite Sisters for the Aged and Infirm, Germantown, N.Y.
Archives of the Catholic University of America, Washington, D.C.
Archives of the Christian Brothers, Lockport, N.Y.
Archives of the Diocese of Pittsburgh, Pittsburgh, Pa.
Archives of the Diocese of St. Augustine, St. Augustine, Fla.
Archives of the Dominican Sisters, Adrian, Mich.
Archives of the Dominican Sisters of St. Catherine de Ricci, Elkins Park, Pa.
Archives of Duquesne University, Pittsburgh, Pa.
Archives of the Henry Flagler Museum, Palm Beach, Fla.
Archives of the Josephite Fathers, Baltimore, Md.
Archives of the Oblates of Providence, Baltimore, Md.
Archives of the Religious of the Assumption, Philadelphia, Pa.
Archives of Saint Vincent Archabbey, Latrobe, Pa.
Archives of the School Sisters of Notre Dame, Baltimore, Md.
Archives of the Sisters of Charity of St. Elizabeth, Convent Station, N.J.
Archives of the Sisters of the Holy Family of Nazareth, Des Plaines, Ill.
Archives of the Sisters of the Holy Family of Nazareth, Torresdale, Pa.
Archives of the Sisters of the Holy Names of Jesus and Mary, Albany, N.Y.
Archives of the Sisters of Mercy, Enniskillen, Northern Ireland.
Archives of the Sisters of St. Francis, Allegheny, N.Y.

Archives of the Sisters of St. Francis, Joliet, Ill.
Archives of the Sisters of St. Joseph of St. Augustine, St. Augustine, Fla.
Archives of the Sisters, Servants of the Immaculate Heart of Mary, Immaculata, Pa.
Archives of the Sisters, Servants of the Immaculate Heart of Mary, Monroe, Mich.
Archives of the Sisters of Social Service, Buffalo, N.Y.
Archives of the Vincentian Fathers, Jamaica, N.Y.
Files of St. Vincent de Paul Regional Seminary, Boynton Beach, Fla.
Files of the Pastor's Office, St. John Bosco Church, Miami, Fla.
Immaculate Conception Rectory, Baptismal and Marriage Registers, Hialeah, Fla.
Office of Hispanic Affairs, Southeast Region (Southeast Pastoral Institute-S.E.P.I.), Miami, Fla.
St. Brendan Convent Chronicles, Miami, Fla.
St. Brendan Rectory, Baptismal and Marriage Registers, Miami, Fla.
St. John Bosco Rectory, Baptismal and Marriage Registers, Miami, Fla.
St. John Vianney Library, Special Collection, Miami, Fla.
St. Mary's Cathedral, Baptismal and Marriage Registers, Miami, Fla.
St. Patrick Church, Msgr. Barry Files and Notebooks, Miami Beach, Fla.
St. Patrick Rectory, Baptismal and Marriage Registers, Miami Beach, Fla.

Newspapers

Banner of the South (Savannah), 1868.
Boston Daily Globe, 1945.
Boston Pilot, 1958–68.
Catholic Mirror (Baltimore), 1870.
Daily News and Herald, (Savannah), 1868.
Davenport Catholic Messenger, 1958–68.
Detroit News, 1960.
Florida Catholic, 1939–44, 1956–57, 1963, 1967.
Florida Times-Union (Jacksonville), 1915.
Georgia Bulletin (Bulletin of the Catholic Laymen's Association of Georgia, Savannah), 1932.
Jacksonville Metropolis, 1919.
Key West Citizen, 1968.
Lake Worth News, 1896.
Miami Daily Metropolis, 1915.
Miami Daily News, 1926, 1945, 1967.
Miami Herald, 1915, 1924–26, 1960–68, 1983.
Morning Star and Catholic Messenger, 1875, 1916.
National Catholic Reporter, 1964–68.
New York Herald Tribune, 1963.
New York Tablet, 1859.
New York Times, 1960, 1967, 1976.

Palm Beach Post-Times, 1928, 1939, 1956, 1981–83.
St. Augustine Examiner, 1859, 1867–69, 1872.
St. Augustine Meteor, 1916.
St. Augustine Record, 1910, 1916.
Savannah Morning News, 1862.
Sunday Mirror (New York), 1943.
Voice, 1959–77.
Washington Post, 1959, 1981.

Books, Articles, and Papers

Abbo, John A., and Hannan, Jerome D. *The Sacred Canons*. Vol. 2. 2d rev. ed. St. Louis: B. Herder, 1960.

Aguirre, B. D.; Schwirian, Kent P.; and La Greca, Anthony J. "The Residential Patterning of Latin American and Other Populations in Metropolitan Miami." *Latin American Research Review* 2 (1980): 35–63.

Ahern, Patrick H. *The Catholic University of America, 1887–96: The Rectorship of John Keane*. Washington: Catholic University of America, 1948.

Akin, Edward N. "The Sly Foxes: Henry Flagler, George Miles, and Florida's Public Domain." *Florida Historical Quarterly* 58 (July 1979): 22–36.

Alma, Mother Maria, IHM. *Sisters, Servants of the Immaculate Heart of Mary, 1845–1967*. Lancaster, Pa.: Dolphin, 1967.

American National Red Cross. *The Florida Hurricane: September 18, 1926*. Washington: National Red Cross, 1927.

———. *The West Indies Hurricane Disaster: September, 1928*. Washington: National Red Cross, 1929.

Ammidown, Margot. "The Wagner Family: Pioneer Life on the Miami River." *Tequesta* 42 (1982): 5–37.

Andriot, John J., ed. *Township Atlas of the United States*. McLean, Va.: Andriot Assoc., 1979.

Around Mercy 5 (December 1980).

Ballinger, Kenneth. *Miami Millions—Land Boom of 1925*. Miami: Franklin Press, 1936.

Barnes, Sandra T. *Ogun: An Old God for a New Age*. Philadelphia: Institute for the Study of Human Issues, 1980.

Barry, Patrick P. Papers. Archives of the Diocese of St. Augustine, St. Augustine, Fla.

Bascom, William. "The Focus of Cuban Santería." In *Peoples and Cultures of the Caribbean*, edited by Michael M. Horowitz. Garden City, N.Y.: Doubleday, 1971.

Bellamy, Jeanne. "Sewell, the Chamber, and the Marketing of Miami." *Update* (February 1980): 2–5.

Berlin, Ira. *Slaves without Masters: The Free Negro in the Ante-bellum South*. New York: Pantheon, 1974.

Biever, Albert H. *The Jesuits in New Orleans and the Mississippi: Jubilee Memorial*. New Orleans: Hauser, 1924.

Billinger, Robert D. "With the Wehrmacht in Florida: The German POW Facility at Camp Blanding." *Florida Historical Quarterly* 58 (October 1979): 160–73.

Black, Jan Kippers; Blutstein, Howard I.; Edwards, J. David; Johnson, Katheryn Therese; and McMorris, David S. *Area Handbook for Cuba*. 2d ed. Washington: G.P.O., 1976.

Bouscaren, T. Lincoln, S.J., and Ellis, Adam C., S.J. *Canon Law: A Text and Commentary*. Milwaukee: Bruce, 1957.

Boyd, Mark F.; Smith, Hale G.; and Griffin, John W. *Here They Once Stood: The Tragic End of the Apalachee Missions*. Gainesville: University of Florida, 1951.

Brennan, Mary Elizabeth. "Memories of Msgr. Pace." *Quarterly Bulletin of the International Federation of Catholic Alumnae* 2 (June 1938): 12, 33.

Bresnahan, P. J. *Seeing Florida with a Priest*. Zephyrhills, Fla.: Economy Print Shop, 1937.

Brocker, M. "Cuba's Refugees Live in Hope and Despair." *The New York Times Magazine*, May 12, 1962, p. 17.

Browne, Rev. Henry J. "Fifty Years Ago." *The Catholic University of America Bulletin* 23 (January 1956): 5–7.

———. "Pioneer Days at the Catholic University of America—Part I." *The Catholic Educational Review* 48 (January 1950): 29–38.

———. "Pioneer Days at Catholic University of America—Part II." *The Catholic Educational Review* 48 (February 1950): 96–103.

Browne, Jefferson B. *Key West: The Old and the New*. Facsimile of 1912 ed. Gainesville: University of Florida, 1973.

Burnett, Gene. "The 'Binder Boys' Helped Burst the Great Real Estate Bubble." *Florida Trend*, October 1981, pp. 155–59.

Canét, Carlos. *Lucumi: Religión de los Yorubas en Cuba*. Miami: Air Publications Center, 1973.

Cash, William T. *History of the Democratic Party in Florida*. Tallahassee: Florida Democratic Historical Foundation, 1936.

Castro, Fidel. *Revolutionary Struggle, 1947–58*. Vol. 1, *Selected Works of Fidel Castro*, edited by Rolando E. Bonabea and Nelson P. Valdes. Cambridge, Mass.: M.I.T., 1972.

Chalmers, David M. *Hooded Americanism: The First Century of the Ku Klux Klan, 1865–1965*. Garden City, N.Y.: Doubleday, 1965.

Clarét, Antonio María. *Escritos Autobiográficos y Espirituales*. Madrid: Biblioteca de Autores Cristianos, 1959.

Clark, Juan M. *The Cuban Exodus: Background, Evolution, Impact*. Miami: Union of Cubans in Exile, 1977.

Clark, Sir Kenneth. *Civilization: A Personal View*. New York: Harper and Row, 1969.

Clavreul, Henry P. *Notes on the Catholic Church in Florida, 1565–1876*. St. Augustine, Fla.: The Record Co., n.d. [c. 1876].

Code, Joseph Bernard. *Dictionary of the American Hierarchy*. New York: Longmans, Green and Co., 1940.

Coleman, Wesley F. "Site DA-141, Dade County, Florida." *Florida Anthropologist* (September 1973): 126–28.

Connelly, James F., ed. *The History of the Archdiocese of Philadelphia*. Philadelphia: Archdiocese of Philadelphia, 1976.

Conoley, John. "The Present Position of Catholics in Florida." *The Catholic Mind* 15 (June 22, 1917): 269–82.

"Cuba—And Now the Children." *Time*, October 6, 1961, p. 41.

Cuddy, Edward. "The Irish Question and the Revival of Anti-Catholicism in the 1920's." *Catholic Historical Review* 67 (April 1981): 236–55.

Curley, Michael J. Papers. Archives of the Diocese of St. Augustine, St. Augustine, Fla.

———. Papers. St. John Vianney College Seminary Library, Special Collections, Miami, Fla.

Curtis, Georgina Pell, ed. *The American Catholic Who's Who*. St. Louis: B. Herder, 1911.

Davis Aurora E. "The Development of the Major Commercial Airlines in Dade County, Florida, 1945–1970." *Tequesta* (1972): 3–16.

Dewart, Leslie. *Christianity and Revolution: The Lesson of Cuba*. New York: Herder and Herder, 1963.

Dolan, Jay P. *Catholic Revivalism: The American Experience, 1830–1900*. Notre Dame, Ind.: University of Notre Dame, 1978.

Dougherty, Dennis. Papers. Archives of the Archdiocese of Philadelphia, Philadelphia, Pa.

Dubois, Bessie Wilson. "Two South Florida Lighthouse Keepers." *Tequesta* (1973): 41–50.

Dunne, Edmund F. *Our American Sicily*. San Antonio, Fla.: San Antonio Colony, 1883.

Durkin, Joseph T. *Stephen R. Mallory: Confederate Navy Chief*. Chapel Hill: University of North Carolina, 1954.

Dusenbury, George, and Dusenbury, Jane. *How to Retire in Florida*. Rev. ed. New York: Harper, 1947.

Economic Statistics Bureau. *The Handbook of Basic Economic Statistics* 35 (January 1981): 99–101.

Efundé, Agún. *Los Secretos de la Santería*. Miami: Ediciones Cuba-mérica, 1978.

Ellis, John Tracy. *American Catholicism*. 2d ed. rev. Chicago: University of Chicago, 1972.

———, ed. *The Catholic Priest in the United States: Historical Investigations*. Collegeville, Minn.: St. John's University, 1971.

———. *The Life of James Cardinal Gibbons*. 2 vols. Milwaukee: Bruce, 1952.

Estenger, Rafael. *Sincera Historia de Cuba, 1492–1973*. Medellín, Colombia: Editorial Bedout S.A., 1974.

Fagan, Richard R., and Brody, Richard A. *Cubans in Exile: A Demographic Analysis*. Garden City, N.Y.: Doubleday, 1964.

Fagan, Richard R.; Brody, Richard A.; and O'Leary, Thomas J. *Cubans in Exile: Disaffection and the Revolution*. Stanford, Calif.: Stanford University, 1968.

Fairbanks, George R. *The History and Antiques of the City of St. Augustine*. Facsimile of 1856 ed. Gainesville: University of Florida, 1975.

Faver, Hiram, comp. "Record of Trial: State of Florida v. Sr. Mary Thomasine,

SSJ," Law 778, Docket 3, p. 97, St. Johns County Circuit Court Minute Book, 267 (1916).

Fitzpatrick, Vincent de Paul. *The Life of Bishop Curley, Champion of Catholic Education, 1904–1929.* Baltimore: Baltimore Catholic Review, 1929.

Flannery, Austin, gen. ed. *Vatican Council II: Conciliar and Post Conciliar Documents.* Northport, N.Y.: Costello, 1975.

"Flight of the Cuban Refugees." *America,* March 18, 1961, p. 777.

Florida v. "Ex Parte Sr. Mary Thomasine," Law 778, Docket 3, p. 44, Circuit Court, St. Johns County, St. Augustine, Fla., May 20, 1916.

Flynt, Wayne. *Cracker Messiah: Gov. Sidney J. Catts of Florida.* Baton Rouge: Louisiana State University, 1977.

———. "Sidney J. Catts: The Road to Power." *Florida Historical Quarterly* 49 (October 1970): 107–28.

Foy, Felician, OFM, ed. *The 1959 National Catholic Almanac.* Paterson, N.J.: St. Anthony's Guild, 1959.

———, ed. *The 1960 National Catholic Almanac.* Paterson, N.J.: St. Anthony's Guild, 1960.

———, ed. *The 1969 National Catholic Almanac,* Garden City, N.Y.: Doubleday, 1969.

———, ed. *The 1970 National Catholic Almanac,* Garden City, N.Y.: Doubleday, 1970.

Frazure, Hoyt. *Memories of Old Miami.* Edited by Nixon Smiley. Miami: *Miami Herald,* n.d.

Futch, Ovid L. *History of Andersonville Prison.* Gainesville: University of Florida, 1968.

Gabriel, Br. Angelus, FSC. *The Christian Brothers in the United States: 1848–1948—A Century of Catholic Education.* New York: Declan X. McMullen, 1948.

Gannon, Michael V. "Bishop Verot and the Slavery Question." In *Catholics in America, 1776–1976,* edited by Robert Trisco. Washington: NCCB, 1976.

———. *The Cross in the Sand: The Early Catholic Church in Florida, 1513–1870.* Gainesville: University of Florida, 1967.

———. *Rebel Bishop: The Life and Era of Augustin Verot.* Milwaukee: Bruce, 1964.

Geary, Mildred. "History of Mercy Hospital." Archbishop's Office, Archives and Files of the Archdiocese of Miami, Miami, Fla. Mimeo.

Geiger, Maynard. *The Franciscan Conquest of Florida (1573–1618).* Washington: Catholic University of America, 1937.

George, Paul S. "Passage to the New Eden: Tourism in Miami from Flagler through Everest G. Sewell." *Florida Historical Quarterly* 54 (April 1981): 440–63.

———. "Policing Miami's Black Community, 1896–1930." *Florida Historical Quarterly* 57 (April 1979): 434–50.

Gibbons, James. Papers. Archives of the Archdiocese of Baltimore, Baltimore, Md.

Girard, Louis, and Hilaire, Yves Marie. *Une Chrétienté au XIXe Siècle? La Vie Religieuse des Populations de Diocèse D'Arras (1840–1914).* 2 vols. Lille: L'Université de Lille, 1977.

Gleason, Philip. "A Browser's Guide to American Catholicism, 1950–80." *Theology Today* 38 (October 1981): 373–88.

———. "Catholicism and Cultural Change in the 1960's." In *America in Change: Reflections on the 1960's and 1970's,* edited by Ronald Weber. Notre Dame, Ind.: University of Notre Dame, 1972.

———. "In Search of Unity: American Catholic Thought, 1920–1960." *Catholic Historical Review* 65 (April 1979): 185–205.

Goggin, John M. "The Tekesta Indians of Southern Florida." *Florida Historical Quarterly* 18 (April 1940): 274–84.

Gonzáles, Justo L. *The Development of Christianity in the Latin Caribbean.* Grand Rapids, Mich.: W. B. Eerdmans, 1969.

Gonzáles-Wippler, Migene. *Santería.* Garden City, N.Y.: Anchor/Doubleday, 1975.

González, Edward. *Cuba under Castro: The Limits of Charisma.* Boston: Houghton Mifflin, 1974.

Greeley, Andrew M. *The American Catholic: A Social Portrait.* New York: Basic Books, 1977.

Guilday, Peter, ed. *The National Pastorals of the American Hierarchy (1792–1919).* Westminster, Md.: Newman, 1954.

Halsey, William M. *The Survival of American Innocence.* Notre Dame, Ind.: University of Notre Dame, 1980.

Handlin, Oscar. *The Uprooted.* 2d ed. enlarged. Boston: Atlantic–Little, Brown, 1973.

Harner, Charles E. *Florida Promoters, The Men Who Made It Big.* Tampa, Fla.: Florida Trend House, 1973.

Heffernan, John B. "The Blockade of the Southern Confederacy, 1861–1865." *Smithsonian Journal of History* (Winter 1967–68): 23–44.

Hennesey, James. *American Catholics: A History of the Roman Catholic Community in the United States.* New York: Oxford, 1981.

Higginson, Thomas Wentworth. *Army Life in a Black Regiment.* Boston: Lee and Shepard, 1890.

Higham, John. *Strangers in the Land: Patterns of American Nativism, 1860–1925.* New Brunswick, N.J.: Rutgers University, 1955.

History of Nuestra de la Leche y Buen Parto and St. Augustine. St. Augustine, Fla.: Cathedral Parish, 1937.

Hoffman's Catholic Directory. Milwaukee: Hoffman Bros., 1889.

Huck, Gabe, ed. *The Liturgy Documents: A Parish Resource.* Chicago: Liturgy Training Program, 1980.

Hurley, Joseph P. Papers. Archives of the Diocese of St. Augustine, St. Augustine, Fla.

Jackson, Kenneth T. *The Ku Klux Klan in the City, 1915–1930.* New York: Oxford, 1967.

Jahoda, Gloria. *Florida: A Bicentennial History.* New York: Norton, 1976.

Jenna, William W., Jr. *Metropolitan Miami: A Demographic Overview.* Coral Gables, Fla.: University of Miami, 1972.

Johns, John E. *Florida during the Civil War.* Gainesville: University of Florida, 1963.

Jones, B. Calvin. "Col. James Moore and the Destruction of the Apalachee Mission in 1704." *Bureau of Historical Sites and Properties Bulletin* 2 (1972): 25–33.

Kane, Joseph Nathan. *The American Counties.* Rev. ed. New York: Scarecrow Press, 1962.

Kavanaugh, James. *A Modern Priest Looks at His Outdated Church.* New York: Trident, 1967.

Kelly, George A. *Catholics and the Practice of the Faith: A Census Study of the Diocese of St. Augustine.* Washington: Catholic University of America, 1946.

Kendrick, Baynard. *Florida Trails and Turnpikes, 1914–1964.* Gainesville: University of Florida, 1964.

Kenny, Michael. *The Romance of the Floridas: The Finding and the Founding.* Milwaukee: Bruce, 1934.

Kenny, William J. Papers. Archives of the Diocese of St. Augustine, St. Augustine, Fla.

Kenrick, Francis P. Papers. Archives of the Archdiocese of Baltimore, Baltimore, Md.

Kersey, Harry A., Jr. *Pelts, Plumes and Hides: White Traders among the Seminole Indians, 1870–1930.* Gainesville: University of Florida, 1975.

Kiernan, John. Papers. Archives of the Josephite Fathers, Baltimore, Md.

King, Coretta. *My Life with Martin Luther King.* New York: Holt, Rinehart and Winston, 1969.

King, Martin Luther, Jr. *Why We Can't Wait.* New York: New American Library, 1964.

Kiple, Kenneth F. *Blacks in Colonial Cuba, 1774–1899.* Gainesville: University of Florida, 1976.

Kirlin, Joseph L. J. *Catholicity in Philadelphia.* Philadelphia: John Jos. McVey, 1909.

Kuzniewski, Anthony J. *Faith and Fatherland: The Polish Church War in Wisconsin, 1896–1918.* Notre Dame, Ind.: University of Notre Dame, 1980.

Langlois, Claude. *Un Diocèse Breton au Début du XIXᵉ Siècle: 1800–1830.* Paris: Université de Haute-Bretagne, 1974.

Laws of Florida (1971), 239–40.

Laxton, D. D. "The Dupont Plaza Site." *Florida Anthropologist* (June–September 1969): 67–73.

Lazarus, William C. *Wings in the Sun: The Annals of Aviation in Florida.* Orlando, Fla.: Tyncobb, 1951.

Leuchtenburg, William E. *A Troubled Feast: America since 1945.* Boston: Little Brown, 1973.

Linehan, Edward J. "Cuba's Exiles Bring New Life to Miami." *National Geographic,* July 1973, pp. 68–95.

Litwack, Leon F. *Been in the Storm So Long: The Aftermath of Slavery.* New York: Vintage, 1980.

Llerena, Mario. *The Unsuspected Revolution: The Birth and Rise of Castroism.* Ithaca, N.Y.: Cornell University, 1978.

Long, Durwood. "Key West and the New Deal." *Florida Historical Quarterly* 46 (January 1968): 209–18.

Lord, Robert H.; Sexton, John E.; and Harrington, Edward T. *History of the Archdiocese of Boston.* 2 vols. New York: Sheed and Ward, 1944.

Lyon, Eugene. *The Enterprise of Florida: Pedro Menéndez de Avilés and the Spanish Conquest of Florida, 1565–68.* Gainesville: University of Florida, 1976.

McKeown, Elizabeth. "Apologia for an American Catholicism: The Petition and Report of the National Catholic Welfare Council to Pius XI, April 25, 1922." *Church History* 43 (December 1974): 514–28.

McNamara, Robert F. *Catholic Sunday Preaching: The American Guidelines, 1791–1975.* Washington: Word of God Institute, 1975.

McQueen, Don Juan. *The Letters of Don Juan McQueen to His Family, 1791–1807.* Columbia, S.C.: Bostick and Thornley, 1943.

Mahon, John K. *History of the Second Seminole War, 1835–42.* Gainesville: University of Florida, 1967.

Maloney, Walter C. *A Sketch of the History of Key West, Florida.* Reproduction of 1876 edition. Gainesville: University of Florida, 1968.

Marks, Henry S. "Labor Problems of the Florida East Coast Railway Extension from Homestead to Key West, 1905–1907." *Tequesta* (1972): 28–33.

Marschall, John P. "Diocesan and Religious Clergy: A History of a Relationship." In *The Catholic Priest in the United States,* edited by John Tracy Ellis. Collegeville, Minn.: St. John's University, 1971.

Martin, E. M. "U.S. Outlines Policy toward Cuban Refugees." *Department of State Bulletin* 48 (June 24, 1963): 983–90.

Martin, Sidney W. *Florida's Flagler.* Athens: University of Georgia, 1949.

Masó, Calixto C. *Historia de Cuba.* Miami: Ediciones Universal, 1976.

Matter, Robert Allen. "Economic Basis of 17th Century Florida Missions." *Florida Historical Quarterly* 52 (July 1973): 18–38.

———. "Missions in the Defense of Spanish Florida, 1566–1710." *Florida Historical Quarterly* 54 (July 1975): 18–38.

Matthews, Herbert L. *Fidel Castro.* New York: Simon and Schuster, 1969.

Mertz, Paul E. *New Deal Policy and Southern Rural Poverty.* Baton Rouge: Louisiana State University, 1978.

Mississippi Vista: The Brothers of the Christian Schools in the Midwest, 1849–1949. Winona, Minn.: St. Mary's College, 1948.

Moore, John. Papers. Archives of the Diocese of St. Augustine, St. Augustine, Fla.

Morales, Cecilio J. *Hispanic Portrait of Evangelization—Shrine of Our Lady of Charity, Miami, Florida.* Washington: NCCB, n.d. [1981].

"More About Refugee Cuban Children." *Christian Century,* April 18, 1962, pp. 497–98.

Mowers, Bert; Williams, Wilma; Green, Mark; and Coleman, Wesley. "The Arch Creek Site, Dade County." *Florida Anthropologist* (March 1975): 1–13.

Murnion, Philip J. *The Catholic Priest and the Changing Structure of Pastoral Ministry: New York, 1920–1970.* New York: Arno, 1978.

Nelson, Lowry. *Cuba: The Measure of a Revolution.* Minneapolis: University of Minnesota, 1972.

———. *Rural Cuba.* Minneapolis: University of Minnesota, 1950.

O'Brien, David J. *American Catholics and Social Reform: The New Deal Years.* New York: Oxford University, 1968.

———. "The American Priest and Social Action." In *The Catholic Priest in the United States*, edited by John Tracy Ellis. Collegeville, Minn.: St. John's University, 1971.

O'Connor, James. *Origins of Socialism in Cuba.* Ithaca, N.Y.: Cornell University, 1970.

Official Catholic Directory, 1871, 1878, 1903, 1915, 1923, 1934, 1941, 1950, 1958–78. Publisher varies: New York: D. J. Sadlier; Milwaukee: M. H. Wiltzius; New York: P. J. Kenedy and Sons.

O'Mahoney, Jeremiah. "Diocese of St. Augustine." *American Board of Catholic Missions*, 1933–34.

———. "Needs of the Diocese of St. Augustine." *American Board of Catholic Missions*, 1932–33.

O'Neill, William L. *Coming Apart: An Informal History of America in the 1960s.* Chicago: Quadrangle Books, 1971.

O'Rourke, Sr. Alice, OP. *The Good Work Begun: Centennial History of the Peoria Diocese.* Peoria, Ill.: Chancery of the Diocese of Peoria, 1977.

Pace, Edward. Papers. Archives of the Catholic University of America, Washington, D.C.

Page, David. "Bishop Michael J. Curley and Anti-Catholic Nativism in Florida." *Florida Historical Quarterly* 45 (October 1966): 101–17.

———, ed. and comp. *Peregrini Pro Christo.* Orlando, Fla.: Florida Catholic, 1967.

Parks, Arva Moore. "Miami in 1876." *Tequesta* (1975): 89–145.

Pattee, Richard. *The Case of Cardinal Aloysius Stepinac.* Milwaukee: Bruce, 1953.

Paul VI, Pope. *Humanae vitae.* Boston: Daughters of St. Paul, 1968.

———. *Evangelii nuntiandi.* Washington: United States Catholic Conference, 1976.

Pearson, Fred Lamar, Jr. "Spanish-Indian Relations in Florida, 1602–1675: Some Aspects of Selected *Visitas*." *Florida Historical Quarterly* 52 (January 1974): 261–73.

Peña, Raymond. "The Church and the Hispanics." *Origins* 8 (December 7, 1978): 391–93.

Peters, Thelma. *Lemon City: Pioneering on Biscayne Bay, 1850–1925.* Miami: Banyan Books, 1980.

———. "The Log of the Biscayne House of Refuge." *Tequesta* (1978): 39–62.

Pierce, Charles W. *Pioneer Life in S. E. Florida.* Edited by Donald Walter Curl. Coral Gables, Fla.: University of Miami, 1970.

Pius XII, Pope. "De Spirituali Emigrantum Cura." *Acta Apostolicae Sedis* 44 (August 1, 1952): 649–704.

Ponce, Frank. "The U.S. Church's Hispanic Catholics." *Origins* 10 (September 11, 1980): 193–201.

Porter, Kenneth Wiggins. "Florida Slaves and Free Negroes in the Seminole War, 1835–1842." *Journal of Negro History* 28 (1943): 390–421.

Poyo, Gerald E. "Cuban Patriots in Key West, 1878–1886: Guardians at the Separatist Ideals." *Florida Historical Quarterly* 61 (July 1982): 20–36.

———. "Cuban Revolutionaries and Monroe County: Reconstruction Politics, 1868–76." *Florida Historical Quarterly* 55 (April 1977): 407–22.

————. "Key West and the Cuban Ten Years War." *Florida Historical Quarterly* 57 (January 1979): 289–307.

Pozzetta, George E. "Foreign Colonies in South Florida, 1865–1910." *Tequesta* (1974): 45–56.

————. "Foreigners in Florida: A Study of Immigration Promotion, 1865–1910." *Florida Historical Quarterly* 53 (October 1974): 164–80.

Prohías, Rafael. *The Cuban Minority in the United States.* Washington: Cuban National Planning Council, 1974.

Quinn, Jane. *Minorcans in Florida: Their History and Heritage.* St. Augustine, Fla.: Mission, 1975.

————. *The Story of a Nun: Jeanie Gordon Brown.* St. Augustine, Fla.: Villa Flora, 1978.

Raboteau, Albert J. *Slave Religion: The "Invisible Institution" in the Antebellum South.* New York: Oxford, 1980.

Rackleff, Robert B. "Anti-Catholicism and the Florida Legislature, 1911–1919." *Florida Historical Quarterly* 50 (April 1972): 352–65.

Rand McNally Road Atlas. Chicago: Rand McNally, 1981.

Read, William A. *Florida Place-Names of Indian Origin and Seminole Personal Names.* Baton Rouge: Louisiana State University, 1934.

Redford, Polly. *Billion Dollar Sandbar: A Biography of Miami Beach.* New York: E. P. Dutton, 1970.

Regnum Regis 1 (January 1939): 13–15; 2 (October 1940): 34.

Reid, Whitelaw. *After the War: A Southern Tour.* Cincinnati, N.Y.: Moore, Wilstach and Baldwin, 1866.

Relations Mortuaires des Freres des Écoles Chrétiennes, Tome Quatrième (de 1860 à 1863). Versailles: Beau Jne., 1865.

Remington, Frederic. *Crooked Trails.* New York: Harper, 1898.

Reynolds, Edward. *Jesuits for the Negro.* New York: America, 1949.

Robbins, George, ed. *Diary of Rev. H. Clavreul.* Waterbury, Conn.: Connecticut Assoc. of Ex-Prisoners of War, 1910.

Romig, Walter, ed. *The American Catholic Who's Who.* Vol. 10. Grosse Pointe, Mich.: Walter Romig, 1954.

Roth, Very Rev. Benedict, OSB, ed. *Brief History of the Churches of the Diocese of St. Augustine, Florida.* St. Leo, Fla.: Abbey, 1923–40.

Rubin, Wladyslaw. "Religiosidad Popular y Evangelización Misionera," *L'Osservatore Romano,* October 31, 1976.

Ryan, Mary Perkins. *Are Parochial Schools the Answer?* New York: Holt, Rinehart and Winston, 1964.

Ryan, Mary Philip. *Amid the Alien Corn.* Vol. 1, *The Early Years of the Sisters of St. Dominic, Adrian, Michigan.* St. Charles, Ill.: Jones Wood, 1967.

Rynne, Xavier [pseud.]. *Vatican Council II.* New York: Farrar, Straus, and Giroux, 1968.

Sadlier's Catholic Directory. New York: D. and J. Sadlier, 1871; 1878.

Saltrem, P. S., and Mings, R. C. "The Projected Impact of Cuban Settlement on Voting Patterns in Metropolitan Miami, Florida." *Professional Geographer* 24 (May 1972): 123–31.

Santovenia, Emeritorio S., and Shelton, Raul M. *Cuba y Su Historia.* 3 vols. 2d ed. Miami: Cuba Corp., 1966.

Schene, Michael G. "The Early Florida Salvage Industry." *American Neptune* (October 1978): 262–67.

———. "Indian Key." *Tequesta* (1976): 3–27.

Schmeckebier, Lawrence. *Ivan Meštrovic, Sculptor and Patriot.* Syracuse, N.Y.: University of Syracuse, 1959.

Sexton, Virginia S. "Edward Aloysius Pace." *Psychological Research* 42 (1980): 39–47.

Shanabruch, Charles. *Chicago's Catholics: The Evolution of an American Identity.* Notre Dame, Ind.: University of Notre Dame, 1981.

Sheehy, Maurice S. "The Last Days of Msgr. Pace." *Catholic University Bulletin* 6 (May 1938): 3–4.

Sheeran, Clara D. "Msgr. Edward A. Pace—Honorary President and Director of the I.F.C.A." *Quarterly Bulletin of the International Federation of Catholic Alumnae* 21 (June 1938): 11.

Shehan, Lawrence Cardinal. *A Blessing of Years: The Memoirs of Lawrence Cardinal Shehan.* Notre Dame, Ind.: University of Notre Dame, 1982.

Shepard, Birse. *The Lore of the Wreckers.* Boston: Beacon, 1961.

Shofner, Jerrell H. *Nor Is It Over Yet: Florida in the Era of Reconstruction, 1863–1877.* Gainesville: University of Florida, 1974.

Smith, Ignatius, OP. "Msgr. Edward Pace, Apostle of Truth—Funeral Sermon at the Shrine, April 27, 1938." *Quarterly Bulletin of the International Federation of Catholic Alumnae* 21 (June 1938): 8–10.

Smith, Walter J. "Msgr. Pace and Scientific Psychology." *Guild of Catholic Psychiatrists Bulletin* 9 (January 1962): 31–34.

Sorensen, Theodore. *Kennedy.* New York: Harper and Row, 1965.

Sosa, Juan J. "An Anglo-Hispanic Dilemma: Liturgical Piety or Popular Piety." *Liturgy* 24 (November–December 1979): 7–9.

Spalding, Martin J. Papers. Archives of the Archdiocese of Baltimore, Baltimore, Md.

Stoesen, Alexander R. "Road from Receivership: Claude Pepper, the Dupont Trust, and the Florida East Coast Railway." *Florida Historical Quarterly* 52 (October 1973): 132–56.

Suchlicki, Jaime. *Cuba from Columbus to Castro.* New York: Charles Scribner's, 1974.

Suenens, Leon Cardinal. *The Nun in the World.* Westminster, Md.: Newman, 1962.

Tebeau, Charlton W. *A History of Florida.* Coral Gables, Fla.: University of Miami, 1975.

———. *Synagogue in the Central City: Temple Israel of Greater Miami, 1922–1972.* Coral Gables, Fla.: University of Miami, 1972.

Testé, Ismael. *Historia Eclesiástica de Cuba.* 5 vols. Burgos, Spain: Monte Carmelo, 1969.

Thomas, Donna. "'Camp Hell': Miami During the Spanish American War." *Florida Historical Quarterly* 57 (October 1978): 141–56.

Thomas, Emory, M. *The Confederate Nation, 1861–65*. New York: Harper and Row, 1979.

Thomas, Hugh. *Cuba: The Pursuit of Freedom*. New York: Harper and Row, 1971.

Tomberlin, Joseph A. "Florida and the School Desegregation Issue, 1954–59: A Summary View." *Journal of Negro Education* (Fall 1974): 457–67.

———. "Florida Whites and the Brown Decision of 1954." *Florida Historical Quarterly* 51 (July 1972): 22–36.

Trisco, Robert, ed. *Catholics in America, 1776–1976*. Washington: NCCB, 1976.

U.S. Bureau of the Census. *Census of the United States, Population*, 1890, 1950, 1960, 1970. Washington: G.P.O.

———. *Historical Census of the United States, Colonial Times to 1957*. Washington: Bureau of the Census, 1960.

———. *Statistical Abstract of the United States, 1970*. Washington: G.P.O., 1970.

Vanderblue, Homer B. *The Florida Land Boom*. Chicago: Northwestern University, 1927.

Verot, Augustin. Papers. Archives of the Diocese of St. Augustine, St. Augustine, Fla.

Verot, Rt. Rev. Augustin. *A Tract for the Times: Slavery and Abolitionism, Being the Substance of a Sermon Preached on the 4th Day of January, 1861, Day of Public Humiliation, Prayer and Fasting*. Baltimore: John Murphy, 1861.

Walsh, Bryan O. "Cuban Refugee Children." *Journal of Inter-American Studies and World Affairs* 13 (1971): 378–414.

———. "Cubans in Miami." *America*, February 26, 1966, pp. 286–89.

———. "Cubans in Miami: The Political Impact." *Inter-American Scene* 4 (1973): 41.

Washington, Curtis. "Miami Mission," *St. Augustine's Messenger*, January 1946, pp. 2–3.

Weigall, T. H. *Boom in Paradise: Florida—"The East Coast," Its Builders, Resources, Industries, Town and City Developments*. New York: King, 1932.

White, Theodore H. "Summing Up." *New York Times Magazine*, April 25, 1982, pp. 32 ff.

Will, Lawrence E. *Okeechobee Hurricane and the Hoover Dike*. St. Petersburg, Fla.: Great Outdoors, 1961.

Williams, Eric. *From Columbus to Castro: The History of the Caribbean, 1492–1969*. New York: Harper and Row, 1970.

Williamson, Edward C. *Florida Politics in the Gilded Age, 1877–1893*. Gainesville: University of Florida, 1976.

Wilson, George. "Convention of Colored Catholics First Held in the State of Florida." *The Colored Harvest*, June–July 1941.

Wilson, Kenneth L., and Portes, Alejandro. "Immigrant Enclaves: An Analysis of the Labor Market Experiences of Cubans in Miami." *American Journal of Sociology* (September 1980): 295–319.

Wissel, Joseph. *The Redemptorist, On The American Missions—Joseph Wissel—Vol. I*. Reprint of 1920 ed. New York: Arno, 1978.

Woodward, C. Vann. *The Burden of Southern History*. Rev. ed. Baton Rouge: Louisiana State University, 1968.

————. *The Strange Career of Jim Crow*. 3d rev. ed. New York: Oxford, 1964.

————. *Tom Watson: Agrarian Rebel*. New York: MacMillan, 1938.

Wyden, Peter. *Bay of Pigs: The Untold Story*. New York: Simon and Schuster, 1979.

Zubillaga, Félix, SJ. *La Florida: La Misión Jesuítica y La Colonización Española (1566–1572)*. Rome: Institutum Historicum, S.I., 1941.

————, ed. *Monumenta Antiquae Floridae, 1566–1572*. Rome: Monumenta Historica, S.I., 1946.

Sermons, Memorials, Souvenirs and Pamphlets

Brown, Raymond, SS. "Homily at Msgr. Enright Funeral—St. Rose of Lima Church, October 31, 1980." AFAM, Communications Office, October 31, 1980. Audiotape.

Catholic Service Bureau Golden Anniversary, 1931–1981. Miami: privately printed, 1981.

Centennial Souvenir Booklet: Sisters of the Holy Names—Key West, Florida, 1868–1968. Key West: privately printed, 1968.

Clavreul, Henry P. "The Late Bishop Verot—A Sermon Delivered in the Cathedral of St. Augustine, Sunday, July 16th, A.D. 1876, by Rev. Fr. Calvreul, Rector of the Cathedral." St. Leo, Fla.: St. Leo Abbey, n.d. [c. 1876].

Commemorative Booklet of the 25th Anniversary of the Death of Edward A. Pace—1963. St. Augustine: Privately printed, 1963.

Dedication Booklet—St. Raphael Chapel, St. John Vianney Minor Seminary, January 16, 1966. Miami: privately printed, 1966.

50th Anniversary of Msgr. William Barry. Miami Beach: privately printed, 1960.

Flintham, L. S. *The Key West Convent-Hospital*. N.p.: privately printed, n.d. [c. 1900].

Golden Jubilee of Msgr. James F. Enright, May 14, 1977. Miami: privately printed, 1977.

Hisrich, Maria Thecla. *A History of Sacred Heart Parish—100 Years*. Pittsburgh: Pickwick-Morcraft, 1972.

Immaculate Conception Anniversary, 1954–79. Hialeah, Fla.: privately printed, 1979.

Installation Commemorative of Coleman F. Carroll, Auxiliary Bishop of Pittsburgh, August 25, 1953. Pittsburgh: privately printed, 1953.

The Jesuits in Florida: Fifty Golden Years, 1889–1939. Tampa: Salesian Press, 1939.

Living Waters—Centennial Booklet, 1866–1966. Jacksonville, Fla.: Ambrose the Printer, 1966.

Los Cumpleaños de San Agustín—The 375th Anniversary of St. Augustine. St. Augustine: Knights of Columbus, 1940.

Msgr. William Barry, P.A.—Golden Jubilee of the Priesthood, 1910–1960. Miami Beach: privately printed, 1960.

O'Mahoney, Jeremiah, ed. *Fides*. Gainesville, Fla.: Society for the Propagation of the Faith, 1934.

————, ed. *Fides*. Gainesville, Fla.: Society for the Propagation of the Faith, 1937.

St. Brendan Church—Dedication Booklet, May 17, 1981. Miami: privately printed, 1981.

St. Francis Hospital, 1927–52. Miami Beach: privately printed, 1952.

St. Patrick's Patrician Club, 1931–1981. Miami Beach: privately printed, 1981.

St. Rose of Lima Parish—25th Anniversary, 1948–1973. Miami: privately printed, 1973.

Silver Jubilee—Bay Haven, Academy of Assumption, 1942–1967. Miami: privately printed, 1967.

Silver Jubilee—Corpus Christi School, 1947–1973. Miami: privately printed, 1973.

Souvenir of the Silver Jubilee of Reverend Thomas Comber, 1919–1944. Miami: privately printed, 1944.

Sweet, Zelia and Sheppy, Mary H. *The Spanish Missions of Florida.* N.p.: Works Progress Administration, 1940.

25th Anniversary of St. Patrick's, Miami Beach, 1926–51. Miami Beach: privately printed, 1951.

Unpublished Sources

Adessa, Dominick Joseph. "Refugee Cuban Children: The Role of the Catholic Welfare Bureau of the Diocese of Miami, Florida, in Receiving, Caring for and Placing Unaccompanied Refugee Children—1960–63." M.S.W. thesis, Fordham University, 1964.

Birdwhistell, Ira V. "Southern Baptist Perceptions of and Responses to Roman Catholicism, 1917–1972." Ph.D. diss., Southern Baptist Theological Seminary, 1975.

Braun, William P., CSC. "Msgr. Edward A. Pace, Educator and Philosopher." Ph.D. diss., Catholic University of America, 1968.

DePaoli, Ambrose B. "Property Laws of the State of Florida Affecting the Church." J.C.L. thesis excerpt, Lateran Pontifical University, 1965.

Joksina, Alexander Stanley. "Orphaned and Unaccompanied Catholic European Children Immigrating into the United States under the Displaced Persons Act of 1948 as Seen from the Files of the Catholic Committee of Refugees." M.S.W. thesis, Fordham University, 1953.

Kerr, William. "The 1928 Presidential Election and the Catholic Issue in Florida." M.A. thesis, Florida State University, 1974.

Lopez-Blanco, Marino; Montiel, Pedro A.; and Suarez, Luis L. "A Study of Attitudes of Cuban Refugees Toward Assimilation: Selected Attitudes of Cuban Refugees in the Miami Area." M.S.W. thesis, Barry College, 1968.

McGoldrick, Sr. Thomas Joseph, SSJ. "The Contribution of the Sisters of St. Joseph of St. Augustine to Education, 1866–1960." M.A. thesis, University of Florida, 1961.

McKeown, John F. "History of the Church of Florida." 2 Vols. Mimeograph, n.d. [c. 1960].

McMurry, Vincent de Paul. "The Catholic Church during Reconstruction 1865–1877." Ph.D. diss., Catholic University of America, 1950.

McNamara, Robert. "Rochester Catholics in a Time of Change: 'Bare Ruined Choirs'?" Lecture, Jewish Community Center of Greater Rochester, March 9, 1980.

Matter, Robert Allen. "The Spanish Missions of Florida: The Friars vs. the Governors in the Golden Age—1606–1690." Ph.D. diss., University of Washington, 1972.

Moroski, Thomas Leonard. "A Study in the Role of an Institution in the Resettlement of Catholic Orphaned and Unaccompanied Children from Europe." M.S.W. thesis, Fordham University, 1952.

Murphy, Joseph M. "Ritual Systems in Cuban Santería." Ph.D. diss., Temple University, 1981.

O'Neill, Sr. Mary Roselina. "History of the Contributions of the Sisters of the Holy Names of Jesus and Mary to the Cause of Education in Florida." M.A. thesis, Fordham University, n.d. [c. 1935].

Pace, Edward A. "Das Relativitätsprincip in Herbert Spencer's psychologischer Entwicklungslehre." Ph.D. diss., University of Leipzig, 1891.

Pedraza-Bailey, Silvia. "Political and Economic Migrants in America: Cubans and Mexicans." Ph.D. diss., University of Chicago, 1980.

Phillips, Sr. M. Andre, OSF. "The Closing Decades of a Century in the History of the Allegheny Franciscans, 1938–1958." M.A. thesis, St. Bonaventure University, 1967.

Román, Agustín A. "La Piedad Popular Del Pueblo Cubano." M.A. thesis, Barry College, 1976.

Rosen, Bruce. "Development of Negro Education in Florida During Reconstruction." Ph.D. diss., University of Florida, 1974.

Schellings, William J. "The Role of Florida in the Spanish American War, 1898." Ph.D. diss., University of Florida, 1958.

Shehan, John Cardinal. "Memoir: John Cardinal Shehan." Unpublished manuscript, 1981.

Sosa, Juan J. "La Santería, The Lucumi Traditions of the Afro-Cuban Religions." M.Th. thesis, St. Vincent de Paul Seminary, 1972.

Strong, Sr. Miriam, OP. "Refugees from Castro's Cuba—Of Fish and Freedom." M.S.W. thesis, Fordham University, 1964.

Tierney, Kevin B. "American Cuban Relations, 1957–63." Ph.D. diss., Syracuse University, 1979.

Wagy, Thomas Ray. "A South to Save: The Administration of Governor Leroy Collins of Florida." Ph.D. diss., Florida State University, 1980.

Woodbury, Kimball D. "The Spatial Diffusion of the Cuban Community in Dade County, Florida." M.A. thesis, University of Florida, 1978.

Interviews

All interviews are by the author except where noted.

Amia, Sr., CSFN, Philadelphia, Pa., June 24, 1981.
Atkins, Judge C. Clyde, Coral Gables, Fla., October 5, 1981.

Balfe, Rev. William, St. Petersburg, Fla., October 3, 1981.
Barry, Msgr. Dominic, Pompano Beach, Fla., September 25, 1981.
Barry, Msgr. William, Miami Beach, Fla. (conducted by Michael V. Gannon), October 3, 1966.
Benjamin, Mr. and Mrs. Ben, Miami, Fla., October 13, 1981.
Bosco, Bp. Anthony, Pittsburgh, Pa., June 9, 1981 (telephone).
Burke, Rev. Cyril, OP, Miami Shores, Fla., September 20, 1981.
Bushey, Msgr. David, Ft. Lauderdale, Fla., September 19, 1981.
Concannon, Sr. Isabel, CSJ, Pittsburgh, Pa., June 11, 1981 (telephone).
Cummings, Msgr. George, Citrus Springs, Fla., May 22, 1982 (telephone).
Dearden, John Cardinal, Detroit, Mich., June 24, 1981.
Donohue, Mrs. Marjorie Fillyaw, Miami, Fla., October 1, 1981.
Ellis, Msgr. John Tracy, Washington, D.C., August 4, 1981.
Ellis, Br. Patrick, FSC, Philadelphia, Pa., July 14, 1981.
Fitzgerald, Mr. Joseph, Miami, Fla., September 29, 1981.
Fitzpatrick, Bp. John, Brownsville, Tex., October 28, 1981.
Flynn, Sr. Shiela, RA, Philadelphia, Pa., June 26, 1981 (telephone).
Fogarty, Msgr. Noel, Miami Shores, Fla., October 17, 1981.
Genovar, Rev. Lamar, Ft. Lauderdale, Fla., September 26, 1981.
Girdis, Rev. Joseph, Pittsburgh, Pa., June 11, 1981.
Gleason, Sr. Rita, OP, Adrian, Mich., June 3, 1981.
Jordan, Msgr. Harold, St. Augustine, Fla., August 18, 1981.
Kiernan, Rev. John, SSJ, New Orleans, La. (conducted by Rev. Peter Hogan, SSJ), January 10, 1978.
Kindelan, Mr. James, Miami Shores, Fla., September 16, 1981.
LaVoy, Sr. Joyce, OP, Adrian, Mich., June 17, 1981.
Leonard, Bp. Vincent, Pittsburgh, Pa., June 11, 1981.
Lewis, Senator Philip, Riviera Beach, Fla., October 8, 1981.
Luaces, Sr. Henrietta, OSP, Baltimore, Md., July 27, 1981.
Lussier, Sr. Mary Albert, SSJ, St. Augustine, Fla., August 27, 1981.
McCarthy, Rev. Edward, OSA, Philadelphia, Pa., July 2, 1981.
McHall, Sr. Jerome, SM, Pittsburgh, Pa., June 12, 1981.
McKeown, Rev. John, Ft. Lauderdale, Fla., August 16, 1979.
McKeever, Msgr. William, Coral Gables, Fla., September 22, 1981.
McNulty, Msgr. John, St. Petersburg, Fla., October 2, 1981.
Mallen, Rev. Charles, CSSR, Opa-Locka, Fla., October 19, 1981.
Marinas, Msgr. Arcadio, Miami, Fla., September 12, 1981.
Murphy, Rev. Robert, Pittsburgh, Pa., June 13, 1981.
Navarrete, Rev. Anthony, Miami, Fla., October 14, 1981.
Nelan, Msgr. James, Ft. Lauderdale, Fla., September 25, 1981.
Neomisea, Sr. M., CSFN, Philadelphia, Pa., June 25, 1981.
Nevins, Bp. John, Miami, Fla., September 30, 1981.
O'Connell, Rev. Lawrence, Pittsburgh, Pa., June 12, 1981.
O'Donovan, Msgr. Thomas, Pompano Beach, Fla., September 19, 1981.
O'Dowd, Msgr. John, South Miami, Fla., October 10, 1981.
O'Shaughnessy, Sr. Mary Aquinas, SSJ, Lake Worth, Fla., October 6, 1981.
Rastatter, Msgr. Rowan, Pompano Beach, Fla., September 19, 1981.

Reilly, Sr. Kathleen, SSND, Baltimore, Md., July 20, 1981.
Reilly, Msgr. Peter, Coral Gables, Fla., September 22, 1981.
Roberts, Rev. Louis, Boynton Beach, Fla., September 18, 1981.
Román, Bp. Agustín, Miami, Fla., September 11, 1981; October 17, 1981.
Scheer, Sr. Mary Bernadette, OP, Elkins Park, Pa. (conducted by Sr. Martha Marie, OP), October 18, 1981.
Schiefen, Msgr. Robert, Siesta Key, Fla., October 3, 1981.
Symons, Bp. J. Keith, St. Petersburg, Fla., October 2, 1981.
Tanner, Bp. Paul, Boynton Beach, Fla., September 28, 1981.
Unger, Rev. John, Pittsburgh, Pa., June 10, 1981.
Vallina, Rev. Emilio, Miami, Fla., September 12, 1981; October 26, 1981.
Walsh, Msgr. Bryan O., Miami, Fla., October 10, 1981.
Walsh, Msgr. James J., Key Biscayne, Fla., September 26, 1981.

Correspondence

All correspondence is directed to the author.

Carroll, Mr. Gerald V., Rochester, N.Y., July 10, 1981.
Fee, Sr. Elizabeth, RSM, Enniskillen, N. Ireland, May 21, 1981.
Fitzgerald, Mr. Joseph, Miami, Fla., January 6, 1982.
Grzeskiewicz, Br. Richard, FSC, July 5, 1981.
Hughes, Fr. Dennis, March 21, 1982.
Sherry, Sr. Josephine, RSM, Hialeah, Fla., May 7, 1981.
Stieb, Fr. Terry, SVD, December 30, 1981.
Thomas, Br. Martin, FMS, Miami, Fla., August 26, 1981.
Whiteman, Sr. Lorean, SNJM, Albany, N.Y., October 9, 1981.

Index